TIDES IN THE AFFAIRS OF MEN

TIDES IN THE AFFAIRS OF MEN

The Social History of Elizabethan Seamen, 1580–1603

CHERYL A. FURY

Contributions in Military Studies, Number 214

GREENWOOD PRESS
Westport, Connecticut • London

Library of Congress Cataloging-in-Publication Data

Fury, Cheryl A., 1966–
    Tides in the affairs of men : the social history of Elizabethan seamen, 1580–1603 /
Cheryl A. Fury.
        p.   cm.—(Contributions in military studies, ISSN 0883–6884 ; no. 214)
    Includes bibliographical references and index.
    ISBN 0–313–31948–0 (alk. paper)
    1. Sailors—England—History—16th century.   2. Great Britain—History, Naval—
Tudors, 1485–1603.   I. Title.   II. Series.
VD50.F87   2002
359.1'0942'09031—dc21   2001019998

British Library Cataloguing in Publication Data is available.

Library of Congress Catalog Card Number: 2001019998
ISBN: 0–313–31948–0
ISSN: 0883–6884

First published in 2002

Greenwood Press, 88 Post Road West, Westport, CT 06881
An imprint of Greenwood Publishing Group, Inc.
www.greenwood.com

Printed in the United States of America

The paper used in this book complies with the
Permanent Paper Standard issued by the National
Information Standards Organization (Z39.48–1984).

10 9 8 7 6 5 4 3 2 1

Copyright Acknowledgments

The author and publisher are grateful for permission to reproduce portions of the following
copyrighted material:

Portions of Chapter 1 originally appeared as "Education and Training in the Elizabethan
Maritime Community," *Mariner's Mirror* 85 (1999), 147–61. Reproduced by permission of
the Editor of *Mariner's Mirror*.

Portions of Chapter 5 originally appeared as "Elizabethan Seamen: Their Lives Ashore," *The
International Journal of Maritime History* 10, no. 1 (June 1998), 1–40, and is used here with
the kind permission of the International Maritime Economic History Association.

Soli Deo Gloria

Contents

Preface

Early English maritime expansion and, in particular, the Anglo-Spanish war have been analyzed by generations of historians. Until recently, the focus has been placed on events and participants "at the top." This book revisits that period but from a different perspective: the men of the seafaring community and their experiences during a particularly volatile period of maritime history.

Without a doubt, the seafaring community had to contend with simultaneous pressures from many different directions; shipowners and merchants, motivated by profit, hired seamen to sail voyages of ever-increasing distance, which taxed the health and capabilities of crews and vessels. International tensions in the last two decades of Elizabeth's reign magnified the risks to all seamen, whether in civilian employment or on warships. The advent of open warfare with Spain in 1585 ushered in two major developments. First, there was the privateering war against the Spanish empire, seen by seamen as one of the few economic benefits of the conflict. Seamen, however, were not the only ones who went to sea for pillage and plunder; unprecedented numbers of landsmen were also eager to participate in the very popular privateering war. This influx tested the cohesion of the maritime community, largely unprotected by a guild or trade group. The other major development was the introduction of large-scale impressment, a deeply resented aspect of any naval war and one that brought uncertainty and great hardship to seamen and their families.

During the second half of Elizabeth's reign, seamen were forced into their sovereign's service in large numbers, a rude shock to laborers accustomed to a great deal of employment freedom. The Crown wrongly assumed that these men would be content to act out their parts in a play that it had scripted, wherein the needs of a state in crisis would take precedence over seamen's health and ability to earn a living. Without a naval caste of seamen, the Crown was frustrated by the intractability of a labor group accustomed to a high degree of "shipboard democracy" and a higher standard of working conditions. The relationship between the Crown and its seafarers was a "pull-haul" between a government beset by financial problems of fighting a protracted war on several fronts and frustrated by its limited infrastructure, and employees forced to work in dangerous conditions for substandard wages in an expanding economy. The stresses of the war years tell us much about the dynamic of the maritime community, its members' expectations, and their coping strategies.

This book examines a group of laborers whose livelihood, customs, and traditional freedoms were under attack. Unable to take advantage of the increasing societal need for skilled seamen because of the power of the state, the growing numbers of "outsiders," and their weakness as a collective, seamen fought a defensive war; they tried to combat their deteriorating status by holding on tenaciously to their customs in an effort to survive their clash with the state. The fact that seamen were ultimately successful is a testament to the tenacity of early modern work culture.

Acknowledgments

When I was pondering what to write in the preface of this book, my husband suggested that I could summarize my book as a work on "some guys, some boats, and bad food." While that synopsis contains a good deal of truth, I hope that I have taken my analysis beyond those limits. This book explores a number of themes involving the dynamics of the Elizabethan maritime community and the effects of war and commercial expansion upon that group. I have also endeavored to understand seamen as part of the larger society. This is a result of my belief that naval and maritime history should be incorporated into the mainstream of historical scholarship rather than segregated, as has often been the case in the past. In addition to my analysis of seafarers, this study reveals much about the nature of early modern government and the deferential relationship of Elizabethan society. Like all historians, I hope to do my subjects justice and to interpret correctly the nuances of their relationship with each other, the Crown, and those ashore. After spending several years in this pursuit, it is my greatest wish to convey the seamen's understanding of their world and their circumstances to the reader.

This book is the product of living in close proximity with "my sailors." Several people aided and abetted us in our ongoing love affair. I welcome the opportunity to thank those who have given me so much support during the conception, research, writing, and revising of this book. I owe a great debt of gratitude to my Ph.D. supervisor, J. D. Alsop, whose vast knowledge of the period and the subject has been invaluable. His excellent editorial skills and attention to detail have forced me to be more precise in both my writing and analysis. Jim's insights and the benefit of his own research have helped me see the larger significance of my own findings.

I owe a great deal to McMaster University for its financial support and to the staff of the many libraries and record depositories who helped me in my searches. The staff at the Guildhall Library and the Greater London Record Office were especially helpful and generous with their time. I wish to thank the staff of the John Carter Brown Library in Providence, Rhode Island, for their fellowship, which allowed me to spend time using their collection of printed works on maritime matters.

I would like to thank my family, who have never wavered in their support for me or my work. My husband, Andrew, has stood by me throughout the journey, even when he had to take a backseat to my love affair with Elizabethan sailors. His strength helped me to continue my education. My mother has always been my much-needed sounding board. She has provided moral and financial support when it was not forthcoming elsewhere. My sister, Bonnie, helped my education in other ways; her generosity and companionship allowed me to visit parts of England that I would not have seen otherwise. Above all others, she shares my enthusiasm for things British. I would also like to thank my mother-in-law, Wyn Miller, for taking the time to read my work and for being such an ardent champion of higher learning, especially in the arts.

I must also acknowledge my many friends from Hamilton, those at McMaster and outside the institution. I will always treasure my years in Ontario. The friendships that I have forged there were, and continue to be, one of my greatest blessings. Thus, I reserve a hearty thank-you to the crew of the "academic ambulance," in particular, Chris and Patti, who opened their homes and families to a lonely Maritimer. Last but not least, I wish to thank my friends from St. Patrick's Church (the Disco Massers). Their faith, sense of humor, and commitment to music provided a diversion from intellectual endeavors and helped to provide perspective and balance in my life.

Abbreviations

A.P.C. *Acts of the Privy Council*
B.L.   British (Museum) Library
GLRO   Greater London Record Office
HCA   High Court of the Admiralty
PRO   Public Record Office
SP   State Papers (Domestic)

TIDES IN THE
AFFAIRS OF MEN

Chapter 1

Training and Manning the English Maritime Community

The Anglo-Spanish war of 1585 to 1604 brought new opportunities for seamen. In addition to merchant voyages, exploration, fishing, and piracy, privateering[1] and naval expeditions provided employment throughout the late Elizabethan period. Following the outbreak of the war in the 1580s there were changes to the more traditional forms of seafaring. Many voyages combined trade and privateering, blending new and old forms of employment. These new opportunities also drew landsmen attracted by plunder, patriotism, Protestantism, or simply seasonal employment in an era of steady inflation and population growth. Military objectives of the navy and privateers altered the peacetime composition of the maritime community by allowing soldiers and other landsmen aboard in greater numbers. They joined the ranks of those afloat.[2] The end result was a broadening of the maritime community in terms of employment opportunities and membership.[3]

While seamen viewed themselves as tradesmen of the seas, they lacked a nationwide craft infrastructure to enforce uniform training, to monitor hiring practices, or to protect their membership from outsiders. Seamen conducted themselves as individual agents motivated by self-interest. Yet, they had a collective consciousness; they adhered to recognized customs of their trade despite the want of a guild. The established methods of socializing youths, training, and hiring were not affected by the demands of the war. Although the range of employment options increased, seamen used the same criteria to seek employment: adequate remuneration for calculated risk and recognition of their "pseudo-independence."[4] As a trade group, seamen did not—or could not—endeavor to take advantage of the increased demand for their labor; they merely strove to preserve their liberties in the face of wartime impressment, the influx of landsmen, and related developments. Essentially, they attempted to function within the maritime community as they had prior to the war; they clung to established methods of apprenticeship and hiring that had proved adequate for the needs of the maritime community in the past.

While the Crown's expectations of seamen in naval service were contrary to many of the traditions of peacetime seafaring, the state did not attempt to regulate the inner workings of the maritime community. In part, this can be attributed to the limitations of the bureaucracy of the early modern state. The state was either unwilling or unable to eradicate seamen's "pseudo-independence" or bend them to its purposes. However, seamen were weak as a collective; unlike some other trade groups, they could not avoid or mitigate compulsory service.[5] Protest against service and conditions was usually conducted on an individual basis or in small groups (as will be demonstrated below). This could take many forms, including open defiance or passive resistance.

Due to the state's very limited development of a standing navy, Elizabethan England lacked a separate naval class of seamen. Hence, the state's wartime needs necessitated seamen's leaving their more traditional forms of employment for extensive campaigns. Frequently, the end result was forced naval duty for resentful civilian seamen convinced of their customary right to contract out their own labor on their own terms and for relatively short commitments. While few seamen had the financial security not to work for long periods of time, only a very small number were employed continuously; even the poorer seamen had inactive periods. In civilian seafaring, each individual chose when to contract out his labor; seamen's employment schedules were dictated by their own needs as well as the vagaries of the marketplace. Since seamen sought employment on their own terms, they had to be willing to actively seek it: they had to be prepared to travel where jobs were the most abundant and wages were the most lucrative. Procurement of one's next voyage could involve a high degree of mobility. For men accustomed to such self-reliance and freedom in their employment dealings, naval service not only was "inconvenient" but violated their sense of worth and independence. Furthermore, it interfered with each individual's schedule, employment pattern, and earning potential.

The absence of career naval seamen meant that the state did not have a large group of loyal and skilled men bred to accept the greater risks, harsher discipline, rigid hierarchy, lower wages, and poor shipboard conditions associated with the navy. Lack of state or guild standardization of maritime apprenticeship and the absence of a naval training program in peace or war meant that the state had no control over the caliber of men whom it impressed or attracted to its service. Essentially, the Crown relied on traditional approaches to increase, gather, and train manpower in times of national emergency.

The following discussion of the various aspects of manning demonstrates how truly individualistic the members of the maritime community were, how conscious seamen were of the value of their own labor and their customary "rights," and how tenaciously they clung to their traditional practices. The lack of a guild did not obstruct seamen's awareness of themselves as skilled craftsmen. Clearly, this was present and is illustrated through an analysis of seamen's attitudes regarding their labor, the power of the individual to make his own employment contracts, and the traditional freedom to choose the nature of his own work. These themes reinforce E. P. Thompson's observation: "The conservative culture of the plebs as often as not resists, in the name of 'custom,' those economic innovations and rationalizations . . . which the rulers or the employers seek to impose."[6]

Naval activity had hitherto been largely sporadic in nature. However, England's war against Spain was the first to depend so heavily on its navy for a protracted period. Hence, the traditional employment and customs of a major occupational group were subjugated to the military requirements of the state. Because of the different recruitment patterns of the army and the navy,[7] the maritime community was the first economic group to feel the full force of the expanding early modern state. While the state could coerce its seamen to serve, it could not dominate them; their consciousness of their conventional practices and independence was not altered. Forced employment temporarily annulled established customs but did not eradicate seamen's underlying sense of entitlement to certain "rights." Because military service was seen by the Crown in temporary terms, no effort was made to resocialize seamen for their naval roles. The state realized its basic requirements without fundamental alteration or intrusion; the seafaring community therefore retained its customary characteristics and ethos.

APPRENTICESHIP AND EXTERNAL REGULATION

Sixteenth-century society used service as a means to train and educate its young both for life as part of the adult community and for their specific occupations. Although information on Elizabethan maritime apprenticeship is meager,[8] the available sources indicate that formal and informal apprenticeship to the sea had the same basic goals as service on land: technical education and social discipline. Apprenticeship had the added advantage of providing economic benefits and an inexpensive source of labor for the master.

Despite the greatly increased demands for seamen during the war years, apprenticeship and training remained unaltered: standards were upheld through individual instruction and not by any type of collective or state directives or monitoring. The Statute of Artificers (1563) was the only significant attempt by the Elizabethan state to regulate and expand apprenticeship laws for every craft or occupation throughout the kingdom. This legislation required a minimum of a seven-year apprenticeship, but this was very rarely enforced.[9]

The lack of regulations governing maritime apprenticeship can be attributed to seamen's lack of a formal guild, although the Trinity Houses of Hull, Deptford, and Newcastle assumed some of the duties of a guild.[10] These private foundations were principally concerned with pilotage and dispensation of alms but also provided mediation to settle disputes within the maritime community without divisive recourse to law.[11] Proposals for more formal and uniform organizations to regulate the standards of these "craftsmen of the sea" were a feature of the Elizabethan period. England lacked a comprehensive national system to regulate navigators and pilots such as existed in Spain and Portugal.[12] In Spain, for instance, all masters and pilots were examined and authorized by the pilot-major. Master navigator Stephen Borough proposed that England establish a program on the Spanish model. A draft royal commission was drawn up in 1564 naming Borough as "Cheyffe Pilote of this owr realme of Englande." He would be granted the same powers as the Spanish pilot-major; all masters and pilots of ships over 40 tons burden would have to be examined and certified by Borough and his deputies. Seamen navigating without authorization would be fined 20 shillings. Similarly, officers such as boatswains, quartermasters, and master's mates would be required to pass an examination. The commission, however, was never confirmed.[13] Other national programs to educate navigators and pilots in the new mathematical methods of navigation were proposed but came to nothing.[14] Likewise, the idea of a corporation of naval gunners was advanced but never materialized.[15] Although Elizabeth's Parliament enacted "fish days" to foster the fisheries and provide a training ground for seamen,[16] there were no mechanisms to uphold standards outside individual apprenticeship and "natural selection," the elimination of the unskilled and careless as a result of the various hazards inherent in sixteenth-century seafaring. Trinity Houses and merchant companies made efforts to monitor the abilities of their memberships, but evidence suggests that there was a dearth of qualified men within these increasingly technical fields.[17]

The failure to develop such programs can, in part, be explained by inertia. The Elizabethan state normally avoided innovation in favor of convention. The Queen's policy toward her navy was to employ previously tried methods; by enforcing "fish days," she hoped to train and employ seamen and by offering bounties for shipbuilding, she encouraged private employers to construct large vessels that could be hired by the Crown during a crisis without the costs of upkeep and maintenance; impressment furnished seamen for her navy. Privateering was also an old practice; by issuing letters of marque, Elizabeth hoped to wage her war against Spain and turn a profit. In light of these policies, it is not surprising that the Crown was ultimately unwilling to sponsor or fund a national project. The absence of such a program is consistent with the Crown's unstated policy of relying on traditional practices and keeping interference in the maritime community to a minimum. Borough, for example, was named merely as one of the four ordinary masters of the Queen's navy and left to advance his recommendations for skilled mariners within the more limited sphere. Although the Crown briefly considered sweeping regulation of the maritime community, it retreated from such intrusion. The monitoring of skilled navigators was left to the Trinity Houses of the realm. The Crown's neglect of national regulation of skilled seamen was probably influenced by the Trinity Houses; Borough's proposed program would have expropriated their established rights in regard to pilotage. Since Elizabeth confirmed the existing Trinity House charters at her accession, the Crown was left with a conflict between vested interests and innovation. Ultimately, the state was content to utilize the infrastructure already in place.

For their part, most seamen were independent craftsmen who concentrated on their own livelihoods at the expense of the collective. Seamen were used to acting as individual agents who set the terms of their own employment. Borough spoke of seamen skilled in new navigation techniques who "wold not gladly teach [each] other, for hinderinge of their oune lyvinge."[18] Crews could band together when necessity required, but self-sufficiency was deeply ingrained. Without a guild to lead or speak for the collective, seamen were not accustomed to acting or thinking in terms of the greater good of all seafarers. It was left to men such as scholar and propagandist Richard Hakluyt or to a self-promoter such as Stephen Borough to advocate training programs. Yet most shipmasters clung to the traditional methods of navigation; there was a deep distrust of "mathematical seamen."[19] Experience, in most seamen's view, was still the best teacher.[20]

In the absence of guild or state regulation, individual mariners made decisions to apprentice boys to the sea for their own reasons. The needs of the state in wartime were irrelevant to the process; apprenticeship was based on training youth for peacetime roles in the maritime community. The state encouraged parishes to indenture pauper boys as seamen at the local authority's expense as part of the state's attempt to control the growing problem of vagabondage and poverty.[21] This was the Crown's only intervention, and it was not unique to Elizabeth's reign or to periods of sustained naval warfare.[22] Maritime apprenticeship was characterized by continuity, not change.

LEGAL BASIS OF APPRENTICESHIP

A fortunate few seafarers were formally indentured to mariners. Formal apprenticeship within the mercantile marine was usually restricted to those boys whose parents could afford to indenture them or to pauper children educated at the expense of the parish. Not until late in the next century did the state begin to apprentice pauper boys to the navy itself, thereby providing boys with a trade as well as serving its own need for manpower. If these youths survived to complete their training, they would enter the skilled elite of the maritime community. Apprentices' indentures were binding and set out the respective obligations of the servant and master. Masters were bound to educate the boy in their craft, "soe farre as the capacitie of the said [youth] shalbe hable to receyve the same"; they provided meat, drink, bedding, and "washing and wringing" in addition to "all other thinges necessarie for such an apprentice."[23] Many masters agreed to supply clothes "boothe lynnen and woollen, hose and shoes." In return, apprentices were expected to work for their masters, remain unmarried during their indenture, stay out of taverns and alehouses, refrain from playing unlawful games, and generally behave themselves.[24] At the end of service, apprentices were often provided with a double set of apparel, one for holy days and one for workdays.[25] This was standard in many trades, as was a gift of money and tools of the trade at the conclusion of an apprenticeship. For seamen, sea-beds, chests, sea-gowns, and sometimes navigational instruments were to be provided on the successful completion of training. Terms of the indenture could be influenced by the socioeconomic status of the parents and the masters and frequently varied even among individual masters. For instance, the indentures for James Robson's two apprentices were dissimilar; both servants were simultaneously granted their freedom under the terms of Robson's will in 1602, but Richard Wilcocks's indenture promised him 40 shillings, navigational instruments, and two sets of apparel "for the holliday and workday." Edward Collins was to have only 20 shillings and two sets of apparel.[26] Sometimes masters provided a significant amount of money. In their wills some seamen set down generous sums for their charges at the completion of their training; master Philip Grimes gave his apprenticed servant ten pounds, boatswain Thomas Ivett provided his servant with six pounds, while mariners Robert Freeman and John Blome each contributed five pounds for their apprentices.[27] These examples provide an indication of the sums granted in expectation of full and faithful service.[28] A gift of five pounds would be sufficient to equip a youthful skilled seaman and provide him with basic maintenance for a month or two while he sought employment.

Because apprentices were technically indentured to both the master and his wife in the land and sea trades, servants of deceased masters could be expected to fulfill their term in their mistress's service.[29] For example, boatswain Thomas Ivett's third apprentice, Anthony Barber, was given over in his last will and testament to his widow's care and supervision.[30] This bond to both seaman and spouse is reflected in the 1607 will of apprentice John Roche of Whitechapel: "and whatsoever becometh of me in this voyage is due to my Master [Francis Giles] and my dame his wife."[31]

Boys routinely began their training between the ages of 12 and 17 for the land trades.[32] From available documentation we can say that maritime apprenticeships follow this pattern.[33] There were always exceptions to the rule. Boys did go to sea at even younger ages; 30-year-old William Bonfield of Weymouth Melcombe Regis claimed that he had been a seaman for 20 years. It was not unusual to find 10-year-olds aboard, although it is uncertain if they were in apprenticeships. There were also youths who came relatively late to the sea; Masters Robert Duke and Lucas Barfoote were apprenticed at 18, and Master Thomas Kerwoode and gunner James Jennings began their careers at age 20.[34]

The boy's age at the time of the indenture was obviously only one of many considerations; the timing of the indentures was also determined by the parents' ability to pay an apprenticeship premium and to select a suitable master and willingness to part with their son and his economic contribution to the household economy. It was also based upon striking a mutually beneficial agreement between the parties. In the 1580s Richard Caseye Sr. persuaded shipwright Thomas Greaves (or Graves) to take his son,

to serve him as his apprentice which he [Greaves] was verie lothe to doe for that he was so younge but in the end at the erneste requeste of the said Richard Casys father and this Examinate [Greaves's father, Henry] the said Thomas Graves was contente to take him for eighte yeres wherevppon Indentures were drawen accordinglie betwen them for the accomplishmente of the saide yeres.[35]

In another case, Philip Courte went to sea for a trial period before any formal agreement was made; Anthony Moore (whose relationship to Courte is unclear) conferred with master John Lane and

prayed hime to take the boy to sea for a viadge or two, and if he liked of the boy & the boy liked of him, he should haue him for vij yeares and he would be bound for his truthe.[36]

Such evidence suggests an overabundance of would-be apprentices. Clearly, the establishment of an apprenticeship was not simply an economic matter; there was a social component that reveals the importance of personal connections and influence for entry into the maritime occupational elite.

The normal duration of apprenticeship seems to have been between seven and twelve years for both land and sea trades. Variations were frequent. The following brief case histories reveal common patterns. Master Thomas Grey (one of the principal masters of the navy) went to sea as a young boy and became a master around the time he was 19. Similarly, William Allen went to sea at age 10 and became a master at 22. Those who were apprenticed at older ages appear to have had shorter terms. Robert Duke was apprenticed at 18 but became a master when he was 23. Thomas Kerwoode was apprenticed at 20 and became a master at 24.[37] Perhaps late age at the time of apprenticeship and shorter terms can be explained as second indentures; because mortality was high in the sixteenth century, it was not uncommon for the master to die before the period of service was completed, and these circumstances sometimes resulted in new apprenticeship indentures. On his deathbed in 1554, Cornelius Lucas, probably the gunner of the *Primrose*, provided for an overseer to take care of his boy, Henry Sanderton:

I will and desire Thomas Swallowe to be my ouerseer and to receyve my holle wages and to paye my debtes and to take my boye and vse hym as he will. And I giue to Thomas Swallowe all my golde and xij Rialle of plate with all that is myne at portesmouthe saving my Toulles and two monethes wages whiche I giue to hym that kepeth my boye.[38]

An alternative explanation is that these shorter indentures follow upon nonapprenticed prior employment at sea; unfortunately, the earlier life histories cannot be reconstructed. As in the land trades, 24 was viewed by this society as a desirable age to release apprentices from service.[39] Thus, shorter and later apprenticeships could reflect a combination of higher skill levels at the time of the indentures or current cultural concepts.

Servants might be acquitted of the time remaining in their masters' wills, thus giving them a shorter apprenticeship. Boatswain Thomas Ivett had three apprenticed servants; he acquitted two of their time while leaving the third indentured.[40] Mariner John Benn of Essex freed his apprentice Robert Freeman after five years of service but dictated that John Clark must fulfill his term of years.[41] Masters presumably made decisions depending upon the skill attainments of their charges and/or the continuing labor or income needs of their own families following the breadwinners' demise.

Occupational training did not necessarily include schooling. Indentures did not bind masters on this issue. However, the land trades usually included a period of schooling.[42] Unquestionably, literacy and numeracy would have been assets to the maritime elite involved in navigation and seaborne trade.[43] During a voyage to Russia in 1602, the *Speedwell* of London was attacked by a Dunkirk privateer, and pilot John Hare found himself confronted by an old schoolfellow, John Allen alias Sallows, the English master/pilot of the enemy vessel.[44] Master's mate John Parr knew sailor Christopher Mills before they were shipped on the crayer *Greyhound*, for they had once been schoolfellows.[45] Although evidence is practically nonexistent on this point, routine schooling could explain the extremely high rate of literacy among skilled seamen; they were plausibly beneficiaries of the expansion of English educational opportunities in the sixteenth century.[46] Evidence from the Admiralty Court depositions suggests that literacy was extremely widespread among officers and some seamen. Since seafaring life would have been difficult to coordinate with schooling ashore, boys might have been taught on shipboard.

SOCIAL AND FAMILIAL ASPECTS OF APPRENTICESHIP

In her work on sixteenth-century Bristol, Anne Yarbrough claims that apprenticeship "was the single most important channel for . . . the maintenance of traditional values from one generation to the next."[47] Tudor society was based upon the idea of service (both indentured and nonindentured) and educated its young principally through this method. Service was part of the "social ethos" of the Tudor period.[48] Through service boys and girls learned their place within the societal hierarchy in the expectation that they would become contributing members in Tudor society in their own right. This period was the second stage in the progress from child to servant to householding adult. It was significant in that the youth took on greater responsibilities, as masters "have no use for hired infants."[49] Like apprenticeship in the land trades, maritime youths were expected to leave their families and take up residence in the household of their new master.[50] "Binding out" introduced youth to the larger community and allowed for the development of important social ties outside their immediate family. Nonetheless, kinship and social bonds were significant factors in placing a boy in maritime apprenticeship and service.[51] For example, Christopher Coo had "a ladde . . . putt to (him) by his freend to be browght uppe."[52] In his will, sailor James Thornbush of Suffolk committed his sons James and John to the custody of "his loving friend," merchant Francis Foxe, until their respective ages of majority. Because Thornbush's wife was alive at the time that his will was written, he probably had occupational training in mind when he left his sons to Foxe's care.[53]

There is overwhelming evidence that seamen tended to come from seafaring families. Through record linkage of Admiralty records, wills, parish records, and marriage allegations, it is possible to reconstruct numerous seamen's families.[54] In the rapidly expanding London-area maritime communities—in particular, the parishes of Ratcliffe, Limehouse, Wapping, and Rotherhithe, which contained large numbers of seafarers relative to the overall population—it was routine to have sons apprenticed in their fathers' trade. Wages in London tended to be higher relative to those in other English ports, and the fact that so many sons remained in their home parishes after they became masters and officers suggests they could find ready work. The 1629 survey of seamen in London shows that 3,422 seamen lived in the environs of London, and of these, 529 were masters and Trinity House brothers. Numbers of resident seamen in the area had more than doubled between 1582 and 1629.[55] Furthermore, it was not unusual to have brothers or fathers and sons employed aboard the same ship. This is true not just of highly skilled members of the maritime community but also of men farther down the social ladder. While studies of the role of kinship in employment in the early modern period are rare, it has been suggested that kinship bonds played a significant role.[56] The expanding maritime commerce of Elizabethan England provides an interesting case study in the interaction between kinship and apprenticeship within one of the largest, but also the most mobile, employee groups of early modern England.

The Rickman family of Ratcliffe, Middlesex, is an apt illustration of seafaring as an inherited occupation. Robert and Thomas Rickman were both masters of high esteem. The sources are not clear whether the two were brothers or cousins. Thomas died without issue, but Robert and his many sons constituted a formidable seafaring dynasty during the late sixteenth and early seventeenth centuries. At least one of Robert's boys was educated at his side: his 20-year-old son, Henry, served his father aboard the *Trinity* in 1603. Another son, Thomas, was apprenticed as "the boy" of one Master King. At least one of Robert's grandsons also became a mariner. Like the Rickmans, the Goodlad family of Leigh, Essex, made their living from the sea; brothers Richard, John, and William were shipmasters. The latter two had sons whom they apprenticed to the sea. Although the details of their apprenticeship are not known, we do know that, like their fathers, the sons became respected masters and Brethren of Trinity House. Their descendants were ship commanders in 1684 and 1686.[57]

From the few examples where grandsons were produced and can be positively identified through record linkage, it is apparent that occupations could be handed down through generations within an expanding sector of the economy. Nevertheless, there is little evidence that seamen explicitly wanted their sons to be apprenticed to the sea. Even though wills were frequently written during the children's minority, fathers rarely indicate a preference regarding their sons' occupations.[58] Mariner William Palmer of Ratcliffe is typical in that he willed only that his son "be broughte vp in learninge and in the feare of god."[59] One cannot preclude the possibility that the boys' careers had been discussed or determined prior to the writing of the wills. However, many of the children were quite young when the wills were written, and the silence is striking. This silence is particularly noteworthy in cases of deathbed, shipboard wills where the testator was physically separated from spouse and family and would have been more inclined to place on the written record his wishes for his children. As in the Palmer case, preferences were stated, but they were not occupation-specific. No doubt sons' apprenticeship to the sea resulted more from opportunity and connections than parental desire to perpetuate the "family business," especially among the less skilled or less successful, where there was no transfer of capital property (ownership of, or shares in, vessels) between generations.[60]

The effectiveness of the intergenerational socialization process depended greatly upon master–apprentice relationships. There was significant diversity in the character of relations between masters and their servants. In general, masters were expected to serve *in loco parentis*.[61] They were "charitablie to correct" the boys for their "defaltes and offences" and to care for their charges "aswell in sicknes as in helth."[62] However, relations could be turbulent at times. In the course of one voyage in 1575, shipmaster Robert Feewilliams fell out with both his apprentice and the ship's purser. The purser and the master's boy were accused of informing on Feewilliams to Catholic priests at Seville as an act of revenge.[63] The story of Edward Hampton, who ran away from his master because of his alleged illtreatment and refused to return, was probably not uncommon.[64]

The records of the law courts—in this case the High Court of Admiralty—are, of course, dominated by disputes and conflict. The writing of the social history of an occupational group strictly from judicial records clearly privileges the failures in the socializing and employment processes. Complementary analysis of last wills and testaments reveals obverse evidence. Moreover, within the abundant civil disputes of the High Court of Admiralty, master–apprentice conflict is relatively rare, whereas the equally abundant testamentary evidence provides evidence of bonds of loyalty and affection between masters and their charges. For example, mariner Thomas Munson left all his apparel and wages to his servant Thomas Williams.[65] Shipmaster John Fryer bequeathed all his tools and instruments for the sea to his former apprentice, sailor William Roo (or Roe). Fryer also stipulated that Roo should inherit the lease of his house if his immediate family died.[66] It was fairly common in seamen's wills for masters to mention their servants. Mariner John Benn of Essex gave his apprentice John Clark 20 shillings in addition to the terms of the indenture if Clark did "his duetie diligently."[67] In 1562 boatswain John Grebby willed

vnto Nicholas dowlym my prentice his iiij . . . yeres seruice xls. in monney, one Carde with compasses, one Cheste, iiij shertes, one bcd with a Coueringe, one gowne, one black cloke, thre paire of bretches, ij Cassockes and one paire of hose.[68]

There are probably many unidentified apprentices and former apprentices in seamen's wills among the host of men whose relationship to the testator is unexplained. Although apprentices' wills are relatively rare, in recovered records the loyalty and affection were returned. Apprentice mariner John Roche's will acknowledges the gratitude of servant for his master and mistress; he gave Master and Mistress Giles the wages for his last voyage "for the satisfaction of the debt I owe them."[69] As in the land trades, indentured servants of the maritime trades like Roche were made to feel a part of both an economic unit and a household. Apprentice Henry Goslinge gave his master (and uncle) mariner Stephen Talmage half his belongings.[70] In September 1603 Edward Cornewall fell sick on the *Red*

Dragon on her return voyage from the East Indies. He had been the apprentice of William Winter, one of the master's mates, who had predeceased him:

at his deathe [I] was my owne Man and from that tyme my wages was due to my self yett for [the] love I did carrie him I doe giue and bequeathe vnto Ellen Winter wief vnto my late Master William Winter all the wages due vnto me synce his deathe.[71]

Like the community on land, servants and youth were an integral part of Tudor society afloat. While shipboard communities usually excluded women, they mirrored their counterparts on land in terms of hierarchy and in that service was an essential component. The community was a social unit with economic goals; it contained large numbers of youth under tutelage who contributed to the overall productivity. Apprenticeship was comprehensive in its aims; it provided an education, contacts, tools, and money in order to begin a career of one's own. It also allowed the boy a surrogate family and a new network that enlarged his social horizons. The overall goal was to produce a skilled worker who was equipped to fulfill both his social and economic role; he knew his place in Tudor society and was content to function within the confines that birth and training had dictated. The evidence points to effective overall socialization, helping to perpetuate a traditional craft in a time of disruption.

ECONOMIC ASPECTS OF APPRENTICESHIP

Apprenticeship was an important component of the overall economic system of sixteenth-century society. Given that seamen worked and lived largely within their occupational network, it is not surprising that they routinely chose associates in maritime or trade-related activities to train their sons. The selection of a master for an apprentice was influenced by connections within the maritime community and the family's means. While apprenticed maritime youth frequently hailed from moderately prosperous families, more than one boy in apprenticeship could strain the resources of a family, especially if the parents hoped to secure accomplished masters to instruct their offspring. Occupational networks and business contacts influenced the choice of a master for one's son.

One common pattern was for men in related trades to apprentice their sons as mariners. For instance, shipwright Nicholas Diggens's son Nicholas became a successful mariner. Similarly, some seamen learned ship carpentry to increase their marketability. The Bence family of Suffolk included both merchants and mariners. Boys who were apprenticed as merchants became mariners, and vice versa. For instance, John Callice testified in 1577 that he had been apprenticed first as a merchant and then as a mariner. Michael

Geare, a successful privateering captain, had been apprenticed as a mariner but later identified himself as a merchant. Sir John Hawkins, one of Elizabeth's greatest seamen, an architect of her navy and cousin to Sir Francis Drake, probably began his career as a merchant factor watching his father's interests on shipboard. Seafaring and trade were a natural pairing. Merchants were also attracted to sea service in privateers and trading vessels because of potential profitability and to guard the interest of the investors. Given their involvement, it was common for merchant backers to serve as captains. Some merchants drifted from legal trade to piracy; although risky, the latter could be particularly lucrative. One of the most notorious Elizabethan pirate captains, Clinton Atkinson, was a London merchant by trade.[72]

Although masters incurred considerable costs in clothing, feeding, and housing servants, apprenticeship had financial benefits for the master; he profited from the additional labor and collected the wages or shares of any voyages that the boy made. Masters in maritime occupations were relieved of the financial burden of providing food, drink, and shelter for their servants during the voyages since seamen's victuals were not deducted from their wages.[73] The contemporary recognition of a separate stage of apprenticed adolescence translated into distinctive employment and remuneration patterns. On board the *Greyhound*, John Tresolde was seen as a "striplinge of the age of xvj or xvij yeres," and the crew recognized that "neyther was [he] able to doe nor did suche labor as a man oughte to doe."[74] In 1580 Richard Rider received the wages for his apprentice, which were calculated to be "halfe the wages of a man."[75] Because most maritime masters were themselves waged employees, the normal economic pattern was for an individual to contract with his employers for his labor and that of his apprenticed servant(s). For example, shipmaster Bartholomew Hugguet received the wages for his three apprentices.[76] In early modern English urban apprenticeships, the apprentice was normally the servant within an established household headed by an independent master, and the principal economic benefit to the master was the apprentice's labor. There are few parallels on land for a master–apprentice relationship where the principal economic value lay in cash profit from wages. The use of apprenticed labor to acquire wage profits applied also to land-based trades that sent numbers of their occupation to sea, as can be seen in the provision of apprenticed ship surgeons by the masters of the Barber-Surgeons Company of London.[77]

In 1589 the right of the master to his servant's earnings was tested in the Admiralty Court when shipwright Thomas Greaves filed a suit in the court regarding the breach between himself and his apprentice, Richard Caseye Jr. Greaves claimed that he was greatly hindered by the loss of his indentured servant; the shipwright had outfitted his servant for a privateering voyage, and Caseye refused to return to his master after the voyage ended. Greaves maintained that he was entitled to his apprentice's wages in addition to the "service . . . a servante oughte to doe." Thomas's father, shipwright Henry Greaves of Ratcliffe, testified under oath in the Admiralty Court that "yt ys both vse & custome of his knowledge and greate equity also . . . that Masters should haue the gayne of theire prentises viadges which they bring vpp instruct and furnishe to sea." It seems more likely that the real issue was that Greaves felt entitled to the great wealth that Caseye garnered while on his privateering voyage. It was estimated that Caseye amassed £200 worth of silk, gold, and other commodities. Caseye's father told Greaves that "yt was not his service that he soughte but the gayne of his viadge which he sayd he should never haue excepte he won yt by lawe." The court recognized Greaves's rights to the revenue of his servant.[78]

Service could also have economic benefits for the widow of a maritime master. Fisherman Simon Stamford promised his "covenant servant" Harry Gooddin 26s.8d. and a half share in the family's fishing boat in partnership with Simon's son, Thomas, if he completed his time in the service of Simon's wife, Eleanor.[79] While James Robson's will released both his servants from their time, he ensured that his wife, Elizabeth, would receive both their shares and wages from their final voyage.[80]

Families might also benefit from a boy's apprenticeship. Seamen, merchants, and shipowners found it convenient to apprentice their boys to the sea so that they became knowledgable about maritime industries before inheriting vessels, shares in shipping, or trade-related responsibilities. There were obvious advantages to leaving ownership to a skilled seaman. A knowledge of the inner workings of the maritime community was an asset for those men who sought to maximize their profits in the competitive and risky world of sixteenth-century trade.

Ultimately, the servant would also profit from his training. Tutelage under an established master was a definite asset. Maritime apprenticeship was not like guild and land-based apprenticeships, where such training was a legal requirement (except when freedom was accorded by patrimony) to practice the craft. The upper ranks of the maritime community were not closed to those who had not completed an apprenticeship, but covenant servants almost always took their place among the skilled elite and highest wage earners. The few who received formal apprenticeship became masters, pilots, and often shipowners. Apprenticeship in itself offered the opportunity for rapid advancement and command. Because skill in navigation was the dividing line between a seaman capable of command and the rest of the crew, apprenticeship was the surest route of obtaining these skills.[81] With the increase in transoceanic travel, navigational ability grew in value; a completed apprenticeship with an adept navigator increased one's worth on the labor market. Shipowners and merchants were no doubt more willing—at least initially—to entrust their ship and cargo to a man who had learned navigation and business acumen under a shipmaster of ability and reputation than to one who lacked such credentials. A young master would have to sink or swim on his own abilities, but apprenticeship could provide those all-important initial breaks. While knowledge and training were not the only criteria for command, apprenticeship to a shipmaster or pilot "fast-tracked" a small number of youths for positions of authority and virtually assured them of a gainful living. Connections and an element of luck were added assets. Skilled seamen who were relatives of merchants, shipowners, or successful shipmasters were doubly assured of their prospects to command at a young age.[82] While apprenticeship alone could not guarantee the choicest employment opportunities or great wealth, it altered the boy's prospects drastically from that of the majority of his shipmates.

LIMITATIONS OF MARITIME APPRENTICESHIP IN THE SIXTEENTH CENTURY

In 1598 sailor Thomas Chartham of Feversham, Kent, complained that glover Mathew Harte, sawyer Thomas Virgo, and servingman John Hamon left their respective trades in 1595 to operate hoys on the Thames. Chartham protested that they had not "beeyne broughte vpp apprentise vnto any maryner" and were

thereby takeinge from this examinate and others whoe haue duely served Apprentises vnto Seafayreinge men the Lyveinge which they dyd and shoulde gette by followeinge the trade where vnto they haue served and beyn Broughte vpp.[83]

Chartham had little recourse except to appeal to the Lord Admiral to monitor the standards of the craft for the sake of the navy:

her Majestye is disappointed in tyme of service when occasion servethe for theise and suche like vnskilfull persons ether with drawe them selves . . . or beinge constrayned there vnto for lake of skylle and knowledge doe indanger the chardge they take in hande.[84]

In the absence of civic or national regulation, seamen's only hope—a remote one—was an appeal to the state to defend its interests. Chartham was not alone in his complaints. The Trinity Brethren had a history of appealing to the Lord Admiral to guard their asserted rights to conduct pilotage on the Thames; they lacked the authority to uphold standards even in their own limited domain. A formal guild would have preserved standards of the craft by monitoring apprenticeship and safeguarding its membership from infiltration by landsmen. Guilds, however, were invariably municipal, and English seafaring was national and sometimes international in its membership. Even the Thames basin contained an abundance of independent local authorities, dispersed among four counties. Nonetheless, the Tudor state was unused to any role in independent regulation. When the state did require regulation of extramunicipal economic groups, it customarily turned to the church for the necessary administration (as in the regulation of the press, medical practitioners, and midwives); this model possessed little relevance for the merchant marine. The absence of organization meant that seamen were unprotected as craftsmen. The standards of the trade were left solely to individuals to uphold. Lack of a guild compromised the level of training that seamen received; most men never benefited from apprenticeship. Although we have few details, it seems that most seamen learned their trade through on-the-job training, and the majority of fishermen, merchant seamen, pirates, privateers, and naval seamen were never indentured.[85] In the absence of a formal guild or binding regulations, most training was conducted casually. Ordinary seamen professed themselves to be "simple men . . . [with] like skill."[86] Even those who sought proficiency in a maritime craft could seek it through informal training.[87] Many presumably followed the example of Christopher Mills of London, who simply shipped himself with master Robert Bush so that he might learn a mariner's trade.[88] He paid no apprenticeship premium, suffered none of the restrictions placed upon his freedom—sexual, moral, occupational—by apprenticeship, and kept the wages that he earned. The road to the top was longer and harder, but in this expanding sector of the economy many like Christopher Mills of this period found acceptable economic niches, free of patriarchal discipline and insulated by the peculiar life of a recognized subgroup within society.

Thus, seamen had a two-tiered system of training for the highly skilled upper ranks and the less skilled lower echelons; professional wisdom was passed on through formal and informal channels within the maritime community. While informal training might have proved satisfactory for the less skilled seamen, it compromised the overall quality of Elizabethan seamen. Lack of apprenticeship regulation and development opened the door to unrestricted entry, competition, and incompetence in a trade already fraught with life-threatening hazards.

HIRING AND ENTRY INTO SERVICE

As in the case of apprenticeship, seamen's lack of a guild meant that hiring practices were governed mostly by custom and not regulated by a trade organization. Unlike other waged laborers of the period, seamen's hiring practices were not monitored by the polity either.[89] Seamen's employment was based on a peripatetic work pattern, and the individual was responsible for negotiating the terms of his own employment. In regard to specific durations of employment, work-related geographic mobility, and the individual's role in negotiating contracts, seamen had much in common with other laborers of the period such as colliers and farm laborers.[90] Although seamen had a large amount of employment freedom (the converse being the absence of job security) relative to many of the land-based trades, it does not necessarily follow that they were unparalleled in Tudor society. Farm servants, for instance, had a high degree of geographic mobility and entered into their own short-term contracts. These contracts, however, were based upon an annual pattern that was determined regionally.[91] While the hiring practices of some seamen were governed by the seasonal nature of their runs, many types of voyages operated year-round, and hiring was not based upon the seasons.

Owners and merchants usually hired the master if he was not already a shareholder in the vessel. While merchants often sent representatives to take care of their interests on important voyages, the responsibility of representing the interests of the owners normally fell to shipmasters. Since both maritime and commercial interests were at stake, the owners were eager to select a trustworthy man of ability in both areas. Thus, those men hired by the shipmasters were often related to the owners and merchants. The growth of shipping, however, created new places for skilled men of ability.

The rest of the complement was normally hired by the shipmaster but were sometimes retained by the owners of the ship. Contracts were made verbally and rested on a foundation of customary practice and English Common Law.[92] This could present problems for the employees; if the owner disputed the terms at the end of the voyage, seamen had no written proof of their contract.[93] The will of mariner George Warde in 1557 bequeathed his wages to his mother and named his uncle as "myne Attorney to withstande and attempte the lawe against all suche as withholde or kepe awaye any part mencyoned."[94] While shipowners were more likely to make binding written agreements with masters, this was not always the case. Laurence Rowndell of the *John Baptist* made his will during the Guinea voyage of 1564–65 and bequeathed his wages to his executrix. Although Rowndell was probably the master, he acknowledged the possibility that his wife and executrix would never receive her due, in which case the matter would be left "betwene god and theire [the London merchants'] conscience whoe ys a righeous Judge."[95] Judging from the experience of land-based industry, the casual nature of the employment agreements suggests, once again, an abundance of labor.

Predictably, wages and perquisites were crucial to lure men into employment. These themes are discussed fully later. Suffice it to say that seamen (excluding apprentices) were individual agents who sought to hire themselves out for suitable wages in positions that they thought reasonable and to appropriate destinations.[96] Undeniably, it was important for a man of skill to obtain a place in a rating befitting his rank. For instance, a man who considered himself an "officer" might be willing to sail as a mate, but only the most desperate would debase themselves much below their station. For the most part, seamen sought out the most advantageous positions and could be quite mercenary in the pursuit of wages and shares. One seaman boasted "that if the Great Turk would give a penny a day more he would serve him."[97] This statement contains a good deal of truth, although presumably its author intended that it should possess shock value. Some English seamen were unsatisfied with conditions at home and opted for service on foreign ships. For those pursuits judged as being lucrative, there was no shortage of willing men.[98] Certainly, English privateers could be found serving under commissions of foreign princes such as the king of Navarre, the prince of Orange, and Don Antonio of Portugal, although in some instances at least these were merely flags of convenience.[99] Foreign employment could also include laboring for national enemies. Although he ultimately returned to England for employment, William Allen alias Sallows made a career out of plundering his own countrymen on Spanish and Dunkirk ships.[100] He was not alone. Contemporaries recognized that privateering had a great attraction for seamen. Stuart sea captain Nathaniel Boetler wrote in his *Dialogues*: "As for the business of pillage, there is nothing that more bewitcheth them, nor anything wherein they promise themselves so loudly, nor delight in more mainly."[101] Sir Richard Hawkins asserted that seamen's "mindes are all set on spoyle."[102] Such service held the greatest hope of reward—at least in the minds of seamen.[103] When trading voyages and privateering were combined, the employment proved compelling because it offered both the guaranteed wages of merchant voyages and the shares of prizes that the privateers offered. Some seamen preferred to sail the more dangerous runs, which promised higher wages. Frobisher's northwest passage voyages of 1576–78 offered wages at twice the going rate to attract employees, and the trade with tropical West Africa depended upon higher than normal levels of remuneration.[104] Some men sailed almost exclusively on coastal voyages, which held the fewest dangers, especially when compared to risky, long-distance voyages. Mariner Anthony Loveking, for example, made his living sailing on coal runs to Newcastle on the *Margaret* of London.[105] The majority of seamen earned their daily bread from the coasting and short-distance foreign trades: "for every seaman who sailed west with John Hawkins there were a thousand who spent the whole of their active lives at sea but never passed beyond 10° west."[106]

There was great diversity within career patterns. Some seamen testified to serving on the same ship for several voyages with many of the same crewmates and preferred to sail frequently to the same destination. Naturally, there would be a greater sense of security in the familiar routine of the voyage and dealing with the same workmates and owners. Others were not nearly so specialized, and their choices show great variety in both the type of voyages and destinations. Patrick Dalton of Plymouth was the master of the *Jennet* of Stonehouse to Roscoff in April and May 1580. In June and July he sailed the *Greyhound* of Plymouth for Morlaix, while in August and September he took the *Trinity* of Plymouth to Conquet, Brittany.[107]

Seamen's impermanence in regard to employers and type of voyage does not necessarily imply that they were dissatisfied with working conditions or remuneration. In part, career patterns rested upon the seasonal nature of certain routes. Some coasting and most fishing voyages took place from the spring to the autumn. The transport of cargoes of wine to and from Bordeaux was determined by the October and February wine fairs. The salt and grain trade with Spain (prior to the embargo of 1585) was characterized by two major periods of activity.[108] While there were exceptions, many types of voyages proceeded in the winter months. Since seamen were hired by the voyage, most were not able to support themselves if there were long intervals between the time that their ships returned to port and the next departure. It was easier for a mariner to find job security with merchant companies, such as the Levant or East India Companies, that operated several ships. Reputation was critical. Cargoes were expensive, and a master or skilled seaman who showed himself trustworthy and capable could expect to be hired for additional voyages.[109] Those seamen who aspired to higher wages, a better rating with more responsibility, or improved shipboard conditions could seek their fortunes elsewhere; as in the case of other mobile labor groups, moving on to a new master allowed for the possibility of improving one's lot.[110]

Seamen were willing to take risks, but they did have their limits. Recruitment was difficult for voyages of exploration, and impressment frequently had to be used in addition to, or in lieu of, higher wages.[111] Drake concealed the true nature of his voyage of circumnavigation largely because he would have found it difficult to recruit seamen; he told his crew that he was sailing to Alexandria.[112] Martin Frobisher's northern voyages were not attractive to seamen, and, in spite of exceptionally high wage rates, prisoners had to be used to meet the shortfall.[113] Shortages of manpower, however, were almost exclusively a naval problem, where service was poorly rewarded. With the exception of the navy, hiring practices were essentially the same; seamen negotiated with masters or owners for wages, perquisites, and position. While elements such as skill level, experience, and the "going rate" limited seamen's expectations, they were still entitled to make their own choices and calculate their own risks. It was forced, unprofitable service that—as we shall see—seamen resented so deeply.

While seamen normally had a great deal of freedom in choosing their employment, they were hampered by various factors. Employment was not always available in the seaman's home port. Seamen frequently moved as a result of apprenticeship and to seek employment after the completion of their training. It is clear from Admiralty depositions that many seafarers came from far afield to pursue their careers.[114] The records are biased toward seamen living in London and the surrounding area; the large number of Londoners probably reflects the high population and higher wages of the capital,[115] its importance as a port, and the fact that witnesses would be more readily accessible to the court. In comparison to other ports, London demonstrates a tendency to draw seamen from greater distances. Men residing in London originated in ports such as Weymouth, Melcombe Regis, Lyme Regis, Bristol, Leigh, Plymouth, Portsmouth, Newcastle, and Hull. Some came from Wales, Scotland, Ireland, Danske, the German states, and Sweden. Within a Tudor populace with a generally high degree of geographic mobility, seamen were an especially migratory lot.[116] Other itinerant groups such as farm laborers benefited from the fact that contracts terminated at the same time every year; in this way, prospective employees knew when positions were opening. Positions aboard ships involved in seasonal traffic opened at roughly the same time every year. However, most types of voyages were not confined to specific months, and thus there was no given time to seek employment. Seamen had to rely on chance, word of mouth, and connections in order to find employment. They did not have anything equivalent to the hiring fairs that matched farm laborers with masters. In periods where employment opportunities were scarce, seamen had to travel farther from home in search of work.[117] Employment opportunities were also limited by reputation. Considering the number of libel cases in this period, reputation was a matter of considerable importance.

While information on the process of hiring seamen in the sixteenth century is practically nonexistent, advertisements were probably made through networks of kinship, friends, and word of mouth. Taverns were a popular place to exchange information; merchant seamen who joined pirate ships were often approached in alehouses. One has only to read Admiralty Court depositions to see that taverns figured largely as a popular haunt for seafarers. The search for employment was probably helped by the fact that seamen were recognized by their distinctive manner of dressing. A grocer and his apprentice who bought goods from two strangers took them to be seafarers because they wore "saylers apparell." An Admiralty officer who was looking to impress seamen for naval duty approached one John Richard on sight, presumably because of manner of dress.[118]

SEAFARING AS SEASONAL EMPLOYMENT

Seafaring was a significant form of seasonal employment. Men from related trades such as fishmongering and rope making joined the ranks of seamen. Fishermen and seamen also found their way into other groups of the maritime community. In addition, it was usual for men in many coastal communities in England to combine seafaring and farming.[119] While some inexperienced landsmen like the tailor Isaac Hampton of Kent joined the ranks of unskilled or semiskilled labor, others went to sea frequently enough to work their way up to skilled positions. George Foster combined the occupations of gunner and cutler. Salter and mariner Thomas Brooke of London observed that "he liveth by the sea partly and partly by the lande." James Woodcot's career as a mariner was an illustrious one: he became a master, pilot, and a member of Trinity House. However, he also was identified as an ironmonger. There was no shortage of men in unrelated trades sailing as seamen: tallow chandlers, tailors, painters, vintners, butchers, yeomen, grocers, and sheer men.[120]

Positions on ships were welcome by landsmen hit hard by steady price inflation, overpopulation, unemployment, and underemployment in late Tudor England.[121] The shipboard community utilized such men "to drudge" as manual laborers.[122] Evidence is extremely thin, but G. V. Scammell postulates that wage laborers and small tenants would have been especially vulnerable to hard times and would have augmented the ranks of the expanding maritime community.[123] The evidence consulted for this study can neither confirm nor refute this assumption. Once in a while, the flow could be reversed: inheritance, marriage, or profits could provide seafarers with the ability to limit maritime employment to occasional work.

While seafaring had traditionally been a significant form of seasonal employment in coastal locations, the need for manpower and the lure of pillage during the war years drew landsmen into the maritime community in greater numbers. Demands for financial backing ensured that wealthy gentlemen became privateering captains, officers, and investors. Societal hierarchy, patronage, and the need for governance ensured that men from the upper echelons commanded naval vessels in spite of bitter criticism from accomplished seamen like Walter Raleigh, who complained that landsmen were made commanders "by vertue of the purse" and "speciall favour of Princes."[124] Military objectives of the navy and privateers altered the peacetime composition of the maritime community by allowing soldiers aboard. Consequently, this influx of landsmen not only diluted the numbers of skilled seamen on shipboard but created tensions. Drake's speech during his voyage of circumnavigation encapsulates his frustration:

it doth even take my wits from me to think on it. Here is such controversy between sailors and the gentlemen and such stomaching between the gentlemen and sailors, that it doth even make me mad to hear it. But, my masters, I must have it left. For I must have the gentleman to haul and draw with the mariner and the mariner with the gentlemen. What! let us show ourselves all to be of a company . . . I would know him, that would refuse to set his hand to a rope, but I know there is not any such here.[125]

The presence of greater numbers of unskilled landsmen after 1585 disturbed the traditional shipboard equilibrium by upsetting the customary balance between command and consultation. Both privateering and naval expeditions required heavy manning, which also decreased communication between the crew and master.[126] Ultimately, these factors compromised what has been termed the "maritime democracy of the medieval age."[127]

As we shall see, at least in regard to privateering and naval duty—the areas where landsmen were concentrated—seamen lost much of their voice in shipboard affairs.

Overall, by-employment affected the maritime community in many ways. Part-time seamen ensured that maritime employment would be linked to the wider economy. Additional labor was necessary for this period of expansion. However, maritime by-employment ultimately compromised the position of seafarers. The availability of unskilled labor served to keep wage rates low. It also diluted the ethos of maritime life in the two important "new" areas of the late sixteenth century: privateering and the navy. The presence of a significant number of landsmen in the maritime community attenuated the tendency for seamen to view themselves as a community set apart (physically and socially) from the greater society.

JOINING A PIRATE CREW

Seamen's search for employment was not limited to the "legitimate" maritime community; they were willing to move outside the law to find satisfactory remuneration and conditions. Contemporary opinion stated that seamen fell into "unlawful courses" because of poverty and idleness.[128] Seamen Stephen Dingley, Nicholas Crammer, and William Randall said that "soe longe as they wente abrode they had money to serve theire turnes, but when they lay still they were allwayes beggerly & in wante." Henry Mainwaring, "the great pirate-turned-admiral of James I's reign," claimed that common seamen turned to piracy because they "are so generally necessitous and discontented." Captain John Young requested that shipowners compensate seamen adequately for their labors, or else "necessity will force them to steal." Insolvency was undoubtedly a motive for some seamen to accept employment from pirates. Sailor Thomas Freeman went with Captain Clinton Atkinson from Portsmouth, he said in his defense, because he was "in povertye and greate nede." Three mariners claimed that they joined Captain William Arnewood at Studland in 1583 "beinge destituted of service." Thomas Cowdell claimed he was "out of service" and thus joined Arnewood. Many men who joined had been discharged from military or naval service, and they were very likely in want as well. Bands of vagrants, migrants, and other "ill-disposed persons" committed crimes because of indigence.[129] These were explanations that Tudor Englishmen could understand and that spoke to contemporary experience, particularly during the economic crisis of the 1590s.

Depositions within the Admiralty Court are not as useful as we might hope in revealing why seamen joined pirate crews. Many examinants claim that they were kidnapped or tricked into joining. Captured crewmen of Arnewood's testified that he hired them on the pretense that they were going to serve in Flanders. This seems to have been a popular ruse among pirates; Thomas Walton alias Purser confessed that he alleged that he held a commission from Don Antonio of Portugal as a subterfuge to aid in hiring a crew. According to his statement under oath, ship carpenter Richard Johnson of Norfolk merely sought passage home from the Isle of Wight in late 1598 or early 1599. He claimed that, despite the fact he was on board a pirate ship, he did not partake in any illegal activities. Johnson was "wantinge money to goe home by lande, he sought passidge at the cowes & so fell into this mischeife." While some seamen might have been duped, more were likely lying to avoid condemning themselves from their own testimony. When Arnewood was captured, he refused to answer certain questions in the Admiralty Court on the grounds "he will not accuse himselfe." In 1580 several seamen claimed that they were hired to go on a trading voyage for Bordeaux on the *Philip and Joyce* and did not know until the voyage was under way that they were to go "vppon adventure and purchase." Mariner James Willys of Newcastle upon Tyne affirmed that he was lodged at the White Horse in Wapping in 1587 when sailor William Tooley, also from Newcastle, and a group of other seamen approached him. They announced that they were going to go to Southampton to serve upon one of the Queen's ships and welcomed him to come along. Willys said that he had no money to go so far but would accompany them on any merchant voyages. Tooley raised the money by selling a taffeta doublet and bore Willys's charges to go to Southampton. The group was recruited in a victualing house in Handfast (now Standfast) to sail on Clinton Atkinson's pinnace, which took a French and a Scottish ship. Willys tried to convince the court that he had fallen in with the wrong crowd and had abandoned "that kinde of liffe" at his first opportunity for more legitimate employment. Daniel Buckley claimed that he went to sea only once with his brother, pirate Charles Buckley, "and woulde not goe to the seas with his said brother eanye more but lefte him of his said trade." Potential pirates were probably recruited, in part, through networks of friendship and kinship as in the lawful maritime pursuits.[130]

Like privateering, piracy was perceived as a quick route to wealth. However, some seamen were drawn to serve on pirate vessels for other reasons. Pirate captains could be very generous and charismatic. Arnewood was known to have "vsed his men well," and even captured seamen testified to being "well vsed and mutche made of" by pirates. Curious and casual visitors to pirate ships were often "intertayned" and treated hospitably. Pirate captains do not seem to have been the rogues of legends; gentlemen, government officials, respectable women, and, occasionally, children went aboard pirate ships for business and to socialize. Clinton Atkinson admitted that on his ship he "kepte open howse and sundrie Jentilmen and others came on borde him and made merye."[131]

Pirate captains could be masters of public relations. Gifts and flattery endeared them to many officials. Presents could range from provisions to exotic pets. Several vice admirals' deputies were in possession of parrots given to them by pirates; two such birds and a monkey found their way to the Lord Admiral's cook, who gave the monkey to the Admiral's wife, "the oulde Lady howarde."[132] Atkinson admitted such gifts were to earn "good willes and favoers."[133] Even in those instances when pirates demanded provisions and supplies at sea from their countrymen, they frequently compensated them generously for their troubles.[134] Many sixteenth-century pirates do not deserve the reputation of amoral cutthroats that legend has accorded them. Evidence suggests that many English pirates were eager not to alienate their countrymen unnecessarily. While business interests led them outside the boundaries of legal trade, few of these men lived exclusively outside the law. No doubt most "pirates" were seamen who were flirting with "casual and rather timid piracy" and whose continued existence depended upon moderate, socially acceptable behavior.[135]

The atmosphere of acceptance contributed to seamen's willingness to partake in illegal actions. Elizabethan piracy "almost attained the dignity of a recognised profession."[136] The Crown made sporadic efforts to control the growing tide of disorder in the second half of the sixteenth century through commissions, inquiries, and campaigns.[137] However, "professional" pirates were often viewed with indifference by those ashore and in many cases were protected by local officials and gentry. There was no end of abettors willing to assist pirates in victualing, housing, and providing services for them ashore. For example, Arnewood/Arnold and his crew had meat and drink at victualing houses "as other Masters and maryners of shipps."[138] In 1583 John Pope of Gosporte, bailiff to the Bishop of Winchester, acknowledged that he frequently lodged known pirates and those "whom he suspected not to be honeste." He had been advised by a local official that he could lodge pirates if

they vsed them selves honestlye and payde for that they tooke he had not to chardge them, and said that this examinate mighte as well lodge them, as other men both in Portesmouth and other places there abowte.[139]

Captain Vaughan and his crew were known to be pirates in Portsmouth, but they walked the streets and "were not molested nor trowbled." Officials found that they could not capture accused pirate Charles Buckley because "he had suche freindes in the Cuntreye." Pirates provided a service; they had no shortage of customers willing to buy their wares and often had clients at the highest levels of society. In a letter of 1590 the Lord Admiral wrote that the Queen and the Privy Council were "disquieted" that sundry of "her Majesties good subiectes [were] drawn into question and trowble in buyenge & receavinge such goodes soe taken." It was alleged that justices and local officials frequently accepted gifts and bribes in return for immunity.[140] Successful pirates had friends in very high places. Captain Haines and his pirate crew,

affirme that theye had better freindes in Englande then eanye Alderman or merchante of London had naminge Sir Christopher Hatton duringe whose life as they sayde theye knewe whither to goe and therewithall wisshed for his longe liffe.[141]

Corrupt officials, piracy, and misguided privateering contributed to the growing lawlessness at sea during the war years.

Captain John Young claimed that "when they [seamen] are once entered into that trade [piracy], they are hardly reclaimed."[142] While this is true of some of the more professional buccaneers, many "pirates" wove comfortably back and forth between various groups of the maritime community as well as vacillated between legal and illegal activity. Although evidence is slim, there seemed to be a high turnover of personnel on pirate ships, which supports the contention that piracy was at least in part a stopgap measure for seamen looking for employment.[143] Most of the ordinary seamen of the pirate crew of Captain Thomas Walton alias Purser, "came but latelye." One "pirate" "hath his fathers lyvinge and vsethe Fishinge." A number of men who were accused of being pirates had served in the navy. For example, sailor William Hockeridge of Ratcliffe was a mariner of the Queen's ship *Advice* and was discharged in 1594. His friend, shipmaster John Bedford, convinced him to go to sea under "Wicked Will" Smith; he was assured of "good purchase within [a] fewe dayes." There was also traffic going the other way. The Crown used pirates to wage war because they were "commonly the most daring and serviceable in war."[144] In part, the shortage of trained seamen willing to serve contributed to the Crown's readiness to accept sea rovers into naval service.

The Crown had a long history of employing pirates to serve the state. Privateering was essentially state-sanctioned piracy that assisted the war effort by draining Spain's resources. Many pirates proved willing privateers, and some were offered pardons in exchange for service to the state.[145] Doubtless, it proved convenient for pirates to fashion themselves as patriots and pillage on the right side of the law. Husbandman John Boise went to Studland in 1583 to find his son Stephen, a member of pirate captain Holborn's crew. Boise located Stephen at Studland,

makinge mery on lande in an ale house with other of his companye, where this examinate fell to perswade him to leave thatt yll kinde of life, and to retorne home with this examinate. To whom this examinate('s) sonn made answere that one Master Sackford of the Courte had procured them good commission from her Majestye to take Spanerdes and theire goodes and that whiche theye had taken was good prize bye vertue of the said Commission.[146]

The services of such experienced sea rovers helped England wage a successful war of attrition.

While "career pirates" were probably quite rare, piratical acts were not. "Pirates" could be privateers who crossed the line into illegal activity. There was no end of "grevous complaintes" to the Queen, the Privy Council, Lord Admiral, and the Admiralty Court regarding the "manifeste violatinge and abvse of their [privateers'] saide Reprisalls."[147] The examples of greed, violence, illegal captures, and pillaging fill the pages of the Admiralty Court depositions. Richard Hawkins observed: "yea I haue seene the common sort of Mariners, vnder the name of pillage, maintaine and iustifie their robberies most insolently, before the Queenes Maiesties Commissioners, with arrogant and vnseemly termes."[148] To what degree these unlawful acts were premeditated is pure speculation. Many piratical acts resulted from "sudden opportunity."[149] The freer discipline of privateers could give way to license.[150] Most illegal deeds appear to have resulted largely from pillaging fervor and the economic necessity of capturing prizes to pay the backers and the crews. Seamen readily defended their shares and actions as their rightful compensation for a voyage. Richard Hawkins maintained that "the Mariner is ordinarily so carried away with the desire of Pillage, as sometimes for very appearances of small moment, hee looseth his voyage, and many times himselfe."[151] Ignorance of the law and of the exact nature of Admiralty commissions might have also played a role among ordinary crewmen. While the Admiralty Court depositions give witness to the great number of ill-gotten gains, economic necessity (and perhaps a degree of ignorance) led many to defend their deeds.

With the exception of the more "notorious pirattes" like Captains Stephen Haines, Clinton Atkinson, William Vaughan, William Arnewood alias Arnold, or Thomas Watson alias Purser, the evidence suggests that most of their crews did not live permanently outside the law or form a separate criminal caste. The seamen's depositions indicate that most participated in the legitimate or legal maritime community in addition to their sojourns into illegal activities. Motives were varied for seeking such employment, but it appears to have been transitory work. In many cases, pirates were privateers in error or seamen in search of work. Most "pirates" were a part of the larger maritime community and accepted as such. It is likely that the transitory nature of this sort of employment precluded the development of a separate subculture. Pirate ships also had apprentices and boys aboard to learn seamanship. Most of those who were termed as "pirates" originated from a common labor pool that supplied seamen for both lawful and unlawful employment.

NAVAL POLICY AND MANNING

Elizabeth I's intention to rule over a Protestant nation within a predominantly Catholic Western Europe had certain political ramifications, as did her countrymen's belief that the Iberian powers could not defend their monopoly on the New World. Given these somewhat antagonistic policies, her island kingdom would be well served offensively and defensively by a successful "blue-water strategy." Elizabeth's first Parliament of January 1559 was unified in its decision to keep the navy "ever in readiness against all evil haps."[152] Throughout her reign, the Crown continued to provide moderate support for a national policy that sought to promote shipbuilding and an increase in seamen.[153]

The navy depended on the common labor pool of the maritime community. For the health of her navy and commerce, Elizabeth had seen fit early in her reign to promote the "nursery of seamen" by legislating "fish days" (days when the Crown mandated the eating of fish). In addition, in 1582 William Cecil ordered the Lord Admiral, the Earl of Lincoln, to compile information on numbers of seamen and merchant ships with their tonnage. A 123-page report was produced on these subjects, broken down by county. The following year Cecil licensed a commission to look into the condition of the Queen's fleet. The commissioners, in turn, ordered the vice admirals, Admiralty officers, Lords Lieutenant, and mayors of port communities to conduct a survey of seamen. This information equipped the Crown to formulate a naval policy.[154]

The Crown's naval policies were relatively successful, not least because they were limited in objective and undertaken during a period of commercial expansion. England's merchant shipping and fishing fleet increased significantly throughout the period; as we have seen, the tonnage of the merchant fleet more than doubled between 1560 and 1629, and manpower rose steadily. The principal issue was how the regime would acquire access to this manpower resource.

IMPRESSMENT

Sir William Monson, a naval captain in the late Elizabethan period, remarked that naval seamen's "usage had been so ill that it is no marvel they show their unwillingness to serve the Queen." Raleigh acknowledged that seamen worked for their sovereign "with a great grudging" and viewed such duty as equivalent to being galley slaves. At the core of the matter were not only their poor usage but the loss of freedom to make their own employment contracts. Forced service was greatly resented by seamen because it intruded on their traditional "rights" and freedoms. A seaman of the *White Hind* of London in 1584 expressed a common attitude that "he knew his tymes for labor . . . and would go [to] sea when [it] pleased him." Nineteen-year-old mariner William Rogers was pressed by Captain Richard Nashe in 1590 under a commission to serve in Sir Francis Drake's squadron. Like most seamen, Rogers deeply resented being obliged "to goe to sea . . . against his will." Nashe had Rogers and other impressed seamen appear before the mayor of Tinbury in Pembroke, who told them they had to serve. Even in the face of this coercion, Rogers "refused to serve the said nashe & would gladly haue byn cleare of him." In March 1589 Chris Cockery was pressed with his ship, the *Talbot* of Hull, and her crew to carry the Queen's soldiers. The master and crew were loath to serve, "and thinkinge to avoide the same both he and his men hid them selves, whereof complainte was made to the Lord Treasorer and the said Cockery threatned to prison for neclectinge the Quenes service." Other than patriotism, naval service had few attractions for seamen.[155]

Exact numbers do not exist, but volunteers were a minority in the navy. Gentlemen captains and volunteers were eager to serve their Queen, but they also stood the greatest chance to be recognized for courageous service and, unlike most seamen, had financial security. They were also free from most naval discipline and at least some of the unpleasantries of shipboard life. Maximizing one's income was critical for the great majority of seafarers and their families. Unlike privateering or piracy, naval service offered little hope of rich "booty" for the average seaman. Merchant voyages promised regular and higher wages without the hazards of life on men-of-war. Raleigh claimed that seamen's aversion to the sovereign's ships resulted from their "feare of penurie and hunger," the "case being cleane contrary in all Merchants ships."[156] Naval wages were lower than in other areas of maritime employment, and if payment was made at all, it was often delayed for long periods.[157] The prompt payment of wages was especially important to seamen with dependents. Unpaid and idle seamen could pose a threat to the social order; they were much more likely to commit crimes for basic subsistence or to join to ranks of the able-bodied poor on parish relief. Because naval service offered few incentives, the Crown had to resort to methods of coercion to furnish manpower for the navy.

The problem of manning the navy was an age-old one. The usage of impressment predates the statute of 1378 that dictated that seamen between the ages of 18 and 60 were eligible for the monarch's service.[158] Essentially, there were two main methods of impressment used in this period. First, the Privy Council used the 1583 survey of seamen as a starting point to determine quotas for each coastal area. Vice admirals were then obliged to impress the required number and have them ready for embarkation on a designated day. The second method was reserved for emergency situations, when valuable time could not be wasted on the bureaucratic chain of command. In these cases, the Queen simply authorized a local official to impress the stipulated number of men.[159] The Elizabethan navy relied on both forms, but the first method was the most common.

Seamen were entitled to "press and conduct money" (advances on their wages). A levy of seamen in the Cinque Ports in 1602 ordered officials to

give them [the sailors] twelve pence for imprest money and after the rate of a half-penny the myle for their conduct from thear [the Ports] to Chatham in Kent, and chardge them uppon payne of death to present themselves before the officers of the navye by the laste daie of the present January to be disposed into soch shippes as shalbe meete.[160]

Conduct money was variable according to how far the seamen had to travel for service; one shilling was typical for press money.[161]

While many seamen accepted press money, this did not necessarily mean that they intended to serve. Some sought ways to collect the money "and then plucke their heads out of the coller."[162] Resistance to service took other forms as well. Desertion (examined later) was undeniably a problem. Straggling seamen were a great source of discontent among commanders. Clearly, seamen were in no hurry to report for duty; if service could not be evaded, it could be postponed to the last possible moment. Sometimes opposition could take violent forms. The need to press men for the Queen's ship, the *Antelope*, resulted in a brawl between sailor John Richard and an impressment official in April 1589. Richard testified that the official tried to give him press money, but Richard was already pressed to sail with the Earl of Cumberland aboard the Queen's ship, the *Victory*. Cumberland, aboard the *Victory*, and a small number of privateers were sent to the Azores by the Queen around the same time to intercept Philip II's treasure fleet. Thus, Richard threw the money upon the ground and attempted to flee. He contends that the official threatened "he shoulde goe before the Constable and serve or he woulde kill him." Richard Sharp, a wax chandler in a nearby shop, corroborated Richard's story; Sharp intervened to stop two strangers fighting in the street "chardinge them in her majestys name to kepe the peace." Sharp heard the official threaten to kill Richard, to which Sharp answered that "he muste not presse men with swordes, but ife that he had any commission to presse men vse it in good order as it oughte to be vsed."[163] In their defense, impressment officials were under considerable pressure to furnish seamen and ships in less than advantageous circumstances. In this case, the impressment official's account is never recorded, but it is understandable why he might resort to violence to cope with seamen's defiance of his commission. Contemporary opinion held that Admiralty officials were instructed to fill their quotas "vppon paine of there lives."[164] It was a difficult task to fill the ranks of the navy given seamen's passive and active opposition.

There is abundant anecdotal evidence that the quality of seamen secured by impressment was fairly low. In 1597 the Earl of Essex released many of the seamen impressed by the press masters because they "knew not one rope in the ship." Commanders made regular complaint of the caliber of men under their charge; "tailors, potters, and the like" and "men of all occupations, some of whom did not know a rope and were never at sea" found their way on board.[165] Raleigh's orders for a 1617 voyage acknowledged the presence of "landlubbers"; they were to "learne the names and places of the ropes, that they may assist the Sailors in their labours upon the decks, though they cannot goe up to the tops and yards." Contemporaries alleged that local officials (mayors, justices, and constables, for instance) used the press system as an opportunity to rid their jurisdictions of "infirm persons," "idlers and boys," "rogues taken up in the streets," and "the scum and dregs of the country." Again, use of undesirables to man the navy was not new. Henry VIII used "ruffians, vagabonds, masterless men, common players and evil-disposed persons" in his navy. Frequently, the most skilled seamen possessed the status and financial resources necessary to evade the press through bribery or influence.[166] In 1597 it was reported that men could suborn press officials for one pound a head.[167] Raleigh claimed that "either the care therein is very little, or the bribery very great, so that of all shipping" the monarch's ships "are ever the worst manned."[168] He stated that

the [impressment] Officers doe set out the most needy and unable men, and . . . doe discharge the better sort, a matter so commonly used, as that it is growne into a Proverbe amongst the Saylers, That the Mustermasters doe carry the best and ablest men in their Pockets, a Custome very evill and dangerous.[169]

For the more skilled seamen, it was worth their while to pay one pound or more to rid themselves of service, as they could make a much greater profit in other forms of maritime employment, with less risk. However, the state's power and need for manpower compelled large numbers of capable men to serve along with "the dregs."

The Crown did resort to drastic methods to see that seamen served the state. Given the shortage of naval gunners in the early years of the war, they were forbidden to leave the realm in 1586 in anticipation of a Spanish invasion.[170] In March 1590 the Privy Council ordered the deputy lieutenants of seventeen maritime counties to conduct a general survey of mariners, gunners, fishermen, and other seafaring men within their counties so that officials would have a roll identifying particular individuals by age and distinguishing marks. Unfortunately for our purposes, few returns from this survey survive. The Crown was in such want of experienced men that it dictated that the enrolled members of the maritime workforce

shuld by proclamacion in her Majestie's name be commaunded uppon paine of deathe not to departe from theire habytcion and dwelling place, so as thei might allwaies hereafter be forthcominge within three howres warninge, to be emploied as there shuld be occasion in her Majestie's service. . . . And because divers maryners and gonners might be absent in voyages . . . yt was thought necessary that the foresaid Justices and Vice-admyrall shuld give commandement to th'officers of the portes, creekes, harboroughes and villages on the sea syde to sende a note unto them . . . the names of soche maryners and seafaring men as were absent and to what places thei did saile, givinge expresse chardge to the said officers as the said marryners and others shuld retorne . . . from theire said voyages that they might be enjoyned and comaunded not to departe againe, but to be forthecoming in soche sorte as was directed for the rest.[171]

While the order was almost certainly a temporary one, the intrusion into seamen's freedom and livelihood is evident. Officials in Essex wrote to the Privy Councillors of the

generall grevaunce & Complainte which is made amongst them [the seamen of Essex] for beinge Restrayned to theire attendaunce at three howers warninge, whereby they are barred from theire vsuall trade of Lyveinge, And whereine (if they be not shortlie in some sorte eased as they affirme) they shall not be able to mayntayne themselves, & theire famylles.[172]

It is clear why naval service and Crown restrictions were resented among seamen.

Despite seamen's aversion to service, the ramshackle bureaucracy of the early modern state served England extremely well in time of crisis. In 1588 the naval administration managed to muster over 16,000 men to defend the country.[173] Given the limited size of the maritime community in the early 1580s, naval duty put serious constraints on the maritime population. We do know that the coastal towns claimed seamen were in short supply. The Cinque Ports (towns on the Channel coast) were especially hard hit. Under these conditions ship complements contained "poore Fishermen and Idlers" who were "insufficient for such labour." Although fishermen were accustomed to the sea, commanders found them to be "poor, unserviceable and of weak spirit."[174]

Like other areas of the maritime community, naval seamen had to contend with landsmen in their ranks. With the exception of those officers of gentle birth, the evidence suggests that the quality of landsmen who filled the ranks of the navy was low enough to compromise the overall quality of manpower. In turn, their presence damaged the limited bargaining power that seamen might have had in regard to the naval bureaucracy. Without their presence, the state might have been forced to raise wages to supply a higher caliber of seamen.[175]

Although the war with Spain forced England to maintain a regular naval presence, the Crown did not seriously contemplate a standing navy until 1603.[176] The Queen lacked both the will and the necessary finances; it was much cheaper to impress merchant vessels and men as the situation demanded.[177] John Hawkins did lower manning rates for the navy shortly before the coming of the first *Armada* in an attempt to reduce shipboard mortality caused by overcrowding. Hawkins recommended that naval ships be manned one man to every two tons burden as opposed to three men to five tons. There is no evidence that manning rates changed in other segments of the maritime community. Merchant ships were usually manned at a rate of one man for every five net tons. Some historians estimate that it was even lower.[178] Instead of a standing navy, the Crown managed to wage a successful war of attrition with Spain on the strength of privateers and occasional naval expeditions.

Yet the failure to develop a naval class of seamen had consequences. The lack of a standing navy prohibited willing men from forging a career in the navy. Impressment was useful in that it forced some seamen to serve, but the most skilled and affluent men—those seamen of whom the Crown was in the greatest need—frequently managed to elude the trap set for them. It is little wonder that the Queen's government accepted the services of former pirates who traded their expertise for the silent inaction on standing charges. Impressment did little to develop a body of trained men at the Crown's disposal who were schooled in waging war upon the seas; privateers and pirates were experienced in pillaging and plunder, but they were not accustomed to discipline or the carrying out of large-scale naval campaigns. Impressment did nothing to establish an "esprit de corps"; the majority of seamen fulfilled their service under duress and then sought a discharge in order to find more desirable employment. Demobilization simultaneously released thousands of seamen at a given port; this created obvious problems for men hoping to find placements in a finite number of mercantile voyages. Reintegration proved hazardous to earning potential; lucrative or previously held positions might have been lost in the meantime. Generally, seamen who served in the Elizabethan navy were much more interested in their own individual pursuits than waging war for the good of the nation. In many ways England's successes at sea were both determined and tempered by the self-interest of its seamen.

CONCLUSION

Established forms of training and apprenticeship were not altered by the war. The state recognized the need for seamen and made attempts to increase England's number of fishermen and other seafarers. Evidence supports the view that numbers of skilled seamen grew.[179] While efforts were made to increase overall numbers, no attempt was made to monitor the quality of training; proposals for national programs to educate seamen came to naught. The maritime community was left to its own devices, and experienced seamen instructed novices largely through informal tutelage.[180] While wartime experience created a group of men familiar with naval campaigns, a separate naval class did not emerge due to the state's refusal to fund a sizable standing navy or intervene actively in the running of the internal workings of the maritime community. A common labor pool furnished seamen for all groups of the maritime community. Thus, seamen were trained for civilian employment; they were more conscious of personal motives than the goals of the Crown. They were imbued with a clear sense of the workings of the peacetime economy and their own place within it. They resented the intrusion of the state, as it circumvented their established customs in terms of determining their own employment and shipboard con-. ditions and imposed instead hazardous, ill-paid work and martial discipline.

Seamen could show great versatility in their choice of employers. Career patterns were varied. Remuneration (which is discussed more fully later on) was a central consideration. Seamen made employment contracts on the basis of their skill and experience and the risks that they took. Those who could not find suitable legal employment might resort to voyages on pirate vessels. The questionable legality of some privateering ventures created a gray area between the two sides of the law. This was a development of the war years. Seamen traversed the line of legality frequently; privateers often captured unauthorized plunder, while noted pirates can be found serving the Crown or conducting legitimate trade. Many seamen defy categorization as to the segment of the community to which they belonged. Traffic between the various groups of seamen was not particular to this period; however, the war introduced new employment choices and widened the breadth of the community to include welcomed and unwelcomed options. Privateering and naval voyages both sought military objectives; privateering, however, was clearly seen as a positive advancement by most seamen because many of the benefits and traditions of established forms of seafaring were respected. It also allowed seamen the possibility of financial benefit for their risks and skill. The unpopularity of naval service was due to the elimination of these factors in combination with such issues, as we shall see, as harsher discipline, the virtual elimination of the customary seamen's voice in shipboard affairs, inadequate health care for the sick, and the greater dangers involved in naval campaigns.

Undeniably, Elizabethan seamen had a clear idea of their "rights" and expectations in regard to the contracting of their labor. It is impossible to ascertain how far this attitude toward their own labor extended through English society, because seamen were the only large-scale mobile and contract-based sector of the wage-earning population to find its traditional work culture challenged by an intrusive state. When seaman West asserted in the High Court of Admiralty in 1584 that "he knew his tymes for labor . . . and would go [to] sea when [it] pleased him," he was articulating a conception of the ownership of labor understandable in the preindustrial economy of wage labor. The sentiment survived due to the irregularity of large-scale naval warfare in early modern England and the relative ineffectiveness of the Tudor state.

The war years introduced both new opportunities and onerous service for seamen. Due to the lure of booty, much needed by-employment, and the huge numbers of men required for service, landsmen infiltrated the ranks of the seafaring community in sizable numbers, disturbing shipboard dynamics and lowering the standards of the maritime craft, which had few means to limit its membership or uphold its professional standards. While landsmen were required to fill the ranks of the navy, they also competed with career seamen for the more coveted positions (on privateers, for instance). Potentially, increased demand for seamen during this period could have raised both the status and compensation for seamen. This did not occur in any significant way. Landsmen readily provided labor. Only in the navy were seamen at a premium during this period. Any bargaining power that seamen might have had there was erased by the state's right to compel its seafaring subjects to serve. Those who evaded the press, bribed their way out of naval service, defrauded officials, straggled behind, or deserted were acting on their established civilian practice to negotiate the terms of their own employment. There is ample evidence that more rewarding seafaring pursuits found adequate manpower while the navy scoured the country for men to its fill its ranks. In theory, wartime conditions were such that seamen could have profited from the demands for their labor. In practice, the inflow of landsmen and the prerogatives of the Crown combined to eradicate these favorable conditions. Ultimately, seamen's status and independence were compromised during the reign of Elizabeth. However, their sense of their own worth and their expectations of traditional privileges and customs remained intact within a traditional work culture.

NOTES

1. Privateering expeditions were commissioned by the government. Letters of marque granted the bearers the right to take prizes during wartime and interrupt the commerce of the enemy.

2. Kenneth R. Andrews, *Elizabethan Privateering: English Privateering during the Spanish War 1585–1603* (Cambridge: Cambridge University Press, 1964), 40.

3. Measuring the membership of the maritime community can be done only in the broadest of terms. The most complete surviving surveys were conducted by the Crown in 1582–83, before tensions with Spain had escalated into open warfare. We do know that expansion of the maritime sector continued throughout Elizabeth's reign, drawing men to the sea in increasing numbers. The dramatic expansion in shipping following the first decade of Elizabeth's accession continued throughout her reign and beyond it; the total tonnage of English shipping more than doubled from 1572 to 1629. Christopher Lloyd, *The British Seaman 1200–1860* (London: Collins, 1968), 34; R. W. Unger, "The Tonnage of Europe's Merchant Fleets 1300–1800," *The American Neptune* 52 (1992), 254; Ralph Davis, *The Rise of the English Shipping Industry in the Seventeenth and Eighteenth Centuries* (1962; rpt. Newton Abbutt, U.K.: David and Charles, 1972), 2–10; N. J. Williams, *The Maritime Trade of the East Anglian Ports 1550–1590* (Oxford: Clarendon Press, 1988), 215–24; Kenneth Andrews, *Ships, Money and Politics: Seafaring and Naval Enterprise in the Reign of Charles I* (Cambridge: Cambridge University Press, 1991), 203–5. It is a safe assumption that manpower increased proportionately because

manning rates remained fairly constant. G. V. Scammell, "Manning the English Merchant Service," *Mariner's Mirror* 56 (1970), 132.

The Crown's surveys during the early 1580s found that there were between 16,255 and 17,157 seafaring men in the realm. William Laird Clowes, *The Royal Navy: A History from the Earliest Times to the Present*, vol. I (London: Sampson, Marston, and Co., 1897), 439; Lloyd, *The British Seaman 1200–1860*, 34. The 1583 survey showed that there were 16,255 men in England "accustomed to the water": 1,484 masters, 11,515 mariners, 2,299 fishermen, and 957 Thomas wherrymen. See Clowes, *The Royal Navy*, vol. I, 439. Presumably, apprentices and ship's boys were not included as they were technically not subject to impressment (these surveys would ultimately be the basis for mustering seamen). Given seamen's high degree of mobility and long absences, many escaped enumeration. The surveyors' methodology allowed for grave inaccuracies. In Devon, for instance, the important ports of Dartmouth and Plymouth were not included; Joyce Youings's work shows that the survey underestimates the number of Devon shipmasters by 50 percent. Joyce Youings, "Ralegh's Country and the Sea," *Proceedings of the British Academy* 75 (1989), 282. Thus, we have reason to assume that thousands of England's seamen were never accounted for in these surveys. Part-time seamen and pirates no doubt are also underrepresented. Moreover, landsmen who would take to the sea during the war years would soon swell the numbers of the maritime population. Although contemporary sea captain William Monson was in all likelihood magnifying the situation, he claimed that "the number of seamen and sailors are increased treble" by the privateering war alone. William Monson, *The Naval Tracts of Sir William Monson*, vol. IV, ed. M. Oppenheim (London: Navy Records Society, 1913), 21. Undeniably, after 1585, the "sweet trade of privateering" attracted thousands of Englishmen to the sea. Lloyd, *The British Seaman 1200–1860*, 36–38.

4. Monson, *Naval Tracts*, vol. IV, 245. The nature of this term is explored fully in the pages to come. For our purposes here, we can define seamen's pseudo-independence as freedom from guild regulation and the ability to negotiate the terms and times of one's employment.

5. For example, company negotiations with the state afforded the barber-surgeons of London some protection from impressment; although the state's quota had to be met, the company chose the men for sea and army duty. This proviso was one of the conditions of their charter. The membership of the College of Physicians managed to avoid sea service altogether. Since physicians treated internal ailments, they would have been better suited (in theory) to treat the greatest killers of the fleet: diseases and epidemics. Lloyd, *The British Seaman 1200–1860*, 43; J. J. Keevil, *Medicine and the Navy 1200–1900*, vol. 1 (Edinburgh: E. and S. Livingstone, 1957), 70; Kenneth R. Andrews, *Trade, Plunder and Settlement: Maritime Enterprise and the Genesis of the British Empire 1480–1630* (Cambridge: Cambridge University Press, 1984), 28.

6. E. P. Thompson, "Eighteenth-Century English Society: Class Struggle without Class?" *Social History* 3 (1978), 154.

7. Unlike seamen, the nation could scarcely afford gainfully employed militiamen to leave their regular work for long periods. Thus, Elizabethan troops that were sent abroad depended on local levies of civilians, generally drawn from the unemployed, underemployed, and less skilled sector of society. Few of these men

had any training in the art of war. C. G. Cruickshank, *Elizabeth's Army*, 2nd ed. (London: Oxford University Press, 1966), 12, 25, 131–33.

8. E. G. Thomas, "The Old Poor Law and Maritime Apprenticeship," *Mariner's Mirror* 63 (1977), 153.

9. Penry Williams, *The Tudor Regime* (1979; rpt. Oxford: Clarendon Press, 1983), 153–54.

10. See *Trinity House of Deptford Transactions, 1609–35*, ed. G. G. Harris (London: London Record Society, 1983), ix, xiv; G. G. Harris, *The Trinity House of Deptford, 1514–1660* (London: Athlone Press, 1965).

11. This function was a central feature of all formal guilds in this period, indicative of the presence of strong employment-centered conceptions of community.

12. G. V. Scammell, "European Seamanship in the Great Age of Discovery," *Mariner's Mirror* 68 (1982), 363–64. There is evidence that Henry VIII modeled the Trinity House at Deptford on the Spanish model of pilotage, the India House at Seville. See Alwyn A. Ruddock, "The Trinity House at Deptford in the Sixteenth Century," *English Historical Review* 65 (1950), 463.

13. David W. Waters, *The Art of Navigation in England in Elizabethan and Early Stuart Times* (London: Hollis and Carter, 1958), 105.

14. Scammell, "European Seamanship in the Great Age of Discovery," 364.

15. Public Record Office State Papers (Domestic) 12/147/189.

16. G. V. Scammell, "The Sinews of War: Manning and Provisioning English Fighting Ships, c. 1550–1650," *Mariner's Mirror* 73 (1987), 356. "Fish days" were not a new concept. Edward VI enacted legislation that made Fridays, Saturdays, and Ember days fish days under penalty of fines and imprisonment. M. Oppenheim, *The Administration of the Royal Navy, 1509–1660* (1896; rpt. Hamden, Conn.: Shoe String Press, 1961), 108; 2 & 3 Ed. VI c.19, 5 Eliz. c.5, *Statutes of the Realm*, vol. IV, part 1 (London: Dawsons of Pall Mall, 1963), 165, 422, 424.

17. Williams, *The Maritime Trade of the East Anglian Ports 1550–1590*, 230.

18. Waters, *The Art of Navigation*, 105.

19. Lloyd, *The British Seaman 1200–1860*, 29.

20. Andrews, *Trade, Plunder and Settlement*, 29–30.

21. See *Kingston upon Thames Register of Apprentices 1563–1713*, ed. Anne Daly (Guildford: Surrey Record Society, 1974), viii. The original act was 27 Henry VIII c.12 (1530–31) but was reenacted under Edward and Elizabeth. 1 Ed. VI c.3 (1547); 3 and 4, Ed. VI c.16 (1549–50); and 39 Eliz. c.3 (1597–98). Thomas, "The Old Poor Law and Maritime Apprenticeship," 153, 160. The increase in vagabondage prodded the Crown into passing legislation to set the able-bodied poor to work. G. Renard and G. Weulersse, *Life and Work in Modern England* (1926; rpt. London: Routledge and Kegan Paul, 1968), 93, 96.

22. Thomas, "The Old Poor Law and Maritime Apprenticeship," 153.

23. John Webb, "Apprenticeship in the Maritime Occupations at Ipswich, 1596–1651," *Mariner's Mirror* 46 (1960), 31.

24. Contemporaries like William Gouge also believed that this relationship had a spiritual component: "it followeth that seruants in performing duty to their master performe duty to Christ, and in rebelling against their master they rebell against Christ." William Gouge, *Of Domesticall Duties* (London, 1622), 641.

25. Webb, "Apprenticeship in the Maritime Occupations," 31; See also Public Records Office (London) (hereafter PRO), PROB 11/124/230, 11/65/33.

26. PRO PROB (wills, Prerogative Court of Canterbury) 11/102/182.

27. PRO PROB 11/92/79: Guildhall Ms. 9171/22/228v; PRO PROB, 11/57/271, 11/65/11-v; see Daly, *Kingston upon Thames*, xv; Webb, "Apprenticeship in the Maritime Occupations," 31.

28. The possibility exists that the sums bequeathed to apprentices in wills were higher than those given at the end of contracts. Some prudent testators felt the need to purchase future loyalty for their widows.

29. Anne Yarbrough, "Apprentices as Adolescents in Sixteenth Century Bristol," *Journal of Social History* 13 (1979), 69. See also W. L. Goodman, "Bristol Apprentice Register 1532–1658: A Selection of Enrolments of Mariners," *Mariner's Mirror* 60 (1974), 29–31; Webb, "Apprenticeship in the Maritime Occupations," 34.

30. Guildhall Ms. (wills, Commissary Court of London) 9171/22/228v. See also PRO PROB 11/124/230, Guildhall Ms., 9171/18/274, 9171/18/260v.

31. Guildhall Ms. 9171/21/92v.

32. Yarbrough, "Apprentices as Adolescents," 68. There was no fixed age for children to leave home. In the case of servants in husbandry in rural areas, children began their training anywhere from 10 to 14. Ann Kassmaul, *Servants in Husbandry in Early Modern England* (Cambridge: Cambridge University Press, 1981), 70. London apprentices, especially migrants, were markedly older (late teens and early 20s) at the time of the signing of indentures. Steven Rappaport, "Social Structure and Mobility in Sixteenth-Century London: Part I," *London Journal* 9 (1983), 115–16.

33. Unfortunately for posterity, apprenticeship records rarely record the age of the boy at the time of indenture. Most evidence involves backward projections from subsequent testimony under oath and is necessarily imprecise.

34. PRO HCA, 1/44/220, 13/33/312v, 13/34/120–21v, 13/28/74–75v,13/30/268v–69, 13/30/268v, 13/32/357v–58v. See also PRO HCA 13/30/132–33.

35. PRO HCA 13/27/309v. Unfortunately, we do not know Caseye's age.

36. PRO HCA 13/31/164.

37. PRO HCA, 13/28/127–28, 13/33/312v, 13/28/74–75v, 13/30/268v.

38. P.E.H. Hair and J. D. Alsop, *English Seamen and Traders in Guinea 1553–1565: The New Evidence of Their Wills* (Lewiston: Edwin Mellen Press, 1992), 192.

39. Webb, "Apprenticeship in The Maritime Occupations," 32; Daly, *Kingston upon Thames Register*, x.

40. Guildhall Ms. 9171/22/228v. For other examples, see also PRO PROB 11/65/33, Guildhall Ms. 9171/18/72.

41. PRO PROB 11/57/271.

42. Yarbrough, "Apprentices as Adolescents," 69–70.

43. Joyce Youings, *Sixteenth-Century England* (1984; rpt. London: Penguin Books, 1988), 100. Senior ships' officers, in addition to the purser, were routinely associated with merchandising, either in their own right or as agents for commercial principals.

44. PRO HCA 1/46/110.

45. PRO HCA 1/40/42–43, 1/40/44v, 1/40/47.

46. Scammell, "Manning the English Merchant Service," 136; Joan Simon, *Ed-*

ucation and Society in Tudor England (Cambridge: Cambridge University Press, 1966), 294.

47. Yarbrough, "Apprentices as Adolescents," 67.

48. Scammell, "The Sinews of War," 352.

49. Kassmaul, *Servants in Husbandry*, 70, 72.

50. Yarbrough's study, for example, shows that 78 percent of Bristol apprentices did not originate in the city. Yarbrough, "Apprentices as Adolescents," 68.

51. Scammell, "The Sinews of War," 361; Webb, "Apprenticeship in the Maritime Occupations," 30.

52. Scammell, "Manning the English Merchant Service," 137.

53. PRO PROB 11/98/142v.

54. Most of the men examined here were masters and thus had almost certainly been apprenticed. The families involved were primarily from the London area, and this evidence tends to point to kinship's being a greater determinant in apprenticeship than Webb's study of Ipswich suggests.

55. Andrews, *Ships, Money, and Politics* 223–24; Kenneth R. Andrews, "The Elizabethan Seaman," *Mariner's Mirror* 68 (1982), 255.

56. D. Cressy, "Kinship and Kin Interaction in Early Modern England," *Past and Present* 113 (1986), 38–40, 44, 50–51.

57. PRO HCA, 1/40/118v, 24/52/61; Guildhall Ms., 9171/19/90, 9171/20/211v, 9171/22/252, 9171/22/574, 9171/24/116v, 9171/24/27v; PRO PROB 11/108/361v; PRO, HCA 13/31/44, PROB 11/108/361v, HCA 1/36/310–311; Guildhall Ms., 9171/24/116v, 9171/24/361; PRO E101/64/24; PRO, PROB, 11/121/100, 11/121/346v, 11/182/299v, 11/142/292v, 11/144/368v, 11/279/38, 11/277/80v; Harris, *The Trinity House of Deptford 1514–1660*, 273. See PRO PROB, 11/395/26v, 11/388/291v.

58. Approximately 200 wills were consulted in which seamen had male children in their minority.

59. PRO PROB 11/102/237.

60. Guildhall Ms., 9171/20/80-v, 9171/24/33, 9171/24/361. Vessels or shares in vessels were commonly bequeathed to immediate family members. Sons frequently inherited their fathers' shares, but seamen were prepared to will them to wives and daughters. Sometimes shares were sold, and the money was put into a more secure investment. See G. V. Scammell, "Shipowning in the Economy and Politics of Early Modern England," *Historical Journal* 15 (1972), 397–401. PRO PROB, 11/60/15, 11/58/28v, 11/57/201.

61. Steven R. Smith, "The Ideal and the Reality: Apprentice–Master Relationships in Seventeenth-Century London," *History of Education Quarterly* 21 (1981), 450.

62. Webb, "Apprenticeship in the Maritime Occupations," 31.

63. PRO HCA 13/22/121. See Chapter 4 for additional examples of Feewilliams's allegedly bellicose personality.

64. PRO HCA 1/45/303v.

65. PRO PROB 11/102/394v.

66. GLRO DW/PA/5/1588/58.

67. PRO PROB 11/57/271. See also PRO PROB, 11/63/4v, 11/65/11-v, 11/65/33, 11/70/139, 11/102/249v, Guildhall Ms. 9171/18/71v–72, 9171/18/274, GLRO DW/PA/5/1575/23, DW/PA/5/1598/89.

68. Hair and Alsop, *English Seamen and Traders*, 283. For other examples of apprentices mentioned in wills of seamen employed in the Guinea trade, see also 167, 186–87, 192–93, 215, 333.

69. Guildhall Ms. 9171/21/92v. We do not know whether this "debt" was monetary or personal, but the latter is more likely. A monetary debt owed equally to a master and his wife would have been unusual, especially when it was repaid by a bequest to the master alone.

70. PRO PROB 11/86/74.

71. PRO PROB 11/102/179.

72. Guildhall Ms. 9171/19/114v; PRO PROB 11/143/239v; PRO HCA, 13/35/130, 13/31/81v; PRO PROB, 11/108/244, 11/118/338, 11/121/79, 11/102/162; Goodman, "Bristol Apprentice Register," 28; PRO HCA 1/40/22, 1/40/45, 1/40/47, HCA 25/3 unfoliated. Youings, "Raleigh's Country and the Sea," 269–70. See also John Webb, "William Sabyn of Ipswich: An Early Tudor Sea-Officer and Merchant," *Mariner's Mirror* 41 (1955); Williams, *The Maritime Trade*, 232; PRO HCA 1/42/26.

73. F. W. Brooks, "A Wage Scale for Seamen, 1546," *English Historical Review* 60 (1945), 242.

74. PRO HCA 13/24/130v.

75. PRO HCA 24/51/91. A youth employed as a farm laborer was generally paid half an adult male's wage. Kassmaul, *Servants in Husbandry in Early Modern England*, 72.

76. PRO HCA 13/32/1–2.

77. J. D. Alsop, "Sea Surgeons, Health and England's Maritime Expansion: The West African Trade 1553–1660," *Mariner's Mirror* 76 (1990), 218.

78. PRO HCA 13/27/311. Greaves had at least one other apprentice to assist him. PRO HCA, 13/27/310, 13/27/310, 13/31/98–99, 13/27/310v, 13/27/304, 13/27/309-v, 24/56/27, 13/27/311, 24/56/27.

79. Guildhall Ms. 9171/18/274.

80. PRO PROB 11/102/182.

81. The exception was captains and military officers on naval and privateering vessels. While some were seamen, most often landsmen became captains, lieutenants, and soldiers in charge of the military objectives of the voyage. Such officers almost always left navigational matters of the sailing of the ship to the seafarers on board.

82. Davis, *The Rise of English Shipping*, 117, 128.

83. PRO HCA 1/45/50-v.

84. PRO HCA 1/45/50v.

85. Youings, "Raleigh's Country and the Sea," 289.

86. Shipwright John Vallre of the *Lion*, testifying in 1602 on the taking of the ship by pirates. PRO HCA 13/35/382.

87. Scammell, "Manning the English Merchant Service," 137.

88. PRO HCA 1/40/44v.

89. While the level of involvement is in question, hiring fairs are the best example of official intervention in hiring procedures of waged laborers. See Michael Roberts, "Waiting upon Chance: English Hiring Fairs and Their Meanings from the 14th to the 20th Century," *Journal of Historical Sociology* 1 (1988), 124–28.

90. See David Levine and Keith Wrightson, *The Making of an Industrial Society*

Whickham 1560–1765 (Oxford: Clarendon Press, 1991), 184, 187–91, 192; Roberts, "Waiting upon Chance," 125, 128, 131–32; A. Hassell Smith, "Labourers in Late Sixteenth-Century England: A Case Study from North Norfolk [Part II]," *Continuity and Change* 4 (1989), 376, 380.

91. Kassmaul, *Servants in Husbandry in Early Modern England*, 49, 50, 55.

92. C. H. Dixon, "Seamen and the Law: An Examination of the Impact of Legislation on the Merchant Seamen's Lot, 1588–1918" (Ph.D. diss., University of London, 1981), 13. This also parallels Elizabethan collieries where overmen were bound to the owners to manage pits and hire workers for an agreed season much as a shipmaster was bound to hire a crew, deliver cargo, and conduct trade. Levine and Wrightson, *The Making of an Industrial Society*, 183–85. Verbal contracts were a feature of employment pacts among other sectors of Elizabethan labor. Kassmaul, *Servants in Husbandry in Early Modern England*, 179.

93. As late as 1729, Parliament legislated that masters and mariners were to have all agreements pertaining to wages in writing. See Anno 2 Geo. II. Cap. 36 in *A Collection of the Statutes Relating to the Admiralty, Navy, Ships of War, and Incidental Matters; to the 8th Year of King George III* (London: Mark Baskett, 1768), 370–71.

94. Hair and Alsop, *English Seamen and Traders*, 282. Oppenheim submits that postvoyage confrontations were common. Oppenheim, *A History of the Administration of the Royal Navy, 1509–1660*, 243. Evidence from the Admiralty Court depositions suggests that wage disputes were not frequent. However, most seamen were not in a financial position to seek redress in the court. In lieu of this, some cases were handled by informal arbitration at the Trinity Houses, while other seamen petitioned the Lord Admiral directly for redress. This is discussed more fully in the next chapter.

95. Hair and Alsop, *English Seamen and Traders*, 324.

96. PRO HCA 1/42/57v; Pauline Croft, "English Mariners Trading to Spain and Portugal, 1558–1625," *Mariner's Mirror* 69 (1983), 252–53; Andrews, "The Elizabethan Seaman," 254–55.

97. Scammell, "Manning the English Merchant Service," 136.

98. Scammell, "Shipowning," 401; G. V. Scammell, "The English in the Atlantic Islands c. 1450–1650," *Mariner's Mirror* 72 (1986), 308.

99. PRO HCA, 1/42/2, 1/42/33, 1/42/14, 1/42/14v, 1/43/47, 1/43/206v, 1/44/67v, 1/42/88v, 1/42/7, 1/42/21, 1/42/57, 1/42/66, 1/42/23v. In some cases, serving foreign princes was a way to avoid English restrictions.

100. PRO HCA 1/46/104v–15.

101. Nathaniel Boteler, *Boteler's Dialogues*, ed. W. G. Perrin (London: Navy Record Society, 1929), 37.

102. Richard Hawkins, *Observations of Sir Richard Hawkins*, ed. James A. Williamson (1622; rpt. London: Argonaut Press, 1933), 112.

103. Scammell, "The English in the Atlantic Islands c. 1450–1650," 308; Andrews, "The Elizabethan Seaman," 253.

104. Andrews, "The Elizabethan Seaman," 255; Hair and Alsop, *English Seamen and Traders*, 119–23.

105. PRO HCA 13/32/76v–77.

106. Williams, *The Maritime Trade of the East Anglian Ports 1550–1590*, 215.

107. Youings, "Raleigh's Country and the Sea," 285.

108. For greater detail of seasonal voyages see Williams, *The Maritime Trade of the East Anglian Ports, 1550–1590*, 239–45.

109. Davis, *The Rise of the English Shipping*, 128–29.

110. Kassmaul, *Servants in Husbandry in Early Modern England*, 55, 61.

111. Hair and Alsop, *English Seamen and Traders*, 116, 122, 147–48.

112. Julian S. Corbett, *Drake and the Tudor Navy*, 2nd ed., vol. I (New York: Burt Franklin, 1899), 216.

113. Scammell, "Manning the English Merchant Service," 133; Scammell, "The Sinews of War," 357. The practice of using convicts as unwilling labor on high-risk voyages originated earlier. See Webb, "William Sabyn of Ipswich," 211.

114. Geographical mobility is drastically understated in Admiralty depositions. Most men stated only their current parish of residence, which was probably all that was required of them by Admiralty officials.

115. Andrews, "The Elizabethan Seaman," 249, 255.

116. See John H. Farrant, "The Rise and Decline of a South Coast Seafaring Town: Brighton, 1550–1750," *Mariner's Mirror* 71 (1985), 63; Peter Laslett, *The World We Have Lost—Further Explored*, 3rd ed. (London: Methuen, 1983), 75.

117. Davis, *The Rise of the English Shipping*, 116.

118. PRO HCA 1/43/12; G. E. Manwaring, "The Dress of the British Seaman," *Mariner's Mirror* 9 (1923), 162–73, 322–32; PRO HCA, 1/44/194, 1/44/194, 13/27/324v.

119. Farrant, "The Rise and Decline of a South Coast Seafaring Town," 63; Donald Woodward, "Ships, Masters and Shipowners of the Wirral 1550–1650," *Mariner's Mirror* 63 (1977), 242–43; Youings, "Raleigh's Country and the Sea," 287.

120. PRO HCA, 1/42/13, 13/26/70v–71, 13/26/70v, 13/29/188v. Woodcot was possibly the master of the Trinity House. See Harris, *The Trinity House of Deptford*, 73; Hilary P. Mead, *Trinity House* (London: Sampson, Low, Marston, and Co., 1947), 36; Guildhall Ms. 9171/21/165v–66. Apparently, Woodcot worked in both trades until the time of his death. The entry recording his burial in Stepney parish identified him as both ironmonger and mariner. GLRO X24/70/43v; PRO HCA, 13/25/205-v, 1/43/181v, 1/44/205, 1/42/13, 1/44/9, 1/42/77v, 1/44/23, 1/44/73; Scammell, "Manning the English Merchant Service," 138.

121. Scammell, "Manning the English Merchant Service," 138. From the 1540s the population increased at a rate of 1 percent annually. Just prior to the invasion attempt of 1588, Elizabeth governed 3.8 million subjects. In the 1590s population growth slowed to 0.5 percent per annum because of a series of disastrous harvests and the effects of disease and mortality among soldiers and seamen. Youings, *Sixteenth-Century England*, 139, 149, 151. See also D. C. Coleman, *The Economy of England* (London: Oxford University Press, 1977), 21–30.

122. Scammell, "Manning the English Merchant Service," 138; Farrant, "The Rise and Decline of a South Coast Seafaring Town," 63.

123. Scammell, "Manning the English Merchant Service," 138.

124. Walter Raleigh, *Judicious and Select Essayes and Observations* (London: Humphrey Mosele, 1650), 4.

125. Corbett, *Drake and the Tudor Navy*, vol. I, 249.

126. Andrews, *Trade, Plunder and Settlement*, 27.

127. Ibid., 206; Andrews, *Elizabethan Privateering*, 40–41, 234–35.

128. Andrews, "The Elizabethan Seaman," 251; PRO HCA, 1/42/18, 1/42/20, 1/43/12, 1/44/17, 1/45/87v–88.

129. PRO HCA 1/44/17. Mainwaring, quoted in Andrews, "The Elizabethan Seaman," 249–251; PRO HCA, 1/44/17, 1/44/186, 1/42/20, 1/42/18, 1/42/15v. Ex-military personnel in general experienced problems fitting back into the labor market. Gareth Stedman Jones, *Outcast London: A Study in the Relationship between Classes in Victorian Society* (Oxford: Clarendon Press, 1971), 77, 97. Scammell, "The Sinews of War," 360.

130. PRO HCA, 1/42/14v–17v, 1/42/2, 1/45/87v–88, 1/101/14, 1/42/12, 1/40/126v, 1/43/12, 1/43/79. Criminal bands on land were recruited through the same connections. See John Bellamy, *Crime and Public Order in England in the Later Middle Ages* (London: Routledge and Kegan Paul, 1973), 69–88.

131. PRO HCA, 1/42/15v, 1/42/23, 1/42/18, 1/43/111, 1/41/185v, 1/43/43, 1/41/18v, 1/43/50v, 1/41/121, 1/43/169, 1/43/172v, 1/43/93v, 1/42/30.

132. PRO HCA, 1/42/26v, 1/43/32v. See also PRO HCA, 1/41/169v, 1/41/189. The woman referred to was Howard's wife, Catherine (Carey), whom he married in 1563. *Burke's Peerage* (London: Burke's Peerage, 1967), 709; L. M. Hill, *Bench and Bureaucracy: The Public Career of Sir Julius Caesar, 1580–1636* (Stanford, Calif.: Stanford University Press, 1988), 17.

133. PRO HCA 1/42/26v.

134. PRO HCA, 1/43/148, 1/43/151, 1/43/160v.

135. David Mathew, "The Cornish and Welsh Pirates in the Reign of Elizabeth," *English Historical Review* 39 (1924), 342.

136. M. Oppenheim "The Royal and Merchant Navy under Elizabeth," *English Historical Review* 6 (1891), 473.

137. PRO HCA, 1/40/62, 1/101/10, 1/101/12v, 1/43/1, 1/43/4, 1/40/58v, 14/21/61 14/21/75, 14/21/80, 14/21/83, 14/21/99, 14/21/126, 14/21/130, 14/22/52, 14/22/58, 14/22/214, 14/22/245, 14/30/85, 14/34/5, 13/34/8, 14/34/16, 1/44/220; Hill, *Bench and Bureaucracy*, 9.

138. PRO HCA 1/43/6v.

139. PRO HCA 1/43/42-v.

140. PRO HCA, 1/43/181v, 1/41/18v, 1/41/125, 1/41/142v, 1/41/145v, 1/43/81, 1/43/36, 1/43/128v; Mathew, "The Cornish and Welsh Pirates in the Reign of Elizabeth," 337–39, 340; PRO HCA, 14/27/112, 1/42/28-v, 1/42/42, 1/43/66v.

141. PRO HCA 1/41/116v. Hatton was the lord chancellor of England, the admiral of the Isle of Purbeck, vice admiral of Dorset, and a favorite with the Queen. While he was very interested in maritime matters, Haines's accusations cannot be substantiated. Haines's actions suggest that he did believe that he was sheltered from the authorities. Alice Gilmore Vines, *Neither Fire nor Steel: Sir Christopher Hatton* (Chicago: Nelson-Hall, 1978), 172; C. L'Estrange Ewen, "Organized Piracy round England in the Sixteenth Century," *Mariner's Mirror* 35 (1949), 38.

142. Quoted in Andrews, "The Elizabethan Seaman," 251.

143. PRO HCA 1/42/4. In the case of criminal bands on land, John Bellamy argues that gangs' cohesion tended to be brief. See Bellamy, *Crime and Public Order*, 83; PRO HCA, 1/43/25v, 1/41/112v, 1/41/180v, 1/46/50v–51, 1/43/12, 1/44/126v, 1/44/217v, 1/40/6, 1/44/120v, 1/44/120v.

144. Quoted in Andrews, "The Elizabethan Seaman," 251.

145. Ewen, "Organized Piracy," 31; PRO HCA, 14/36/165, 14/36/167.

146. PRO HCA 1/43/47-v. The reference is likely to Henry Seckford of the Queen's Privy Chamber.

147. PRO HCA 13/27/112.

148. Hawkins, *Observations*, 112.

149. Ewen, "Organized Piracy," 32.

150. Peter Padfield, *Armada* (London: Victor Gollancz, 1988), 95.

151. Hawkins, *Observations*, 101.

152. D. W. Waters, "The Elizabethan Navy and the Armada Campaign," *Mariner's Mirror* 35 (1949), 91.

153. Ibid., 91. For information on the royal bounty for construction of large ships suitable for service in times of war, see Brian Dietz's "The Royal Bounty and English Merchant Shipping in the Sixteenth and Seventeenth Centuries," *Mariner's Mirror* 77 (1991). This bounty was not particular to Elizabeth's reign; the earliest recorded royal bounty for large ships was 1449. For greater detail regarding the Crown's initiatives, see M. Oppenheim, *A History of the Administration of the Royal Navy and of Merchant Shipping in Relation to the Navy 1509–1660*, 19, 167–71.

154. Ronald Politt, "Bureaucracy and the Armada: The Administrator's Battle," *Mariner's Mirror* 60 (1974), 119–20; PRO SP 12/156/45/76–140v.

155. Monson was referring to the lack of charity for sick seamen and the irregularity of seamen's pay. Monson, *Naval Tracts*, vol. IV, 244; Raleigh, *Judicious and Select Essayes and Observations*, 30; PRO HCA, 13/25/176v, 1/44/2, 1/44/3, 1/44/3, 13/28/8.

156. Raleigh, *Judicious and Select Essayes and Observations*, 30.

157. Michael Duffy, "The Foundations of British Naval Power," in *The Military Revolution and the State, 1500–1800*, ed. Michael Duffy (Exeter: University of Exeter, 1980), 68.

158. Ibid., 69.

159. Politt, "Bureaucracy and the Armada," 124.

160. J.J.N. McGurk, "A Levy of Seamen in the Cinque Ports, 1602," *Mariner's Mirror* 66 (1980), 139.

161. Ibid., 141; Padfield, *Armada*, 94.

162. Hawkins, *Observations*, 22.

163. The official might have been trying to find men for the Portugal expedition of 1589 under Drake and Sir John Norris. There were two ships in that expedition named the *Antelope*, but neither was the Queen's. See *The Expedition of Sir John Norris and Sir Francis Drake to Spain and Portugal, 1589*, ed. R. B. Wernham (Aldershot, U.K.: Navy Records Society, 1988), 332–33; PRO HCA 13/27/324v; Corbett, *Drake and the Tudor Navy*, vol. II, 336; PRO HCA 13/27/324-v.

164. The commission was reputed by Peter Hills, one of London's most respected mariners and shipowners, to contain these words. PRO HCA 13/35/394v.

165. Scammell, "The Sinews of War," 356–58; Lloyd, *The British Seaman 1200–1860*, 39; Youings, "Raleigh's Country and the Sea," 268; David Hannay, "Raleigh's Orders," *Mariner's Mirror* 3 (1913), 213; Keevil, *Medicine and the Navy*, 78.

166. Scammell, "Sinews of War," 358.

167. Ibid.

168. Raleigh, *Judicious and Select Essayes and Observations*, 36.

169. Ibid., 36–37.

170. Waters, "The Elizabethan Navy and the Armada Campaign," 104.

171. *Acts of the Privy Council* vol. XVIII, 1589–90, ed. John Roche Dasant (Norwich: Her Majesty's Stationery Office, 1899), 401.

172. PRO SP 12/231/46.

173. Figures are taken from lists of seamen required to man the fleet in the summer of 1588. *State Papers Relating to the Defeat of the Spanish Armada*, vol. II, 2nd ed., ed John Knox Laughton (Aldershot, U.K.: Temple Smith for the Navy Records Society, 1987), 331. These figures are not the total numbers impressed. Overall numbers would be far greater if they included men who were discharged or those who died on shipboard. Keevil, *Medicine and the Navy*, vol. I, 76.

174. Scammell, "The Sinews of War," 356; Raleigh, *Judicious and Select Essayes and Observations*, 37.

175. Hawkins did convince the Crown to do this, but naval wages were still inadequate. This is discussed in Chapter 4. See Oppenheim, *The Administration of the Royal Navy, 1509–1660*, 134.

176. The plan for a general levy met opposition just as Charles I's plan would. Scammell, "The Sinews of War," 355.

177. Duffy, "The Foundations of British Naval Power," 49.

178. Oppenheim, *The Administration of the Royal Navy, 1509–1660*, 134; Scammell, "English Merchant Shipping Service," 132.

179. Oppenheim, *Administration of the Royal Navy, 1509–1660*, 167.

180. In the eighteenth century, there were a great number of navigational books published to assist mariners. In 1777 mariner William Hutchinson published *A Treatise on Practical Seamanship*, lamenting that sea officers had to learn navigation largely by the "slow progress of experience" and from "their own and other people's misfortunes." See William Hutchinson, *A Treatise on Practical Seamanship* (Liverpool: Cowburne, 1777), address.

Chapter 2

Authority, Discipline,
and the Maritime Social Order

The maritime community paralleled Tudor society in terms of a clear hierarchy and a system of expectations that bound the society together. Walter and Wrightson describe early modern society on land in the following terms:

it seems clear that, given the very limited coercive powers at their disposal, the position of the ruling class was upheld by a comparable complex of relationships and expectations between individuals and groups occupying different positions in the hierarchy of wealth and power. . . . These relationships . . . derived their binding force from the fact that they served above all to provide protection against the myriad insecurities . . . of a hostile environment. That force could be maintained, however, only if expectations were met, relationships serviced and renewed.[1]

Sixteenth-century English society maintained order principally through assent, not coercion. To a great degree, the order and discipline of shipboard communities depended on seafarers' willingness to obey directives. Despite the fact that seamen were frequently regarded by their social superiors as being "untaught and untamed creatures," "voyde of reason as of obedyence," and "without government,"[2] they were generally receptive to carrying out orders from those in authority; this was part of the seamen's psyche. The smooth running of the ship and the safety of all aboard depended on orders being enforced throughout the chain of command; N.A.M. Rodger, a specialist on the Georgian navy, says that this "was not a matter of unquestioning obedience . . . but of intelligent co-operation in survival."[3] It was not enough, however, for captains, masters, and officers merely to issue orders. If a crew decided to ignore its officers, there was little means of enforcement. In this regard, authority figures were probably more vulnerable at sea than on land. Compliance and order rested on the fulfillment of expectations and, to a lesser degree, a code of censure that acted as a deterrent.

As in the general population, seamen's "acceptance of subordination" was in no way a "degeneration into submissiveness."[4] Indisputably, many seamen were given to bouts of impetuousness, outbursts of violence, and a degree of unmanageability. One has only to consult the High Court of the Admiralty depositions for abundant evidence. The words of Sir Richard Hawkins, an experienced sea captain and member of one of Elizabethan England's most prominent seafaring dynasties, encapsulate widespread sentiment regarding the notorious intractability of seamen; he speaks for many of his colleagues who governed, or tried to govern, merchant, naval, and privateering crews:

but Mariners are like to a stiffe necked Horse, which taking the bridle betwixt his teeth, forceth his Rider to what him list mauger his will: so they hauing once concluded, and resolved, are with great difficultie brought to yeelde to the raynes of reason.[5]

No doubt some of the friction between those in command and their underlings stemmed from what the latter saw as transgressions of their rights and unfulfilled expectations. Seamen, especially skilled ones, had a clear sense of their dues. Captain William Monson summed up the most frequent grievances of seamen as products of the times:

When they have inexperienced, needy, commanders; bad and unwholesome victuals, and complaining of it can have no redress; cutting their beef too small; putting of five or more to four men's allowance; want of beer; longstaying for their wages.[6]

Since the foundation of order was conceived of as consensus, authority had to rely on techniques of persuasion. Few of those in positions of maritime command could claim that their authority and position were dictated by virtue of birth. Authority figures in the maritime hierarchy normally achieved their position through skill and training and not by accident of birth.[7] Thus, maritime hierarchy was more vulnerable to challenges than the hierarchy and social structure of the land community, with the ingrained structure provided by property. It was even more essential that channels be in place for the common sort to express their views and grievances. Seamen had a strong tradition of consultation and petition. With the introduction of impressment on a large scale during the war, the Crown compromised these traditional practices but could not eradicate them. As we will see, in the seafaring community the maintenance of order remained a process of cooperation between the various segments. In this way the maritime community was very similar to Tudor society on land.

The traditional techniques of persuasion, consultation, reconciliation, and arbitration were not always sufficient to reach an accord. Sometimes more extreme measures were needed to draw attention to a problem. Even in its most radical form, early modern English social protest was rarely, if ever, intended to overthrow the system. The men of the *Golden Lion*, in the sole recorded court-martial for mutiny in the later Elizabethan navy, assured their captain that unacceptable conditions drove them to desert the naval campaign in 1587. They identified themselves as the "Quenes men and yours" despite their resolve to desert their posts.[8] To borrow Wrightson's words, "there was order in this disorder."[9] The mutineers articulated both a sense of life-threatening injustice and comprehension of their liability; they were loath to starve, and so "they would rather truste to the Quenes mercye . . . and they would awnswer yt at home that they had donn."[10] Their actions are consistent with disturbances ashore: popular protest emerged from the perception that common rights were being eroded or neglected. Both ashore and afloat, food and starvation lay at the center of articulated sociopolitical challenges. Mutineers frequently acted out of concern for their food supplies. Authorities on land and at sea recognized the rights of the populace to protest about "subsistence matters"; certainly, these issues were a common catalyst for popular disturbances.[11] Those in positions of authority acknowledged that verbal and written petitions and orderly demonstrations and protests focusing on food were legitimate means of bringing attention to the problem. When complaints and disquiet moved outside the boundaries of accepted channels (as in the case of mutiny or riots ashore), then retribution could be cruel indeed. Retribution within the maritime community was achieved through its own, hitherto unstudied system of justice and punishment. An analysis of this system sheds light upon the inner workings and the subculture of the seafaring community as well as its relationship with the dominant (land) culture.

BASIS AND NATURE OF AUTHORITY

Maritime discipline was, in good measure, determined by the basis and limits of authority. Royal commissions entitled the bearer to wield great powers while at sea. Therefore, only those who had proven themselves loyal servants to the Queen were so endowed. In his *Dialogues*, Captain Nathaniel Boteler notes that "this [responsibility] is not to be entrusted with every Commander, much less every Master."[12] Furthermore, such men were given royal commissions only if the Crown thought that the expedition warranted it. Although their authority was extensive, the vast majority of captains and masters in the navy, privateering expeditions, or the merchant marine did not receive royal commissions and therefore did not enjoy the range of powers of those who had commissions.

Naval commanders who were granted royal commissions for specific voyages had a wide latitude in regard to the direction of the voyage. They also had the power to try and punish offenders who disrupted the voyage. In "capital causes [such] as murders, mutinies and the like," only a commander with a royal commission had the authority to execute those who transgressed maritime law.[13] Nevertheless, even a naval commander's authority had limits. With or without a royal commission, a naval commander who had overstepped his bounds would be called to account for his actions when he returned home. Although much could be forgiven in the interest of national security, few naval commanders were a law unto themselves.[14] Their conduct of the campaign and their treatment of their subordinates were subject to the Crown's scrutiny.

Privateers received their authority from the Lord Admiral; this was achieved through letters of reprisal.[15] Although privateering captains represented the pinnacle of power on their warships and were sanctioned by the Crown to assist in the war effort at sea, they did not have the same powers as naval commanders. They were, however, accountable to the Crown; bonds for good behavior were posted before letters of marque were granted. Those who failed to adhere to the terms of the commission were prosecuted in the High Court of the Admiralty.[16]

While it was the responsibility of the Lord Admiral and the Admiralty Court to ensure that privateering did not descend into piracy, owners and backers determined the precise nature and overall objectives of the expedition. In both privateering and merchant voyages, those in charge (whether captains or masters) normally had a say in the direction of the voyage relative to their stake and investment in the undertaking and the latitude accorded them by the backers and owners. Once a ship was at sea, officers' discretion could be considerable, especially if there were no owners, backers, or factors on board.

Unlike naval seamen and privateers, civilian seamen were not responsible to the Crown. Although they were obliged to conduct their business within the boundaries of English maritime law, they did not have special commissions from, or bonds with, the Admiralty. Shipmasters in the merchant marine, whether owners or part-owners themselves, had authority to conduct the trading voyage from the owners and merchants involved. Their powers were determined prior to the ship's departure from port. For instance, in the early 1580s Master Stephen Hare of the *Minion* had been given the authority from the owners and merchants to displace from office those "he shoulde dislike of."[17] Theoretically, owners, merchants, and backers had a say in shipboard regulations, but orders normally followed a common format based on maritime tradition.[18]

While captains, masters, and crews frequently received their orders before disembarkation for privateering expeditions and trading voyages, merchants, owners, and backers sometimes chose to make the voyage themselves or send representatives to ensure that the voyage ran according to their directives. Whether they were physically present on shipboard, owners, merchants, and backers relayed their wishes through written and verbal orders. If crews veered far from, or ignored, the objectives set for them by the backers and owners (however loosely or forcefully communicated), owners and backers might choose simply to end their dealings with the principal officers responsible, or they might elect to have the matter heard as a civil suit in the Admiralty Court. As in the case of naval commanders, privateering captains and masters of the merchant marine might pride themselves on their powers, but ultimately they had to answer to higher authorities for their actions.

From these different sources of authority emerged different limits to the extent of punishment. Only those commanders officially empowered by the Queen could take a man's life for acts of disobedience. In most cases the men were naval commanders. During the naval strike on Cadiz in 1587, Drake stated that he had

from Her Maiestie sufficient Jurisdiccon to correcte and punnishe with all severitie as to me in discretion shalbe meete, Accordinge to the Qualitie of the offences, all those sceditious persons which sholl be in the whole fleete.[19]

There were occasions when the Crown did grant these powers to non-naval commanders; letters-patent for Richard Grenville's projected voyage in 1574 to *Terra Australis* gave the commander far-ranging powers over "persons of the companye rebellyously or obstinatly resisting against there commandementes or aucthoritie." For the duration of the voyage the commander had the authority

to slaye execute and put to death or otherwise correct without other Judiciall proceedinges but by the lawe martiall accordinge to there discression, and that all paynes & execucions of deathe so to be done and inflicted shalbe accompted & judged lawfully done as by our speciall will & commandement & by the law martiall.[20]

Promoters of the first Guinea voyage of 1553–54 were also granted the right to employ martial law.[21] Given the grave responsibilities that went along with royal commissions, it is not surprising that relatively few were issued.

No examples of executions on merchant voyages or privateering expeditions emerge from the records. In these cases, serious crimes committed on shipboard were handled after the conclusion of the voyage by the High Court of the Admiralty. With the exception of capital crimes, most seamen in the maritime community lived under the threat of traditional penalties for specific offenses that were dictated largely by maritime tradition; the real difference between the various groups of the maritime community was the scope that discipline could encompass.

Despite its source or its scope, captains and masters encountered challenges to their authority. Problems sometimes arose if the chain of command was unclear. The almost total absence of mutiny in the Elizabethan navy was, in part, due to its well-defined hierarchy and stricter discipline; all were subject to a general or commander. However, there was room for confusion in other segments of the maritime community. Shipboard disputes regarding authority did emerge from time to time. The case of Thomas Watts contra Robert Feewilliams (or Fitzwilliams) in the High Court of the Admiralty is an apt illustration of turmoil at the highest levels of the command structure. Watts's brother and father were part-owners of the *Examiner* of London along with Feewilliams and Thomas Sewell. Feewilliams was made master of the privateering voyage in 1588; there was no dispute on this issue.[22] Watts was presumably made captain, but this point is contentious. Some crew members claimed that they saw the documentation on parchment that a privateering commission named Watts as captain. Despite the fact that most of the crew regarded Watts as the captain, Feewilliams refused to accept that

Roberte Feewilliams wente master of the said shippe the viadge . . . and in the viadge outwardes he disliked that Thomas Wattes tooke uppon him to be Captaine, and openly sayd he was noe Captaine there or had to doe with the men or victualls and that John Wattes his brother requested him to suffer . . . Thomas Wattes to goe with him in the shippe.[23]

The quarrel regarding Watts's office escalated to the point that Feewilliams attacked the "capon face captain," injuring his head and arm. The master's mate of the *Examiner* intervened and prevented Feewilliams from running Watts through with a pike and having "a pounde of his bloode." Ultimately, the master took the ship's boat and deserted his ship, stating that "he was sory he had not killed the said Captaine." Watts brought a suit in the Admiralty Court in November 1588 for his injuries.[24] It is difficult to ascertain where the fault lies regarding the origin of the problem. Were the other owners unclear in communicating Watts's role to Feewilliams? Was it merely a case of the master and part-owner resenting Watts's instatement in a superior position by his family members? We can see from the case of Thomas Watts contra Robert Feewilliams the disruptions that disunity of command could cause when proper authority was lacking or unclear.

In another case, dissension in command brought a ship to a virtual standstill. In 1601 William Ivy was acting as lieutenant for a privateering expedition, although he was a master-mariner. Ivy, the master, William Russel, and the master's mate, Richard Mathew, opposed the captain, William Craston. The company appeared to be divided on whether the expedition should continue. Tensions came to a head when the master commanded the sails to be unfurled to make for home. Captain Craston countermanded the order, threatening that anyone who carried out the order would be made to eat the foresail. Master Russel alleged that he "was putt in as much trust for the viadge as he [Craston] was." Weapons were drawn, and insults were hurled, the captain saying the master knew no more than a "sheepes heade."[25] Despite the temporary breakdown of authority, stability was restored, and the expedition did continue.

As these cases illustrate, order in the seafaring community was relatively solid despite the fact that ripples of dissension reverberated from the top to the bottom of the social pyramid from time to time. The grumbling of naval seamen tended to focus on specific complaints, especially payment of wages and poor provisioning. To date there is no evidence that naval mutinies were caused by direct challenges to those in authority. In the only court-martial of the period, the men deserted Drake because of unacceptable risks. There were no attempts to displace Drake or other officers in command. There were challenges to those in authority in the merchant marine, but these seem to have been relatively rare. Those seamen who were displeased with their master and the manner in which he conducted the voyage tried to complete their voyage (and thus collect their full wages). An incompetent or exacting master could be avoided when the time came to make future employment contracts. For those who wanted immediate severance, desertion was an option. Privateering voyages were the most prone to challenges to authority because of the looser discipline, the absence of wages, and the inexperience of many gentle-born and affluent captains. Monson wrote that "seamen are much discouraged, of late times, by preferring of young, needy, and inexperienced gentlemen captains over them."[26] Such challenges often emerged out of the desperation of seamen who could not afford to return home empty-handed; many sought to direct the voyage for greater profits.

In addition to the problem of an uncertain hierarchy, problems arose periodically if the objectives of the voyage were ill defined. This was more likely to happen on "mixed" voyages that combined trade and privateering or naval campaigns and privateering expeditions than on voyages where objectives and the nature of authority were clearly set out. Contradictory objectives and problems of command frequently went hand in hand; unclear aims and priorities invited dissension, confusion, and challenges to authority.

Naval campaigns conducted during the later Elizabethan period were notorious for their abandoned strategies. The Crown wanted the best of both worlds. By virtue of letters of reprisal, the Crown encouraged its seamen to hinder or destroy Spain's ships and intercept its merchant ships on their trade routes. Yet the Queen, her Privy Councillors, the Lord Admiral, and Admiralty officials regularly made complaint when seamen did not follow the guidelines of the letters of reprisal and Crown proclamations. In order to save money and effort, the Crown left non-naval seamen to conduct the war largely on their own terms and with their own resources with little intervention or direct control; English seamen and merchants—seeing profits to be had—made the cause of the realm their own. When it wished to do so, the Crown was hard put to reclaim control of the rudder and navigate the war according to its own course. With the vast majority of naval campaigns conducted on a joint-stock basis and manned by civilian seamen with a pronounced tradition of independence, the Crown's naval objectives were often compromised for the pursuit of profit. Because of its insistence on waging the war on a shoestring budget and employing ad hoc methods of fighting the enemy at sea, the Crown simply could not contain the war afloat within its own parameters. Despite the efforts of commanders, rarely were the Queen's wishes and the investors' purses satisfied from a given voyage. Conflicts that arose from contradictory objectives and questions of priority could (and did) wreak havoc during many voyages and expeditions.

The confusion that resulted from mixed voyages is best exemplified by the trial and execution of mutineer Thomas Doughty during Drake's voyage of circumnavigation of 1577–80. This incident illustrates the problem of royal and private orders. Unquestionably, Drake followed court-martial procedure; he impaneled 40 dignified jurymen to hear the evidence against Doughty, who had repeatedly challenged his authority. In addition, Captain Winter, a friend of the defendant, was chosen as the foreman by the others. Doughty was found guilty and executed. The legality of this action is still debated by historians. What was the extent of the commander's jurisdiction? Much of the controversy rests on the indefinite nature of the mission. Was it an official expedition supported by the Queen? Did Drake possess the Queen's commission, which empowered him to conduct a court-martial? We do know that John Doughty appealed the right of Drake to execute his brother and that the suit ultimately failed. The Crown supported Drake's cause and his contention that he was justified in executing mutineers. Apparently, neither contemporaries nor historians were aware of the precise limits of Drake's authority.[27]

The maintenance of order and authority is not merely a matter of legality but also depends upon the conduct of those in positions of power. To a great extent, authority was maintained through deference, and deference required respect. Those who had positions of authority were expected to live up to shared expectations. Hence, those who did not perform their role in a satisfactory manner compromised authority. Inept captains and masters were a source of great discontent and animosity among seamen. In

1592 Richard Sanders, the boatswain of the *Gift of God*, claimed that the master, James Lyle, "duringe the sayd voyadge, would sundrye tymes be overcome withe drinke, blaspheme god withe oathes & cursinges & misvse his companye." These bouts of drunkenness convinced Sanders that Lyle had shown himself a "man not sufficiente att those tymes to take chardge of suche a shippe as was the Gifte, or to governe suche a company."[28]

Aboard the *White Hind* of London, two crewmen called their master

rascall knave and boye and woulde make him a boye, and to his greate discreaditt reported he was not a sufficiente Master, nor able to take chardge, and often tymes they have threatened to beate him.[29]

In 1591 Captain Barnstraw lost control over the crew of the *Tiger* in dramatic fashion. His efforts to keep the privateers from "breaking bulk" (dividing up the booty) until they got back to England were totally ineffectual. It was said that "the boy in the shipp had as much command & governmente all the viadge as the said Barnstrawe the Captanne had For he could beare noe sway." Hendrick Arnold, the steward's mate, claimed that Barnstraw was "greatly reviled" by the crew, who called him "coppernose & that he was fitter to drincke . . . then to be a Captanne." Significantly, Barnstraw could not even earn his officers' loyalty or respect. When the captain criticized the crew for embezzling goods, order broke down; the master's mate and the quartermaster threatened to cast the captain overboard, and one of them allegedly struck at him with a dagger.[30]

Contemporary wisdom recognized that commanders should rule "both in fear and love."[31] In the words of historian Bernard Capp, those in positions of authority were to observe a "brisk paternalism."[32] A commander who was seen as unjust or excessively harsh risked extreme reactions from his crew, including desertion or mutiny. The extreme actions of Master Nicholas Roberts of the *Charity* toward one of his crewmen, sailor Samuel Ley, prompted a mutiny of sorts or at least an act of gross insubordination. There had been many signs of the master's drunkenness and irresponsibility during the course of the voyage. Roberts's unfair punishment of Ley was the final straw. The master was "dronncke and malitiously bente" and mistakenly believed Ley had been in a brawl ashore the previous day. He had the sailor pinioned to a capstan bar with a rope tied around his neck. Roberts denied Ley the opportunity to speak and clear his name. Quartermaster William May informed Roberts that he would not see an innocent man strangle and attempted to untie Ley. Roberts allegedly assaulted May, while another member of the crew cut the ropes and freed the hapless Ley.[33] While it was necessary for captains and masters to discipline those who threatened the maintenance of order, it was equally important that they should not abuse their power or be seen to treat their men unfairly. Those in authority who did not live up to the expectations of their subordinates jeopardized the deferential relationship that was the basis of the maritime hierarchy. Because rank was earned, not inherited, it cut to the quick to call a master a "boy" or to question his sobriety.

METHODS FOR REGULATION OF SOCIAL RELATIONS

The maintenance of order was a two-edged sword. Obedience was not given blindly; the crew's opinions and expectations had to be taken into account. Wrightson makes the point that passive acquiescence was not equivalent to positive affirmation.[34] Order was assured only if these expectations were (or were seen to be) met. While those in authority were eager to achieve harmony, they also had to convey the fact that they negotiated from a position of strength. Maintaining the "face of authority" in a paternalistic society was an important consideration.[35] However, the overriding concern was to achieve harmony for all involved. The maritime community had various ways to achieve accord among its members: persuasion, consultation, arbitration, and petition, methods that aided the community in its pursuit of harmony.

N.A.M. Rodger states, "Where modern officers expect to command, mid-eighteenth-century [naval] officers hoped to persuade."[36] The same can be said for the officeholders of the sixteenth-century maritime community, regardless of whether they occupied positions in the navy, on pirate or privateering vessels, or in the merchant marine. Even Drake felt the need to use rhetoric and persuasion to justify his actions to his men. Drake's most famous speech was a plea for unity.[37] During the 1587 naval mutiny on the *Golden Lion*, Captain Marchant and Master Bigate reasoned with the men and attempted to placate them. Bigate endeavored to ascertain the source of the work shutdown. Sensing the seriousness of the situation, Bigate also solicited the captain's help. Marchant went

to the mayne maste, demaunded, whie they did not as the master comaunded them, and, as yt will be proved he comaunded them in her maiesties name to doe yt. The moste parte of them awnswered hime that they would not, but that they would goe for England, for the winde is nowe good, and that they would not goe backe againe and be starved for wante of victualls; the captaine awnsweringe them againe sayd, Contente yourselves, what victualls soever are in the shipp you shall have yt, and therefore holde yourselves contente untill wee mete with our generall.[38]

Captain Marchant, William Boroughs, Bigate, and Cornelius the gunner tried to persuade the men to wait for Drake to discuss the source of their discontent. Marchant promised the men riches but "sawe that by no perwasioun they would alter there mynds."[39] Captain Clifford of the Queen's ship *Spy* was nearby and witnessed the "broyle" aboard the *Lion* and tried to influence the men. Bigate had said to him: "Alack sir! I am but one mann, I have donn as muche as I can to perswade them but by noe intreatye can make them to tarrie."[40] William Towerson, leader of a trading expedition to Guinea in 1558, had to "move" the men to continue the voyage, as they were dejected about high mortality among the crew and "would not tary." Towerson's persuasion, his insistence on the need to continue in order to "make our voyage," had some influence, as the expedition did not make for England immediately. Nonetheless, Towerson had "much a doe with froward Mariners," and, lacking some of the powers of earlier Guinea traders, Towerson was reduced to begging his men.[41] Given the limited resources of authority figures while at sea, there was a great need to persuade and coax unwilling crews into conformity. This necessity reveals the fragile basis of command afloat.

Looser discipline in commercial voyages meant that non-naval mariners had a freer atmosphere in which to seek redress. This climate of relative openness was recognized by contemporaries. Boteler criticizes the dynamic in non-naval vessels for breeding "unusual and new distempers":

I am persuaded that they have been rather fuelled than quenched by an over indulgency, in that these men have found their tumultuous clamours and demands answered and satisfied by this rude (or rather rebellious) course of seeking them; a precedent that may be doubted of worse consequence than hitherto hath been felt.[42]

Those in command of naval vessels were concerned that, encouraged by the established customs in other sectors of the maritime community, seamen would expect the same latitude in the navy. Given the lack of a naval caste of seamen and the common labor pool, Boteler and his ilk were powerless to eliminate what they perceived to be trends that threatened order in the navy.

In privateers, commanders were expected to confer with their men on important matters. On issues such as "consorting" (crews working together), the crew expected the majority to rule. To a limited extent, they had some say over their membership. The privateering crew of the *Salamander* refused to allow Edward Marlow to be lieutenant for the voyage; for unspecified reasons "the company would not allowe him for that place."[43] In addition, privateering crews normally established the allotment of shares for each man on each voyage, although a basic pattern was followed. The power of the collective had considerable jurisdiction in this regard. On a privateering voyage in 1603, sailor John Stone of the *Affection* lost his right leg in battle, and the crew voted to give him two additional shares by way of compensation.[44] Conversely, in 1595 one crew voted to decrease a seaman's share for his misbehavior.[45]

The merchant marine also had a strong tradition of consultation. Crews customarily gave counsel on jettisoning cargo, accepting extra freight, and cutting down masts in storms. During his appearance in the Admiralty

Court in 1579, Master John Giles reported that he had to refuse to take certain cargo aboard the *Hopewell* of London "for that he could not gett the good will of his companie when first he made metyon therof vnto them." Changes to the itinerary were seen as a legitimate concern to all. Seamen on the *Prudence* of London "seamed altogeather unwillinge to goe or saile the saide viadge for Frannce because of the dunkerkers." The Admiralty's records demonstrate that consultation was conducted on a great variety of issues. In 1602 the complement of the *Speedwell* consented to surrender the ship to the Dunkirkers. The men of the *Minion* conferred on whether Stephen Hare, the master, should go ashore in Brazil to answer to the Justices for certain religious books they had on board: "all the companye . . . gave theire consentes and subscribed that the Master shoulde not goe on shore vnlesse they had pledge for his saffetye."[46]

Consultation, on the other hand, was very restricted in the navy. Given its rigid hierarchy and strict discipline, it is not surprising that the navy attempted to limit consultation to the highest echelons. Wider consultation, when it occurred, was usually in the midst of crisis.[47] Matters involving national security were entrusted to the most experienced and senior naval officers, and the "meaner sort" were not given a voice in such weighty concerns. Ultimately, decisions were made by naval commanders (unilaterally or on the advice of other officers); these men would be answerable to the Crown for the conduct of the voyage. Even if the navy had adopted the more egalitarian and open atmosphere of non-naval vessels, coordination of fleets to achieve military objectives virtually negated the opportunity for large-scale and frequent discussions, except in rare circumstances. Sheer numbers prevented the navy from operating in the same fashion as a small contingent of privateering vessels. Good relations within the shipboard community were vital, given the close quarters and time spent aboard. A smoothly running ship tended to be a more efficient one. When techniques such as consultation and persuasion failed to achieve the desired level of internal harmony, other methods were used. Arbitration between individuals and groups was a practice of long standing on land.[48] Good relations between neighbors and coworkers were deemed important in any sixteenth-century community. Arbitration was an important extrajudicial tool to settle disputes that threatened the harmony of the group. The maritime community also utilized this technique, conducting the proceedings on an informal or formal basis.

Although efforts were doomed to failure, Captain Thomas Watts and Master Robert Feewilliams of the *Examiner* were pressured by the crew to settle their differences, and their dispute was temporarily resolved; the two "were at sondry variances and many wordes passed betwixte them yet they were made freindes and remayned togeather."[49] Similarly, on board the *Mary Anne*, John Smith and Richard Graston, who had a long history of animosity, resolved their quarrel and by "mediation of frendes they putt the same to compromise."[50] Arbitration could also be conducted in a formal manner. Matters regarding wages, ownership, and similar issues were sometimes by agreement of parties directed to the Brethren of Trinity House for settlement rather than taken to law in the High Court of the Admiralty. A dispute between Captain Christopher Newport and his crew over wages is a case in point. Only after arbitration failed did the crew seek justice from the Lord Admiral.[51]

While a court of law represented the final step in any attempt to settle a dispute, it was desirable for all parties to reach an accord before the courts were involved. In theory, if an agreement was reached speedily and in an informal manner, it might prevent deep-seated resentment and anger from festering. For this reason most trade guilds of the period explicitly prohibited members from taking a dispute to law, insisting instead upon third-party mediation. Once an issue was before the courts, both sides were usually entrenched in their positions. Furthermore, the cost of having a suit heard in a court of law could be quite expensive and would thus raise the stakes and make winning that much more important.[52] Informal and less costly methods of achieving settlement were therefore more desirable.

Undoubtedly, the maintenance of law and order was a process that demanded participation by all, to varying degrees. While numerous tensions could and did result from shipboard life, the community had means to mend the tears in the social fabric that disturbances and breaches of discipline caused. Rituals emphasizing unity and reconciliation strengthened morale. On board the *Golden Dragon* of London in 1592, Captain Christopher Newport urged his men to reconcile and toast each other before battle began with a Portuguese carrack:

masters nowe the tyme is come that eyther we must ende our dayes, or take the said carricke & wisshed all the company to stande theire chardge like men and if eny displeasure were amongst eany of them to forgett & forgive one an other, which every one seemed willinge vnto, & then the said Keyball (the master) tooke a canne of wyne & droncke to John Locke (the master's mate), & John Locke droncke to him agayne & soe throughe out the shipp every one droncke to the other whereby he is persuaded that all the company were good freindes one with an other.[53]

Before Doughty's execution, Drake assembled his men for confession and taking of the Blessed Sacrament.[54] Solidarity in religion and religious ritual could act as a unifying force and soothing influence.[55]

PETITION AND PROTEST

In general, an outlet for discontent is a desirable safety valve for any community seeking to maintain some level of order. Non-naval seamen had ample opportunity to air their views. Because the navy, merchant marine, and privateers drew from the same pool of labor, the navy had little hope of eradicating the underlying attitudes and sense of entitlement of the experienced seamen. In the absence of a professional naval caste, some concessions were made; while opinions from the nonelite were not solicited in the navy, there was a limited program for the expression of grievances and opinions. The *Instructions to the English Fleet* (1589) stated that

if your company find themselves aggrieved for their victuals, or upon any other occasion, that they make choice of two or three of the most sufficient men to complain in a civil manner, not in a mutinous and uncivil sort.[56]

We do not know how widespread petitioning in the navy was. Lord Admiral Howard's letters in the State Papers Domestic show that he was aware of the complaints of his men and sought remedy. The Lord Admiral was not alone; it was not uncommon for officers and naval officials to point out the men's grievances to the Crown. Bernard Capp's study of Cromwell's seamen demonstrates that mid-seventeenth-century naval officers and seamen were very forthcoming about their grievances and that the Protectorate was responsive to these complaints.[57] In his study of the Georgian navy, N.A.M Rodger points out that the absence of official mechanisms for complaint did not stop eighteenth-century naval seamen from making their grievances known.[58] Therefore, it is clear that naval seamen in the sixteenth, seventeenth, and eighteenth centuries had little compunction about addressing those in authority. The Lord Admiral wrote to Secretary of State Walsingham in July 1588, "I cannot stir out but I have an inf[inite number] hanging on my shoulders for money."[59]

Before the crew of the *Golden Lion* resorted to mutiny, they petitioned their captain for redress. The men explicitly identified themselves as being loyal to their Queen but desired Marchant "as you are a man and beare the name of a captayne over us, so to weighe of us like men." The crew obviously saw themselves as aggrieved:

lett us not be spoyled for wante of foode, for our allowaunce is so smale we are not able to lyve any longer of it; for when as three or foure were wonte to take a charge in hande, nowe tenn at the leaste, by reason of our weake victuallinge and filthie drinck, is scarce able to discharge it, and yet growe rather weaker and weaker. . . . Wee were preste by her Majesties presse to have her allowaunce, and not to be thus dealt withall, you make no men of us, but beastes. And therefore wee are not determyned to goe any further.[60]

The petition of the crew of the *Delight* of Bristol is comparable in tone and format. In this case, though the voyage had royal backing, it was not a naval expedition. Disease, dissension, and scarcity of victuals had demoralized the men; they "thought [it] good to shew unto you (being our

Master) our whole mindes and griefes in writing." The demand of the crew was unmistakable:

wee doe againe most humbly desire you to consider and have regard unto the premisses, as you tender your owne safetie and the safetie of us which remaine alive, that wee may (by Gods helpe) returne backe into England, rather then die here among wilde and savage people: for if wee make any longer abode in this place, it will bee (without all doubt) to the utter decay and losse, both of our selves, and of the shippe.[61]

It is apparent that there is no real threat to authority from the men. This is a classic example of a petition that seeks remedy. In this situation it obtained the desired response: the ship headed for home.

Protest and petition were sometimes verbal. In the freer atmosphere of privateering and merchant vessels, crews were less inclined to compose a formal petition.[62] The crew of the *True Love* complained to the master, John Harper, during a fishing voyage in 1601 that the habits of his teenage apprentice, Thomas Adams, were unbearable. Adams

was givn to suche filthiness that he dyd his excrementes in his cloathes from tyme to tyme and thereby was soe filthey and . . . noysome withe the stinche of the said filthines th[at] he muche greeved, troubled and annoyed no[t] this examinate alone but all the reste of his companye soe as the said [crew] perswaded this examinate to stripe him to lette him overborde into the Sea to make him cleane, and then to giue him freeshe cloathes to whose perswasion this examinate yealded.[63]

Adams was lowered into the ocean and given a dunking at the behest of his crewmates. Mariner Nicholas Simondes of the *Phoenix* protested his beating at the hands of the master's mate, Robert Salmon. He had informed Salmon that "he came not into the shippe to be beaten of him."[64] Simondes sought out the master ashore to inform him that his back was bruised from the buffeting that he had received. In 1591 the crew of the *Bark Hall* protested against Lieutenant John Hills's continued presence on the privateering voyage. Hills desired the crew to cut back their allowance of victuals so they might prolong the voyage: "& aftrwardes the company disliked of him & were vnwillinge to continewe longer at sea in his companye."[65] The ship returned to England.

Although they were relatively rare in this period, seamen were capable of mounting protests on land as well. The Crown was very apprehensive about the seamen and soldiers who formed "disordered assemblies" in London in August 1589. The men had participated in the Portugal expedition and demanded their wages before they dispersed. Afraid that their protests would turn into riots, the Crown took action to pay the men and to strengthen security in the capital.[66] This technique was used again in 1592 to pressure the Crown to give seamen their wages.[67] Similar protests during

the next century illustrate that the 1589 and 1592 incidents were not aberrations in the study of early modern seamen. In the late 1620s angry
naval seamen crowded into London to show their displeasure with the
Crown for not having paid them. Unpaid naval seamen began rioting in
London, Harwich, and Portsmouth in October 1653. Parliament was so
intimidated by this last demonstration that it passed an article of war that
dictated that naval seamen rioting ashore could be executed. Despite its
limited financial means, the Protectorate made great efforts to pay and
placate its seamen to avoid such unrest, but demonstrations remained commonplace.[68]

These methods for the regulation of social relations were traditional
means by which the maritime community sought to maintain peace and
cooperation; give-and-take between those in authority and the rank and
file was vital to internal harmony and continued cooperation. Such methods
were well practiced in the traditional, peacetime seafaring population.
Given the common labor pool, these practices could not be eradicated from
the naval community despite the fact that the authority of naval commanders was bolstered by martial law. It became apparent to the naval
officers that, although the needs of the Crown during wartime were bound
to compromise the freedoms of England's seamen, the safety valves that
operated in the peacetime seafaring population were necessary in the naval
community as well to preserve the fragile bond that existed between seafarers and a government waging a protracted naval war.

DESERTION

Protest could take an active or passive form. For instance, John Cooke
resisted Drake's attempts to unify the crew after the Doughty affair. He
"bore a grudge" against the commander for what he saw as the murder of
an innocent man and "gentleman of honest conversation." He elected to
protest by excusing himself from attendance at Drake's service of reconciliation.[69] Some men preferred (when possible) to absent themselves altogether from a disagreeable working environment. In theory, desertion from
the navy could bring stiff punishment, but the threat of retribution for
deserting naval service was not sufficient to prevent men from running
away, and the Crown seldom (if ever) executed deserters in practice. In
September 1580, for example, the Privy Council acknowledged that "divers
of the mariners appointed to serve in her Majesties shippes have, contrarie
to their duetie, withdrawen themselves." Desertion from the navy was so
prevalent that in 1585 Sir John Hawkins proposed that wages should be
raised for naval duty to stop "the best men" from defection and avoiding
service. Even with the increase in pay, desertion remained "a scandall too
rife amongst our Sea-men."[70]

On the eve of his departure from Plymouth in 1591, circumnavigator

Thomas Cavendish complained to Sir Richard Hawkins that his impressed men had absconded with their pay:

These varletes within a few dayes after his departure, I saw walking the streetes of Plimouth, whom the Iustice had before sought for with great diligence, and without punishment. And therefore it is no wonder that others presume to doe the like.[71]

Desertion in the merchant marine or privateering expeditions was a popular form of individual or group protest. It also served to rid the shipboard community of its disaffected element. Non-naval seamen could desert their ship with impunity. On a merchant voyage to Brazil in 1581, three of the men of the *Minion* complained to their master over the state and quantity of their provisions. The master was sympathetic in that he "toulde them there was noe better there to be had and willed them to be contente." But he also "willed them to houlde theire peace and tempre theire speeches better or else he would stretche them longer then ever god made them." Unsatisfied, a small contingent left the ship and refused to come back "excepte as theye sayde they mighte have a newe master." Two of the mariners who departed the ship, Christopher Newport and Abraham Cocke, were anything but scoundrels. Both went on to become respected subjects and naval captains.[72]

Examples of desertion are plentiful. Mariner William Valentine alias Baughe left the *Edward Cotton* of Southampton because he "gott nothinge but strokes and soe returned home." After his participation in the illegal capture of a Portuguese caravel in 1603, mariner William Hamblet forsook the men of the *Blessing*; he and other crew members "would not goe eany more to sea on those affaires & so this examinate lefte them." An officer of the privateering vessel *Tiger* wished to put into Newfoundland for repairs rather than return home because "all his men would forsake him yf he wente againe for England." Desertion was an important weapon in the arsenal of disquieted seamen.[73] Whether they actually departed from the ship, the threat of desertion might well be enough to persuade officers that they should be more accommodating. This caveat had much more force if the ship was far from England and a significant number of men, particularly if they were skilled men, intended to jump ship.

MUTINY

Mutiny was a more extreme form of protest than desertion and one more threatening to authority.[74] Boteler referred to seamen as "surly natured patients" and claimed that "the insolencies of these men are so overgrown of late as upon every slight occasion they have nothing more ready in their mouths than that mutinous sea cry, 'One and All.' "[75] However, mutiny was not simply a matter of unmanageable mariners in rebellion. The act was a clear indication that the reciprocal relationship of the common sort to their superiors had faltered. Invariably, the governors were perceived to have failed the governed by not providing "protection against the myriad insecurities . . . of a hostile environment"; they had overlooked both their duties as rulers and the "rights" of those being ruled. Seamen did not expect perfection in an imperfect and frequently harsh working environment; as long as a remedy to problems and predicaments was being actively sought by those in authority, the social order was secure, and tumult was staved off.[76]

Although tensions reached a breaking point in both the *Delight* of Bristol and the *Golden Lion*, a crucial difference explains the absence of mutiny in the former and the insurrection in the second; authority responded in one instance and not in the other. The words of the crew of the *Golden Lion* illustrate this point: "They said againe, they have had manye faire woordes, but nothing performed in dedes."[77] In 1588 rampant disease, delayed pay, and insufficient victuals in the navy created conditions conducive to disturbance. However, the navy suffered no reported incidents of mutiny. In part at least, unrest was contained because the Lord Admiral was believed to be sympathetic to the grievances of the men, and authority was seen as working for the alleviation of suffering. Howard wrote:

We think it should be marvelled at how we keep our men from running away, for the worst men of the fleet knoweth for how long they are victualled; but I thank God as yet we are not troubled with any mutinies, nor I hope shall not; for I see men kindly handled will bear want and run through the fire and water.

In a crisis the Lord Admiral acted. He wrote to Walsingham in July 1588, "There was a fault, which I will not write of; but how, I will tell you when I come up; and if I had not in time looked into it, we should have had much more misery amongst some than we have." His compassion for his men is evident. In August 1588 he wrote to Lord Treasurer Burghley advising him of the need to assist the diseased seamen in port. This "most pitiful sight" inspired him to action: "I am driven myself, of force, to come a-land, to see them bestowed in some lodging." In addition, he claimed that he was "driven to make Sir John Hawkyns . . . relieve them with money as he can (do)" while he and the other commanders "do all we [can to re]lieve them."[78]

Clearly, insurrection was on the horizon. Hawkins, the Treasurer of Marine Causes, spoke of the need to satisfy the men "to avoid exclamation [unrest]."[79] Lord Henry Seymour, the Admiral of the Narrow Seas, warned the Lord Treasurer in July 1588 that he

would do very well to help us with a pay for our men, who are almost 16 weeks unpaid; for what with fair and foul means, I have enough to do to keep them from mutiny.[80]

However, the responsive nature of those in authority contained the unrest to a manageable degree and, thus, avoided insurrection.

With the exception of the mutiny of 1587, the Elizabethan navy was relatively free of disorder. Even in this instance the mutiny was not widespread; it involved a single ship in the fleet and no violence. During the late Elizabethan era, strict discipline and martial law had some role in maintaining good order in the navy, but we must also credit the naval commanders (particularly Lord Admiral Howard and John Hawkins), who made great efforts to care for the men under their command.[81] While harsh discipline and unpleasant conditions were resented by seamen impressed into the navy, men were usually willing to endure them until the end of the campaign, when they would be free to return to their homes and other forms of seafaring.

Mutiny was more common on non-naval ships. Privateers were inordinately prone to disturbance. This probably stemmed from the absence of wages, the lure of plunder, the fear of failure, and the frenzy that usually accompanied the taking of a prize. While conditions on the Queen's ships were bleak, those on privateering vessels were often worse. In the navy there were regulations and standards for manning rates and provisioning. Although these standards were frequently compromised, at least there were established guidelines in place. There were no such regulations for privateering vessels. Because provisioning was one of the greatest costs in outfitting a privateering expedition, backers were keen to make a greater profit by cutting corners wherever possible. Since privateering expeditions had no trouble attracting seamen, backers did not have to worry unduly about shipboard conditions.

Other circumstances gave rise to unrest. Privateering drew sizable numbers of affluent landsmen into its ranks. Those without experience were obvious targets for disgruntled crew members. Another factor was the lack of authority held by captains and masters; no doubt, retribution and authority seemed more remote when dealing with commanders without the Queen's commission. Lacking the deterrent of harsh punishments, non-naval crews had fewer reasons to endure hardship or unpopular decisions.

One of the most clear-cut cases of mutiny on a non-naval vessel involved Robert Holland, a gentleman shipowner of London. Holland maintained that the crew took his ship, the *Grace* of Dartmouth, in 1600 and made off with her while he was ashore on the Isle of Rhodes.[82] Their reasons for doing so are unknown. The motivation for the abduction of the ship and cargo seems to have been simple greed: seamen trying to get what they perceived to be their rightful share (or more) of purchase, plunder, or pillage.

In January 1603 William Pearse, a gentleman captain of the *Elizabeth* of Plymouth, was faced with a mutiny when he unilaterally decided to release a captured ship of Venice. Richard Cornelius alias Noyler, a mid-

shipman, Roger Peek, master's mate, and John Evans, the boatswain, informed their captain that "theye would not be made fooles." With the
exception of a handful of men, the majority of the *Elizabeth*'s 100-man
complement intended to keep the prize and throw the captain overboard
if he refused. The captain later escaped from his crew while in port and
sought passage back to England.[83]

Master William Russel, mentioned previously, was persuaded that his
privateering expedition should return to England because of the grumbling
of the crew. He feared that if order did collapse, there would be no hope
of restoring it. They had captured a French ship in 1602 but released her
because she was a questionable prize. To aggravate the situation, victuals
were running low. Russel claimed that the

compainie beinge offended because theye mighte not make spoile of what theye
tooke, fell into a mutynie, & pertended, theye should starve in the Streightes, if
theye mighte not enioye what they tooke.

Russel's fear of the crew's wreaking havoc did not materialize, nor did the
expedition return home. The captain's supporters wanted to continue to
seek more prizes, and they carried the day, not necessarily because the
captain had more authority but because his faction was numerically
larger.[84]

The breakdown of authority could be unnerving for commanders. In a
statement in which he sought to distance himself from an illegal act, Jasper
Norris, the gentleman captain of the *Flying Dragon*, bemoaned his lack of
control over his men upon the illegal capture of a Scottish ship and claimed
that he "was like to haue byn slayne amongst them for vrginge to haue yt
restored." Nevertheless, few commanders lost their lives as a result of mutinies. Henry Hudson is the most infamous exception to the rule. During
his search for the Northwest Passage in 1610–11, his crew left him and his
officers in a boat at sea and returned to England. Far from home and with
only a few days' provisions left, one of the chief mutineers reportedly said
that he knew the ramifications of his actions, but "he would rather be
hanged at home then starved abroad." It is important to remember that
this was the anomaly. During the mutiny of the *Golden Lion*, the men,
after debate, simply let Captain Marchant go aboard the *Spy*, which remained loyal to Drake. By harming the authority figures, mutiny would
have decisively stepped outside the boundaries of popular protest and into
the realm of disorder.[85]

Mutinies had much in common with charivaris and riots on land. All
three had the same impetus. Like riots, mutinies were a "temporary and
exceedingly fragile assertion of authority by subjects." Such actions were
designed to draw the attention of those in authority to an injustice that
had been hitherto overlooked. Subordinates sought to point out the "mal-

feasance of their governors."[86] While the outcomes of charivaris, riots, and mutinies were sometimes uncertain, there was a protocol to all three. They were seldom challenges to power per se; they were "extrainstitutional" as opposed to being "anti-institutional." Like riots, mutinies were not irrational acts but reactions to grievances.[87] They were extreme responses to problems and threats to the well-being of the community or a sector of the community. Although Charles Tilly was writing specifically about riots, his words also describe political charivaris and mutinies:

[A riot] embodied a critique of the authorities, was often directed consciously at the authorities, and commonly consisted of the crowd's taking precisely those measures its members thought the authorities had failed their own responsibility to take.[88]

Since those in authority had neglected to address the problems, it was the duty of those in subordinate positions to take action. Such reactions were both a "cry for help" to those in authority and an affirmation of the social structure. Therefore, the restricted mutinies of the Elizabethan period were the maritime equivalent of political charivaris and riots.

FUNCTION AND PRACTICE OF DISCIPLINE

Authority, law, discipline, and order were intimately connected. Douglas Hay's seminal work asserted that the law

was critically important in maintaining bonds of obedience and deference, in legitimizing the status quo, in continually recreating the structure of authority which arose from property and in turn protected its interests.[89]

In practice, early modern law distinguished between "errors" and "crimes." One of its functions was corrective; the law chastised the "errant brethren" within the community. But it also rid the community of the reprobate who threatened the overall order and protected the populace from moral contagion. This "domino theory of human character"[90] is evident in maritime law:

it is for want of good and severe justice at the first, for that one diseased sheep may corrupt a whole flock. . . . For it is not possible to govern aright, without good discipline in warlike affairs upon the seas.[91]

Like the legal system on land, maritime law functioned very differently in theory and in practice. In theory, disciplinary measures at sea and on land could be brutal, and the rhetoric of law enforcement emphasized the need for fierce deterrents. Much of English maritime law was based on the Laws of Oléron, which stated:

I. Whosoever shall kill any man a shipboard, shall be bound to the back of the party killed and thrown into the sea with him.

II. If one should be killed on land, the party should be bound in like manner and buried alive with him killed.

III. Whosoever shall draw any knife or weapon with an intent to draw blood, or by other means shall draw blood, shall lose a hand.

IV. Whosoever shall strike one, without drawing blood, with his hand or otherwise, shall be ducked three times at the yard-arm.

V. Whosoever reviles or curses another, for so often as he hath reviled shall pay so many ounces of silver.

VI. Whosoever steals shall have his head shorn and boiled pitch poured on it, and feathers strewed upon the same whereby he may be known; and at the first landing place where he shall come, there to be towed ashore.[92]

Because the Laws of Oléron provided the basis for the regulations of fleets and for individual vessels in this period, the tripartite division of the maritime community had a common disciplinary tradition to draw upon. The following punishments were typical for Elizabethan vessels: "putting one in the bilboes during pleasure; keep them fasting; duck them at the yard-arm under the ship's keel; or spread them at the capstan, and whip them there at the capstan or main mast; hang weights about their necks till hearts and backs be ready to break; or to gag or scrape their tongues for blasphemy or swearing."[93] While we must acknowledge that individual captains and masters exercised their own discretion, these articles suggest that, in practice, seamen were disciplined in a harsh fashion, often using "shaming punishments" so popular in early modern Europe, but not in the brutal manner recommended by the Laws of Oléron.[94] The death sentence for the principal mutineers of the *Golden Lion* in 1587 was regarded by the jury as being "iuste and necessarye for avoydinge the like hereafter, which elles muste needes growe to the utter dissolucon of all her Maiesties service for the sea hereafter."[95] As Oppenheim points out, the death penalty for mutiny or desertion "did little but hold the penalties *in terrorem* over them [seamen], and did not affect their independence of action if they were content to forfeit their pay." Even for novice seamen, ignorance of the law was not a viable excuse for misbehavior; instructions for the fleet in 1589 commanded that regulations be read two or three times a week "to the intent that these orders may come to the knowledge of every man."[96] Shipboard regulations were read aloud and posted on the mainmast in privateers and merchant vessels.[97]

FINES AND DEMOTION

Seamen might rightly be accused of being somewhat more "inclined to bloody-mindedness . . . than your tame landlubber."[98] While violence was prevalent, it was not the sole means of interaction or punishment. Unruly members of all facets of the maritime community were threatened with financial loss. In 1595 seaman Valentine Wood had his shares on a privateering voyage decreased from two or two and a half to a single share by consent of the company of the *Virgin* of London "in rescpekte of his insufficentcy by some disorder or misdemenners by him vssed at the sea."[99] Demotion and fines could cost seamen dearly. In 1593 the crew of the *Anne* gave depositions containing details of the removal of John Brookes from his office as master's mate. Along with the financial penalty, Brookes had to deal with the loss of his privileges. The master told steward Thomas Rose that he should not "geve him eany meate excepte he came at meales, and would take his victuals with the reste of the mariners whereas before he did eate with the Master at his messe in the cabon."[100] Richard Earsewick was removed from his position of the *Minion* by the master for insubordination and stirring up dissension. In addition, he endured the physical punishment of being tied to the mainmast with a "base" chamber about his neck. Nevertheless, he and the man accused of being his accomplice "were kepte on borde but not as prisoners or without necessarye victualls for theire dyett For they had suche provision as other men had." Earsewick in particular seemed to want for little except his office; it was said he was allowed to drink wine "as other men drincke water."[101] Francis Drake was reputed to be the strictest disciplinarian in the Elizabethan navy. However, even he used demotion as a way to quell disruption. Initially, he removed accused mutineers Borough and Doughty from their offices.[102] This was important in that it provided an intermediate disciplinary step that preceded court-martial.

Within the established guidelines and regulations, discipline was a matter of discretion of the master or captain. Contemporary seamen claimed discipline was dished out in liberal doses aboard naval vessels. It was said that this was the chief reason for their hesitance to serve the Queen. Monson wrote,

It is strange what misery such men will choose to endure in small ships of reprisal, though they be hopeless of gain, rather than serve her Majesty, where their pay is certain, their diet plentiful, their labour not so great. Nothing breeds this but the liberty they find in the one, and the punishment they fear in the other.[103]

Boteler corroborated Monson's view; he refers to the "loose liberty and undisciplined life that they take to themselves . . . especially in that of the private men-of-war."[104] Somewhat stricter measures were required out of the necessity of keeping a naval fleet together and to achieve strategic goals. In addition, many of the men in the navy were impressed and did not always serve willingly.

The right to impose martial law and to impress seamen was coveted by non-naval commanders, shipowners, and investors. The ability to resort to martial law was a boon to commanders and backers of risky merchant or privateering voyages or voyages of exploration. While backers and officers were eager to maximize profits by undertaking treacherous journeys, seamen were just as eager to terminate a voyage when shipboard conditions and risks had become unacceptable. Marital law was a useful tool to coerce men to work when the risks were great. Thus, promoters wanted to convince the Crown to grant them royal commissions. In the 1560s one promoter tried to persuade William Cecil that he needed recourse to martial law in order to undertake a trading voyage to Guinea. He complained that seamen were unruly, and when they were at sea, "they wil do as they lyst . . . except authorytee cause them to feare."[105] Without this power, employees could attempt to exercise their own discretion regarding when a voyage should be aborted. In an age of maritime expansion and increased risks, this age-old custom was an impediment to profits.

Although most contemporaries speak of the need for harsh discipline in order to avoid shipboard anarchy, there were those who adhered to the "carrot" rather than the "stick" approach. John Hawkins and Lord Admiral Howard were two leading exponents of the former. Hawkins tried to improve shipboard conditions and wages for seamen on his private voyages and in the navy. Lord Admiral Howard's letters to the Queen and her inner circle demonstrate his compassion for his men. Howard's view can be summed up in his letter of June 1588: "men kindly handled will bear want and run through the fire and water."[106] However, these men were in the minority. Most sixteenth-century commanders held that strict discipline reinforced by the Queen's authority was the obvious solution to seamen's recalcitrance and disorderly behavior.

VIOLENCE

It is not surprising that physical punishments were an integral part of the disciplinary practice of the maritime community[107] given the overall level of violence in sixteenth-century society. A contemporary seaman summed up the prevailing attitude toward corporal punishment; he referred to two seamen as "a cowple of Skurvy boyes that made an vprore, and yt were a good deede to . . . beate them."[108] This idea would remain fashionable long after the reign of Elizabeth. One career seafarer in the late seventeenth century claimed that "when they [seamen] do anything it is with a grumbling, unwilling mind, so that they must be forced and drove to it."

It was reported that most Restoration commanders thought it "folly to say that good words only without blows will wholly command an English seaman."[109]

There are many examples of officers' resorting to violence in an effort to discipline their men. Silvester Glassope, master and owner of the *William Bonaventure*, came aboard his ship to find members of his company "brawlinge and redye to fall togeather by the eares." Upon discovering that John Wornell's "evil speeches" were the cause of the disturbance, the master gave the offender "a cowple of boxes on the eare."[110] Boatswains thought nothing of resorting to blows to "persuade" a seaman to perform his duties. When Henry Inkersall, the boatswain of the *Richard* of Arundel, commanded Philip Noves to fall to his labor, and the mariner refused, the boatswain picked up a stick and struck Noves on the shoulder.[111] In another case, master's mate Robert Salmon hit mariner Nicholas Simondes with the helm of his hatchet for his insubordination, "evell language," and calling the carpenter's mother a "hoores burd." Initially, Salmon only chastised Simondes verbally: "what meaneste thowe to call an honeste womans sonn hoores burde." Simondes's refusal to let the matter drop prompted Salmon to hit him three or four times with the helm of his hatchet. Salmon warned him that "yf he woulde not houlde his peace he woulde sloppe his mouth with the said helme." When Simondes persisted, the master's mate followed through with his threat.[112] Harsh discipline was not limited to the men aboard. Edward Hampton, the ship's boy of the *Content* of London, was hit with a rope's end by the boatswain for not performing his labor and whipped by Master Edward Crane for being intoxicated and threatening to murder the crew.[113]

In this regard, naval discipline was no different from discipline in other sectors of the maritime community or the land community. During the naval expedition of 1596 to Cadiz, boatswain Hugh Turner of the *Alcredo* found seven or eight of the crew in the forecastle talking and singing despite the master's call to assemble. Turner chastised the men and bestowed blows among the group with a rope's end. When one died thereafter, the beating was considered commonplace; it never "did him eany harme or was eany cause of his deathe."[114] Examples of beatings for idleness and misbehavior are routine in the Admiralty depositions.[115]

Discipline was not the responsibility of only those in authority. While violence often characterized relations between seamen, crew members were constantly intervening in disputes and breaking up brawls. Since it was usually in the interest of the community to maintain order, the task of controlling the unruly fell to the entire crew, although the burden was borne more by officeholders. Two seamen of the *John and Frances* tried to check the fray that broke out between two of their fellows, even though the protagonists had weapons. The master's mate of the *William Bonaventure* managed to wrest John Wornell off the master, Silvester Glassope, who was about to be thrown in the Thames. The master's mate of the *Examiner* blocked the master's attempt to run the captain through with a pike.[116]

FORMAL AND INFORMAL LAW

Just as there was a distinction between the theory and practice of discipline, there could also be a discrepancy between formal and informal law. Whereas seamen believed that the maintenance of order was usually in their interest and participated accordingly, they did not always find it so. Like the land population, "acceptance of their [the elite's] authority by the mass of the common people was partial and conditional." Historian Eric Hobsbawn claimed that social criminality "occurs when there is a conflict of laws, e.g. between an official and an unofficial system." Thus, even in a deferential society unpopular laws were sometimes disregarded by the nonelites who voiced an alternative vision of order.[117] While it was the role of the property owners to draw up and implement laws, they had to take into account customs and expectations of the rest of society. These customs and expectations were often articulated as customary rights. When it came to unpopular laws, the governed could passively or actively resist authority. As we will see, in these instances, such laws could be difficult to enforce.

In 1598 Richard Burden, an officer of the Admiralty Court, attempted to apprehend one William Gibson of the *George*. Burden complained to the court that he requested the aid of all the men present on the ship in making the arrest but "noe man answered or would doe eany thinge." Because of their passive resistance, Gibson managed to flee the authorities in a boat. The master of the ship was charged with assisting Gibson in his escape.[118] In addition to crewmates, there was no end of "enablers" on land who were willing to assist seamen fleeing the law. Predictably, mariners' family members were ready to resist Admiralty officials. Local officials were sometimes willing to protect seamen from the Admiralty as well. Francis Cotton, esquire, refused to allow Henry Mott, an officer of the Admiralty, to arrest various seamen on the Isle of Wight. Mott showed Cotton the writ of contempt that he possessed from the Admiralty Court with little effect. When Mott claimed that he would appeal to Judge Julius Caesar, Cotton replied, "Tush man I knowe him well enoughe he is Master of the Requestes and I respecte him not a button."[119]

Resistance to Admiralty officers did not always take such a passive form. Unfortunately for many hapless officials, the officers personified the Admiralty's unwelcome interference into the lives of seamen and the coercion of formal law. William King, an officer of the Vice Admiral in Essex, detailed his problems arresting certain errant seamen who "contemptuoslye withstoade his authoritye." He had had ongoing problems with one Thomas Hankyn, who had resisted his authority on various occasions and had also "reviled the said Coarte and the Viceadmirall and vttered such vile and vnsemly speeches agaynste him as are not here with modestye to be sett downe."[120] Admiralty official Thomas Walthowe was attacked by seaman Lawrence Dutton with a sword when he tried to arrest him for illegal plunder; Dutton swore "greate oathes" and "sayde he cared not for the judge of the Admiralty nor his warrante." The wife of Richard Prideaux attacked Admiralty officials with a knife to protect her husband. Diggory Holman told William Hamlet, an officer of the court, that he would like to heave him overboard and "ferrett the cuntrey" for "all other of his coates, that they should trouble the cuntrey noemore." Overwhelmingly, the resistance was in the form of verbal abuse and threatened violence[121]; actual bodily harm was rare. This in itself is suggestive of a code of behavior that pressed upon formal authority to the limit but drew back from violence.

Seldom were seamen as opposed to the Admiralty's jurisdiction as when it involved plunder. Seamen undertaking any sort of privateering activity were forbidden by the Lord Admiral's directives not to break bulk until it was inventoried in port and divided accordingly. The practice of ignoring these directives was rampant. As we have seen in an earlier chapter, impressment was a bone of contention and was another occasion for resistance. In both situations it is evident that seamen felt that their customs, which they saw as rights, sanctioned their resistance to formal law. They guarded their tradition of "pseudo-independence": seamen believed that they had the right to choose the nature of their own employment and were entitled to the fruits of their labor. In these instances, their prerogatives took precedence over the demands of the Lord Admiral and the Queen. The Crown was unsuccessful in altering this mind-set during the period under review.

MERCY

Although law and punishment appeared stringent and inflexible in theory, there was a great deal of scope for discretion and mercy in both shipboard courts-martial and the Admiralty Court. While Drake had a greater abhorrence for the mutinous officeholders of the *Golden Lion*, he also condemned the common men as "accessaryes to this treacherous defection." Notwithstanding, he did acknowledge the possibility of the sovereign's mercy as he passed judgment:

And though it shall please her Majestie to looke upon them with mercye, yett my sentence is theye shall all come to the Corte gate with halters aboute theire neckes for an example of all such offendours.

Drake's prediction that the mutineers would "abyde the paynes of Death; yf not theye shall remayne as deade men in lawe" never came to pass.

Boroughs was treated very leniently, even though Drake condemned his displaced vice admiral to death, and an inquiry charged him with neglect of duty at Cadiz. Boroughs remained in favor (especially with Lord Burghley) and retained his prominent position as one of the principal officers of the navy. Two years later he was promoted to Controller of the Navy. Similarly, the other seamen of the *Golden Lion* suffered no penalty. In fact, the master of the mutinous ship, William Bigate (or Bygot), went on to have a career as an eminent master. He was obviously regarded as a responsible and prominent man in the seafaring community and in his parish. Both he and Boroughs were Elder Brethren in the Trinity House at Deptford, indicating their stature in their occupation. A year after the incident on board the *Lion*, Boroughs commanded the *Bonavolia* against the Spanish Armada. William Bigate's experience earned him a job as an appraiser for the High Court of the Admiralty. In addition, both men were vestrymen and auditors for their parish of St. Dunstan's, Stepney, and Bigate was named as an overseer in other mariners' wills, a mark of his social position as a man of trust. Evidently, such incidents did little or nothing to besmirch the careers of these men.[122] Both remained respected master-mariners and citizens.

In theory those who committed felonies deserved death, although there was always the possibility of royal pardons, which were the prerogative of the monarch. Yet within the routine process of sixteenth-century justice we find a two-tiered system. In practice the courts distinguished between hardened "criminals" and "offenders." Those who were contrite and were judged to be "redeemable" might well escape death. Although both offenses carried the death penalty, naval deserters and mutineers rarely fell into the category of "criminals." In most cases deserters were opportunists who sought more lucrative employment or hoped to escape the harsh realities of naval life. There is little evidence that deserters from the Elizabethan navy were punished. Mutineers were frequently men who fled homeward to escape what they judged to be life-threatening conditions. Such actions were, and had to be, frowned upon; a nation could not wage war if its soldiers and sailors exercised their discretion and decided to flee in the face of danger and hardship. However, fighting men also deserved sufficient provisions, and when they were deprived of the basic necessities to sustain the lives of the crew, it was understandable why some elected to return to England. Thus, few mutineers or deserters showed, or could be demonstrated to have shown, the malicious intent that defined criminals. In the power relationship between the Crown and its seamen, to deprive men of mercy when their reactions stemmed from the Crown's negligence, their officer's mismanagement of critical provisions, or unforeseen circumstances not only was morally questionable but contravened the spirit of Tudor paternalism. Lack of compassion in such cases would undermine the deferential system of authority and justice that was the foundation of sixteenth-century society.

The Crown tended to be most indulgent with those offenders of the lower orders who fell into trouble because of poverty or poor leadership. Both excuses were articulated by seamen in criminal cases in the High Court of the Admiralty. Skilled men probably found tolerance because of England's great need for experienced seamen for the war effort. In 1586 Lord Admiral Howard dismissed any legal actions against four seamen at the behest of Judge Julius Caesar as the men were sufficient for service and condemned for small offenses.[123]

Mercy was extended intermittently to seamen of all backgrounds for their participation in such activities as robbery and piracy.[124] The bounds of mercy sometimes went beyond this; in 1594 the Crown pardoned John Rise and George Gregory, two sailors from Kent, for stealing a horse worth three pounds and other goods worth five pounds. The pardon of Rise and Gregory is remarkable because horse thievery was normally considered to be a crime solely for profit.[125] The justice system made allowances for men who may have been in the wrong place at the wrong time. In 1599 Lord Howard ordered Julius Caesar, Judge of the Admiralty Court, to draw up a pardon for sailor Anthony Man, who was convicted with other crew members for the death of Henry Baker, the master, and the Dutch master of a captured prize. Man's wife, Margaret, petitioned the Lord Admiral for consideration as her husband was not in collusion with the "wicked persons" responsible for the murders and was "not thought fitt by reason of his simplicity" to be acquainted with their plan.[126]

There are many instances whereby skilled seamen were "forgiven" by the Crown for their transgressions. The case of William Goodlad is an apt example. Goodlad, one of the Brethren of Trinity House, was a member of a family of masters and shipowners and related in marriage to other prominent seafaring families of Leigh, Kent. He was obviously well regarded and commanded a ship used to revictual the navy in August 1597 and performed other services to the Crown after that date. However, Goodlad was indicted for resisting arrest in 1598. His defiance for the authority of the Admiralty apparently had no lasting negative effects on his career in regard to the Crown or the rest of the maritime community.[127] Even Robert Feewilliams, whose violent actions on board the *Examiner* brought about a suit in court, managed to retain some measure of respect in his occupational group and in his community. The High Court of the Admiralty appreciated his expertise as a shipmaster enough to use him as an appraiser of a vessel in June 1591, and he participated in the government of Stepney parish.[128]

The Lord Admiral dismissed Bartholomew Earning, captain of the *Godspeed* of London, Anthony Nox, captain of *Anthony* of Portsmouth, and their crews from all legal actions and suits in 1600, when depositions in the court show that these privateers battled each other (some to the death) over a captured prize. Many of the greatest Elizabethan sea heroes came into conflict with the law but escaped punishment. Martin Frobisher was suspected of piracy, Sir John Hawkins was accused of corruption, Drake was accused of deserting his post in 1588, and Hawkins and Sir Walter Raleigh captured illegal goods. The Lord Admiral was once placed in the awkward position of pardoning his own ship and crew for taking a prize without having a commission.[129]

In general, it can be said that despite tough rhetoric to the contrary, the Crown allowed English seamen scope for misbehavior. As individuals or as groups, seamen flouted the law, and the Crown, like a long-suffering parent, not infrequently granted them amnesty. Only the reprobate, the most notorious career pirates, for instance, gave up their lives for their misdeeds.[130]

CONCLUSION

Shipboard communities mirrored land communities in many respects. Tudor society afloat and on land preserved order through reciprocity and consensus. In both cases the elite lacked the infrastructure to impose order through force alone. Punishments worked when they were perceived to be just. Seamen supported maritime authority in most instances and in return expected the recognition of their customary rights. The deferential model allowed for protest if the common sort thought that too much was being expected of them and not enough was being delivered. Generally, protest remained within acknowledged channels. However, when those in authority invariably tried to compromise these liberties, they risked a temporary loss of control. The withdrawal of support for authority exposed the fact that both societal hierarchy and order rested on consensus.

Never did order come close to breaking down altogether. Anecdotal accounts and records of the High Court of the Admiralty (both civil and criminal) demonstrate that seamen were a contentious lot, but order seldom gave way when the ship was at sea. In such cases, some semblance of order was required for the crew to sail the ship back to port. Accounts of very serious breaches of order almost always refer to ships in harbor or allude to temporary, exceptional, and provoked lapses of order. Although commanders often had to address complaints about conditions or changes in the itinerary, and there were bound to be tensions among all-male communities in tight quarters, it was in the interest of the officers and the rank and file to complete their voyage so they could collect their pay and get home safely to sail another day. Simply put, order was almost always in everyone's best interests, and it was internally created, not externally imposed. Generally, only the most unbearable conditions or flagrant abuses of power prompted work stoppage or mutiny. Overall, the system was remarkably stable given the complex and precarious basis on which it rested.

When order did break down, it was frequently the result of subsistence · issues. Like riots on land, mutinies or near mutinies can usually be traced back to food. While complaints of the quality and quantity of provisions were a regular facet of accounts of life at sea, we will never truly know the veracity of the many complaints. Whether they used subsistence matters as a weapon, mutineers understood that issues of survival and nourishment were deemed to be "legitimate" causes for challenges to authorities.

Although order rarely collapsed, it was often compromised—particularly on privateering or "mixed" voyages. The nature of the command structure aboard privateering vessels holds a partial explanation. With the expansion of the maritime community during the war years, the ship's hierarchy took on new members; aboard men-of-war, traditional maritime authority (the master and his officers) was supplanted by captains and other wartime personnel. To aggravate the problem, captains were not always familiar with the sea. Unlike shipmasters, they had rarely worked their way up through the maritime hierarchy or been trained specifically to command a ship and crew. While naval captains were sometimes bolstered by the threat of martial law, privateering captains lacked this authority. Therefore, the truly inexperienced and incompetent were targets for direct challenges when they made unpopular decisions. Such men were especially vulnerable if their commissions or the objectives of their voyages were unclear. When challenges were made, they were generally channeled through those who held positions in the maritime hierarchy. In most cases where a captain's authority was directly questioned, the shipmaster or other senior officers had some involvement, either directly or indirectly. Just as the prudent shipmaster heeded maritime custom and listened (or at least appeared to listen) to the opinions of his crew, the wise captain took into account the opinions of the experienced maritime personnel on board. Mutual respect and a sense of give-and-take helped to stave off potential disturbances. However, given tensions in the dual command structure (military and maritime), the looser discipline, and the desperation of the men to profit from their voyage, privateering vessels remained the most prone to disturbances. If problems were not resolved, they were glossed over; normally, order was resumed in some fashion, at least long enough to get the ship home.

While maritime discipline and justice shared the basic features of the larger society, they were also distinct. Sailors had a reputation for boisterous independence not least because they were given, or seized, the latitude for such behavior. Those in positions of authority in the shipboard community therefore had concerns and difficulties different from those of their counterparts on land. Order was particularly precarious in the shipboard environment as seamen had an option that few landsmen had: they could desert their work environment if the risks were too high. This was not possible for most workers in early modern England because few could disassociate their employment from their personal lives. Although other workers (such as servants or miners) showed a very high degree of mobility and a propensity for short-term employment, few were as mobile or autonomous from the greater community as seamen.[131] Thus, maritime authority had the additional problem of maintaining order among men who were removed from their families and often from the immediate threat of the law and were therefore freer of external constraints.

With the onset of the war with Spain, the Crown and those men who assumed semipermanent naval positions for the duration of the conflict encountered some difficulties when they attempted to impose naval rules on a seafaring population accustomed to self-regulation. The peacetime maritime community had various techniques by which it sought accord: consultation, persuasion, petition, arbitration, and reconciliation; the navy did not utilize or recognize all of these techniques. Perhaps, as a consequence, it had to fall back upon mercy. Although the naval hierarchy tried to implement tighter discipline and curtail the freer practices of the maritime community, impressed seamen managed to make their voices heard just as they had in other forms of sea service. It seems that seamen paid little heed to attempts to prevent them from exercising their traditional freedoms; they offered their opinion even when it was not solicited, deserted, and, on occasion, staged more blatant displays of their displeasure. The frustration of naval writers such as Monson and Boteler, able to criticize the independent seamen but not to reform their behavior, is readily apparent. The threat of martial law failed to quell the sense of customary obligations. The more egalitarian customs of the merchant marine could be eradicated only through the growth of a naval caste unaccustomed to the greater freedoms of other forms of sea service. This was not to come about for some time. Except for the more permanent servants of the Crown, naval service in Elizabeth's reign was sporadic and seen by seamen as an adjunct to their more traditional labors. The more rigid code of behavior was not internalized. It was something to be endured until they were discharged.

Although commanders and officials had considerable theoretical powers that they could use to pressure seamen into conforming to the navy's rigid code of behavior, in practice their use proved difficult and imprudent. The Elizabethan naval infrastructure lacked the personnel and the will to prosecute "errant" seamen to the full extent of its theoretical power. To a great extent, the Crown's actions and dealings with its seamen were circumscribed: law and discipline on land and at sea had to function according to the deferential model. In most instances, the lower orders thought that it was in their interest to take part; those in authority did not want to give them any reason to doubt this assumption. Shipboard communities were similar to the larger society in that they functioned with roughly the same dynamic, parameters, and mechanisms regarding the protection of order for the aggregate. Both governed and governors reacted to crises in the same way as they did on land and used comparable tools for communication and resolution. That they did so without the deferential weight of landed property says a good deal concerning the internalization of values of community and order within sixteenth-century society.

NOTES

1. John Walter and Keith Wrightson, "Dearth and the Social Order in Early Modern England," *Past and Present* 71 (1976), 22–23.
2. Monson, *Naval Tracts*, vol. III, 388; Henry Oughtred, quoted in Scammell, "Manning the English Merchant Service," 135; Andrews, "The Elizabethan Seaman," 246.
3. N.A.M. Rodger, *The Wooden World: An Anatomy of the Georgian Navy* (1986; rpt. Glasgow: Fontana Press, 1990), 207.
4. Keith Wrightson, *English Society 1580–1680* (London: Hutchinson, 1982), 172–73.
5. Hawkins, *Observations*, 12.
6. Monson, *Naval Tracts*, vol. III, 437.
7. This is not to say that there was not a correlation between ranking and socioeconomic background. The highest-ranking officers in the maritime community were usually from more affluent backgrounds than were the common seamen. In the naval hierarchy, captains were often men of gentle birth who had little sea experience.
8. Oppenheim, *The Administration of the Royal Navy, 1509–1660*, 384.
9. Wrightson, *English Society*, 175.
10. Oppenheim, *The Administration of the Royal Navy, 1509–1660*, 390.
11. William Cecil claimed, "Nothing will sooner lead men to sedition than dearth of victuals." Many of his contemporaries shared his view. See John Walter, "The Social Economy of Dearth," in *Famine, Disease and the Social Order in Early Modern Society*, ed. John Walter and Roger Schofield (Cambridge: Cambridge University Press, 1989), 76; Charles Tilly, "Food Supply and Public Order in Modern Europe," in *The Formation of National States in Western Europe*, ed. Charles Tilly (Princeton, N.J.: Princeton University Press, 1975), 385; Wrightson, *English Society*, 173; B. Sharp, "Popular Protest in Seventeenth-Century England," in *Popular Culture in Seventeenth Century England*, ed. Barry Reay (London: Croom Helm, 1985), 273.
12. Boteler, *Boteler's Dialogues*, 18. Boteler's career in the navy spanned the reigns of Elizabeth I, James I, and Charles I.
13. Monson speaks as if most naval commanders were accorded these powers as a matter of course. In his discussion of discipline, he acknowledges that captains had the authority to punish most offenses on their ships, but "if his [a captain's] company grow contumelious or stubborn, he may recourse to the General, who will inflict more stricter chastisement as death . . . which no private Captain can do." Monson, *Naval Tracts*, vol. IV, 15. In his "Notes on Sea-Service," John Young, a veteran of several naval campaigns during Elizabeth's reign, wrote of the

need to avoid serious offenses while aboard naval ships lest seamen "receive marital law, and for other smaller faults smaller punishments." Young quoted in Monson, *Naval Tracts*, vol. IV, 203, 218. Many contemporaries who had served in the navy made reference to the generals' powers to take the lives of their subordinates.

14. Elizabeth reined in her generals at sea on a number of occasions. Owing to the fact that many naval expeditions were essentially "mixed voyages" in which military objectives were undertaken in conjunction with privateering, Elizabeth was fearful that the pursuit of profit would override her instructions. Thus, few commanders had the "absolute charge" of which Monson speaks. Monson, *Naval Tracts*, vol. IV, 1. Oppenheim notes that commanders were, in practice, usually presidents of war councils Monson, *Naval Tracts*, vol. II, 83. They were obliged to solicit the advice of their leading officers. This was especially true of those expeditions headed by the impetuous Earl of Essex, who complained loudly that the Queen obliged him to act in consort with a cocommander or a council Monson, *Naval Tracts* vol. I, 374–75, vol. II, 49, 83.

15. Letters of reprisal or letters of marque were issued by the lord high admiral during wartime. Such letters entitled the bearers to seek out and subdue enemy vessels in retribution for past injuries or to aid in the war effort.

16. The later Elizabethan Admiralty Court was especially active as a court of law, with an expanding jurisdiction during this time. *Select Pleas in the Court of Admiralty*, ed. R. G. Marsden, vol. II (A.D. 1547–1602) (London: Selden Society, 1897), xiii, xvii; Hill, *Bench and Bureaucracy*, 26–27, 30–32.

17. PRO HCA 13/24/218.

18. While the wording may have varied slightly, most shipboard orders were basically the same. Regulations normally dealt with such issues as religious observance on board, messing, the watch, signaling, emergency procedures, and fighting instructions. Freedoms taken for granted on privateering and merchant ships were curtailed on naval expeditions and "mixed" voyages, which combined naval and privateering objectives. Punishments for inappropriate behavior (gambling, blaspheming, and insubordination, for instance) were stricter for naval expeditions.

19. Oppenheim, *The Administration of the Royal Navy, 1509–1660*, 387; John Young's "Notes on Sea-Service" in *Monson's Naval Tracts*, vol. IV, 218.

20. W. Senior, "Drake at the Suit of John Doughty," *Mariner's Mirror* 7 (1921), 291.

21. Hair and Alsop, *English Seamen and Traders*, 148–49. Subsequent voyages to Guinea were undertaken without these powers, a cause of complaint by organizers who hoped to coerce seamen into greater obedience during risky voyages.

22. Kenneth Andrews, ed. *English Privateering Voyages to the West Indies 1588–1595* (Cambridge: Cambridge University Press, 1959), 44. Masters normally were at the top of the command structure on merchant and nonmilitary voyages. If the voyage had military objectives, a captain was usually present and had precedence over the master. Captains were expected to implement strategy, and masters were to see to the running of the ship, because captains were not always mariners.

23. Andrews, *English Privateering Voyages*, 45; PRO HCA 13/27/262.

24. PRO HCA, 13/27/336, 13/27/262v–63v; Andrews, *English Privateering Voyages*, 44.

25. PRO HCA, 13/29/219, 13/34/426v. He also claims that he had a whistle,

a symbol of office, in his possession. PRO HCA, 1/46/17, 1/46/19v, 1/46/25, 1/46/19, 1/46/25v, 1/46/28.

26. Monson, *Naval Tracts*, vol. III, 435.

27. Geoffrey Callender, "Drake and His Detractors," *Mariner's Mirror* 7 (1921), 102, 142, 146; Senior, "Drake and the Suit," 291, 296; Gregory Robinson, "A Forgotten Life of Sir Francis Drake," *Mariner's Mirror* 7 (1921), 14. For greater detail, see Corbett's *Drake and the Tudor Navy*, vol. I, 201 323.

28. PRO HCA 13/30/69v–70v.

29. PRO HCA 13/25/176-v.

30. PRO HCA, 13/29/221v, 13/29/218v–19v, 13/29/220. "Coppernose" was a term for a drunkard.

31. Sir Henry Mainwaring, a seventeenth-century English vice admiral, quoted in Bernard Capp, *Cromwell's Navy: The Fleet and the English Revolution 1648–1660* (Oxford: Clarendon Press, 1989), 221.

32. Ibid., 221.

33. PRO HCA, 13/35/12–13, 13/35/13–14v.

34. Wrightson, *English Society*, 173.

35. Capp, *Cromwell's Navy*, 292.

36. Rodger, *The Wooden World*, 206.

37. Drake, quoted in Corbett, *Drake and the Tudor Navy*, vol. I, 249.

38. Oppenheim, *The Administration of the Royal Navy, 1509–1660*, 389.

39. Ibid., 389, 385, 390.

40. Ibid., 390.

41. J. D. Alsop, "The Career of William Towerson, Guinea Trader," *International Journal of Maritime History* 4(1992), 65–66; Hair and Alsop, *English Seamen and Traders*, 147–49.

42. Boteler, *Boteler's Dialogues*, 44–45.

43. PRO HCA 1/44/46v.

44. PRO HCA 13/36/217v–18.

45. PRO HCA 14/32/130.

46. PRO HCA, 13/23/330v–31v, 13/27/405 13/35/464–66, 13/24/219.

47. For one example, see J. D. Alsop, "A Regime at Sea: The Navy and the 1553 Succession Crisis," *Albion* 24 (1992), 577–90.

48. J. A. Sharpe, "Such Disagreement betwyx Neighbours: Litigation and Human Relations in Early Modern England," in *Disputes and Settlements: Law and Human Relations in the West*, ed. John Bossy (Cambridge: Cambridge University Press, 1983), 174–75.

49. PRO HCA 13/27/262v.

50. PRO HCA 13/25/142.

51. PRO HCA 14/34/69. See also PRO HCA 14/32/91.

52. Part of the hesitation to seek redress within the formal context of the law was the cost. John Banes, a sailor of the *Pearl* of Limehouse, requested Julius Caesar, judge of the Admiralty Court, to order Captain Thomas Best to pay him his wages "being vnable to wage lawe for the same." PRO HCA 14/34/161. See also PRO HCA 14/36/13.

53. PRO HCA 13/30/108v. Also printed in Andrews, *English Privateering Voyages*, 205.

54. Callender, "Drake and His Detractors," 72.

55. Religious observance was a daily routine. See Monson, *Naval Tracts*, vol. IV, 200; Walter Raleigh, *The Works of Sir Walter Ralegh*, vol. VIII (Oxford: Oxford University Press, 1829), 682. See also Chapter 3.

56. Monson, *Naval Tracts*, vol. IV, 197.

57. Capp, *Cromwell's Navy*, 222–23, 289–90.

58. Rodger, *The Wooden World*, 229–30.

59. *State Papers Relating to the Defeat of the Spanish Armada*, vol. I, 273.

60. Oppenheim, *The Administration of the Royal Navy, 1509–1660*, 384.

61. It was part of John Chidley's expedition to the Straits of Magellan in 1589–90. See Andrews, *English Privateering Voyages*, 54, 65, 68, 70.

62. It is possible that formal written petitions were on occasion produced at the behest of shipmasters to cover them from liability or the anger of employers when the ships returned to England and that most petitioning was, in fact, oral and unstructured.

63. PRO HCA 1/46/3v–4.

64. PRO HCA 13/24/329v.

65. PRO HCA 13/30/247v–48.

66. *Tudor Royal Proclamations*, vol. III, ed. Paul L. Hughes and James F. Larkin (New Haven, Conn.: Yale University Press, 1964), 44–47; *Acts of the Privy Council* (hereafter *A.P.C.*), vol. XVIII, 46–49, 54–55.

67. *A.P.C.*, vol. XXXIII, 320. The seamen's riots of 1592 ultimately led to a new pay system the following year. Geoffrey L. Hudson, "The Origins of State Benefits for Ex-Servicemen in Elizabethan England," unpublished paper, 9–11.

68. Nonetheless, such demonstrations were fairly common during the interregnum. Capp, *Cromwell's Navy*, 286–89.

69. Callender, "Drake and His Detractors," 100, 142, 72.

70. *A.P.C.*, vol. XII, 213; *State Papers*, 352; Hawkins, *Observations*, 20.

71. Hawkins, *Observations*, 20.

72. PRO HCA 13/24/232–33; Kenneth Andrews, "Christopher Newport of Limehouse, Mariner," *William and Mary Quarterly* 11 (1954), 30.

73. PRO HCA, 1/42/21, 1/46/143-v, 13/28/302v. See also PRO HCA, 1/42/77, 1/42/41, 1/42/181.

74. The term "mutiny" was an imprecise one during this period. It covered individual acts of violent insubordination as well as group actions. See Rodger, *The Wooden World*, 237–38. It could refer to the unmanageability of an individual and, as well, work shutdowns or "strikes." See Andrews, *Ships, Money and Politics*, 66; Capp, *Cromwell's Navy*, 228–29.

75. Boteler, *Boteler's Dialogues*, 44.

76. Walter and Wrightson, "Dearth and the Social Order," 23, 41.

77. Oppenheim, *The Administration of the Royal Navy, 1509–1660*, 389.

78. *State Papers*, vol. I, 96, 198, 273, vol. II, 96, 183, 283.

79. Ibid., vol. II, 177.

80. Ibid., vol. II, 283.

81. Capp's work on Cromwell's navy illustrates that commanders and officers were often sympathetic to the men's demands. Most of the "mutinies" that took place during this time were "strikes": the ships and crews concerned were usually

in harbor, and unrest was normally directed at the authorities ashore who had failed to pay or provision the navy. Capp, *Cromwell's Navy*, 286.

82. PRO HCA 1/46/101.

83. PRO HCA 1/46/74–77v.

84. PRO HCA 1/46/19v–20v. See also PRO HCA 13/44/68.

85. PRO HCA 1/45/48v; Henry Greene, quoted in Luke Foxe, *North-West Fox or Fox from the North-West* (London, 1635), 103; Capp, *Cromwell's Navy*, 228; Oppenheim, *The Administration of the Royal Navy, 1509–1660*, 390; G. M. Asher, ed., *Henry Hudson the Navigator* (New York: Burt Franklin, 1860), 193.

86. Martin Ingram, "Ridings, Rough Music and the 'Reform of Popular Culture' in Early Modern England," *Past and Present* 105 (1984), 93, 97.

87. John Bohstedt, *Riots and Community Politics in England and Wales, 1790–1810* (Cambridge, Mass.: Harvard University Press, 1983), 5, 11.

88. Tilly, "Food Supply and Public Order in Modern Europe," 386.

89. Douglas Hay, "Property, Authority and the Criminal Law," in *Albion's Fatal Tree: Crime and Society in Eighteenth-Century England*, ed. Douglas Hay et al. (New York: Pantheon Books, 1975), 25.

90. Cynthia B. Herrup, "Law and Morality in Seventeenth-Century England," *Past and Present* 106 (1985), 109–11.

91. Monson, *Naval Tracts*, vol. II, 205.

92. These laws were codified by Richard I and introduced to England in the 1190s. They were based on Rhodian sea law of the 700s. See Dixon, "Seamen and the Law," 13; Monson, *Naval Tracts*, vol. IV, 130–31.

93. See Monson, *Naval Tracts*, vol. III, 436, vol. IV, 200–201, 202–3.

94. Vincent White-Patarino has observed that the punishments employed in the navy during the reigns of Charles II and James II (1660–1688) were much more lenient than the Naval Discipline Act allowed for. Vincent White-Patarino, "Living outside the Ordered Society: Discipline, Violence, and the Shipboard Culture of English Sailors, 1550–1688," unpublished paper, 9.

95. See Oppenheim, *The Administration of the Royal Navy, 1509–1660*, 387–88.

96. Monson, *Naval Tracts*, vol. I, 139, vol. IV, 199.

97. Padfield, *Armada*, 94.

98. Andrews, "The Elizabethan Seaman," 247.

99. PRO HCA 14/32/130. Trinity House later overturned the decision.

100. PRO HCA 13/30/210.

101. PRO HCA, 13/24/218, 13/24/294.

102. Oppenheim, *The Administration of the Royal Navy, 1509–1660*, 382; Corbett, *Drake and the Tudor Navy*, 226.

103. Monson, *Naval Tracts*, vol. II, 237.

104. Boteler, *Boteler's Dialogues*, 35.

105. Hair and Alsop, *English Seamen and Traders*, 147–48.

106. *State Papers*, vol. I, 198.

107. For more information on the relationship between violence and power in this period, see White-Patarino, "Living outside the Ordered Society" and Susan Dwyer Amussen, "Punishment, Discipline, and Power: The Social Meanings of Violence in Early Modern England," *Journal of British Studies* 34 (January 1995).

108. PRO HCA 1/44/223v. Masculinity and the exercise of command or au-

thority were linked in the minds of the speakers. The contrast, though, is always to "boy" and never to woman. On land, a husband who could not control his family was called a "woman." At sea, the prejorative designation within an internalized all-male ethos was to the lowest and most immature rank of seafarer.

109. Quoted in Capp, *Cromwell's Navy*, 219.

110. PRO HCA 13/25/48v.

111. PRO HCA 13/28/25v.

112. PRO HCA 13/24/329–30. For more on Salmon, see *State Papers*, vol. I, 324–25.

113. PRO HCA 1/46/303.

114. PRO HCA 1/44/170v–71v.

115. See also PRO HCA 1/44/5v.

116. PRO HCA, 1/45/132v, 13/25/48v, 13/27/262v–63v.

117. E. J. Hobsbawm, "Social Criminality," *Bulletin of the Society for the Study of Labour History* 25 (1972), 5–8; quoted and discussed in Joanna Innes and John Styles, "The Crime Wave: Recent Writing on Crime and Criminal Justice in Eighteenth-Century England," *Journal of British Studies* 25 (1986), 395–96; Wrightson, *English Society*, 173.

118. PRO HCA 1/45/53–54.

119. PRO HCA 13/32/295v. Cotton was possibly a justice of the peace, but his office is not specified in the deposition.

120. PRO HCA 13/25/109v–10. See also PRO HCA 13/26/334.

121. PRO HCA, 13/26/334, 13/32/297v–98, 13/33/324v–26.

122. Oppenheim, *The Administration of the Royal Navy, 1509–1660*, 382–83, 387; *Trinity House of Deptford Transactions, 1609–35*, 944; Mead, *Trinity House*, 36; Corbett, *Drake and the Tudor Navy*, vol. II, 107; PRO HCA 14/32/137; Leslie Stephen and Sidney Lee, *Dictionary of National Biography*, vol. II (Oxford: Oxford University Press, 1917), 867; PRO HCA 24/58/72; GLRO, P93/DUN/327/5, P93/DUN/327/13, P93/DUN/327/20, P93/DUN/327/21; Guildhall Ms., 9171/20/341, 9171/18/313; PRO PROB 11/102/75.

123. PRO HCA 1/3/39. Capp suggests that the Protectorate was extremely lenient with deserters because it needed skilled men for the war effort, and desertion was so widespread that punishing them would have resulted in a "bloodbath." Capp, *Cromwell's Navy*, 284. This was probably the case during the war with Spain. Had skilled seamen been readily available, the Crown would have had more scope to punish deserters.

124. For example of royal pardons to seamen, see PRO, SP 12/29/172, SP 12/234/Nov. 9, 1590, SP 12/264/July 27, 1597, SP 12/267/June 24, 1598, SP 12/July 16, 1598, SP 12/274/Jan. 27, 1600; PRO HCA, 1/4/37, 14/36/165, 14/36/167. For examples of the Crown's leniency, see PRO HCA, 1/3/39, 1/4/37, 14/33/7, 14/32/28.

125. PRO SP 12/249/Aug. 10, 1594. Because of the nature of the crime, 95 percent of convicted horse thieves were hanged. Herrup, "Law and Morality," 114–15.

126. PRO HCA 14/33/133–34. See also PRO HCA 1/3/39.

127. *Trinity House of Deptford Transactions 1609–35*, 12, 77; PRO, E 101/64/28/3, E 101/64/24; PRO HCA, 1/45/57, 1/4/56.

128. PRO HCA 24/60/113; Greater London Record Office, P93/DUN/327/5, P93/DUN/327/33.

129. PRO HCA 14/34/201; *State Papers*, lxxvi; Oppenheim, *The Administration of the Royal Navy, 1509–1660*, 392; Robinson, "A Forgotten Life of Sir Francis Drake," 17; PRO HCA, 14/30/43, 14/30/104, 14/33/7.

130. For example, see PRO HCA 1/101.

131. See Farrant, "The Rise and Decline of a South Coast Seafaring Town," 63; Peter Laslett, *The World We Have Lost—Further Explored*, 3rd ed. (London: Methuen, 1983), 75.

Chapter 3

Maritime Subculture, Labor Relations, and the Role of Custom

The examination of hiring practices has demonstrated that there was an established tradition of individualism within the maritime community. In part because seamen lacked a national structure to impose a wage scale and regulate the terms of their employment, they were "free agents." They contracted out their own labor, had autonomy to negotiate the terms of their own employment with employers, and had a say in the manner and method of payment. Moreover, many seamen wisely opted to conduct some private trading in order to supplement their wages. They were accustomed to looking out for themselves and relying on their own efforts to secure a decent living. During the last two decades of Elizabeth's reign, this tradition of personal control of employment and leisure was undermined by the wartime demands of the Crown. Without question seamen's individualism and customary freedoms were at odds with the Crown's age-old right of impressment, which affected the composition of the maritime community, dictated when seamen should work, and had a negative impact on the seamen's financial state. The war decreased their occupational freedom; naval duty dictated that seamen would serve aboard a warship on a given voyage at a specific rate, well below what they could command for other types of maritime employment. There was no opportunity for private trading and little hope of benefiting from booty. Thus, service to the Crown carried a financial penalty for seamen and their dependents. Because naval wages were below market value, and payment was routinely delayed, seamen had little compunction about embezzling to make up for lost income. However, seamen resented the intrusion upon their employment freedoms more acutely than the loss of income.

Although it was common knowledge that seamen detested naval service, and many tried to evade it through desertion or bribery, most tacitly bowed to the Crown's authority. Perhaps it is more precise to say that most seamen tried to ignore all but the most blatant encroachments upon their usual freedoms and carry on as they had in peacetime. On the whole, they relied on the strength of custom to govern their employment obligations to the Crown, rather than attempt innovative solutions, such as organizing themselves into a collective.

Despite their obvious independence and itinerant existence, the ties that bound the maritime community together were very strong indeed. The shipboard economy and system of debt were important pillars of the maritime community; they had a vital role in each man's livelihood, and both depended upon and enhanced economic and social bonds within the community.

Financial and commercial exchanges were only one practice that created and perpetuated cohesion within the seafaring population. Undoubtedly, maritime subculture engendered solidarity among men of the sea as well. English seamen had an elaborate system of customs, rituals, symbols, and codes. Much of their subculture was shared with foreign seamen; the folklore of the sea, seamen's dances, songs, and idiom all sprang from their lives afloat and were uniquely their own.

The Protestant faith fostered cohesion within the English sector of a wider European maritime community. Although shipboard orders imposed regular Protestant worship, the practice of shipboard religion was an established custom of the maritime community that needed no enforcing. The Crown was concerned about ensuring that seamen's practices and beliefs were orthodox, but there are few traces of the old faith among the maritime community by the 1580s. The outbreak of war with Spain exacerbated and emphasized religious differences and tensions between Catholic and Protestant seamen.

The interplay between religion and the Anglo-Spanish war had important consequences for the English maritime community. Religious rhetoric provided the English maritime community with a noble motive—or an acceptable justification—for waging battles against the Spaniards.[1] Furthermore, their collective and individual successes instilled pride in their abilities and their identity as an uniquely English maritime group.

RITUAL AND SUBCULTURE

While seamen spent much of their time at sea, isolated from land dwellers, they were still privy to "a common stock of popular culture." This is witnessed in methods of protest and religion. Nevertheless, isolation was bound to breed a distinctive subculture.[2] While it was not unusual for craftsmen and occupational groups to develop their own subcultures, the maritime subculture was so distinctive and pervasive that many English observers would deem seamen to be "a nation by themselves."[3]

Like other itinerant occupational groups that endured physical isolation, seamen had a highly developed "system of shared meanings, attitudes and values, and the symbolic forms (performances, artifacts) in which they are expressed or embodied."[4] Seamen possessed their own idiom and colloquialisms. "Landlubbers" were effectively excluded from this language, which sprang from the extensive terminology related to seafaring life. One outsider commented on his first exposure to the shipboard environment: "Nor could I think what world I was in, whether among spirits or devils. All seemed strange; different language and strange expressions of tongue." Sir William Monson observed that the "sea language is not soon learned, much less understood, being only proper to him that has served his apprenticeship"; to the untrained ear, seamen's jargon sounded like "a barbarous speech which he [a nonseaman] conceives not the meaning of." In particular, seamen had a reputation for cursing and swearing. An early eighteenth-century observer commented that such habits were "so common among our Seamen, that they can scarcely speak without such horrid Imprecations and blasphemous Oaths, as no Christian can hear without horror."[5] Monson went on the say that seamen "are stubborn or perverse when they perceive their commander is ignorant of the discipline of the sea, and cannot speak to them in their own language." Nautical glossaries testify to the extensive nature of seamen's distinct vocabulary.[6]

Seamen's songs not only employed their unique jargon but also reflected the work rhythms of their occupation. Chanteys were exchanges between a leader and a chorus, "one who sings and orders and the labourers who sing in response."[7] Seamen's dances were designed for confined areas. Both forms were tailored to shipboard life. Thus, their working environment and the rhythm of their labor had a direct influence upon the character of their popular culture, and that culture reinforced their "otherness."

Music figured prominently in maritime subculture because it provided relief from the monotony of life at sea.[8] While musicians were kept on board naval, exploration, and privateering fleets to give signals, they were also used to entertain the men. Among the items salvaged from Henry VIII's flagship, the *Mary Rose*, were a wooden shawm, three tabor pipes, several small reed pipes, a wooden whistle, and the remnants of two stringed instruments. The ship's musicians played on board Humphrey Gilbert's *Delight* as the ship and crew tried to weather an Atlantic storm: "like the swan that singeth before her death, they in the *Delight* continued in sounding trumpets, with drums and fifes, also winding the cornets and hautboys." Musicians were common aboard ships that were traveling in groups, as they were used to convey signals between vessels in a fleet, especially when fog or high waves limited visibility. The appreciation of music was shared by pirates as well. In the early 1580s a pirate crew kept a young boy with a fiddle on board their ship "to make them merye." While affection for music was in no way particular to seamen, it is apparent that much of their subculture, that is, their language, songs, and dances, evolved from their unique work environment.

The system of shared meanings, however, went far beyond simple terminology and usages. Like all subcultures, there was a complex code of nonverbal communication, symbols, and rituals that only those of the maritime community understood. For instance, crews took their orders from the calls of the boatswain's whistle. While whistles worked well for conveying messages on any given ship, other forms of nonverbal communication were needed for fleets. By the sixteenth century there was an intricate code whereby messages could be transmitted by firing the ship's ordnance, displaying lanterns, striking sails, or waving flags or through musical signals. Crews could indicate their friendliness or their aggression to other crews without exchanging a word. Given the international nature of seafaring, many elements of this coded language were held in common by European seamen. If a ship struck her topsails, the crew was signaling its intention to yield and allow a search for contraband. When a Portuguese ship with a lucrative cargo of sugar had the misfortune of encountering the English privateering vessel *Disdain* in 1592, John Endicke, the English shipmaster, waved a sword at the Portuguese. The young ship's surgeon, Martin Pelham, "also waved her [the Portuguese ship] with his hatt & then caste his hatt overborde and commanded them of the prize to strike for the Queene of Englande." The Portuguese opted to surrender:

and they of the prize asked what shippes those a heade were, and answere was made from the disdayne they were the Queene of Englandes shippes and then the said portiugall prize strake her topp sayles & yelded.[9]

By waving an unsheathed sword at the Portuguese company, the men of the *Disdain* were giving a clear indication of their intention to fight if necessary. The custom of "waving amaine" was widespread among the maritime community. This practice was not limited to English seamen. The crews of two French warships considered Englishmen Lutherans and "thoughte yt lawfull to take eany englishe mens goodes if they could." When they encountered the English privateering vessel *Centaur* in 1595, the French seamen

of eyther shippes aforesaid called the Esperannce & princesse with swordes drawen wayved the englishe men amaine, and one of the officers of the princesse with a sworde drawen in his hande did bid the companye of the centaure amaine englishe dogges and shott two shott[s] at the Centaure.[10]

Throwing beverages into the water was another sign of defiance and aggression.[11] Francis Auston, master's mate of the *Samaritan*, testified before the Admiralty Court that he and his crew had fired on a Dutch ship because its company had refused to strike their topsails in deference to Queen Elizabeth. The Dutch crew demonstrated their willingness to fight when one of their number "did weave a naked sworde vppon the poupe and caste a cann of drincke towardes" Auston and his company "in dispighte and defiannce." The English seamen testified that "the waving of a naked sworde and castinge of a cann over borde are signes and tokens of hostility and Defiance at sea." The gunner's mate, William Hanson, corroborated Auston's account; these actions "are vsvall and knowen signes of warre." Similarly, pirate captain Tom Clark saluted his victims with a glass of wine and then threw the glass into the sea before he robbed them.

While these gestures needed no explanation to seamen in the sixteenth century, they might also be accompanied by verbal provocations.[12] When the crew of the Queen's ship *Guardland* commanded the *Black Bull* of Hamburg to strike her topsails to salute Queen Elizabeth in 1591, the Germans "skornefullie denyed [to strike their sails], vttering . . . vnseemely & vnreverent speeches." The standard incitement was to insult the English Queen. Thomas Atkins, master of the *Mary Fortune* of Lynn, described his company's battle against a ship of Hamburg in the mid-1590s: the Germans goaded the English company by yelling, "Skite vppon the Quene of England." When Flemish seamen encountered a fleet of English privateers at sea, they angered them by "sayenge skite vppon the Queene with other vnsemely wordes, and bade them come on borde yf they durste."

Given the importance of alcohol[13] to the seafaring community, seamen routinely incorporated beverages into their rituals. During the Interregnum, naval administrators were deeply concerned with the "mad, savage spirit" of drunken seamen ashore. An eighteenth-century observer commented, "Liquor is the very cement that keeps the mariner's body and soul together." This was true of the sixteenth-century population as well. Toasting with alcohol was a ritual that could foster a sense of fellowship and mark important events. Raleigh's shipboard orders recognized that the custom of "drinking to healths" between meals was dangerous because it diminished the ship's provisions. While toasting might be deemed little more than good manners, there were occasions when toasting had much weightier functions. Captain Christopher Newport, one of England's most distinguished seamen during the reigns of Elizabeth and James I, used the custom of toasting to boost morale and create solidarity among the company of the *Dragon* of London in 1592. Prior to engaging in battle with a Portuguese crew Newport spoke to his men:

Masters nowe the tyme is come that eyther we muste ende our dayes, or take the said carricke & wisshed all the company to stande to theire chardge like men and if eny displeasure were amongst eany of them to forgett & forgive one an other which every one seemed willinge vnto, & then the said Keyball [the shipmaster] tooke a canne of wyne & droncke to John Locke [his mate], & John Locke drancke to him agayne & soe throughe out the shipp every one droncke to the other . . . [and] all the company were good freindes one with an other.[14]

   Drinking had several important social and business functions.[15] Pirates often lured potential customers and employees aboard by offering them alcohol. Their vessels were "hospitality suites" where pirates conducted business. Seamen frequently made employment contacts in taverns and ale-houses ashore. Raleigh combed drinking establishments along the Thames to find seamen for his voyages. It was routine for English seamen in foreign or domestic ports to go aboard other ships or to row ashore to "make merry" or "to make good cheare." Merchant William Farnanlles of the *Bartholomew* left 10 shillings for his crewmates "to praye for me and to drynke . . . together" after his funeral service. In his will mariner Rowland Jordan left the large sum of £6 13s. 4d. for the company of the *George Bonaventure* "to drinke withall."[16] It seems apparent that alcohol fulfilled the symbolic function of celebrating and reinforcing camaraderie and community identity within a shifting, itinerant male society of seafarers. For pirates or others to lure unsuspecting victims through the promise of drink was thus a contravention of the maritime symbolic code,[17] and to cast a drink overboard—instead of offering it—was naked hostility.
   Rituals were also used to mark significant milestones within the maritime community. For instance, on their voyage of circumnavigation, Drake and his men struck the topsails of their ship when they entered the Straits of Magellan in homage to their Queen. The christening of ships and boats was a long-standing ritual. Similarly, seamen maintained an age-old tradition of celebrating the crossing of the equator.
   Seamen also had their own rituals to mark the passing of their members. In early modern society, family, friends, and neighbors congregated around the deathbed of the dying person. We know that seamen observed this ritual in their shipboard communities. During the sixteenth century, one aspect of this shipboard death ritual was developing greater importance: the practice of will making.[18] With the explosion of long-distance voyages during this time and the high rates of shipboard mortality, ever greater numbers of seamen met their demise far from home. Seamen dying at sea had to make arrangements for their personal effects, wages, trading commodities, debts on shipboard, and possessions left behind in England. In the general absence of their next of kin, seamen counted on their crewmates to carry out their last wishes or, at least, relay them and the wills to those who were charged with that duty. Given that the demands of their occupation increasingly took them far from their homes, the reasons behind the growing importance of communal shipboard will making in seamen's

deathbed rituals during the sixteenth century are readily apparent.[19] Wills in Tudor England generally acknowledged ties to kin, neighbors, and servants, many of whom would have been present at the making or reading of the will; shipboard wills similarly focus upon the immediate ship's company, and this indicates considerable ties that bound the maritime community together. For example, Richard Hexum, hired as a gunner for the East India fleet, was so scrupulous about his debts to his crewmates that he willed "that all my debtes in the ship which I do owe to be firste paide."[20]

Those who died at sea were committed to the depths by their crewmates; although we do not know the specifics of this service, we do know that seamen conducted funerals according to the "rite of the sea."[21] Their wills provide evidence to support the contention that shipboard funeral services were distinctive from those of the land community. In their wills, seamen recognized that, because of their geographic mobility, they probably would not be buried in their home parishes. However, there are instances where seamen specifically requested that they be buried at sea whether they died at sea or on land. In his will of 1589, shipmaster Thomas Rickman noted that he wanted to be buried at sea "accordinge to the manner thereof." John Wardell made a similar request in his will, which was written and probated in 1598; Wardell wanted his "bodie to be interred after the mariner Custome." Contemporary seamen recognized a distinctive form of death ritual that was particular to their occupation. Rituals and customs such as these served to foster a sense of unique identity by marking rites of passage and special occasions in a distinctive manner.

The shipboard environment naturally exerted a huge influence on maritime customs and subculture. The ship's mainmast was the focus of many shipboard activities. Here religious worship took place, seamen were punished, and crews congregated for meetings and to sell items. Auctions at the mainmast were routine; in their wills dying seamen frequently requested that their personal effects and any items that they had purchased for the purpose of trade be sold at the mainmast.[22] Custom dictated that privateers must meet at the mainmast to share their spoils. Clearly, the mainmast was the public, communal locus of shipboard life, and, as such, it came to be viewed as more than merely a convenient open space; in the cramped quarters of a sixteenth-century ship it was where seamen came together as a community.

Although seamen were not divorced from the land population in their religious convictions, their worldview was colored by superstitions and beliefs spawned by life at sea.[23] The experiences of generations of seafarers had created a very rich tradition of beliefs and folktales. Every sixteenth-century seaman knew that ships were intrinsically lucky or unlucky. The men of the English maritime community had determined that the Queen's ship *Revenge* was a ship of "no good hap" even before she was shot through by the Spaniards in 1591. Sir Richard Hawkins called the ship "the unfortunatest ship the late Queene's Majestie had during her Raigne." Seamen had long believed that electricity glowing from the ship's masthead indicated that St. Elmo was with them during a storm. Seamen on John Hawkins's third trading expedition to the Spanish Main claimed to have seen a merman off the coast of Bermuda who "shewed himselfe three times unto us from the middle upwards, in which parts hee was proportioned like a man, of the complection of a Mulato, or tawny Indian." Ghost ships, mermaids, and sea monsters were a part of every seaman's belief system. Seafarers had always been a superstitious lot, and strange sights in foreign lands only reinforced this. Frobisher's men, for instance, undressed an Inuit woman to ascertain if she was a witch or a devil. While members of the land population might give credence to such beliefs, there was more emphasis placed upon creatures and phenomena of the deep in seamen's worldview. Such figures and strange happenings loomed large and were a very real part of seamen's universe. It is evident, then, that seamen viewed their universe with a different emphasis from that of those who spent most of their days on land, adding to a sense of group identity that transcended mere common employment.

Given that the shipboard environment was normally an all-male community, the resulting subculture and belief system exuded machismo. Seamen's code of honor was intimately tied to the importance of behaving "like a man."[24] As in the case of Captain Christopher Newport, who pleaded for his crew "to stande to theire chardge like men" prior to battle, commanders and officers often appealed to seamen's sense of male honor. Master Thomas White of the *Amity* of London advised his men to take heart during a crisis and "willed them to shewe themselves like men." When the crew of the hoy *William* entreated the company of the *Thomasyn* to alter their course for the safety of both vessels, they cried, "Aloofe Alooffe yf you be men keepe your loofe, or else you will over ron vs." When an English ship encountered eight Turkish galleys in 1563, the owner of the ship "manfully encouraged his companie, exhorting them valiantly to shewe their manhoode, shewing them that God was their God."

Conversely, to disparage someone was to call or compare him to a boy.[25] Two disgruntled seamen of the *White Hind* of London had little regard for their master and called him

rascall knave and boye and woulde make him a boye, and to his greate discreaditt reported he was not a sufficiente Master, not able to take chardge, and often tymes they have threatened to beate him.

A similar incident occurred aboard the *Phoenix* in the early 1580s, when seaman Nicholas Simondes found fault with William Baker, the ship's carpenter, for his lack of strength in helping Simondes load hogsheads of wine.

Simondes insulted Baker's honor by saying that he "woulde make the shippe boye yf he were on borde to doe yt." When Richard Buckley, master of the *Anne* of London, removed his mate from office, he made his great displeasure known by saying that his mate "should haue noe more to doe in the shipp then the leaste boy of the shipp."

How unique was seamen's subculture compared to that of other early modern occupational groups? Although seamen's idiom and rituals were particular to their subculture, the existence of their own idiom and rituals did not make them atypical of tight-knit occupational groups in preindustrial Europe. Undeniably, aspects of their subculture were shared by non-seafarers; the importance of music and drinking, for instance, was not limited to seamen. Drinking rituals were used by other occupational groups to achieve or reinforce unity.[26] In all likelihood, their code of honor was not particular to seamen; however, machismo was probably of greater importance in all-male communities. No doubt this code was especially pronounced among soldiers and seamen who manned warships.

Seamen's subculture, however, was unusual in the sense that it was nurtured in isolation, and, as a result, it was particularly rich and pervasive. The markings of this subculture, in dress and behavior, were so obvious that, at a glance, seamen were readily identifiable to each other and to the rest of the population. The fact that most seamen were considered "outsiders" in mainstream society suggests that they were marginal men because of their differences from the land population as a whole; in other words, the strength of their subculture limited them from "blending in" with the land population.[27] This is not to say that there were not similarities with the larger culture, simply that these similarities were not as immediately identifiable as their differences and that contemporaries emphasized uniqueness, not commonality.

WAGES AND BENEFITS IN MARITIME COMMERCE

There was no standard wage scale for seamen during the Elizabethan period.[28] Non-naval seamen, as free agents, were entitled to contract out their labor to their best advantage. Deftness in negotiating, the individual seaman's reputation and skill, the duration and destination of the voyage, his level of responsibility, and the "going rate" were all factors that determined how much a seaman was paid. In addition, seamen received money for loading and unloading cargo. "Primage" may have been required by the master or owner in the terms of the seaman's employment or paid in addition to his regular wages. There was also variation in how and when seamen were paid. Although most seamen on merchant journeys were paid by the voyage and received the bulk of their wages at the conclusion of the voyage, others were paid by the month, some were given a share of the freight and the right to load cargo, and, occasionally, seamen bargained for their wages after the completion of the voyage.[29] It was not uncommon to find that crewmates had negotiated quite different arrangements with the owners or the master.

Some seamen were given press money, or advances, before their journey, presumably to help them pay off outstanding debts, obtain the necessities for the voyage, and, in cases of married seamen, to support their families in the breadwinners' absence. Press money was an advance on the seaman's wages and would be deducted from the final pay accordingly. Sums advanced varied from voyage to voyage and from person to person. Again, this seems to have been a matter of personal need and negotiation with the owners or the shipmaster.[30]

According to Richard Hawkins, the advancing of press money was a custom that was much abused[31]:

for that such [seamen] a goe to the sea (for the most part) consume that money lewdly before they depart, (as common experience teacheth vs:) and when they come from [the] Sea, many times come more beggerly home, then when they went forth, having received and spent their portion before they imbarked themselues, are forced to theeue, to cosen, or to runne away in debt.

There were seamen who supplemented their incomes by entering into employment contracts, accepting press money, and then deserting before the ship left port: "others, to benefit themselues of the Imprest given them, absented themselues; making a lewd liuing in deceiving all whose money they could lay hold of: which is a scandall too rife amongst our Sea-men." The English navy was not alone in experiencing these problems. Promoters of the Guinea trading voyages sought the Crown's permission to impress mariners and to impose martial law; with royal authority behind them the promoters believed that they could discourage seamen from taking advances of clothing and money and then vanishing.[32] These practices could be very costly for owners and backers. In 1590 renowned mariner Thomas Cavandish complained that many of his men had "absented themselues in Imprests," which had cost him £1,500 in lost wages. When the East India Company tried to discontinue the practice of granting seamen an advance on their wages in 1623, the crew of *Charles*, then ready to set sail from England, refused to leave port. The Honourable Company ultimately gave the men their press money. Despite the abuses of the system, the expectation that seamen would receive wages prior to their voyage was too firmly entrenched in seamen's culture and employment needs to be weeded out easily.[33]

In addition to the variation in methods and types of payment, there was a great deal of diversity in how much seamen were paid. Skilled seamen such as masters and pilots, especially those who had been apprenticed, earned much more than unskilled and semiskilled men. K. R. Andrews maintains that the master's wage was normally four or five times that of the common seaman, twice that of his mate, and three times that of his other officers.[34] My own research suggests that this was not always the case. Andrews's assessment holds true only for the Elizabethan navy.[35] However, on merchant and privateering vessels, the disparity between the wages for highly skilled positions such as pilots, master's mates, and masters was not always so great; this explains why trained shipmasters occasionally sailed in subordinate positions. But wages did differ significantly, even among seamen with commensurate skill. Most shipmasters could expect to earn £5 or £6 per month in wages and by selling their shares in commodities aboard the ship.[36] Those with talent and connections could make much more. Shipmaster Roger Hankin, for instance, was hired by the East India Company for its first, exploratory voyage for the grand sum of £10 per month with an additional gratuity of £50.[37] This is in stark contrast to the 10 to 20 shillings a month that an ordinary seaman could expect to earn.[38]

Despite the fact that many shipowners were part-owners of vessels and almost always had some share in the ship's cargo for their own personal profit, not all masters derived substantial benefit from their position. The owners of the ship *Samaritan* promised shipmaster John Baynard

that if he would play the good husband he should haue an eight parte of the said shipp & pay for yt as he earned yt, but he was so poore a man that he could not forbeare his wages or eany thinge which he earned towardes the payenge for of the said shippe.

Neighbors and friends testified before the Admiralty Court that Baynard was a poor man, and his will as well as that of his widow illustrate that he never succeeded in owning any part of the *Samaritan*.[39]

While Baynard was representative of a number of shipmasters who struggled in vain to obtain a share in a vessel, he stands in contrast to a number of his fellow shipmasters whose wills show that they amassed a considerable personal estate from their days at sea.[40] When he wrote his will in 1602, shipmaster William Goodlad described his extensive estate in Leigh, Essex, which included houses, property, and shares in shipping. To ensure that his young children received their inheritance, Goodlad demanded that his widow should be bound for the large sum of £400 if she should remarry. When he died in the early 1590s, mariner Rowland Jordan left cash bequests of £550 to various relatives and friends. Thomas Grove, one of Masters of the Navy and the mayor of Rochester, had amassed substantial properties and goods from his maritime career; as a measure of his wealth Grove left cash bequests of £300 in 1604 to each of his three sons and £250 each to his three daughters and an unborn child.

The study of seamen's incomes appears to be a straightforward matter since there are examples in the Admiralty Court records and wills whereby seamen record how much they were paid monthly or for a given voyage. Unfortunately for our purposes, this is far from true. Seamen's incomes were rarely limited to their wages alone. Shipboard apprentices and servants were accorded wages for the voyage, and the master was entitled to such moneys in addition to his own wages. Shipmaster Bartholomew Hugguet earned six pounds per month aboard the *Constantine* of London, while his three servants earned 18 shillings, 17 shillings, and 16 shillings per month. Given that they were employed for 20 months, Hugguet made a tidy sum. In addition, skilled seamen often had shares in vessels and freight, and even the poorest seamen usually did some trading on the side. Hair and Alsop's research on seamen in the Guinea trade reveals that all crew members were allowed to carry out private trading, and they were permitted to purchase goods from the ship's lading on credit. Seamen's wills illustrate that they frequently obtained goods during their travels that they hoped to sell. Wills that resulted from the high mortality of the first East India voyage in 1601–3 show that a number of these seamen had purchased china dishes.[41] In his will of 1622, Henry Rickman, master's mate of the *Charles*, dictated that all those mentioned in his will should receive white sugar candy in addition to all the bequests. Obviously, Rickman had purchased a generous quantity of candy with the intention of selling it for profit. As in the case of impressment money, seamen saw private trade as a customary perquisite. In a period of dramatically decreasing profits during the reign of Charles I, the East India Company attempted to eliminate this practice; as a result, some men refused to work for the Company, while others insisted on a raise in their wages to compensate them for this loss. Hence, it is apparent that seamen's wages were only part of their total income.[42]

To a great extent incomes were dependent upon not only wages and private trading but the frequency and duration of voyages. Most seamen were accustomed to periods of inactivity. Although those returning from voyages had a reputation for spending their money "lewdly" once ashore,[43] even the thriftiest unskilled and semiskilled seamen quickly fell into the ranks of the idle poor.[44] It was not uncommon for unemployed seamen in the less affluent segments of the maritime community to find themselves in debtor's jail or collecting parish relief. Gunner Nicholas Williams claimed in 1591 that he and his colleagues "had money to serve" as "longe as they wente abrode [at work] . . . but when they lay still they were allwayes beggerly & in wante." In 1601 Richard Paine alias Allen of Wapping, told the Admiralty Court that he had not been to sea for three months, and consequently his mother had maintained him. Sailor John Middleton acknowledged in his will his debt to his sister Jane, who had "byn all wayes my trustie freind and Carefull of me, and I haue had her Purse readdie att all tymes."

Seamen's wills reflect an ever-present, complex network of debt.[45] In the main, seamen owed sums within the maritime and commercial community; wills "reveal a shipboard community linked, not only by perils at sea and ship-discipline, but also by a web of inter-indebtedness." The shipboard economy was based upon credit. This is not surprising given the fact that most seamen did not receive the bulk of their wages until the successful conclusion of a voyage. Early Elizabethan evidence demonstrates that while seamen often owed the promoters, merchants, and senior ships' officers money for goods that they purchased for the purpose of trading, seamen also borrowed money for personal reasons and needs. Robert Guyle of the *Primrose* owed the master of his ship 2 shillings, "which I borrowed to by a paire of bootes." It was standard practice that a testator requested, as did seaman William Butler, "that all my debtes maie be paide whatsoever which I owe." When he wrote his will in 1598, Richard Popes, the ship's carpenter of the *Alcredo*, was indebted to his late servant Robert Buck 24 shillings as well as 2 shillings due to the boatswain of the ship, while the cockswain and the steward's mate each owed him 5 shillings, and the surgeon's mate owed another 2 shillings.

We are handicapped in our study of debts because those testators who did leave a list of their obligations seldom tell us what the nature of their relationship was to those identified or why the money was borrowed or lent. Nonetheless, from the information that does exist, it appears that seaman to seaman debt was the most common. Even pirates were a part of this network, albeit they could exert greater coercion in their credit dealings. In 1584 the infamous sea rover Charles Jones took mariner Robert Hopkins's motley cassock "and promised he would geve him as good a thinge for yt . . . at theire nexte meetinge with him at St. Ellyns."[46] Kinship debts also figure prominently. Many seamen owed or had lent money to their kinsmen (sons and sons-in-law in particular).[47] At the time of his death, fisherman Nicholas Smarthew owed £3 6s. to Walter Bunday, who was betrothed to his daughter Margaret. Mariner Thomas Bence bequeathed £10 to his brother-in-law because he had been "chargeable" to him. There are also debts, presumably for services, to tailors, glovers, and haberdashers. Seamen tended to owe money to hosts and hostesses for lodging ashore. Those who fell sick at sea not infrequently owed money to surgeons or caregivers.

We see evidence of a higher standard of living among the wills of wealthier seamen.[48] Nicholas Diggens owed the large sum of £20 to Richard Nottingham, Clerk of the Trinity House, for a gelding. Although he had already received £16 at the time that he wrote his will in 1602, sailor Charles Marshall of East Greenwich in Kent was owed £42 by one of the Queen's coachman for a house. At the time of his death in 1602, seaman John Howsego was owed £130 for lands and houses that he had sold. Although a large number of seamen refer to their debts in vague terms in their wills, requesting payment or collection of them by their executor/executrix, we can piece together a fairly clear picture of the nature of this credit system. While some did owe small sums for goods or services, most looked to fellow seamen and kinsmen (who were often seafarers) for money. The wills of seamen who died during a voyage provide evidence that almost all had debts in the ship; few who died during a voyage were free from some form of financial obligation to their crewmates.

One of the most interesting facets of this early modern credit economy was that debts and loans were seen as commodities, things to be bequeathed to others.[49] In cases of kinship and affective relationships, debts might be forgiven as an act of charity or in lieu of a bequest.[50] In his will of 1614, shipmaster Abraham Bonner acquitted his sons of the debts that he had paid for them. When he died in 1577, shipmaster Robert Barrett forgave John Freake Miller 40 shillings; Miller was described by Barrett as a "trustie and beloved freinde" and named as one of the overseers of Barrett's will.

This system of credit that characterized the maritime community relied on the fact that most men repaid their debts. The evidence of seamen's wills suggests that their obligations weighed heavily on their minds. Testators ordered overseers or executors to pay or collect their debts and frequently specified a set time period. Mariner John Walker was perhaps exceptional in that he went to sea "without being in debt vnto no man a shillinge," but he cautiously made provisions for his executor to pay anyone who could prove that he owed them money.[51] This example illustrates Walker's pride and care in being able to function successfully within a credit economy focused upon his peers. In his will of 1601, sailor John Stamford alias Brown acknowledged that he owed many debts to persons "who haue no evidences [written debt obligations] for the same,"[52] which he felt honor-bound to pay as his just debts. Stamford was not exceptional; most loans were arranged on the "honor system." Seamen's wills suggests that, in most cases, formal bonds existed only in circumstances where a sizable sum (several pounds or tens of pounds) had changed hands. References to bonds generally appear only in the wills of the most affluent seamen, those involved in shipowning or substantial forms of investment. This credit-based economy was thus conducted largely through informal arrangements, difficult and expensive to pursue through a court of law. This in itself constitutes firm evidence of a close-knit, self-regulating maritime community. The practice was indicative of the bonds of trust and camaraderie that existed among these men of the maritime community; the fact that it continued in operation indicated that these bonds held.

Even in cases where debts could not be paid on demand, it was important for debtors to reassure those to whom they were indebted that the loan would be repaid.[53] When William Chester, carpenter of the *Alcredo* of London, demanded the repayment of a debt that sailor John Norway of the *Margaret and John* owed him, Norway offered to pay the debt in Venetian currency. The two haggled over the exchange rate and could not reach an agreement. Norway entrusted Chester with a quantity of cloth in pawn until they met again and the debt could be paid. Similarly, one Smythe, who was probably a boatswain, owed Thomas Deale of Margate 8s. 6d. for meat and drink that he had consumed at a local inn or alehouse; Smythe promised him his silver whistle and chain until such time as he could repay his debt and redeem his whistle.

Seamen's ability to pay their debts was dependent not only upon their ability to secure employment but upon the successful completion of the voyage. In cases of shipwreck or damaged cargo, employers were not obliged to pay the crew.[54] Most seamen were not prepared financially for such an eventuality. Ship's carpenter Lionel Gardiner told the Admiralty Court that he was unsure if he would receive his wages from a voyage where the ship was cast away: "for that it is not a thinge vsed or questioned neyther did theye doubte but by gods grace to haue broughte backe the said shippe againe in good safetie." During a voyage in 1597, the crew of the *Charity* was held responsible for missing cargo, and eight shillings were deducted from every man's wages. Each man on the *Gift* was docked four months' pay in 1603 when the crew illegally seized a foreign ship without possessing the necessary letters of reprisal from the Admiralty. This practice extended to errant individuals who had caused damage to the ship or cargo; the gunner of the *Refuge* of London had his wages garnisheed because he accidentally dropped some of the ship's furniture overboard during the voyage.

Extensive work on the fragmentary records of Trinity House at Deptford has not uncovered any examples of crews being paid when the ship and cargo were lost;[55] instead, the Masters tried to ensure in these instances that the crews were given some compensation for their efforts.[56] For example, they ruled that the crew of the *Advantage* of London should have partial wages for the successful leg of their journey; the crew completed their voyage to Ireland, but their ship "miscarried" while en route to Bordeaux, France. Although the crew managed to save much of the ship's lading and furniture, the owner did not "afforde them any thinge of his goodwill for their paynes." Similarly, the Masters of the Trinity House ruled on a wage disagreement in December 1591 between the mariners and the owner of a ship that had been castaway:

we canott se any resone to the contrary but that the poore maryners shoolde have ther harborowe wages which was to them dewe be fore the shipe went out of the theames, acording to ancient order & custome tyme out of mynde And for any other wages we doe nott se howe thaye maye recover for that the shipe and al the goods was loste.

Although the foregoing examples indicate that there were disagreements between seamen and their employers over pay, relatively few such cases exist proportional to the large number of voyages that took place throughout the Elizabethan period.[57] In part, this is due to the destruction of the early records of the Trinity House at Deptford, which acted as an arbitrator, forestalling recourse to a devisive contest in a court of law. However, not all seamen elected to have their grievances heard at the Trinity House; some sought redress through the Crown and Admiralty officials. Many of those who hoped for recompense were not able or willing to launch a formal suit in the Admiralty Court but instead made use of petitions to draw attention to their grievances.[58] In 1592 the crew of the *Amity* of London, who described themselves as "being many verie pore men, vnable to go to Lawe herein," petitioned the lords of the Privy Council to order Admiralty judge Julius Caesar to examine the shipmaster and owners, whom they accused of defrauding them of their wages and shares. Sailor John Barnes also petitioned Caesar for the wages due him, "being vnable to wage lawe for the same otherwise your sup[plicant] is likelie to perish for want of money." It is obvious that even those seamen at the lower levels of the hierarchy of the maritime community were aware of established customs regarding the terms of their employment and the payment of their wages. Although seamen lacked a national wage scale and a national guild, the practices regarding the payment of wages were so well established that even those who could not afford to seek formal justice were ready to fight for their due under maritime custom. For the most part, however, Elizabethan seamen appear to have preferred negotiation and arbitration to divisive legal contests, which were costly in respect to money and harmony and rarely conducted on a level playing field. The first line of defense against perceived injuries was generally moral persuasion, as in the case of the early Elizabethan shipmaster Lawrence Rowndell, who on his deathbed wrote into his will that if his employers failed to pay his widow the wages due, then it would be "between God and their conscience who is a righteous judge."[59] Divine judgment, negotiation, and arbitration fitted into the traditional, custom-driven worldview of Elizabethan seamen; appeal to the law or authority was an avenue of last resort, exercised in the face of perceived lack of good faith.

On the whole, employer–employee relations seem to have been fairly harmonious. Tensions sometimes arose in situations where "gray areas" existed in seamen's wage scale, giving occasion for dispute and misunderstanding. Cases such as how much a man should be docked for misbehavior depended on the owners' or shipmasters' discretion, thus leaving the door open for controversy. It appears that the maritime community had a fairly elaborate set of established parameters and customs that governed wages and the payment of those wages; this helped to lessen the "gray areas" and minimized possible conflicts. The self-regulating system worked remarkably well as long as employers and employees lived up to their sides of the bargain. When shipowners or shipmasters tried (or were perceived as trying) to contravene these customs or shirk their responsibilities, seamen were eager to defend their "rights." As many historians have pointed out, early modern work culture was extremely durable, and workers were ready to protest when they believed that their livelihood or traditions were being compromised.[60] Thus, the relative absence of complaints speaks favorably of employer–employee relations. Nonetheless, we do see flashes of an "us versus them" mentality between seamen and their superiors. Throughout the late sixteenth century, we find examples of irate shipowners and naval and privateering captains who complained that they could not rule their men, that they could not stop seamen from running off with their impress money, that they had difficulty getting stragglers aboard, that they could not restrain them when there was plunder to be had. In other words, tensions habitually arose in situations where employers were at odds with, or tried to reform, seamen's work culture. Some were the temporary clashes of war, while others were the product of a far enlarged pool of labor and a rise in depersonalized relationships on larger vessels.

Seamen could mount resistance and be very unaccommodating when they chose to be, often in situations where they were pushed beyond their limits by profit-driven shipmasters and merchants or when their customs were not respected or their expectations met. Although there was frequently friction aboard dangerous voyages of exploration or prolonged trading voyages,[61] privateering voyages had a well-deserved reputation for being the most troubled. Contemporaries placed the blame on loose discipline, but this is only part of the explanation. Although the practice of privateering during time of war originated centuries earlier, privateering during the Elizabethan era began in earnest in 1585, and its customs were not as widely known as those in the peacetime sectors of the maritime community. Initially, there were many "gray areas" that the Crown tried to clarify through regulations and edicts during the course of the war years. Seamen sometimes had a very different idea of what constituted "good prize" than did Admiralty officials or the captains and masters who were bound by financial obligations to uphold the Crown's directives. Furthermore, privateering vessels were frequently captained by inexperienced landsmen, ignorant of seamen's traditions and expectations. These men were seen as outsiders. In such circumstances, seamen were predisposed to an "us versus them" stance. For the most part, however, seamen, like other preindustrial workers and their employers, recognized a high degree of interdependence; although tensions flared periodically in response to disruptions to their work culture or unmet expectations, they quickly subsided and did not constitute class struggle. As elsewhere, paternalism governed early modern labor relations, and most workers were comfortable with their place, knew their duties, and resented those who sought to impose new rules.[62]

PROFITS AND CUSTOMS OF PRIVATEERING

Despite the overcrowded shipboard conditions and the fact that they were not guaranteed any return for their efforts, Elizabethan seamen flocked to join the many privateering voyages that left English ports every year. Elizabethan and Jacobean naval commander William Monson remarked, "It is strange what misery such men will choose to endure in small ships of reprisal, though they be hopeless of gain."[63] Almost all privateering crews were paid only shares of the goods taken. As one participant told the Admiralty Court in 1589, men on privateering expeditions understood "that all such prizes as should be taken should be shared to every one proportionably according to their adventure" and that they "were not hired . . . to receave wages but wente for theire shares."[64] Only in cases where trading voyages were combined with privateering did seamen receive wages (in addition to their shares).[65] Generally, crews on privateering expeditions were allotted one-third of the value of the prizes taken. These shares were divided according to shipboard hierarchy; the captain normally received eight shares, the master seven shares, and so on down the ranks of the crew. Ordinary seamen usually received a share or two.[66] In cases where seamen were maimed, and their livelihoods were affected, the crew might vote extra shares to those men.[67]

Often seamen had the option to dispose of their prize goods themselves or to sell their shares to the owners, victuallers, or officers for a set price per share.[68] This decision was naturally based on individual circumstances; each seaman had to decide which course of action would produce the greatest benefit. It was usually easier to sell one's shares on shipboard than to try to dispose of goods such as unrefined sugar or hides.

Given the uncertainties involved in serving on privateers, why did seamen seek employment on these voyages? While an unsuccessful voyage could spell disaster for married seamen, bachelor seamen were in a better position to weather the storm; shipboard living meant that, at the very least, seamen were provided with free accommodations and food for the duration of the voyage. Although the risks (to one's health and of coming home empty-handed) were greater aboard privateering vessels than on merchant voyages, individual seamen appear to have sought employment on these expeditions to maximize earning potential and because privateering crews were not hampered by strict discipline.

The looser discipline of privateering expeditions did not mean that seamen were devoid of responsibilities; as on merchant voyages, seamen working on privateering ships were liable for the safe conduct of the ship and any goods on board. If confiscated goods or the ship's lading were damaged, charges were deducted from the crew's shares. Despite his many risks, the seaman on a privateering voyage could be assured of one important consideration: he would have a say in conducting the expedition. Any change in the destination or duration of the voyage could affect seamen dramatically in terms of their health and livelihoods. Thus, commanders were required by maritime custom to consult the crew on all matters of import.[69] One example of the importance assigned to consultation involved decisions to sail in consort with other privateers. Some seamen were hired to serve aboard a vessel that was part of a privateering fleet. By entering into an employment contract with the owners, backers, or commanders, seamen were aware of and therefore consenting to a consort agreement. However, English privateers often encountered other privateers while at sea. Since cooperation between such vessels offered obvious advantages, captains and masters were inclined to form partnerships with those privateers combing the same area. In these cases, the crew had the final say whether to consort. Maritime custom dictated that seamen could vote on matters that affected their livelihoods and altered the terms of their verbal employment contracts. The decision to consort was a risk; while extra ships and manpower might reap greater rewards, there was also the danger that the association would not be profitable. In situations where consort ships took little at sea, the resolution to divide prizes "ton for ton and man for man" would decrease each seaman's overall take.

Part of the lure of privateering expeditions was the seamen's customary right of "pillage," in addition to any shares in the adventure.[70] This was a valued perquisite; Captain Nathaniel Boteler claimed, "As for the business of pillage, there is nothing that more bewitcheth them, nor anything wherein they promise to themselves so loudly nor delight in more mainly." Pillage consisted of goods and valuables below the value of 40 shillings that did not belong to the cargo proper. Custom decreed that items above the value of 40 shillings were to be brought to the mainmast and divided according to rank. Custom also dictated that the captain of the victorious vessel was allowed to confiscate the best piece of ordnance, the master took the best anchor and cable, and the boatswain was granted the main topsail.

Specific rules determined by maritime custom and Admiralty decree regulated plunder and pillaging. However, these regulations were frequently ignored by seamen.[71] Lord Admiral Howard and his Admiralty officials were well aware by 1590 of the "manifeste violating and abvse of theire [the privateers'] said Reprisalls"; a decade later the Lord Admiral complained that he was besieged daily with complaints of disorders stemming from letters of marque and that English privateers subdued both enemy and allied ships "in felonious and piraticall sorte." In the heat of confiscating a prize, the Admiralty's regulations and commanders' orders often gave way to "the fury & madness of insolente and lawles people." For instance, when English privateers captured the extremely lucrative *Madre de Dios* in 1592, the ship was accidentally set on fire "by the disorder of the men with candles in their rifling." While there might have been some ignorance concerning regulations, most seamen were well aware of the Admiralty's directives outlining what ships and goods constituted legal prize and the extent of pillage. The case of the *David* of London is an apt illustration. When the men of the *David* captured the *St. John the Baptist* in 1597, the English seamen boarded the prize "In greate hast & layde handes on the money, & were soe vnrewly that the Master could not beare sway amongst them, and . . . every one gott what he could lay handes on." Despite this, George Wright, a servant of one of the London merchants who had invested in the voyage, testified that he and his colleagues on the *David*

were not soe simple but well knew, that if they offered the Florentynes eany wronge, there [voyage] would be overthrowen & restitution must be made by them or the merchantes.

Even those in positions of authority were not above such actions. William Green, the master of the *David*,

delvered vpp much money to the merchantes & swore vnto them he had noe more wishing he mighte never see [his] wiffe & children if he had eany more, But afterwardes beinge disquieted aboute the same he brought out vij or viij hundreth dollers & delivered them to the merchantes.

In their zeal to wring an admission from captured seamen that their ships contained contraband Spanish goods, English seamen used some questionable methods to illicit confessions. Torture was commonly alleged.[72] One English crew forced a French seaman to confess that the goods on his ships belonged to Spaniards "by reason of a matche put betwene his bare toes and sett on fiere." The same crew tied up another Frenchman, "and some of the company begone to payre the nayles of his toyes." Such tactics almost always solicited the correct response. English seamen routinely stripped captured seamen and merchants of their valuables and clothing and treated them harshly. When the *Hopewell* of Dublin was spoiled by English privateers in the late 1590s, one Irishman aboard the *Hopewell* reported that he was "greatly misvsed & beete"; the privateers demanded "of him his clothes, & because this examinante had a smale ringe on his finger, he [an English seaman] drewe his dagger & sware he would cutt of [f] his finger if he pulled not of his ringe & gave yt [to] him." A Portuguese man whose ship was captured by English privateers of the *Primrose* voiced a widespread complaint: "the company of the shipp vsed them selves rather like brute beastes then men."

Given the fact that similar protests flooded the Admiralty Court during the war years, it is not surprising that much of Lord Admiral Howard's correspondence to Judge Caesar during this period referred to such abuses and the necessity for "some further stricte and sever courses helde with suche offendors."[73] In a letter of 1592, the Lord Admiral wrote to Caesar concerning the need for "spedy reformatione" of the disorders that resulted from the mariners' "mutynous cariadge and embeselinge of suche goodes as they take by virtue of comissiones of reprisall to the defrawdinge of the owners of the ships" and the backers.

Although the Admiralty tried to inhibit such abuses, its attempts were largely ineffective. Written privateering commissions warned commanders not to

break bulke wast spoyle sell or diminishe any such shipps goodes money & merchandizes vntill they shalbe adiudged in her Majesties high Courte of the Admiralty to be lawfull prize.[74]

As a condition of granting letters of reprisal, the Admiralty required captains to post a bond to ensure that bulk would not be broken while at sea. Despite strict prohibitions to the contrary, crews often distributed prize goods while at sea or sold them in foreign ports. In 1589 Howard complained that many English privateers were taking their prizes into Ireland to be sold, which defrauded the Queen and himself of their dues.[75] Howard had Judge Julius Caesar insert a clause in all commissions

to inhibite them [privateers] from comonge either in the Streightes [of Gibraltar] or barbarie, or for sellinge anye of the goodes taken by them in anye other place then onelie within this realme of England.[76]

Despite directives that all goods were to be inventoried and judged by the Admiralty Court, embezzling aboard privateers was, and remained, endemic.[77] The end result was that the Queen was frequently deprived of her customs duties and the Lord Admiral his tenth. Howard was keenly aware of this problem: "the Queene, and myselfe [are] deceaved of suche dueties, as of right belonge vnto us." Howard wrote to the mayor of Plymouth in 1591 that "many tymes bullaine, pearles and many other goodes of great valewe are secretly both by day & night conveyed ashore" by seamen. Given the confusion that reigned during boarding and the difficulty of monitoring privateering crews and their practices, there was a degree of tacit acceptance; when Sir Richard Leveson captured a Spanish carrack off the Spanish coast in 1602, the Crown stated that "we doubte not but that there is and wilbe much embesyllinge." In September 1592 the Lord Admiral's frustration is evident in his correspondence:"dayly experience sheweth that theise abvses and outradges are rather continued & increased then eany thinge diminished and amended."

Many ship's officers and port authorities tried to adhere to the Admiralty's regulations; searching vessels for embezzled goods was routine.[78] Seamen, however, were willing to go to almost any lengths to augment their incomes. Sailor Isaac Backler of the *David* of London testified that he had hidden a bag full of money from the prize in his breeches. Although this money was later discovered by the ship's officers, he successfully managed to hide another stash. Some of Backler's crewmates hid $300 or $400 in the ballast. In another case, mariner Thomas Pinchbacke of the *Affection* of London testified that he and his crewmates had taken a Spanish prize in 1594 carrying hides, sugar, and ginger. Pinchbacke admitted that

he had gotten togeather aboute fifty poundes of ginger which Master Wattes seazed . . . at his oastes house & more he had not savinge a cappe full of ginger which he sould for ijs viij d or iijs.

Pinchbacke went on to accuse his crewmates of similar activities: "[S]ondry others of the companye workinge vnder houlde gott a pounde or two of ginger at tymes whiche they caried away in theire breeches." Following the capture of a Portuguese vessel in 1590, the men of the *Elizabeth* of London embezzled some of the goods off the prize and smuggled them ashore in the nighttime. The goods that remained were taken ashore and placed in the Customs House in Cornwall for inspection by the Admiralty.

Although most seamen were probably aware of the Admiralty's regulations, crews resented any intrusion into what they regarded as their right to reap the fruits of their labor. Gentleman Jaspar Norris told the Admiralty Court that he and his father, the captain, lost control of their crew when the men spotted and subdued a Scottish ship that was returning from Spain. The Norrises tried to keep the goods together "until it was affirmed they were good prize." However, "the mariners were soe vnruly that they would haue the goodes shared, and shared them against the will of this examinantes father & this examinante [Norris]." Norris testified that he objected to distributing the goods at sea "& would haue had yt restored," but "he was like to haue byn slayne amongst them for vrginge to haue yt restored."[79] Even in cases where seamen adhered to the Admiralty's regulations, they still felt that they were entitled to compensation for their voyage. Although mariner William Sterling complained before the Admiralty Court about his crewmates' conduct in regard to the capture of a French ship in 1590, he had no compunction about taking three pounds' worth of powder from his own ship as indirect recompense for his labor.[80]

Seamen were ready to defend their interests not only in regard to the Admiralty and their commanders but also in the circumstances where other English seamen tried to infringe upon their claims.[81] In situations where competing English ships subdued a common prize, crews were ready to resort to violence to defend their own interests. When the seamen of two separate English privateering expeditions laid claim to the same prizes in 1602, "there was greate emnity amongst them." Tobias Cox, the captain of the *Diamond*, maintained that his company subdued three ships when other English privateers happened along and laid claim to the captured vessels. Tempers flared on both sides:

> the mariners of the Refusall & her pinnace & this [respondents'] mariners were readye to goe togeather by the eares with them of the Lions Claw, the Channce & the Triall for theire comminge on borde and clayming of parte of the goodes which they had not to doe with all.

English privateering crews that had not agreed to consort together were rivals, and crews could be fiercely territorial. Crewmates closed ranks to protect their interests from other seamen in the same way that they protected their interests from "outsiders."

Seamen were considered ready to protect their interests and earnings (however they came by them) in the face of any threat. Admiralty officials believed that most seamen would risk their souls through perjury to guard their booty. In 1592, following the capture of one of the most lucrative prizes of the war years, the *Madre de Dios*, Admiralty officials recognized the futility of trying to recover embezzled goods from the seamen: "we hold it loste labor and offence to God to minister oathes unto the generallitie of them."[82] Since administration of oaths was the universal method of securing reliable evidence in all civil and ecclesiastical courts, this admission of defeat is strong evidence of the perceived existence of a maritime subculture that would close ranks to protect its own.

Greed is only a partial explanation for the abuses that took place aboard English privateering vessels. Seamen were also motivated by a sense that they should be compensated for their labor and for risking their lives to capture enemy vessels. In part, desperation fueled frantic pillaging and embezzling; in the words of the Lord Admiral, "people in want are disposed to be mutinous."[83] Most of the men who were employed on these voyages were on, or uncomfortably close to, the edge of subsistence and trying to obtain some measure of financial reward. It is not coincidental that the tide of maritime violence reached its peak in the 1590s, when population pressure on land was likewise peaking.[84] The essence of privateering was risk. Sometimes the gamble paid off, and seamen could return home with a handsome return for their labor. However, an unsuccessful voyage could spell disaster for seamen; few could afford the financial setback that resulted from the Admiralty Court's decision that confiscated items were "not good prize" or when an expedition returned home empty-handed. One seaman was understandably bitter when the Admiralty Court questioned the legality of certain prizes that his crew had captured:

> he was wounded & maimed by a shott that came from the Eagle & that is all the good that he hath gotten as yet by the shipp For he was not eany partner in the pilladginge & the goodes are not as yet devided, nor his shares allowed him.[85]

Furthermore, the explanation for the continuing state of affairs in the face of the Admiralty's regulations and attempts to impose these regulations lies in the evidence that ships at sea were basically independent jurisdictions. The Admiralty's punitive power seemed remote to men far from home and determined to obtain maximum profit for their adventures. Given the tradition of consulting that empowered even the ordinary seaman, the temptation of quick riches, the fact that commanders of privateering expeditions lacked the authority to resort to martial law (which naval commanders had access to), and the well-established practice of collecting perquisites by pre-industrial laborers, we can appreciate why contemporaries believed discipline to be almost absent from privateering expeditions.

The reality of privateering expeditions was that seamen on successful voyages would profit from their time at sea, but rarely did they strike it rich. In general, a seaman might hope to receive somewhere between four or five pounds for a single share of a successful privateering adventure.[86] One might well wonder if this was adequate compensation for men who habitually risked their lives in battle and boarding. With a few exceptions, the promise of sudden wealth from privateering was an illusion. The fortunate few who did better their station in life from letters of reprisal kept the hope alive. An occasional seaman "came home . . . from the sea with his dusblett [sic] quilted full of goulde."[87] The gap between expectation and disappointing results understandably fueled frustration and lawless behavior. Some cautious tradesmen who were hired to go on privateering voyages did not elect to have shares as did the seamen aboard. Robert Harwin, ship's carpenter of the *Refuge*, "chose rather to haue wages, then to hazarde his viadge vppon taking of prizes."[88] This illuminates the attitudinal gulf that separated Elizabethan seamen from landsmen.

Privateering reveals much about seamen's subculture. Seamen had definite ideas about their entitlements, which, obviously, were divergent from the Admiralty's regulations. As the Lord Admiral's correspondence and the depositions of the High Court of the Admiralty demonstrate, these divergent codes and expectations often clashed. In these situations, seamen closed ranks to protect their own from the intrusion of "outsiders." "Protectionist strategies" were not unique to seamen, but this tendency to close ranks does seem to be more developed among workers who were isolated from the larger society.[89] The Crown, shipowners, and ship's captains sought to purge seamen's work culture of its less desirable elements and to impose their own regulations on seamen, but the persistence of complaints about abuses and embezzling at sea suggests that their efforts were largely ineffectual.

NAVAL WAGES AND LABOR RELATIONS

The Crown enjoyed the right to compel seamen to serve in the navy during times of national emergency. Because the navy did not distinguish between volunteers and conscripts in regard to treatment or pay, and naval duty was very unpopular, it is not surprising that the Elizabethan navy consisted largely of impressed seamen. Short of desertion or mutiny, naval employment offered virtually no freedom for seamen. While the Crown was obliged to compensate the men of the maritime community for their ships and labor, as an employer, the Crown did not allow seamen to negotiate the terms of their employment. Given the tens of thousands of men who served in the navy during the war years, there was little room to take into account such factors as each seaman's reputation or skill to settle on the terms of his employment. Because of its medieval right to coerce men to serve, the Crown was not obliged to take into consideration such factors as the dangers that would be incurred in a naval expedition or the duration or destination of the voyage. The right of impressment guaranteed that the Crown did not have to make naval service alluring to seamen or compete for their services on a "free market." Therefore, naval duty negated seamen's customary freedoms in regard to negotiating the terms of their own employment.

For the most part, each seaman was paid monthly according to his rating. Prior to 1582, seamen were, in theory, given the same rate of pay. Officers were then accorded additional sums called "dead shares" proportional to their ratings. After 1582 the method of naval payment was altered; ordinary seamen and officers were given a fixed rate per month according to their position. Some monetary concessions were made to masters and pilots who commanded larger ships, thereby compensating each man "according to the greatness of his charge." One account from the early years of Elizabeth's reign shows a wide divergence in naval pay for masters; a master of the largest naval vessels was paid 40s. per month, a master of a lesser ship received 31s. 8d., and a master of the smallest type of vessel was accorded 16s. 8d. for his services.[90] Thus, efforts were made to compensate the most skilled seamen who commanded large vessels and hundreds of men. Nevertheless, the navy's wages were in no way comparable to the "going rate" in other types of maritime employment.[91] Raleigh claimed that seamen disliked naval service because "they stand in feare of penurie and hunger." These fears were not unfounded. Naval seamen were not well compensated. Officers, for instance, could earn in wages alone anywhere from 30 to 100 percent more in civilian service. An ordinary seaman could also expect to earn much higher wages on a merchant ship. The minimum wage aboard the *White Lion* of London on its voyage to Ayamonte in 1596 was 19 shillings per month, almost twice that of naval wages. Moreover, naval harbor wages were substantially less than the monthly rates that seamen received while at sea.[92] Naval expeditions were notoriously slow in preparing for sea, and the government preferred wherever possible to keep ships in harbor to minimum expenses. In an era when wages were not keeping up with inflation, and, in all likelihood, standards of living were deteriorating on land, it was especially important that seamen maximize their income.[93] Small wonder seafarers served their Queen with "great grudging."

There were some formal attempts to offer seamen a more competitive wage. In hopes of luring the "better sort" of seaman to the Queen's service, Sir John Hawkins used his influence with the Crown and within the naval bureaucracy to enact change. By lobbying the Crown and reducing the manning rate of naval ships, John Hawkins succeeded in raising the basic wage of naval seamen from 6s. 8d. per month to 10s. per month in 1585. Although the Crown wanted a higher caliber of seaman, it was not willing to pay the price; seamen were granted a pay raise because Hawkins's reforms reduced manning rates, thereby guaranteeing that there would be fewer men aboard each ship. Hence, this pay raise did not cost the Crown anything. Ultimately, this pay increase failed to attract a higher caliber of seaman, for naval wages still lagged well behind those of other maritime sectors.[94]

In addition to the deterrent of low wages, the Queen's service had none of the other incentives of non-naval maritime employment. Unlike privateering, naval voyages did not offer crews the hope of maximizing their earning potential by capturing lucrative prizes. Only in a handful of instances did the Crown grant rewards for seamen who distinguished themselves. In 1587 one month's extra pay was given to the crews of three pinnaces that had captured Spanish prizes. In 1588 100 men who manned the fireships that broke up the Armada's tight formation were given five pounds to be divided among them.[95] These insignificant and infrequent rewards do not compare to the anticipated profits of successful privateering. Furthermore, naval service almost never offered seamen a voice in the destination or duration of their voyage. Naval expeditions did not proffer seamen the opportunity to trade commodities to enhance their basic wage. In addition, naval wages were rarely paid as regularly as on merchant ships. Seamen employed on merchant ships were accustomed to prompt payment of their wages. When wages were withheld in civilian sectors of the maritime community, crews complained loudly. In 1583 the men of the *Mary Anne* of London protested that three or four days had elapsed since the end of their journey, and they had not been paid; they were said to be destitute since in London and in limbo, as they could not seek new employment.[96] In comparison, payments to naval seamen were frequently months in arrears, without redress. Next to their victuals, naval seamen's wages were their largest source of discontent.

Complaints of nonpayment or delayed payment of naval wages were numerous and continuous throughout the war. Sometimes wages were deliberately held back to discourage the men from "slynking away."[97] Dishonest officers and naval officials conspired to profit at seamen's expense. Captains and pursers in particular were rumored to have pocketed some of the money earmarked for the crews. Unquestionably, the problem went much deeper. The limited bureaucracy of the Navy Board, which had been established for the upkeep of royal ships and dockyards in the reign of Henry VIII, was also responsible for paying those employed by the navy. No one disputes that the Navy Board fell far behind in its payment of wages time and time again during the war. However, historians are divided as to the source of the problem. Most authorities blame Queen Elizabeth's notorious stinginess.[98] Certainly, the Queen's parsimony is well documented. However, there is also evidence to support the less-favored opinion: that the limited government bureaucracy simply buckled under the strain of the unprecedented demands of the war years.[99] Low wages and slow payment of those wages were only a symptom of the larger problem, that the demands of the war had taken seamen out of their natural environment. These men were trained for small-scale maritime commercial employment, where opportunity existed for each man's voice to be heard. Instead, the needs of the wartime state drew these men forcibly into the large machine that was the Elizabethan navy.

Many conscientious naval officers and officials were moved by the financial plight of the men.[100] In July 1588 commanders begged the Crown to pay its seamen. Hawkins also reported that the men had been long unpaid and needed relief. The unrest that resulted from unpaid wages threatened to disrupt the war effort in that all-important summer of 1588. Lord Henry Seymour, who commanded a squadron in the Narrow Seas, admonished Secretary of State Walsingham to assist England's naval commanders:

You shall do very well to help us with a pay for our men, who are almost 16 weeks unpaid; for what with fair and foul means, I have enough to do to keep them from mutiny.

William Borough, expert navigator and commander of the *Bonavolia* in 1588, wrote to Walsingham that one shipmaster had heard the seamen "use speeches that they would have their pay ere they went to the seas; but I hope they will not stick upon it now." Without a doubt, the nonpayment of wages was a major grievance.

In such circumstances seamen clung to established maritime practices. Unlike other employers, naval seamen could not take the Crown to court or seek arbitration at a Trinity House for nonpayment of wages. Seamen had little recourse but to petition the Crown for payment of the moneys due them. In 1586 the men who had served Sir Francis Drake on a quasi-official voyage complained to the Crown:

whereas divers of the souldiers and mariners make complaints against Sir Francis Draque for default of paiement in respect of their service, forasmuch as there were Commissioners appointed to heare their complaintes . . . wherein Sir Frauncis

Draque maie likewise be harde, causing present paiement to be made of so moch
as shall be due unto every of them.[101]

   While most seamen sought peaceful resolution to their complaints by
seeking redress through their commanders or directly from the Lord Admiral or Privy Council, they were capable of more threatening forms of
protest to obtain their overdue wages from the Crown. Commander John
Norris warned Walsingham in April 1589 that infinite spoils would be
committed upon the country if the men of the Portugal expedition were
discharged without their wages.[102] We cannot be certain that Norris believed in the reality of infinite looting; perhaps he thought that an argument
premised upon the need for order would carry more weight with the council
than one focused upon the moral obligations of paternalism. In any case,
the Crown did not heed Norris's warning, and the men were still unpaid
in early July 1589. The Privy Council, however, did acknowledge the need
to pay the demobilized seamen and soldiers "if not to their full satisfaction
yet in some convenient proportion till further order might be taken."[103]
Presumably, no such action was taken, and by the end of the month the
impatient seamen and soldiers had grown unruly. The Privy Council wrote
to the Lord Mayor of London,

Praying him that, whereas he had taken order and appeased in time the disorderly
proceeding of certain mariners and other lewd fellows that did yesterday gather
together in a mutinous sort at the Royal Exchange, to take order likewise if any of
them should persist in any such tumultuous sort, that they might be apprehended
and to be laid by the heels. And in the mean season that they might be willed to
repair unto the town clerk and there to deliver up their names, with the time of
their service, by whom they were imprested, under whom and in what ship they
served, and what they had already received, and what they claim to be due unto
them, to the end that . . . [they] repair hither of Sir Francis Drake . . . [and] the same
might be examined.[104]

Although the Crown found such demonstrations a threat to the maintenance of order, seamen's actions were typical of early modern protesters.[105]
Because petitions were ignored, seamen took matters into their own hands.
In such circumstances seamen were quite capable of banding together temporarily to achieve limited goals.
   While Elizabeth's Privy Councillors did not welcome seamen's demonstrations, their readiness to look into seamen's grievances indicates that
they recognized an obligation to protect and assist. The Crown's treatment
of its seamen had been contrary to maritime custom and the spirit of the
moral economy. The Crown understood its responsibilities and recognized
the need to act in this situation; the survival of the deferential society was
based upon paternalistic response. It was clear that seamen were entitled
to their earnings from the Crown. However, seamen's traditions and ac-

tions were not always above reproach. Our examination of piracy, desertion, and mutiny has revealed that seamen's established practices were
sometimes considered illegal by the Crown. Many seamen serving in the
navy, for example, believed that they were owed not only a "living wage"
but the benefits and perquisites that they had come to expect from other
types of maritime employment. No doubt many knew that embezzling was
illegal, yet seamen were eager to secure sufficient rewards for their efforts.
Unpaid and underpaid seamen frequently misappropriated items from their
ships.[106] In 1590 the boatswain of the Queen's ship the *Bonaventure* admitted that he had stolen £8 worth of silk from a prize "thinkinge to enioy
the same for his share having longe served in her Majesties shippe." The
use of "share" is telling evidence of his private-enterprise mind-set. When
a group of seamen were brought before the Admiralty Court because they
had stolen gunpowder off the Queen's ship, seaman Stephen Dingley defended his thievery because the Queen "was in his debte for the portiugall
viadge." Crews reportedly embezzled £1,000 worth of powder on Drake
and Hawkins's 1595 voyage alone. When a Dutch seaman was captured
by one of the Queen's warships, he made the mistake of chastising his
English captors for embezzling. He

sawe some of them [the English seamen] begin to share the merchantes money, and
sayd vnto them, what doe you meane to share in this sorte, yf yt be prize as you
imagyn, yt ys the Queenes, and you haue your wages, and what doe you meane to
make such sharinge & spoile wherevppon the englishmen misvsed this examinante
callinge him theife & villaine & gave him bloes also, and havinge a longe bearde
they haled & pulled him soe mirciously sondry tymes by the same that this examinante was forced to cutt yt of[f].

Whatever seamen's motives or justifications for their actions, it can be
stated that shipboard environments contained their dishonest elements.
Theft was a crime that was severely punished, as it destroyed bonds of
shipboard unity.[107] Despite the threat of punishment and crewmates' censure, chaplain Richard Madox wrote of his 1582 voyage that "God in his
wrath permitted that we should be daily afflicted with the private crime of
thieves."[108] This thievery consisted mainly of seamen's stealing from the
ship's cargo or helping themselves to additional provisions. Although there
are a few examples in the Admiralty Court depositions of seamen's stealing
from their crewmates, they seemed more inclined to pilfer the ship's lading,
supplies, or furniture than steal from their fellows. Many seamen believed
(or convinced themselves) that they were merely taking what was due them
for their labors. It is safe to say, however, that peculation was especially
rife aboard naval ships, where seamen were especially dissatisfied with their
compensation and usually served under compulsion. Since the majority
lived close to subsistence, and uncertainty characterized their lives ashore

and afloat, seamen tried to augment their earnings whenever opportunities presented themselves. Yet intertwined with the obvious elements of avarice and desperation, we can also sense another factor at work: seamen's sense of entitlement to fair compensation for their labor.

SEAMEN'S BELIEFS AND THE PRACTICE OF SHIPBOARD RELIGION

We have seen that the Crown was quick to castigate seamen as embezzlers and liars. Were these men rogues as their superiors thought? What was the nature of seamen's belief system? Were they loyal Protestants, as their Queen hoped? We now turn to an examination of seamen's belief system and explore the nature of their faith and how it was manifested.

Catholic foreigners were quick to declare that English seamen were heretics and "Lutheranos." Even before the outbreak of the war, Englishmen in Lisbon in the 1570s were "reviled and termed lutherianes dogges slaves and suche vyle termes."[109] It is quite apparent that the Spaniards believed Englishmen to be firm Protestants, and English seamen abroad proudly proclaimed that they considered themselves such. In the 1560s the apprehended 25-year-old John Frampton attempted to say the Ave Maria for the Inquisitors but left out significant portions. Furthermore, he gave his captors detailed descriptions of the religious beliefs propagated by the Church of England. Frampton gave a clear espousal of Protestant doctrine; he denied the existence of purgatory and claimed that the Pope, confession, mass, and holy water were not necessary for salvation.[110] In 1568 Portuguese sailor Miguel Ribeiro observed the religious practices of shipmaster Robert Barrett and his English crew firsthand. In 1570 he testified against Barrett before the Inquisition:

I had the opportunity of eating and drinking with him. I noticed that he did not cross himself and ask for a blessing on the table, either when he sat down to eat or when he got up; all he did being to cross his hands over his breast and look up to heaven when seating himself. . . . Every day when I was there, Barrett and those who accompanied him brought out a rush basket filled with books which they put down upon the deck of the ship, and everyone took his copy, Barrett with the rest, and they sat down in two rows and began to sing, each one with the open book in his hand. Happening to take up one of these books, I saw some of the Psalms of David therein. . . . And so they would sing for half an hour or so . . . and the English pilot would shout something which I did not understand, and the others would respond just as when we respond "Amen."[111]

During one of Sir Francis Drake's attacks on the Spanish Main in the mid-1580s, the indigenous inhabitants heard rumors of the coming of non-Spanish people who "heard no mass and went not to confession, nor had amongst them priests or friars."[112] From Inquisition accounts, Elizabethan seamen emerge as Protestants with a firm grasp of the essence of their faith. Boatswain Andrew Acton of the *Rose Lion* of London expressed a commonly held view: "he is a protestante by profession as all his cuntrey men are or should be."[113]

Material evidence offers proof of the Protestantism of the late Elizabethan maritime community.[114] While the Armada seamen and the Anglo-Catholic seamen of the *Mary Rose* carried religious medals and rosaries, one was more likely to find religious tracts aboard Elizabethan vessels. The Inquisition frequently made search of English ships for heretical materials, including prayer books and Protestant devotional literature. Because seamen usually conducted their own religious services, as in the aforementioned 1568 incident, shipmasters or other officers had religious literature to assist them. In his will of 1565, Lawrence Rowndall, the shipmaster of the *John Baptist*, made a bequest of his service book and his paraphrase of the four Gospels; presumably, Rowndall used these books to conduct shipboard service. While it was not uncommon for seamen to bequeath religious literature to their friends and family in their wills, they do not mention rosaries or religious medals, nor do they request prayers for the health of their souls.

In addition, actions testify to seamen's Protestant beliefs.[115] When Drake and his men were laying siege to the Spanish Main in 1585–86, they showed the inhabitants the "bestial fury of heretics" by robbing Catholic churches, destroying numerous religious images, and even allegedly hanging two elderly monks. In the mid-1580s three seamen of the *Thomasin* went ashore in St. Lucas for fresh water,

and as they were fillinge the same, certayne preistes and Friars with other lay people passed by with the sacramente, and because two of the said mariners did not knele downe and use reverence, they were caried presentlye to the holy house and are condempned to deathe.

In this instance, shipmaster Patrick Johnson was required to post a bond of 1,000 ducats to ensure that the *Thomasin* would not depart until he had received permission from the Inquisition. The master was well aware that his company was Protestant; Johnson gave the order to set sail, "fearinge leste his two mariners ymprisoned mighte confesse some matter to endaunger the saide shippe." In a similar incident, the crew of the *Emmanuel* was arrested in Spain in 1584 and condemned to death; the ship's carpenter had not removed his hat when a procession of the Blessed Sacrament passed by. These recorded clashes indicate a reluctance on the part of common seamen to temporize or blend into the background while in Catholic ports.

Ample evidence in seamen's wills demonstrates their devotion to the Protestant faith. The custom of leaving money to the church and the poor

remained popular, as elsewhere in Tudor society,[116] but there were no instructions for the beneficiaries to pray for the testator's repose.[117] Some
seamen chose the very Protestant option of paying a preacher or minister
to give a sermon.[118] In 1601 sailor Alexander Eylmer willed "that at the
day of my Funerall when the people shall be, or are gathered togeather,
that some learned man shall make vnto them a sermon, to the edifienge of
those that shall be there presente." Eylmer left 10 shillings for this purpose.
Furthermore, he stipulated that the unpaid wages from his last voyage were
to procure "some learned devine" to give sermons in two other parishes.[119]
Seaman William Rafe bequeathed 10 shillings to Master Duffield, vicar of
Stepney, "beseechinge him therefore to preache a sermon at my buryall."[120]
In addition to the edification of the living through sermons, some seamen
were concerned with the training of Protestant clergymen.[121] Mariner William Feres left the significant sum of £5 to his partner's son on the condition
that "he studie divinitie and not folowe the lawe." In 1575 mariner John
Benn left money for four sermons and £2 10s. for one or more poor scholars seeking education in "godlie studyes." All aforementioned examples are
drawn from the wills of the ship officers; as members of the maritime elite,
they were likely to possess disposable income at the times of their deaths,
possessed higher levels of literacy,[122] and could have viewed themselves as
examples of moral leadership and devotion within their community. Although each side in the sixteenth-century religious divide concentrated on
the differences that separated them rather than their common customs and
experiences, the Reformation did not alter that, as a group, seamen were
convinced that their existence was subject to God's will. Seamen's last testaments provide ample evidence that they believed that Providence directed
their lives. Although the language is probably formulaic,[123] there is no reason to doubt that the sentiment was genuine.[124] Seaman John Iveson wrote
his will in 1600 because

[I] am bound forth by the permission of god . . . in the good shipp called the red
dragon of London on a voyage to the East Indians And whether I shall liue and
returne home againe of the same voyage or not is in the handes of the Lord.

Mariner James Penne also surrendered himself to God's plan; he was bound
for the sea "and not knowinge how soone it will please god to call me
consideringe the Frailtie and instabilitie of mans lyfe." Sailor Henry Barret
was "bounde to the new founde landes (god willinge) and because our
affaires are daungerous I am mynded to set downe my minde in wrytinge
towching such wordlie goods as god hath lent me." This belief system was
reinforced by shipboard worship. Luke Foxe's orders for a voyage undertaken in 1631, for instance, recommended that at twice-daily prayers the
crew should commit

our selves, both Soules and bodies, ship and goods, to Gods mercifull preservation, wee beseech him to steere, direct, and guide us, from the beginning to the end of our Voyage.

Life and death were controlled by God, as were sickness and health.[125] When he wrote his will, mariner James Woodcot was "in perfect health thanks be to god." Woodcot, however, was in the minority; most of those who wrote wills did so because of illness. Mariner William Roger was typical in that he stated the reason for writing his will was that he had been "vicited with goddes handes." While much of this language was based upon a predetermined model, the same sentiment is present in the Admiralty Court depositions where seamen's voices are heard more distinctly and with less coaching. Following his death at sea, Richard Clerk's shipmates testified that he had died from natural causes, for Clerk told them that "god hath layde his visitation vppon him, and that he was contented." Clerk's acceptance may be seen in the context of making a "good death," which was so important in the early modern period.[126] Expressions such as "God's will" and "God's grace" were ubiquitous in contemporary idiom; the language undoubtedly reflected the faith of the age.

As an indication of their belief in Providence, seamen were ready to credit their safety and their hardships to the will of God.[127] When the men of the *Tiger* managed to get their leaky ship back to England in 1591, the master, William Ingatt, proclaimed that it "was the worcke of god." Mariner John Hoames of the *Little Mary Marten* readily credited the Almighty for the temperate weather that allowed his crew to get to land: "by godes greate goodnes happeninge fayre weather, theye at laste recovered the shore." His crewmate Edward Williams supported Hoames's assessment: "had not godes marcyes byn the greater," they would not have gotten ashore. As historian J. R. Hale has pointed out, almost every account of seamen's voyages contains a tale of peril that could not have been overcome without God's assistance.[128]

While Providence governed men's lives, prayer was a powerful means of influencing the outcome. Given the many hazards of seafaring, seamen were often in situations where they resorted to collective petitioning. There are numerous examples of crews' engaging in group prayer during times of distress.[129] When Drake's ship *Golden Hind* hit a rock in 1580, the company prayed for deliverance *before* manning the pumps. Similarly, when the *Falcon* encountered a storm on the return voyage from Portugal, the crew "comittyd them selves to god, bequeathed [that] . . . the powre of god shoulde deliver them . . . and labored at the pumpe." When John Hawkins's ship sprang a serious leak during a storm, he announced that they "were but dead menne." Not one of his crew "could refrain his eyes from tears." Hawkins then "began to enter in prayer, and besought them to pray with him, the while indeed he yet letted not with great travail to search the ship fore and aft for leakes." In 1593 the men of the *Toby*, wrecked on a storm-tossed Barbary coast, "committed our selves unto the Lord and beganne with dolefull tune and heavy hearts to sing the 12 Psalme. Helpe Lord for good and godly men." While crews realized the necessity of using human ingenuity to overcome dangerous situations, they were quick to ask for divine assistance. Given the inevitable "togetherness" that resulted from shipboard living, the bond created by shared experiences, and the common goal of each crew, seamen prayed as a group and petitioned God with a united voice. Elizabethan seamen would have been the first to reject any place for atheists or agnostics aboard their vessels.

While it is difficult to gauge accurately the depth of English seamen's spirituality, we do know that regular worship was a facet of the shipboard environment in all sectors of the maritime community. For their part, the Crown and shipowners concurred that it was a "necesitie that such . . . companie[s] . . . be exercised in Religion."[130] Surviving shipboard orders from all sectors of the maritime community show the importance placed on worship afloat. Religion was vital for the health of each man's soul as well as for morale and discipline.[131] There was little need to stress such practices; shipboard worship was already an established and essential part of maritime life and culture.

There is evidence of clerics on ships from the earliest times. However, crews that enjoyed the presence of a clergyman were definitely in the minority.[132] In general, English chaplains were found only on some of the ships involved in large-scale maritime undertakings: naval expeditions, fishing fleets, privateering consorts, and voyages of exploration. Willoughby and Chancellor had a "minister" with them on their 1553 expedition to the northeast, but no chaplain accompanied Hawkins's commercial voyages in the 1560s. During his long voyage of circumnavigation, Drake had one chaplain to minister to his small fleet. Fenton's 1582 expedition destined for the Moluccas had two chaplains. No clergyman appears to have sailed on the many trading voyages to Guinea before 1582. The Crown, however, insisted that a small contingent of chaplains be a fixture of all Elizabethan naval campaigns. Yet, even in these circumstances, not every vessel had the luxury of a clergyman. For example, in that all-important summer of 1588 there were only 13 preachers serving a fleet of 34 royal ships and 163 hired armed merchantmen.

Orders for commercial and naval voyages inevitably stressed the necessity of regular worship, so seamen had an established tradition of managing their own religious worship in the absence of ecclesiastics.[133] Due to the lack of clergymen afloat and out of respect for the Blessed Sacrament, this shipboard practice of lay worship existed long before the Reformation, prior to Luther's doctrine of the "priesthood of all believers."[134] These religious services were unique not only because of their reliance on lay participation but because they were based around shipboard rhythms. The essence of shipboard worship then changed little after the Reformation(s).

The absence of a cleric seems to have made little difference to the basic format of worship afloat. During Elizabeth's reign, the practice of shipboard religion varied only slightly from vessel to vessel.[135] Captain Luke Foxe's orders were typical. He recommended,

That all the whole Company, as well officers as others, shall duly repaire everyday twice, at the Call of the Bell, to heare publike Prayers to be read, (such as are authorized by the church) and that in a godly and devout manner, as good Christians ought.

Similarly, papers were fastened on the mainmasts of the ships of Fenton's fleet in 1582, "with prayers for morning and evening." Pursers hired by the Muscovy Company were instructed to call the men together for morning and evening prayer. The orders for Edward Cotton's commercial voyage to Brazil in 1583 stated that crew must "[o]bserve and keep the daily order of common praier aboard the ship & the companie to be called thereunto, at least once in the day, to be pronounced openly." Prayers and psalms at sunrise and sunset were the basis of all shipboard religious services. Other additions might supplement the basic format:[136] Spanish prisoners who became Drake's enforced guests speak of Bible reading and sermons. John Hawkins's men were likewise treated to gospel readings. Chaplain John Walker of the Fenton expedition of 1582 claimed that the crews were very receptive to preaching and the discussions that sometimes followed: "the maryners who never heard a sermon in their lyves are marveouslye delyghted." This quotation provides evidence that seamen, especially those who spent much of their time at sea, were accustomed to their own particular sea services, which were conducted by nonecclesiastics. Undoubtedly, those men who spent time ashore and attended religious services in English parishes would have been more familiar with preachers and sermons than those whose religious experiences were limited to a shipboard environment normally devoid of clergymen. While sermons and Bible readings became the cornerstone of the new faith, this did not alter the fact that Protestant and Catholic sea services had the same structure and that both were quintessentially maritime in that they revolved around the seamen's work patterns.[137]

Like the old faith, Protestant worship was adapted to the shipboard environment and seafaring tradition; the seamen's workday was interspersed with prayers.[138] On Foxe's ship it was recommended that "all men doe duely observe the Watch, as well at Anchor, as under Sayle, and at the discharge thereof, the Boatswaine or his Mate, shall call up the other; all praising God together, with Psalme and Prayer." Raleigh's orders for a Guiana voyage in 1617 dictated that divine service should be read in the morning, before dinner, and before supper and that a psalm should be sung "at the setting of the watch." Aboard John Hawkins's vessels, there was more emphasis placed upon the nocturnal setting of the watch:

when night fell and the new watch began to come on deck and the hourglass was turned, everyone on board the ship would assemble around the mainmast, kneeling and bareheaded, and the quartermaster would begin to praying, and everyone would recite the Psalms of David, Our Father, and the Creed, in the English language.

Like the Catholic maritime tradition, Protestant religious celebrations were adapted to the shipboard environment. Because the vessel was one's workplace and living quarters, it was only natural that a ship could be turned into a church as well; Drake's men, for instance, trimmed their ships with flags and banners for Sunday service.[139] Celebrations focused around the mainmast, a habitual site for group meetings and activities, and worship was, as we have seen, structured around the seamen's workday.

Opinions in England varied as to the extent that the Protestant religious message had penetrated the seamen's mentality and subculture. In an intellectual climate that allowed for ignorance in matters of religion but not atheism, it is reasonable to assume that, at the very least, most Elizabethan seamen professed adherence to the basic tenets of Christianity. Yet officials seemed to doubt even this on occasion. It was the judgment of Admiralty officials that oaths should not be administered to seamen lest they damn their souls by perjury; seamen would "rather hazard their soules in the hands of a mercifull God, by periury, than their fortunes gotten with perill of their lives."[140] Jonas Hanway commented in the eighteenth century that "our seamen are generally as insensible of danger to their souls as dauntless with respect to their bodies" and that "no people stand more in need of religious admonition."[141] While seamen were accustomed to their own services, some evidence suggests that they resented having to attend the overzealous, structured services conducted by trained clerics.[142] One of Hawkins's seamen reported that "half of the men on the flagship say when called to prayers—Body of God, what an amount of singing, praying and preaching: may the Devil fly away with the preacher!" When chaplain Richard Madox of the Fenton expedition attempted to teach some of the boys Solomon's Proverbs, pilot Thomas Wood "wold not in any case [agree] that his boy shold lern any such thing for he browght hym not hyther for that purpose."[143] Yet Madox's fellow chaplain, John Walker, believed that the men were wonderfully reformed "both in rule of lyfe and relygyon." The Crown's increasing concern with securing religious uniformity at home in the 1570s and 1580s had its parallel at sea, and, as we have seen, ecclesiastics became more prevalent on English naval vessels during the 1580s. Whether this was for reasons of shipboard discipline or to keep a tighter rein on the seamen's normally self-reliant tradition of shipboard worship is unclear. Was the Crown trying to ensure that the normally independent maritime community would be imbued with the official Protestant message? Given that Protestantism was a relatively recent innovation in England and that there was some question as to how firmly it had taken root in the lives of the ordinary people,[144] the Crown sought orthodoxy. Uniformity became increasingly important throughout the 1580s; during the war with Spain, the Crown believed that English Catholics posed a threat as a "fifth column."[145] Hence, shipboard orders for English vessels emphasized the fact that divine service afloat should accord with worship on land.[146] In addition, naval orders often forbade seamen from theological disputation. The Crown dictated

that noe man souldier or other marriner doe dispute of matters of religion vnles it bee to bee resolued of some doubts and in such case that hee confer with the ministers . . . for it is not fitt that vnlearned men should openlie Argue of soe high and mysticale matters.

In civilian service, shipboard orders specified that "no man shall speake any vile or misbeseeming Word, against . . . the Religion established" and that service must conform with that of the Anglican Church on land. Those regulations suggest the presence of lively religious plurality at sea, not indifference. Furthermore, as on land, absence from service carried penalties. On John Hawkins's ships, "all attended, under pain of twenty-four hours in irons."[147] Occasionally, a boatswain would have to administer a rope's end to seamen who dodged service.[148] Whether required because of the presence of religious diversity or indifference, the punishments emphasize the contemporary belief in the necessity of communal faith and worship.

As a result of these control mechanisms implemented by the Crown and shipowners through their orders and the presence of Protestant clergymen and the newness of Protestantism, there was insufficient time during Elizabeth I's reign for a distinctive and developed maritime form of Protestantism to evolve. The fact that the practice of shipboard religion remained unique owes much to the retention of its maritime customs and patterns.[149] It is evident that Protestant seamen preserved their emphasis on lay worship while at sea. Although the number of Protestant chaplains afloat was increasing, in general lay seamen still conducted religious celebrations. Given the shortages of qualified clergymen on land and the unpleasantness of shipboard life, which would surely deter all but the most ardent preachers, maritime worship retained its emphasis on lay worship simply out of necessity. Doubtless, the scarcity of clergymen on ships can also be traced to the parsimony of the Crown and thriftiness of shipowners; why put clergymen on the payroll when seamen were accustomed to looking after their own worship? For its part the Crown hired ministers but spread them very thinly. Given time, a distinctive Protestant maritime tradition was bound to develop, but that lay well in the future; not until 1662 was a seamen's service first included in the English Prayer Book.[150]

While there is little doubt that most late Elizabethan seamen adhered to the Protestant faith and that there were numerous "godly seamen," religious fervor became entwined with pragmatic interests. Religion was a factor in the Anglo-Spanish war; most Englishmen and Englighwomen viewed it as a struggle between Protestant and Catholic, good against evil. In addition to being an important part of sixteenth-century maritime culture, religion provided an ideological basis for the war while fostering a strong esprit de corps. One must recognize, however, that at least some of the anti-Spanish and anti-Catholic rhetoric of the war years obfuscated a less noble goal: commercial interests. Anglicanism's struggle to survive and the importance of uniformity were not lost on seamen. Yet in many minds the religious struggle became virtually inseparable from the war over trade zones. Chaplain Richard Madox noted that the English seamen enjoyed throwing rosaries belonging to captured Catholic crews overboard and calling the Pope "a rascally Jew swindler." He also observed that many of the English seamen who

dyd cowterfet [the] most holynes wer now furthest from reason affyrming that we cold not do God better service than to spoyl the Spaniard both of lyfe and goodes, but indeed under color of religion al ther shot is at the mens mony.[151]

While seamen readily used religion as a rallying cry, few seamen were the stuff of John Foxe's martyrs. It is not in dispute that many were subjected to the rigors of the Spanish Inquisition. However, few did their penance as willing martyrs to the Protestant cause. Once in the hands on the Inquisition, it was not uncommon for men to deny their Protestantism. A minority of those who were captured were burned at the stake; these were the devoted men who Inquisitors decided would never convert to the "True Faith." When given a choice, many of Hawkins's men remained in the New World and embraced the old faith.[152] Under torture Englishmen were often ripe for conversion. One such Englishman was willing to pay any price if his captors ceased the torment: "O God, you are pulling me apart—have mercy!—What do you want me to say?"[153] One of Hawkins's unfortunate seamen who was captured by the Spaniards in Mexico in 1568 chastised his cellmate:

[f]or thou hast done nothing but babble without regard to what thou hast said; and I may tell thee that I myself am a prisoner for having talked too much and I assure thee that I would willingly wear a penitential garment for half a dozen years only to be assured that the Inquisitor will not burn me, and if I escape that fate

and get out of here I will sew up my mouth with thread and will not utter a single word all the rest of my life when among Spaniards.[154]

Although there is convincing proof that, as a group, seamen were not "vile and vngodly" men as they were sometimes accused of being,[155] it is also clear that when faced with potential martyrdom, few opted to die as champions of their faith. While some died because of their religious zeal, many died because of their inability to talk their way out of the flames and into the galleys and penitential garb.

From our examination of seamen's beliefs and the practice of shipboard worship we may draw the following conclusions. As in the general population, faith varied from person to person. On the whole, evidence suggests that by the late sixteenth century English seamen held Protestant beliefs. Try as they might, when faced with the threat of a painful death at the hands of the Inquisition, English seamen were incapable of pretending they were Catholics. This is telling indeed. It is apparent that the practice of this faith among shipboard communities fell within the range of Anglican orthodoxy. While the Reformation changed the substance of English seamen's beliefs, it did little to alter the fact that seamen praised God as they always had, with prayers and songs conducted by laymen and on a schedule determined by shipboard rhythms. There was some resentment of religious services conducted by clerics imposed from on high and alien to the ship, its inhabitants, and their culture, but there was no resistance to religious services per se. The religious tradition was an established and accepted part of the seamen's work culture and their lives at sea. The established church and state enjoyed little direct success in its ministries, and here, as elsewhere, seamen's subculture proved to be resentful and impervious to external efforts at change. Independence was not a valued trait.

CONCLUSION

The English maritime community was characterized by a unique mixture of solidarity and individualism. While seemingly contradictory, these two traits existed side by side; seamen's customs emphasized both attributes. Seamen reveled in their independence to negotiate their own terms of employment, to engage in private trade, to judge the times of their labor, and to worship in their own lay fashion. The men of the maritime community were nothing if not self-reliant.

Elizabethan seamen cherished their self-reliance and their individual liberties, regarded and guarded as "custom." As E. P. Thompson has pointed out, customs often became "second nature"; as such, people are very resistant to externally imposed change or reform.[156] Despite the fact that seamen were faced with a prolonged conflict that intruded on many peacetime forms of maritime employment, they did not move into unchartered waters in the form of attempts at a permanent or semipermanent trade group. They accepted impressment as an unwelcome duty of seafaring men in time of emergency and, as a group, did not attempt to coerce the Crown. Instead of altering the structure and form of protest, they elected to rely on the traditional methods: verbal and written petition, desertion, mutiny, and, above all, studied indifference.

Seamen were effective when they chose to act collectively. The demonstrations in 1589 and 1592 illustrate that seamen were quite capable of banding together en masse to protest their conditions if the need warranted. Contemporary opinion is unanimous: seamen were always ready to voice their opinions to their superiors whether or not that opinion was solicited. English seaman and naval administrator Nathaniel Boteler commented that

the insolencies of these men are so overgrown . . . as upon every slight occasion they have nothing more ready in their mouths than that mutinous sea cry "One and All," and on the shore you have seen some of them affronting Justice in the very High Streets of the City.[157]

Seamen's "strike proneness" or willingness to protect their work culture was recognized by contemporaries; this tendency seems to have been particularly pronounced in occupational groups like seamen who worked and lived in relative isolation. Thus, seamen possessed both the consciousness and the spirit to defend their traditional work environment.

If this united front was effective in pressuring the Crown, we may well ask why seamen did not sustain it to achieve better conditions in the navy. In order to understand seamen's behavior, we must look once again to the deferential society in which they lived. From our perspective, we can see that seamen's interests were often divergent from those of their employers. However, seamen saw themselves as part of an organic whole; early modern laborers, including seamen, did not perceive themselves to have "a separate labour interest distinct from and opposed to" their employers. In the words of Patrick Joyce, a specialist on the subject for a later period, the "relationship between superior and inferior is perceived as one of partnership or inter-dependence, however bogus in reality this may be."[158] From his research on preindustrial laborers, John Rule has observed that

a period of hostility might produce a flourish of rhetoric which sounds like the instinctive reaction of class, but which might be straightaway followed by expressions of a desire to return to a properly ordered world in which masters and men alike know both their place and their obligations.[159]

Therefore, seamen were not unusual in their readiness to defend their "traditional" ways; on the contrary, their protection of custom and the fact that they disbanded their pressure groups after their grievances were addressed indicate that they were typical among preindustrial laborers. In particular, our period witnessed a very modest peacetime navy and virtually no career-long service for common seamen in the royal navy. Therefore, Elizabethan seamen attempted to avoid the Crown and its oppressive restrictions, not confront it.

Given the turbulent times, the desire for harmonious labor relations between employers and seamen was not enough to ensure the protection of maritime customs. Considerable pressures were exerted upon these traditions during the late sixteenth century. The privateering and naval wars brought an influx of untrained, intruding landsmen. Seamen had no way to stop this dilution. Naval duty compromised seamen's freedoms in regard to contracting out their own labor as well as reducing their earning potential. Naval warfare stressed strict discipline and a rigid command structure that left little room for such maritime customs as consultation. The realities of sixteenth-century seafaring compromised seamen's customs in the sense that larger crews reduced the influence of each individual within the company. Despite all these obstacles, seamen clung to their established ways. Their work culture was compromised, but their expectations were not affected. This tenacity was not at all unusual among preindustrial laborers.[160]

Seamen's preservation of tradition and their protection of a culture of individual liberties were their strength and the source of their collective consciousness. The lack of a sustained front or efforts to establish a trade guild was in no way an indication of a lack of solidarity among the maritime community. A number of factors point to a very strong internal unity. Their occupation demanded cooperation; in order to sail a ship, there must be teamwork. They also shared a subculture, work culture, and worldview reinforced by a camaraderie and dependence bred of shipboard living; each man realized that his livelihood and safety depended on his crew members. They worked together, prayed together, lived and often died together; for the duration of their voyage, the fate of each man was dependent on his fellows. Furthermore, they traded commodities among themselves, lent and owed each other money, formed business partnerships together, and apprenticed their sons to other members of the maritime community. While the realities of shipboard life necessitated almost constant togetherness at sea, seamen were routinely found in clusters ashore as well; they lodged, ate, drank, and socialized with other seamen. The "ties that bind" were not limited to the shipboard environment. As we shall see in Chapter 5, seamen's bonds of commonality were the basis of many of their relationships on land.

Both the strength of their subculture and their physical isolation divided them from the land population. To a certain degree seamen have always been "outsiders" among the land population. While they were not divorced from the larger culture, the men of the sea had their own dialect, manner of dress, songs, dances, folklore, and rituals that were uniquely their own. Although religion and the heightened nationalism of wartime stressed seamen's unity with the land population, the pervasiveness of their subculture and their distinctiveness isolated them from the land population even when they were on shore.

The Reformation and the Anglo-Spanish war enhanced English seamen's perception of themselves as a group apart. The events of the sixteenth century drove a wedge between the men of the European maritime community. Religious and political differences obscured the kinship that bound all men of the sea. This affinity is apparent not only in the shared experience of life at sea but also in the format of religious worship and the common code of rituals and customs. However, English seamen of the period saw little of the commonality. Instead, those seamen who sailed on long-distance voyages and campaigns proclaimed their Protestantism and enriched themselves on the spoils of war. During the last years of Elizabeth's reign many of these men were drunk on their own successes and were infused with a sense of their own uniqueness—separated from both Catholic seafarers and the "landlubbers."

We must be cautious not to paint all the men of the maritime community with the same brush. This sense of esprit de corps was exhibited largely among those seamen who were involved with the fight with Spain or affected directly by the political and religious tensions. To what extent did this spirit infiltrate the maritime community as a whole? It is difficult to say. It is unlikely that many seamen who were engaged in fishing and coastal trade or sought to conduct peaceful trade hoped for a cessation of hostilities and the end of impressment. These men—the more staid, the less adventurous—probably saw no advantage to war with Spain. Yet even among this group, such men were required to spend time in the navy and to fight for "the cause." Hence, it would have been difficult for the majority of seamen to remain unaffected by the war. This did not prohibit some healthy (and unhealthy) competition among English seamen; we have seen that competing privateering crews could have bitter rivalries. On the whole, however, English seamen were a united group with their own subculture and bonds of financial interdependency. At the very least, long-distance seafarers, armed with the new faith and a forum and reason in which to defend it, willingly portrayed themselves as frontline fighters in the war against Catholicism. The Protestant religion, the profits that could be made from the war, and their many maritime successes gave these men a vibrant esprit de corps. While English seamen enjoyed a sense of solidarity prior to the war because of their shared experiences and adherence to shared values and customs, the existence of a common enemy or prey created an even greater degree of unity. At a time when all seamen's customary freedoms were under threat from the exercise of the Crown's prerogative, during an age when the nature of seafaring was changing and endangering traditions, the men of the English maritime community were forging a stronger sense of themselves as individuals and as a collective.

We should, however, stop short of suggesting that seamen had their own · distinct culture; they did share elements of the larger culture. Their understanding of the "rules" of protest demonstrates that they were not isolated from the workings of the larger society. Instead, we can put seamen's subculture in the same category as that of other itinerant, wage-based occupational groups whose codes of behavior, symbols, and rituals were nurtured in a high degree of isolation.[161] Such groups were probably marginalized because, externally, they looked different and spoke in what was tantamount to their own language; however, when one scratches the surface of these occupational groups, it is apparent that they functioned according to the same dynamics as the larger culture.

NOTES

1. A number of studies illustrate that the English Protestant tradition was very much in favor of a "just war"; England's war against the Catholic powerhouse of Spain was seen in religious, if not apocalyptic, terms. Timothy George, "War and Peace in the Puritan Tradition," *Church History* 53 (1984), 492–503; John Hale, "Incitement to Violence? English Divines on the Theme of War, 1578 to 1631," *Renaissance War Studies* (1983), 487–511; Paul A. Jorgensen, "Elizabethan Religious Literature for Time of War," *Huntingdon Library Quarterly* 37 (1973–74), 1–17; Paul A. Jorgensen, "Moral Guidance and Religious Encouragement for the Elizabethan Soldier," *Huntingdon Library Quarterly* 13 (1950), 241–59; Carol Wiener, "The Beleaguered Isle: A Study of Elizabethan and Early Jacobean Anti-Catholicism," *Past and Present* 51 (1971), 27–62.

2. As specified in Peter Burke's *Popular Culture in Early Modern Europe*, the term "subculture" has been selected because seamen's customs and rituals formed a cultural nexus that was "partly autonomous rather than wholly autonomous, distinct yet not completely severed from the rest of popular culture." Peter Burke, *Popular Culture in Early Modern Europe* (New York: Harper and Row, 1978), 42.

3. The phrase is the Earl of Clarendon's, quoted in Andrews, *Ships, Money and Politics*, 82. This observation has been made about other marginalized and isolated laborers such as miners and longshoremen. C. R. Dobson, *Masters and Journeymen: A Prehistory of Industrial Relations 1717–1800* (London: Croom Helm, 1980), 30.

4. Burke, *Popular Culture*, prologue.

5. *An Inquiry into the Causes of Our Naval Miscariages: With Some Thoughts on the Interest of this Nation as to a Naval War, and of the Only True Way of Manning the Fleet* 2nd ed. (London, 1707), 7.

6. Quoted in Rodger, *The Wooden World*, 37; John Fry, ed., *Seafaring in the Sixteenth Century* (San Francisco: Mellen Research University, 1991), passim; Monson, *Naval Tracts*, vol. III, 434.

7. The observation was made by Friar Felix Fabri in the 1480s. Burke, *Popular Culture*, 43–44. See also L. G. Carr Laughton, "Shantying and Shanties," *Mariner's Mirror* 9 (1923), 52.

8. Margaret Rule, *The Mary Rose* (1982; rpt. London: Conway Maritime Press, 1986), 198–99; J. R. Hale, *Renaissance Exploration* (New York: W. W. Norton and Co., 1968), 94–95; PRO HCA 1/43/54.

9. PRO HCA 13/30/176.

10. PRO HCA 13/31/99v–100.

11. PRO HCA, 13/26/85–88, 13/26/85v–86; A.P.C., vol. XV, 113.

12. PRO HCA, 14/29/59, 13/31/67-v, 13/30/91-v. See also PRO HCA, 13/26/85–86, 13/27/369–71, 13/27/378v–81.

13. Capp, *Cromwell's Navy*, 249; John Laffin, *Jack Tar: The Story of the British Sailor* (London: Cassel and Co., 1969), 83; Raleigh, *The Works of Sir Walter Raleigh*, vol. VIII, 686–87.

14. PRO HCA 13/30/108v.

15. PRO HCA, 1/41/50v, 1/43/66v, 1/43/109, 1/45/94v; John C. Appleby, "A Nursery of Pirates: The English Pirate Community in Ireland in the Early Seventeenth Century," *International Journal of Maritime History* 2 (1990), 20–21. Appleby maintains that pirate captains were extremely generous to those ashore who would trade, provision, and shelter them. Neville Williams, *The Sea Dogs: Privateers, Plunder and Piracy in the Elizabethan Age* (New York: Macmillan, 1975), 156, 227; PRO HCA, 1/44/105, 1/44/162, 1/44/163v, 1/44/212v, 1/45/100v; Hair and Alsop, *English Seamen and Traders*, 235.

16. PRO PROB 11/82/325v. It was not unusual for seamen who died at sea to leave money for a banquet for their crewmates. Presumably, these meals included drinking. This was a common practice among the Brethren of the Trinity House at Deptford as well. See PRO PROB, 11/113/236v, 11/63/4v, 11/186/354–55; Guildhall 9171/24/277-v; GLRO X/32/7/631v–32.

17. Alsop, "A Regime at Sea," 584–85. During this pivotal time, one of the commanders was lured ashore by the promise of drinking. He was then arrested for disloyalty to Queen Mary.

18. For an in-depth treatment of this subject see Hair and Alsop, *English Seamen and Traders*, 73–99.

19. Ibid., 73.

20. PRO PROB 11/102/249v.

21. This was the precursor of the special form of prayer at sea that was added to the Prayer Book in 1662. Because of our limited information, it is impossible to state whether the sixteenth-century version of the rite of the sea differed from that which was included in the Prayer Book in the seventeenth century. Guildhall Ms., 9171/19/90, 9171/19/45v–46; Hair and Alsop, *English Seamen and Traders*, 327, 218, 220, 223.

22. PRO PROB, 11/102/180v, 11/102/181v, 11/102–182-v. See also PRO PROB, 11/102/220v, 11/102/149-v, 11/102/261v, 11/102/22, 11/102/237; Hair and Alsop, *English Seamen and Traders*, 254, 323–24, 325–27, 332–33; PRO HCA 1/46/127; Andrews, *Elizabethan Privateering*, 41.

23. Walter Raleigh, *The Last Fight of the Revenge* (London: Gibbings and Co., 1908), 27–28; Hale, *Renaissance Exploration*, 88, 90. Rayner Unwin, *The Defeat of John Hawkins* (Middlesex: Penguin Books, 1960), 243; Burke, *Popular Culture*, 45.

24. PRO HCA, 13/30/108v, 13/30/22v–23, 13/25/138v–40v. See also PRO HCA, 1/45/102, 1/45/105v; Alsop, "A Regime at Sea," 583; Richard Hakluyt, *The*

Principall Navigations Voiages and Discoveries of the English Nation (1589; rpt. Cambridge: Hakluyt Society, 1965), 150.

25. PRO HCA, 13/25/176-v, 13/24/329, 13/30/210.

26. Rudolf Dekker, "Labour Conflicts and Working-Class Culture in Early Modern Holland," *International Review of Social History* 35 (1990), 395.

27. See Chapter 5.

28. The masters of the Trinity House at Hull did attempt to draw up a wage scale for seamen in 1546, but it was never implemented. Brooks, "A Wage-Scale for Seamen, 1546," 234–46; Harris, *The Trinity House of Deptford*, 260.

29. Brooks, "A Wage-Scale for Seamen, 1546," 235–36, 241; Ruddock, "Trinity House at Deptford in the Sixteenth Century," 466.

30. Hair and Alsop, *English Seamen and Traders*, 124–25. In 1597 press masters in the navy were instructed to give out small sums to each man. PRO SP 12/263/June 15, 1597; it seems that most seamen were given 12 pence as press money. *State Papers Relating to the Defeat of the Spanish Armada*, vol. I, 89; and PRO HCA 13/27/324v. In addition to this, the navy gave out "coat and conduct" money, which was based upon how far the seaman had to travel to board his ship. The Crown paid 1/2 penny per mile and an additional 4 shillings. PRO SP, 12/26/137, 12/29/7. In 1597 the Crown recommended giving each man 5 shillings to travel home after the completion of the expedition. PRO SP 12/264/112.

31. Hawkins, *Observations*, 20–21.

32. Hair and Alsop, *English Seamen and Traders*, 147–48.

33. Hawkins, *Observations*, 20; K. N. Chaudhuri, "The East India Company and the Organization of Its Shipping in the Early Seventeenth Century," *Mariner's Mirror* 49 (1963), 37.

34. Andrews, *Ships, Money and Politics*, 71.

35. PRO SP, 12/12/100/93, 12/152/19, 12/268/54, 12/270/171.

36. PRO HCA 13/32/2–3v. On occasion, they might get much less than this. John Hills was a respected seaman but received only £20 to act as purser and master for a voyage that lasted ten months. PRO HCA 13/24/193–94. At the time of his death in 1577 shipmaster Robert Barrett earned £3 15s. per month. Guildhall Ms. 9171/16/336v. Master's mate William Fettey listed his monthly wage as £4 10s. per month. It was not unusual for pilots to receive £5 per month or more; pilot Christopher Moises was paid £6 per month in the mid-1590s which he claimed were good wages. PRO HCA, 13/33/35v–36, 13/33/42–43, 13/31/81, 13/25/314–15.

37. Andrews, *Trade, Plunder and Settlement*, 28.

38. Ibid., 26. See also PRO HCA, 13/25/157–59, 13/31/201v-2, 13/35/344–45v.

39. PRO HCA 13/36/305–306v. An assessment of Baynard's estate was not listed with his will, but his widow, Katherine, was said to be worth just over fifteen pounds at the time of her death, roughly a year later. Guildhall Ms., 9171/19/67, 9171/18/451, 9171/19/67.

40. PRO PROB, 11/121/100-v, 11/82/325v, 11/105/55–56.

41. PRO PROB, 11/102/178, 11/102/179v–80, 11/102/180v, 11/102/181v, 11/102/220v, 11/102/237, 11/104/51-v.

42. PRO HCA 13/32/2–3v; Hair and Alsop, *English Seamen and Traders*, 20. While private trade seems to have been a routine undertaking for most seamen, it

was not always the case. In 1556 the Muscovy Company forbade its seamen to engage in private trade. Hakluyt, *The Principall Navigations*, 310; Guildhall Ms. 9171/24/116; M. L. Baumber, "An East India Captain: The Early Career of Captain Richard Swanley," *Mariner's Mirror* 53 (1967), 276. Lack of evidence inhibits the study of seamen's total incomes. We simply do not have enough information. In many cases it is possible to explore seamen's estates for their total worth. This can be done through the study of wills. From time to time in the Admiralty Court seamen estimate the value of their estates, once their debts were paid. Even the assessment of wages is plagued by the fact that we are seldom given all the information that we need in a single deposition or set of depositions: information that provides us with a picture of what a seaman's skill level was, what type of voyage, he went on, the length of the voyage, and the amount and manner in which he was paid. Rarely do seamen furnish us with data on their incomes garnered from private trade.

43. Hawkins, *Observations*, 21.

44. Guildhall Ms. 9234/3/61; PRO HCA, 14/27/144, 1/45/175, 1/44/17, 1/45/184; Guildhall Ms. 9171/22/604.

45. Hair and Alsop, *English Seamen and Traders*, 3, 287; PRO PROB 11/102/231; Guildhall Ms. 9171/20/71v.

46. PRO HCA 1/43/151.

47. Guildhall Ms. 9171/20/260v; PRO PROB 11/112/338.

48. PRO PROB, 11/143/239v, 11/102/26v, 11/102/197v.

49. PRO PROB, 11/80/335v–36, 11/98/142v, 11/105/55–56, 11/103/219–20, 11/102/236v, 11/102/180v, 11/108/361v–62; Guildhall Ms., 9171/24/116v, 9171/20/194, 9171/19/159v, 9171/19/364, 9171/19/454, 9171/19/159v, 25,626/2/341-v.

50. PRO PROB 11/124/230; Guildhall Ms. 9171/16/330v. See also Guildhall Ms., 9171/11d/183, 9171/16/336v; PRO PROB 11/102/179.

51. Guildhall Ms. 9171/17/249.

52. PRO PROB 11/97/182v.

53. PRO HCA, 13/36/293v, 1/43/5.

54. PRO HCA, 1/46/178, 1/45/36v, 14/32/91, 13/36/333. Presumably their wages were garnisheed to pay legal damages.

55. *The Trinity House of Deptford Transactions, 1609–35*, 4.

56. PRO HCA, 14/36/196, 14/28/70.

57. For other examples see PRO HCA, 13/24/193–94, 13/25/248v–49, 13/25/249v.

58. PRO HCA, 14/29/128, 14/36/161.

59. Hair and Alsop, *English Seamen and Traders*, 144.

60. Thompson, "Eighteenth-Century English Society," 54; Rab Houston, "Coal, Class and Culture: Labour Relations in a Scottish Mining Community, 1650–1750," *Social History* 8 (1983), 9–17; John Rule, *The Experience of Labour in Eighteenth-Century English Industry* (New York: St. Martin's Press, 1981), 194, 212–13; Dobson, *Masters and Journeymen*, 19, 30, 41.

61. Alsop, "The Career of William Towerson," 45–82.

62. Rule, *The Experience of Labour in Eighteenth-Century English Industry*, 209–13.

63. Monson, *Naval Tracts*, vol. II, 237.

64. PRO HCA 13/27/242v–45v.

65. There seems to have been some room for negotiation with the owners prior to the voyage. There are a few examples of men who sailed on privateering expeditions who received wages while their crewmates received shares. PRO HCA, 13/31/230v–31, 13/31/33v–34v.

66. Ruddock, "The Trinity House at Deptford in the Sixteenth Century," 469; captains usually received eight shares. PRO HCA, 13/34/128v, 1/42/154. Masters were entitled to seven shares. PRO HCA, 1/46/57v, 13/31/272v–74, 13/31/328v–30, 13/33/323–24v, 13/34/37–38v, 13/34/287–88v. Master's mates had six shares. PRO HCA, 13/27/169v, 13/31/168–69v, 13/31/184v–86v, 13/31/276v–77v, 13/33/245–46, 13/34/60–61v, 13/34/232v–33v, 13/36/214. A gentle-born lieutenant received seven shares. PRO HCA 13/32/299v–300v. Surgeons received five shares. PRO HCA, 13/31/215v–16v, 13/31/292v–94v, 13/33/371–74. A midshipman (a rating that was very rare in this period) received five shares. PRO HCA 13/31/284–85v. Quartermasters, boatswains, stewards, corporals, and carpenters had four shares in most cases. (Quartermasters) PRO HCA, 13/28/329v–30, 13/31/22v–23v, 13/31/169v–70v, 13/31/282v–83v, 13/32/9–10, 13/32/356-v, 13/34/37–38v, 13/34/237v–38v, 13/36/216–17; (Boatswains) PRO HCA, 13/27/165-v, 13/31/34v–35v, 13/31/277v–79, 13/33/206v; (Corporals) PRO HCA 13/36/217v–18; (Stewards) PRO HCA, 13/31/146–47, 13/31/327–28v, 13/34/238v; (Carpenters) PRO HCA, 13/32/5–8, 13/34/235–36. Gunners received four to six shares. PRO HCA, 13/28/12v–13v, 13/32/357v–58v, 13/31/281–82, 13/31/279v–80v, 13/31/214v, 13/34/234v–35. Coopers had three shares. PRO HCA 13/27/91v–93. Gunners' mates and boatswains' mates also received three shares. PRO HCA, 13/33/209v–12, 13/33/247-v. Ordinary mariners had one or two shares. PRO HCA, 13/31/217-v, 13/32/358v. Some were accorded additional half shares. Presumably, those men with more experience warranted more than novices. PRO HCA 13/34/238v–39v. Apprentices were accorded a share or half a share, payable to their masters. It must be noted that these rates were not fixed. We do find examples where seamen were given slightly less or slightly more. See PRO HCA, 13/30/266–67, 13/31/143v–44v, 13/31/209v–10v, 13/31/211v–13, 13/31/213–14, 13/31/290v–92, 13/32/335, 13/33/47v–49, 13/33/243–44, 13/34/16v–19, 13/34/37–38v, 13/34/62v–63v, 13/34/289–92v, 13/34/294–98, 13/34/332–34v, 13/34/334v–35v, 13/34/339v–40, 13/36/218v–20.

67. PRO HCA 13/36/217v–18.

68. Andrews, *Ships, Money and Politics*, 37; Andrews, *Elizabethan Privateering*, 44.

69. Andrews, *Elizabethan Privateering*, 41.

70. Boteler, *Boteler's Dialogues*, 37. Clothing was the exception. Andrews, *Elizabethan Privateering*, 41; Ruddock, "Trinity House at Deptford in the Sixteenth Century," 469.

71. PRO HCA, 14/27/112-v, 14/35/110, 14/29/154, 14/29/161; Monson, *Naval Tracts*, vol. I, 290–91; PRO HCA, 1/45/7–7v, 1/45/9, 1/45/21v–22.

72. PRO HCA, 1/42/113, 1/45/42v–43v, 13/36/45v.

73. PRO HCA, 14/35/110, 14/29/81.

74. PRO HCA 25/3/part III/83.

75. PRO HCA 14/26/67.

76. PRO HCA 14/35/110.

77. PRO HCA, 14/35/110, 14/28/44; PRO E 351/2505; PRO HCA 14/30/85. See also PRO HCA, 14/26/67, 14/26/97, 14/26/162.

78. PRO HCA, 1/44/54–56, 1/45/22-v, 13/31/122, 13/29/46v–48.

79. PRO HCA 1/45/48v. It is possible that Norris found that it was convenient to place the blame for breaking bulk on the crew. Even if Norris was perjuring himself, there are many more complaints of captains who lost control of their men while at sea, and the ready proffering and acceptance of these claims reveal contemporary beliefs in the spontaneous and irrepressible unity of crews confronted with the opportunity for pillage and plunder.

80. PRO HCA 1/42/183-v.

81. PRO HCA, 13/35/374, 13/35/374v.

82. Keevil, *Medicine and the Navy*, 138.

83. Quoted in Evelyn Berckman, *Creators and Destroyers of the English Navy* (London: Hamish Hamilton, 1974), 29; PRO SP 12/209/112.

84. The 1590s was the most difficult decade of the sixteenth century. R. B. Outhwaite, "Dearth, the English Crown and the 'Crisis of the 1590s,' " in *The European Crisis of the 1590s: Essays in Comparative History*, ed. Peter Clark (London: George Allen and Unwin, 1985), 23–43. Andrews, *Trade, Plunder and Settlement*, 247. Although wages were increasing throughout the century, they were not keeping pace with the cost of living. Thus, seamen's lot was getting more difficult throughout the sixteenth century. Andrews, "The Elizabethan Seaman," 255–56.

85. PRO HCA 13/31/285.

86. Andrews, *Elizabethan Privateering*, 44.

87. PRO HCA 13/28/237.

88. PRO HCA 13/31/230v–31. See also PRO HCA 13/31/33v–34v.

89. Dobson, *Masters and Journeymen*, 19, 27, 30, 41.

90. Oppenheim, *The Administration of the Royal Navy, 1509–1660*, 152; *State Papers Relating to the Defeat of the Spanish Armada*, vol. I, lxviii; Bodleian Library, Rawlinson Ms. C. 846/127–129.

91. Raleigh, *Judicious and Select Essayes and Observations*, 30; Scammell, "The Sinews of War," 35–36; Croft, "English Mariners Trading to Spain and Portugal, 1558–1625," 253.

92. Oppenheim, *The Administration of the Royal Navy, 1509–1660*, 154. See also PRO, E 351/2387, E 351/2359; *A.P.C.*, vol. XV, 120.

93. Andrews has pointed out that although seamen's wages doubled and possibly tripled between the 1540s and the 1630s, when weighed against the cost-of-living index compiled by Phelps Brown and Hopkins, seamen's standard of living was quite possibly in decline. Preliminary evidence for the period 1570–1620 shows that wages were not keeping pace with the cost of living. Andrews, "The Elizabethan Seaman," 255; Arthur Bryant, *Freedom's Own Island* (1986; rpt. Great Britain: Grafton Books, 1987), 124; Raleigh, *Observations*, 30.

94. PRO SP, 12/264/11, 12/264/20, 12/283/March 8, 1602; Lloyd, *The British Seaman*, 39; Corbett, *Drake and the Tudor Navy*, vol. I, 382–83.

95. Oppenheim, *The Administration of the Royal Navy, 1509–1660*, 135.

96. Croft, "English Mariners Trading to Spain and Portugal," 253.

97. *A.P.C.*, vol. XV, 120.

98. Oppenheim, "The Royal and Merchant Navy under Elizabeth," 488; Oppenheim, *The Administration of the Royal Navy, 1509–1660*, 142; Monson, *Naval Tracts*, vol. I, 175; William Laird Clowes, "The Elizabethan Navy," in *Social England*, vol. III, ed. H. D. Traill (Cassell and Co., 1895), 470; Herbert Richmond,

The Navy as an Instrument of Policy 1558–1727, ed. E. A. Hughes (Cambridge: Cambridge University Press, 1953), 27, 35, 42.

99. *The Defeat of the Spanish Armada*, vol. I, ed. John Knox Laughton (New York: Burt Franklin, 1971), lvii–lviii; Ronald Pollit, "Bureaucracy and the Armada," 119–32. This theory is argued convincingly by Outhwaite in "Dearth, the English Crown and the Crisis of the 1590s," 23–43.

100. *The Defeat of the Spanish Armada*, vol. I, 273, 361, 283, 336.

101. A.P.C., vol. IV, 223–24.

102. PRO SP 12/223/590.

103. *The Expedition of Sir John Norris and Sir Francis Drake to Spain and Portugal, 1589*, 204. See also PRO SP, 12/228/10, 12/228/17, 12/228/22.

104. *The Expedition of Sir John Norris*, 210. Seamen's grievances concerning delayed payment caused them to repeat this tactic in 1592.

105. Dekker, "Labour Conflicts and Working-Class Culture in Early Modern Holland," 377–420; Walter and Wrightson, "Dearth and the Social Order in Early Modern England," 22–42.

106. PRO HCA, 1/44/9v, 1/44/16v; Oppenheim, *The Administration of the Royal Navy, 1509–1660*, 165; PRO HCA 13/28/237.

107. Because of the devastating effect that thievery could have on a crew's morale, courts-martial during the Georgian period punished it more severely than mutiny or desertion. Rodger, *The Wooden World*, 227.

108. Richard Madox, *An Elizabethan in 1582: The Diary of Richard Madox, Fellow of All Souls*, ed. Elizabeth Story Donno (London: Hakluyt Society, 1976), 241.

109. PRO HCA 13/22/237-v.

110. British Museum Library, Lansdowne Ms. 389 f.327–332. Frampton was a distinguished merchant. See Lawrence C. Wroth, "An Elizabethan Merchant and Man of Letters," *Huntingdon Library Quarterly* 17 (1954), 299–314.

111. P.E.H. Hair, "Protestants as Pirates, Slavers, and Proto-missionaries: Sierra Leone 1568 and 1582," *Journal of Ecclesiastical History* 21 (1970), 204. Barrett was a kinsman of both Hawkins and Drake. He was also John Hawkins's most trusted aide in his early voyages. Barrett was captured on Hawkins's infamous third voyage to the Spanish Main and burned by the Inquisition. A. L. Rowse, *The Expansion of Elizabethan England* (1955; rpt. London: Reprint Society, 1957), 53–54; Unwin, *The Defeat of John Hawkins*, 247.

112. G. Jenner, "A Spanish Account of Drake's Voyages," *English Historical Review* 16 (1901), 52.

113. PRO HCA 13/31/333–334v.

114. Felipe Fernandez-Armesto, *The Spanish Armada* (Oxford: Oxford University Press, 1988), 52; Hair, "Protestants as Pirates," 204; Hair and Alsop, *English Seamen and Traders*, 325–27. For other examples, see PRO HCA, 13/30/73-v, 13/24/218–19.

115. Jenner, "A Spanish Account of Drake's Voyages," 56–57, 58, 61, 66; PRO HCA, 13/25/406v–7v, 13/26/232–33.

116. R. T. Vann, "Wills and the Family in an English Town: Banbury, 1550–1800," *Journal of Family History* 4 (1979), 357.

117. For an isolated early Elizabethan case of a seaman specifying prayers for his soul in 1562, see Hair and Alsop, *English Seamen and Traders*, 285.

118. Guildhall Ms., 9171/12v/80, 9171/17/15, 9171/16/424v, 9171/23/62; GLRO, X/32/30, X/32/31 (Edward Master), DW/PA/5/1575/23; PRO PROB, 11/63/4v, 11/76/296v, 11/102/75-v, 11/102/179v. Some seamen left bequests to ministers with no specific instructions for a sermon. PRO PROB, 11/82/325v, 11/102/205v, 11/108/361v, 11/112/134v; Guildhall Ms., 9171/24/116v, 9171/18/413v, 9171/27/116v.

119. PRO PROB 11/102/107-v. In the early modern period, the funeral service was intended to instruct the mourners. Ralph Houlbrooke, "Death, Church, and Family in England Between the Late Fifteenth and the Early Eighteenth Centuries," in *Death, Ritual, and Bereavement*, ed. Ralph Houlbrooke (London: Routledge, 1989), 33.

120. Guildhall Ms. 9171/17/37.

121. PRO PROB, 11/57/201v-2, 11/57/270v.

122. For a discussion of the relationship between piety and literacy, see D. Cressy, *Literacy and the Social Order: Reading and Writing in Tudor and Stuart England* (Cambridge: Cambridge University Press, 1980), 1, 3–6, 13, 15, 44, 85, 183; Margaret Spufford, "First Steps in Literacy: The Reading and Writing Experiences of the Humblest Seventeenth Century Spiritual Autobiographers," *Social History* 4 (1979), 407–35.

123. Vann, "Wills and the Family in an English Town," 360; Hair and Alsop, *English Seamen and Traders*, 94; J. D. Alsop, "Religious Preambles in Early Modern English Wills as Formulae," *Journal of Ecclesiastical History* 40 (1989), 19–27.

124. Guildhall Ms., 9171/19/349, 9171/19a/161; PRO PROB 11/102/58v; Foxe, *North-West Fox or Fox from the North-West Passage*, 174.

125. Guildhall Ms., 9171/16/47, 9171/21/165v; PRO HCA 1/44/171.

126. Lucinda McCray Beier, "The Good Death in Seventeenth-Century England," in *Death, Ritual, and Bereavement*, 43–61.

127. PRO HCA, 13/29/198v–99, 13/25/160v–61.

128. Hale, *Renaissance Exploration*, 90.

129. Williams, *The Sea Dogs*, 138; PRO HCA 13/24/80v–83; Hair, "Protestants as Pirates," 211; Hakluyt, *The Principal Navigations*, vol. V (London: J. M. Dent and Sons, 1927), 74.

130. The quotation is taken from a letter from the Privy Council to the bishop of Bath in 1578. Their lordships were requesting the bishop's permission to hire one of his clerics to serve aboard one of Frobisher's voyages to Baffin Island. Gordon Taylor, *The Sea Chaplains: A History of the Chaplains of the Royal Navy* (Oxford: Oxford Illustrated Press, 1978), 26.

131. In the eighteenth century Jonas Hanway articulated the relationship between submission and religion: "When a seaman stands in no awe of God, what kind of obedience is to be expected to his master or officer?" See Jonas Hanway, *The Seaman's Faithful Companion Being Religious and Moral Advice to Officers in the Royal Navy, Masters in the Merchant Service, Their Apprentices, and to Seamen in General* (London: John Rivington, 1763), 20.

132. Hair, "Protestants as Pirates," 212; Hair and Alsop, *English Seamen and Traders*, 327; Taylor, *The Sea Chaplains*, 44.

133. Taylor, *The Sea Chaplains*, 24; Fernandez-Armesto, *The Spanish Armada*, 54–59.

134. It was not deemed proper for the Blessed Sacrament to be subjected to the hazards of the rolling and pitching of the ships. Therefore, mass was not said once the ship set sail. This stands in stark contrast with religious practices of some Catholic armies that heard mass daily. Fernandez-Armesto, *The Spanish Armada*, 56.

135. Foxe, *North-West Fox or Fox from the North-West Passage*, 173; Madox, *An Elizabethan in 1582*, 130; Taylor, *The Sea Chaplains*, 37; Hakluyt, *The Principall Navigations*, 310, 187.

136. Taylor, *The Sea Chaplains*, 25, 37; Williams, *The Sea Dogs*, 131.

137. Fernandez-Armesto, *The Spanish Armada*, 56, 64.

138. Foxe, *North-West Fox or Fox from the North-West Passage*, 173; Hannay, "Raleigh's Orders," 212; Hair, "Protestants as Pirates," 211.

139. Williams, *The Sea Dogs*, 131.

140. William Camden, *William Camden's Annales or the History of the Most Renowned and Victorious Princesse Elizabeth, Late Queen of England*, 3rd ed., trans. R. N. Gent (London: Benjamin Fisher, 1635), 414.

141. Hanway, *Seaman's Faithful Companion*, 20, 2.

142. While there were sporadic complaints about zealous preachers who elongated the basic shipboard service, there seems to have been little or no resistance to frequent religious observance at sea. Hair, "Protestants as Pirates," 211.

143. Madox portrays Wood as a chronic complainer who, "with a bawling mouth," was guilty of "blasphemous bragging ageynst God and man." Madox, *An Elizabethan in 1582*, 148–51, 26.

144. J. J. Scarisbrick, *The Reformation and the English People* (Oxford: Basil Blackwell, 1984), 137, 145–61.

145. Stuart E. Prall, *Church and State in Tudor and Stuart England* (Arlington Heights, Ill.: Harlan Davidson, 1993), 89; A. L. Rowse, *The England of Elizabeth* (1950; rpt. London: Cardinal, 1973), 482–501.

146. PRO SP 12/257/45; Taylor, *The Sea Chaplains*, 56; Foxe, *North-West Fox or Fox from the North-West Passage*, 173–74.

147. Taylor, *The Sea Chaplains*, 25. Those who abjured from service on land risked stiff financial penalties if prosecuted. Seamen faced physical punishment for absences from service and, given the claustrophobic nature of shipboard life, stood a much greater risk of detection than those on land.

148. Hair, "Protestants as Pirates," 211.

149. Despite the best efforts of Parliament and the vastly increased number of zealous chaplains to evangelize the seamen of the parliamentary navy, Capp asserts that few seamen could be considered "Puritans." Capp, *Cromwell's Navy*, 308, 323. This suggests that seamen's religious beliefs, like their subculture in general, were very tenacious and resistant to change.

150. Hair and Alsop, *English Seamen and Traders*, 327.

151. Madox, *An Elizabethan in 1582*, 144, 247.

152. F. Aydelotte, "Elizabethan Seamen in Mexico," *American Historical Review* 68 (1943), 6–7.

153. Hair, "Protestants as Pirates," 219.

154. Aydelotte, "Elizabethan Seamen in Mexico," 13.

155. This was an English seaman's assessment of the crew of a foreign ship he sailed on. PRO HCA 1/46/96.

156. E. P. Thompson, *Customs in Common* (London: Merlin Press, 1991), 1–4.

157. Boteler, *Boteler's Dialogues*, 44.

158. Patrick Joyce, *Work, Society and Politics: The Culture of the Factory in Later Victorian England* (New Brunswick, N.J.: Rutgers University Press, 1980), 91.

159. Rule, *The Experience of Labour in Eighteenth-Century English Industry*, 209.

160. Ibid., 194, 212–13.

161. The most obvious parallel was the collier subculture. Like seamen, colliers were considered "a race apart," but the evidence suggests that differences were exaggerated. Houston, "Coal, Class and Culture," 4–14.

Chapter 4

Victualing, Morbidity, Mortality, and Health Care

Sixteenth-century seamen were confronted with a significantly enhanced problem of morbidity and mortality rates, which went hand in hand with the growth of long-distance and long-duration journeys. When the merchant seaman was impressed into the navy, his customary freedom to assess the hazards inherent in any given voyage was denied, and he was forced to endure the hazards and conditions encountered aboard the Queen's warships. A naval seaman frequently lacked the basics for survival: edible provisions, hygienic living and working conditions, and suitable clothing.[1] Non-naval segments of the maritime community, particularly merchant companies, were more astute than the Crown in realizing that to maximize profits and achieve the goals of the voyage, the crews must be kept healthy. The English commercial leadership made some attempts to improve the lot of Elizabethan seamen in order to attract and preserve the labor force. While many of their experiments were ineffective or only partially successful, the search for solutions was ongoing and of some interest in charting employer–employee relations in an expanding sector of the early modern economy.

Although the Crown also needed healthy seamen to achieve its military objectives and secure profits for the private backers (most expeditions being conducted on a joint-stock basis), it effected only a minimum of measures to prevent, contain, and treat shipboard illness and disease. The elimination of seamen's liberty to set their own terms meant that the navy was not nearly as concerned to make service attractive to potential employees as other sectors of the maritime community were. The Crown accepted the very unsatisfactory status quo and did little to improve the lot of naval seamen. Given this approach, it should not be a surprise that the navy experienced the manpower problems that it did or that seamen resisted service. Moreover, those aspects of naval service that were improved upon were not the result of the Crown's initiative; the impetus for change came largely from career seamen who bestrided naval and non-naval segments of the maritime community and were in positions to observe and implement measures from the commercial sector. Because the Crown, overwhelmed by multiple tasks and concerned to keep expenses to a minimum, was resistant to change, improvements were frequently left to individual commanders to implement at their own discretion and charges. For the most part, the Crown was content to rely on traditional methods of running its navy and providing for its seamen. The unprecedented number of men who served and the duration of the war did little to change this general attitude. It thought in terms of responding to immediate crisis and not in terms of a coherent policy. It was resistant to those within the naval bureaucracy, such as Sir John Hawkins, who sought lasting reforms that would assist both the navy (and therefore the Crown) and seamen.

The problems associated with provisioning, health, and health care were not identical in the merchant marine and the navy, but the common ground that these sectors did share was minimized further by the divergent reactions to the necessities of commercial and naval seafaring. Peacetime forms of maritime employment and privateering allowed seamen to weigh the risks of a given voyage against remuneration; acceptable provisions and relatively safe working conditions were high on the list of seamen's priorities when assessing employment opportunities. Once they had entered into an employment contract, seamen expressed the expectation that employers would provide them with sufficient provisions and that they would avoid unnecessary hazards for the duration of their employment. If their expectations were not met, seamen had effective weapons to protest their treatment and conditions; work stoppage and desertion were acceptable ways for non-naval seamen to protest inadequate provisions or an excessively dangerous work environment. Unfortunately for the health of seamen, their freedom to choose or reject work on the basis of provisions and safety, their ability to strike, and the traditional expectation of health care were not upheld within the navy.

What follows is a treatment of naval and non-naval diet and nutrition, disease and health care, and the hazards inherent in sixteenth-century seafaring. To my knowledge, this is the only attempt to cover all of these topics within a single work. J. J. Keevil's chapter on sixteenth-century seamen in *Medicine and the Navy* is, to date, the most comprehensive study on provisioning and health care in the Tudor fleet.[2] His work figures largely in this chapter. While I have taken into account Keevil's analysis and the primary and secondary material that he has used, I have also included a host of other primary and secondary sources that Keevil did not consult. Keevil's purpose was to provide the reader with a general account of naval provisioning and health care. In this regard, he succeeds. However, my intention is to provide a more in-depth treatment by examining both the "small picture" and the "big picture" in more detail. My own research analyzes the navy's victualing records, which support my contention that there was a deterioration in navy victualing during Elizabeth's reign. Keevil's work did not make use of two other sources that are essential: seamen's wills and the High Court of the Admiralty depositions. Both have information on health care, morbidity, mortality, and diet. Such sources are indispensable to uncover information that relates the concerns and experiences of the more obscure members of the maritime community.

I have compared the sectors of the maritime community in terms of risks to seamen and, whenever possible, put my findings on health care and diet into a larger context of the Tudor population. In addition, this study contains one of the most thorough explorations of sixteenth-century charity and relief for seamen to date. Therefore, the following is a more encompassing study of these subjects than has been produced in the past and focuses on the entire maritime community, not just the navy.

SEAMEN'S DIET

Legends of seamen's iron stomachs and their poor diet have been with us for centuries.[3] There is abundant anecdotal evidence to support the notion that the diet of sixteenth-century seamen was, at best, monotonous and unpleasant and, at worst, detrimental to their health. William Clowes, the Lord Admiral's surgeon, described the "rotten and unwholesome victuals" that were served to Elizabeth's seamen:

their bread was musty and mouldie Bisket, their beere sharpe and sower like vinigar, their water corrupt and stinking, the best drinke they had, they called Beueridge, halfe wine and halfe putrified water mingled togither, and yet a very short and small allowance, their beefe and porke was likewise, by reason of the coruption therof, of a most lothsome and filthy taste and sauor, insomusch that they were constrained to stop their noses, when they did eate and drinke thereof: moreover their bacon was restie, their fish, butter and cheese woonderfull bad, and so consequently all the rest of their victuals.[4]

If we accept that some seamen were obliged to eat and drink such putrid fare, how widespread was this problem? Was it simply an accepted fact of life at sea during this era, or was it restricted to certain sectors of the maritime community and particular types of voyages? What were the consequences for seamen in terms of nutrition? What solutions were proffered by contemporaries to deal with deficiencies in seamen's diet?

All seamen tended to share roughly the same diet; salt beef, fish, bacon, biscuits, cheese, and beer were staples. While seamen in all segments of the maritime community were accustomed to flesh and fish days, the "menu" for civilian seamen was by no means as strictly governed or monotonous as in the navy. On paper each naval seaman was to have one pound of biscuit and one gallon of beer every day. He was entitled to two pounds of salt beef on every Sunday, Monday, Tuesday, and Thursday; on Wednesday, Friday, and Saturday he received his gallon of beer and quantity of biscuit with a quarter of stockfish, butter, and a quarter pound of cheese.[5] In addition to the items that constituted naval fare, civilian seamen were accustomed to mutton and fowl as a regular part of their diet.[6] Since many non-naval ships had small crews and lower manning rates in relation to tonnage, there was greater opportunity to carry livestock for the purpose of providing fresh meat for the men.[7] Evidence from the seventeenth and eighteenth centuries suggests that seamen were creatures of habit and were partial to their traditional fare, which had changed very little from Tudor times. Eighteenth-century circumnavigator Captain James Cook maintained that anything unfamiliar in their diet "was sufficient for seamen to reject it."[8] In terms of nutrition, their diet provided more meat than that of their socioeconomic group ashore.[9] Modern physicians and historians who have analyzed seamen's diet during the early modern period maintain that while seamen's diet was sufficient in terms of caloric intake, provisions were frequently in a state that was less than appetizing and "nutritionally disastrous," as they contained little or no vitamin C.[10] Unlike modern-day seamen, their early modern counterparts were not "nutritionally stable"; many of these men were plagued by malnutrition or were on the verge of it before they went to sea.[11] Furthermore, the energy expenditure of Tudor seamen was higher than that of today's seafarers. With so many seamen coming aboard on the verge of malnutrition and in need of a high-caloric diet, their health was precarious at best. Perhaps the only thing more harmful to seamen than a diet devoid of fruit and vegetables was the total absence of food and drink caused by any number of hazards at sea.

Many of the provisioning problems were universal during this time: limited means of preserving food and drink, the rising cost of supplies during the late sixteenth century, shipboard hazards such as vermin, and problems of revictualing in foreign ports. Corruption of victuallers conspired to defraud seamen in both civilian and naval service. The most significant difference was obviously the scale; provisioning for private ventures was done for much smaller numbers of men.

In general, merchant voyages of short distances and coasters had the fewest provisioning problems; they were victualed for brief durations and were never far from fresh water and victuals. However, during this century much of the growth in the merchant marine lay in long-distance voyages; between 1553 and 1603 English seamen began to participate in the Russian, Baltic, Mediterranean, transatlantic, and East Indies trades. Seamen frequently embarked on voyages of uncertain duration and encountered unforeseen hazards along these new routes. Understandably, sojourns into the unknown or relative unknown, sometimes in undercapitalized ventures, resulted in severe victualing problems for Elizabethan seamen, which compromised their diet and their health.[12] In 1579 the crew of the *Mary Frances* was so undervictualed for their journey to Spain, a well-established destination, that "most of the victualls were spente before the viadge was halfe made." Voyages of exploration usually entailed the most grievous hardships for seamen:

the atmosphere of a voyage could turn quickly from one of normality to one of alarm—for almost always the unforeseen involved an extension of time, of food shortage and disease: weeks of unforeseen sailing: months of unforeseen incarceration in the ice. . . . The dread novelty of exploration was delay: more explorers were martyrs to time than to typhoons, more were buried at sea than on the newly discovered shores.

Explorer Henry Hudson's crew exacted the ultimate price from him in 1611 when victuals ran low. His men cast him adrift in the Arctic in retaliation and to preserve the remaining provisions:

Wilson the Boatswaine, and Henry Greene came to this writer . . . and told him that they and the rest of their associates would shift the Company, and turne the Master and all the sicke men into the Shallop, and let them shift for themselves, for there was not 14 dayes victuall left for all the Company, at that poore allowance they were at . . . and . . . they had not eaten anything this three dayes.

The rising tide of lawlessness and violence posed a threat to provisions as well. Robbery at sea was frequent during the war years, and provisions were a valued commodity. Coasters, fishermen, and those on merchant voyages were targets for privateers and pirates.[13] The *Anne Frances* was subdued by a French warship in 1581 that took its cargo, munitions, victuals, the mariners' apparel, and navigational instruments "and lefte them not soe muche as theire leade and lyne, but stripte them of all." The crew and the ship were carried out to sea, and "there lefte . . . all naked," and "if bye god['s] provision they had not byn putt in with the Trade on the quoaste of Britayne and there had gotten victualls and other necessaries of Englyshe men theye had vtterlye perjshed and never gotten home." English seamen of subdued vessels might expect some mercy from English pirates or privateers; they were much more likely to be left "like naked men in the sea" by those not bound by national affiliations.

Privateers and naval seamen had many of the same problems in common. In both cases seamen were being provisioned to go into enemy waters for campaigns of uncertain duration. Because privateers' fortunes depended solely on the capture of legal prizes to recoup their costs and pay the men, the ability to provision for long durations was a definite asset, although it inevitably meant that seamen ate provisions in a decayed state. Because the crews were usually not given wages, victualing was one of the most costly expenditures of outfitting a privateering voyage; victuallers, too, relied on the hope of prizes to recover their investment. Victuallers were routinely granted the very considerable share of one-third of any prizes taken. Thus, while the insufficient quality of provisions could lead to desertion or unrest, and inadequate quantity could force an expedition to turn for home, it was undeniably in the victualers' interest to scrimp on costs in order to obtain a greater profit margin. Since privateers had military goals and sought to capture lucrative prizes, large numbers of men were an advantage. The backers of privateering expeditions were willing to overman their vessels because wages were not a consideration. In many instances, privateering ships were not adequately provisioned for the numbers aboard. Roger Mariner, boatswain of the privateering vessel *Phoenix* of London, told the Admiralty Court that a mess of four men was allowed two and a half pounds of beef with bread and drink each day, which he considered "harde allowance & not sufficiente for theire maintenance savinge some tymes they had a messe of beanes or a dumplinge made of Flower which came out of the Prize."[14] This is in stark contrast to food allotments elsewhere. The navy allowed each man two pounds of beef every flesh day, whereas the men of the *Phoenix* were given little more than that to feed a mess of four. The inclination of privateers was to remain at sea as long as possible. This posed problems when it came to provisions and nutritional considerations.[15] On the *Hope* "homewardes bounde one chiste with suger was dronck with water for wante of other drinck." The 39 men of the *Change* of Plymouth survived on rice and water for 20 days in 1592 until they could put into port for supplies.

Pirates had similar reasons to overman and to keep to the seas for extended periods. In addition, they were circumscribed in where they could obtain provisions. In the early seventeenth century, following the Anglo-Spanish peace, some retreated to Ireland, where they found willing Irish planters who would trade victuals, including "oten & Barly bread, vealle, mutton, & butter," for booty. Captain Arnold alias Arnewood victualed his ship, the *Roebuck*, by contracting butchers to sell him mutton and beef and fishermen to sell him fish.[16] Thomas Walton alias Purser, another famous swashbuckler, exchanged goods and services for provisions; in one instance he claimed that he received 35 cows for victuals in exchange for service to an Irish lord.[17] Although Lord Treasurer Burghley was very concerned that "divers persons are towched to be victualers & relievers of them," not everyone was willing to risk aiding and abetting criminals.[18] Apart from their safe havens, provisions could be costly and difficult to obtain for pirates.

Accidents and hazards that endangered or ruined victuals were common to all deep-sea seamen.[19] Since it did not carry a cooper (as some ships did), leakage in beer casks aboard the *Golden Noble* in the late 1580s caused such extremity that the "Captayne & company wished & prayd to god to sende them to meete with some kinde of drinke." A leak on the *Tiger* spoiled all the victuals on that ship. During his 1593 voyage southward, four-fifths of the victuals on Richard Hawkins's *Dainty* were eaten by rats.

Reprovisioning at foreign ports could be dangerous given international political and religious hostilities and the growing lawlessness at sea.[20] The crew of the *Golden Noble* (mentioned above) were short of victuals and tried to obtain provisions in Barbary. The men encountered obstacles ashore, and the expense proved prohibitive, so they had to exist on a diet of fish and bread for the journey home to England. The stores of fish that they did have were "corrupted & stoncke marvelously & was likely to haue poysoned them all." A fleet of privateers under Sir Anthony Shirley endured starvation rather than put into a Spanish port to obtain victuals:

there was such misery amongst the company . . . for wante of victualls that many englishe men and duch men died, and they grewe soe weake that Sir Anthony was inforced for wante of men to burne one of his shipps called the *George Noble*, & cast of[f] also a galley.

Hostility to Englishmen was not limited to those engaged in privateering or those who attempted to enter Spanish ports. In 1598 the privateering crew of the *Examiner* of London put into Rochelle, France, for victuals, and the townspeople seized their vessel and expelled the English seamen. Master Stephen Hare of the *Minion* encountered problems trying to revictual in Brazil in 1581 because he was "accused to the clergye for matters of Religion." While in a Danish port in 1581, the men of the *Mary* of Sandwich were assured by the bailiff that they were as safe "as in any harboroughe within Englande"; when they were attacked by a warship of the king of Sweden, Danish officials made no move to protect the Englishmen. Those who engaged in long-distance voyages often had to make the difficult decision of whether to risk malnutrition and possible starvation or to go ashore in search of provisions and face the risks inherent in being Englishmen in a strange and potentially hostile land.

The climbing costs of provisioning a ship, whatever its destination or purpose, affected all seamen. The late sixteenth century was a period of inflation and population growth. Between 1585 and 1600 grain prices were almost 50 percent higher than they had been in the previous decade. Crop failure and a trade depression in 1586 caused hardship, as did poor harvests and dearth between 1594 and 1597. By 1600 wage-based workers were worse off than their forebears were at the turn of the previous century.[21] These developments had a significant impact on the diet of all but the wealthy.[22] Years of economic hardship and the subsequent deterioration in diet of the general population affected seamen afloat and on land. The problems inherent in provisioning ships during this period are most evident in the navy's victualing records, to be examined below. Unfortunately, posterity has not bequeathed us any comparable records for provisioning in the non-naval sector of the maritime community. Given the general increase in prices and the decrease in purchasing power, the subsequent deterioration of diet among the land population, and the fact that we know conclusively that the prices of staple items common to all seamen's diets increased dramatically in the late sixteenth century, we may confidently state that provisioning a ship became a more difficult task. Seamen in non-naval employment probably experienced some deterioration in their diet, as did many of their countrymen and women ashore; to what extent is difficult to say from existing records.

Undoubtedly, many factors affected seamen's diets while at sea: substandard provisioning on the part of victuallers or shipowners; unforeseen delays, which meant that provisions ran low; the various hazards of storage (vermin and poor methods of containment and preservation); theft while at sea; and the high cost of provisions. How widespread were these problems? Anecdotal evidence from the period suggests that they were very common indeed. However, for those who plied the waters close to home—North Sea fishermen, coasters, and some pirates, for instance—many of these problems presumably did not have serious nutritional consequences for the men aboard, given the proximity to ports and availability of fresh provisions. For those who ventured farther afield the problems of victualing and revictualing and the consequences of inadequate provisioning became much more serious. Without question, equipping and preserving sufficient food and drink on long-distance voyages were intimately tied with the survival of the crew in terms of morale and nutrition and, ultimately, could determine the success or failure of the voyage. Those who sought to profit from the expansion of transoceanic travel and the growth of the early modern economy began to appreciate the close connection between profit and the health of seamen. In light of these developments, interested parties attempted to minimize the dangers and problems of provisioning in an attempt to maintain the health of seamen. This was a matter of self-interest; hungry, thirsty, unhealthy seamen rarely make for successful voyages.

SOLUTIONS

In view of the link between adequate diet and health, shipboard food and drink were a perennial source of concern and complaint for seamen in all types of maritime employment. The civilian tradition allowed companies to voice their comments and grievances to their superiors.[23] For example, in 1596 the crew of the *Samaritan* had nothing but fish for supper, which caused the men to protest to their master. Complaint was more than an outlet for frustration; group displeasure could force change. On a privateering voyage in 1591, the *Bark Hall*'s company rebelled against their rations being cut and insisted that they return to England. Civilian crews reserved the right to determine when they had reached the end of their endurance; this decision was based largely on the health of the men and the state of their provisions. Although the men of the *Minion* "founde themselves greeved for wante of victualls, and complayned to the Master thereof," shipmaster Stephen Hare was helpless to remedy the situation until they put into port; he "toulde them, there was noe better there to be had and willed them to be contente." Their complaints were ultimately satisfied; once they put into port the master sold his own commodities and some of the merchants' goods in order to furnish the men with victuals. Civilian seamen also had the option of turning down employment if they knew that the ship was poorly provisioned, as was the case with seaman Christopher Moises, who refused a voyage on the *Jonas* because of her inadequate stores. A small contingent of the *Minion*'s crew did desert in 1581 despite the master's efforts to obtain better provisions for the return voyage: "theye fell out with the Master abowte theire victualls and soe by reason of speeches vsed by the Master vppon that occasion they departed awaye." It is evident from these examples that seamen had a number of alternatives in circumstances where the provisioning was not adequate. It is also obvious that negotiation was an essential part of employer–employee relations. Victuallers of privateering expeditions could be replaced if it was discovered that provisions were insufficient. Cheesemonger John Glimston of Ipswich was to have gone to sea on the *Orphan* and to enjoy shares as a victualler, but he was displaced when he failed to provide proper provisions.[24] This is not, of course, to suggest that all incompetent or greedy victuallers were dismissed or that all privateering ships were adequately supplied. It does demonstrate that protest and negotiation did produce beneficial results.

Hair and Alsop's research on the wills of seamen in the Guinea trade demonstrates that the men were concerned with buying supplementary foodstuffs.[25] Seaman Thomas Freeman's will of 1562 shows that he bought oranges, cheese, and hens on credit while on his West African voyage. Some merchants turned a profit by selling dairy products and fruit to civilian seamen eager to supplement their rations at sea. The will of Justinian Goodwin, a factor of the Guinea voyage of 1564–65, left two pounds to the boatswain, carpenter, gunner, cooper, cook, and bower of his ship the *John Baptist* "to bye them fresh victualls." It is difficult to speculate how widespread this practice was because this type of evidence can rarely be expected to be located in surviving documentation. However, at least some individuals augmented their shipboard rations with private stores: "we would be wrong to assume that—short of mutiny—Tudor sailors were merely placid recipients of whatever levels of dietary and health care their superiors chose to provide." The men of the *Phoenix* of London (discussed previously) found their provisioning deficient and those seamen who could afford to purchased their own victuals when in port.[26] In dire situations individual seamen and commanders could be quite resourceful. Beverages, for example, were crucial to survival, but casks of fresh water turned scummy within a few days, and beer was very vulnerable to its environment.[27] When the beer ran out during a return voyage from the Azores, the Earl of Cumberland doled out a few spoonfuls of a mixture of vinegar and rainwater, which kept his men from dehydrating until they reached England.[28] Richard Hawkins employed a distilling mechanism to purify seawater. He wrote of his 1593 voyage aboard the *Dainty*:

our fresh water had failed us many dayes (before we saw the shore) by reason of our long Navigation, without touching any land . . . yet with an invention I had in my Ship, I easily drew out of the water of the Sea sufficient quantitie of fresh water to sustaine my people, with little expence of fewell, for with foure billets I stilled a hogshead of water. . . . The water so distilled we found to be wholesome and nourishing.[29]

Like many discoveries, this knowledge was not disseminated among the maritime community, and those aware of it seemed to abandon it. It was reintroduced in Charles II's reign and improved upon in the mid-eighteenth century.[30]

Forced by circumstances to survive on whatever was available, seamen showed a great deal of adaptability in regard to their food.[31] They caught fish, birds, tortoises, penguins, and rats, which "tasted as well as a rabbit." While passing through the Straits of Magellan on his voyage of circumnavigation, Thomas Cavendish and his men ate "musells and limpets & birds, or such as we could get onshore, seeking them every day as the fowls of the air do." Seamen of the Guinea trade were ordered to catch fish so they could enjoy fresh food. Pilot Thomas Pype sailed on the *Sea Horse* of Danske in 1594 and maintained that had the crew not reached land when they did, they were prepared to eat a horse that they had on board. In 1584 the crew of the *Edward Cotton* survived "not hauving els to eate but grasse."

In times of shortage, seamen tried to obtain provisions from passing ships. Bartering for victuals while at sea was a common practice.[32] Running low on supplies, Master Robert Dale's privateering crew found a well-provisioned ship and traded oars for food in the mid-1580s. Occasionally, pirates could act as victuallers to others while at sea. Captain Arnold and his crew captured a prize with a cargo of herring and sold it to other seamen. Starving seamen were sometimes relieved by the goodwill of their seafaring brethren. When the crew of the *Mary Frances* found themselves

short of bread, they borrowed some for their dinner from a ship lying at
anchor near them. While his assessment is undoubtedly optimistic, quartermaster Nicholas Hurleston told the Admiralty Court that

he thinketh noe english men are soe harde harted but if they mett at sea with eany
in misery & distresse, they will relieve them although noe hope of gaine . . . [was]
to be gotten thereby.

When all else failed, provisions could be taken by force. This was a
favorite method of pirates and privateers. English pirates were more likely
than privateers to subdue their own countrymen to obtain victuals, but
most were willing to compensate them for the seizure.[33] In 1584 Francis
Trasse of Wapping Wall, master of the *Grace of God* of London, was
subdued by pirate Charles Jones, who took his victuals; Trasse "requested
the Captayne not to vse him in such sorte beinge an englishe man and his
contray man, as to spoyle him of his provision." Jones explained that it
was much easier for Trasse to get supplies and that he [Jones] needed certain items from him. Jones willed Trasse to be content, "and he shoulde
be noe looser bye him" and gave him a quantity of canvas in return. In the
early 1580s a pirate informed shipmaster John Hills and the crew of the
Mary Frances that if he "could not have victualls of them by fayer meanes
he would have it whether they would or noe." Hills gave the pirates victuals
and received wax and flax in return. In 1581 Philip Smyth of Devon, master
of the *Primrose*, traded some of his victuals with Captain Haynes for pepper, bedsacks of cotton, monkeys, and parrots. Ironically, pirate Captain
Clinton Atkinson gave his bill for certain provisions that he took "to avoide
the Lawe." In most cases, privateers had no compunction about subduing
seamen from other nations and taking at least some quantity of their victuals without compensation. The crew of the *Tiger* of Drake's fleet in 1585–
86 was not above such actions: "a ship of Saint John de Luce [was] taken
and spoyled. It was laden with New Land fysh." The English privateering
vessel *Alcredo* accosted the *Alexander* of Copenhagen in 1595, taking some
of the Danes' victuals and the ship's boat. The Danes were then allowed
to depart with part of their lading.

Coping strategies had their limitations, but these are the measures utilized
time and again. Those who survived lived to tell tales of resourcefulness
and endurance. They did not petition for fundamental systemic change.
There is little evidence of seamen outside the navy who starved to death
during the period. Of course, the loss of an entire crew and hence the ship
would of necessity not be recorded. But endemic malnutrition almost certainly produced deaths among the weaker, more endangered members of
many ships' crews. Malnutrition was presumably a factor in a number of
shipboard deaths, but no contemporary is known to have identified it as a
primary cause. The opposite was true on land during the harvest failures

of the 1590s.[34] The perception, then, was not that seamen were starving to death but that they were afraid that they might. Presumably, therefore, most captains and shipmasters sought sufficient provisioning before they left port. Once at sea, captains and shipmasters acted to remedy or, at least, to promise to remedy the situation when provisions ran low. Moreover, just because shipowners and officers implicitly acknowledged this obligation, we should not assume that seamen were passive when it came to their diet. What little evidence we do have on the subject suggests that seamen resorted to self-help. We do know that officers often made arrangements for supplements to shipboard fare, and it is likely that others did as well. Even so, in the absence of a clear notion of what constituted a balanced diet or the unknown element that staved off nutritional diseases like scurvy and lacking a means to preserve provisions or protect them from the hazards of shipboard storage, even those men who provided their own food were not safe from the various problems inherent in the seamen's shipboard diet.

NAVY VICTUALS: THE PROBLEM, THE CAUSES, AND THE CONSEQUENCES

In terms of quality, evidence points to the fact that the diet of Elizabethan naval seamen was inferior to that of their predecessors who had served earlier Tudor monarchs. Before 1550 seamen were provided with an assortment of foodstuffs that included much more healthful items such as poultry and fruit.[35] The provisions of Elizabeth's army were superior to the navy's in that there was greater variety, especially on "meat days."[36] Aside from the advantage of relieving monotony and boosting morale, the army's superior provisioning did not provide better nutrition; its ability to acquire additional fresh provisions from the land, however, certainly did.[37] Quantity could also be a problem in the navy. Seamen not infrequently complained to their commanders that their meat was only half the required size.[38] Some commanders, Francis Drake in particular, deliberately left port when they were undervictualed, to save valuable storage space, gambling that they could reprovision during the campaign.[39]

Poor quality and quantity of victuals posed a definite threat to order within the fleet, as they were one of the leading causes of mutiny. Lack of provisions could cripple a fighting force. Samuel Pepys wrote in 1677 that

Englishmen, and more especially seamen, love their bellies above anything else, and therefore it must always be remembered in the management of the victualling of the Navy, that to make any abatement from them in the quantity or agreeableness of the victuals is to discourage and provoke them in the tenderest point, and will sooner render them disquieted with the king's service, than any other hardships that can be put upon them.[40]

Thus, the health and happiness of seamen were intimately connected to their provisions. The Lord Admiral made reference to the fact that even the "worst men" in the fleet knew the state of their provisions.[41] Sir Francis Drake wrote to the Queen in 1588, informing her that he feared desertions if there were not sufficient provisions for the fleet; when a seaman is "far from his country, and seeing a present want of victuals," he "will hardly be brought to stay." Drake's letter carried a dire warning about the importance of adequate provisioning: "Here may the whole service and honour be lost for the sparing of a few crowns." Provisioning and its corollary, survival, were the impetus for the single recorded naval court-martial of the period. In 1587 the seamen of the *Golden Lion* complained:

for what is a piece of Beefe or halfe a pounde amonge foure men to dynner or halfe a drye Stockfish for foure dayes in the weeke, and nothing elles to helpe withall— Yea, wee have helpe, alitle Beveredge worse than the pompe water. Wee were preste by her Majesties presse to have her allowaunce, and not to be thus, dealt withall, you make no men of us, but beastes.

Obviously, the writers appreciated the paternalistic relationship that was the ideal of Tudor society.[42] Although the Crown recognized that it had to feed its fighting men, it was plagued by the financial and logistical problems of providing for thousands of men in an era of inflation and dearth. The precise cause of the problem has been a topic that has generated controversy among naval historians. Much of the attention has focused on the Queen's legendary stinginess as the cause of many deficiencies in naval seamen's diet. Even the antagonists find some common ground here; few would dispute that the naval bureaucracy was hindered by the problem of a very frugal Queen eager to wage war on a budget.[43] The extent to which the Queen was culpable is hotly contested. The majority of historians place the blame largely on the Queen's parsimony.[44] More current scholarship, however, suggests that L. G. Carr Laughton, who once stood virtually alone on this issue, might be correct in looking for another explanation or, at least, contributing factors to the problem. Laughton's skepticism of this unicausal explanation has been bolstered by recent work on the limitations of Tudor bureaucracy; the ramshackle administration of the early modern state barely managed to cope with the demands of the war years.[45]

The Queen's parsimony and the burden placed on the administration of state were not the only factors that compromised the effectiveness of naval bureaucracy and affected the seamen's diet; corruption within the naval bureaucracy was also a problem.[46] The Treasurer of the Navy, Sir John Hawkins, believed that the Queen was continuously being cheated by her servants; yet accusations of corruption were leveled against Hawkins himself on more than one occasion. Sir Walter Raleigh wrote that "the Purveyors and Victuallers are much to be condemned, as not a little faulty in that behalfe, who make no little profit" and "so raise a benefit out of their [the seamen's] hunger and thirst, that serve their Prince and Country painfully abroad." Captain Nathaniel Boteler wrote of "foul cosenage and desperate abuse" in regard to naval victualing. His own experiences suggest that naval seamen, resentful of regular attempts to cheat them of their due, regularly informed their superiors in hope of redress:

I must needs say that in our late, and especially latest, voyages I have more than once found sometimes twenty, sometimes thirty of the common mariners of the king's ship that I then commanded waiting at my cabin door at a dinner time, with their beef and pork in their hands, to let me see how small the pieces were, and how much under the quantity and weight proportioned. And this I indeed found to be true.

Even the most cursory of examinations of the naval provisioning records reveals that the Surveyors of Marine Victuals were struggling to furnish seamen with their apportionment; their efforts were compromised by parsimony, corruption, inflation, and dearth. These latter two factors led to a deteriorating quality and quantity of diet for the majority of Tudor subjects at sea and on land throughout the sixteenth century.[47] The navy's victualing records afford us a rare opportunity to chart the changes in seamen's diet during the war years and to investigate the causes of inadequate victualing.

Edward Baeshe, the Surveyor-General of Marine Victuals during the first half of Elizabeth's reign, had served the Tudor monarchs since the time of Henry VIII; he would die in debt, exhausted by the task of procuring the specified victuals at the Crown's rates.[48] After Baeshe resigned his position in 1587, the task of victualing the navy became even more difficult with the coming of the first Armada in 1588 and the subsequent escalation of naval warfare. The Crown recognized the daunting task of the Surveyor of Victuals and created the position of deputy to the surveyor, but even with their combined efforts, James Quarles and Marmaduke Darell failed to victual the navy within the Crown's budget. They were also faced with the problem of drawing upon an increasingly exhausted market. Although victuallers were still kept on an extremely tight budget, dearth years elicited greater funds for naval victualing from the Crown.[49] The augmented allowance, however, was to continue "onelye vntill it shall please allmightye god to send such plentye as the highe pryces and rates of victualles shalbe deminished." While special concessions were made for periods of scarcity, the Crown routinely cut back its allowances after the dearth had subsided. Therefore, the escalating price of foodstuffs that resulted from inflation was not taken into account by the Crown. It became apparent to the surveyors during the 1590s, "theis late yeres of scarcetie," that the problem of costly victuals was not a temporary one.[50] In 1598 the accounts show that the costs for many items in the seamen's diet had doubled in recent years.[51]

The surveyor compares the difference in the price of provisions between "the former yeres of plenty, and theis late yeres of scarcetie" by contrasting rates for specific provisions during 1597 and an unspecified year that was intended to represent a period before the dearth. The years between 1594 and 1597 are known to have had disastrous harvests, and this is borne out by the victualing records.[52] While naval officials refer to "dearth" in 1590 and 1591, the word is likely being used to mean "dearness" in price rather than scarcity.[53] This suggests that the predearth rates were those of the late 1580s. The surveyor attempts to illustrate that wheat, malt, lings (fish), cheese, and salt showed the greatest increases; most of these items doubled in price or came close to doubling in value. The other foodstuffs listed, beef and stockfish, also rose in price but by a much smaller margin.[54] Dearth was undeniably a short-term cause of the rise in food prices, but the escalation was part of a much larger trend. Food prices were increasing throughout the sixteenth century; between 1500 and 1650, they rose sevenfold.[55] Without question, this trend is evident in regard to the food and drink that formed the foundation of seamen's diets.

In 1599 the Crown finally recognized that

the prices of all victuelles were of Late yeares so raised, and so did then Continew that he [Darell] coulde not provide victuells at such prices as he might have donne when he ent[e]red into those seruices.[56]

Darell's rates went up slightly the next year, but the allowance was still not sufficient.[57] The arrearages in the yearly accounts testify to the surveyors' battle to provision the navy within the Crown's budget. Their accounts also demonstrate that costs were steadily increasing because of a combination of inflation and dearth. This, as we shall see, resulted in the search for cheaper foodstuffs for naval seamen.

The personality of the last Tudor ruler exacerbated these problems.[58] Elizabeth's vacillation is legendary; commanders hurriedly departed with the fleet on more than one occasion in order to avoid countermanding orders from the Queen. Haste to depart often meant that the navy was inadequately victualed; messing arrangements were altered to compensate, thereby decreasing each man's allotment and his caloric intake. Countermanded orders or unexpected demobilization caused supplies to be returned to the royal storehouses for an indefinite period to await a new expedition; not infrequently, naval officials noted in the victualing records that provisions became "slymy and much decayed by long lying." The surveyors were always required to keep a month's worth of victuals on hand. The very limited ability of the age to preserve food coupled with the Crown's aversion to wastage would ultimately compromise the health of the navy's seamen; clearly, some seamen received provisions that had been decaying long before they were delivered to the Queen's ships.

Despite the consequences for seamen's diet and health, the practice of storing large quantities of provisions in case of emergency was necessary.[59] In 1586 there was a hurried preparation for a phantom attack. "Maruelous greate hast [was] made," but the difficult task of obtaining vast quantities of victuals on short notice was aggravated by dearth. Even in years where scarcity was not a factor, procuring victuals swiftly could still be problematic. In May 1590 the surveyors reported that beef "coulde not be provided in all the countrye on such a sodeyne." In July 1601 there was "a wante of some wheate which . . . is not to be had vpon this sodanne . . . without some Inconveinence." Unanticipated and prompt provisioning of thousands of seamen taxed a land already struggling to feed its population. Because of these exceptional conditions, the surveyors were allowed to use their very unpopular right of purveyance[60]; this was a last resort, a measure reserved for the most dire circumstances. While the difficulties are obvious, it is uncertain in some cases how the problem was dealt with or the exact nature of the consequences for seamen's diet. It is quite probable that messing arrangements were altered in times of shortage and that surveyors made do with poor-quality victuals in the 1580s and early 1590s; substitute victuals do not make an appearance in the records until the mid-1590s. Without question, the latter coping strategy, not adopted until the midpoint of the war, was the healthier alternative for seamen's diet.

Finding and purchasing victuals for the navy were only part of the battle; the successful transportation of provisions to the Crown's storehouses and the port of departure was also essential to the survival of hungry seamen. This extremely fragile supply line was further hampered by goods destroyed or damaged in transit, through both human error and mischance.[61] Naval accounts tell us that the state of seamen's provisions frequently deteriorated further once they were aboard. Routinely, biscuit was "consumed into Cromes and Duste by [the] tossinge to and from" of the ship upon the sea. Beer was wasted "with longe tossinge on the narrow Seas." Seepage from the beer harmed other stores. Victuals were eaten by "Battes Rattes Myse and vermin." Furthermore, provisions were stored in the hold, in close proximity to the cookroom. Raleigh complained that this ruined the victuals:

it is a great spoile and annoyance to all [that] the drinke and victualls . . . are bestowed in the hold, by the heat that comes from the cookroome. Besides, it is very dangerous for fire, and very offensive with the smoake and unsavory smells which it sends from thence.

The hold was also near the ballast, the dumping place for all manner of garbage and filth.

Many of the aforementioned problems can be attributed simply to the hazards of life afloat during the sixteenth century. However, the strict financial limitations imposed by the Crown made a difficult task more difficult. Haste and scale further exacerbated problems of obtaining and preserving food and drink. Like victualers for non-naval voyages, surveyors and "middlemen" were anxious to turn a profit from their dealings with the Queen's fleet; the scale allowed for greater scope for profit and corruption within the bureaucracy and along the naval "food chain." Besides overcharging when they could, suppliers made a profit from providing victuals in various states of decay or defaulting on the amounts. Richard Hawkins indicated that this was common practice:

for the company thinking them selues to be stored with foure or sixe moneths Victualls, vpon survay, they find their Bread, Beefe, or Drink short, yea, perhappes all, and so are forced to seeke home. . . . This mischiefe is most ordinary in great actions.[62]

A combination of penny-pinching by the government and suppliers' cutting corners to increase their profit margin jeopardized seamen's health unnecessarily; although the early modern period was hampered by problems of preservation, here was one area where improvements could have been made to ensure a higher quality of diet. For instance, the navy used cheaper, wooden casks to store victuals when ironbound ones would have preserved items longer.[63] Raleigh complained that much beer was wasted because of inadequate casks: "For the Victuallers for cheapnesse will buy stale Caske that hath been used for Herring, Traine Oyle, fish, and other such unsavory things, and there into fill the beere that is provided for the king's ships," and this practice "breeds Infection, and Corrupts all those that drinke thereof." Captain Boteler also criticized the use of substandard casks for "petty saving." Not only was beer important to seamen as the principal liquid in their diet, but it was essential to morale and for its high caloric value. Alcohol made the largest contribution to seamen's energy requirements.[64] In this regard, these "petty savings" had important consequences for seamen. Lack of beer and sour beer were common complaints of seamen throughout the war.[65] The Lord Admiral wrote to Secretary of State Walsingham: "I know not which way to deal with the mariners to make them rest contented with sour beer, for nothing doth displease them more." Low morale was a problem, but substandard beer had much more serious consequences for seamen; as thousands of seamen awaited the arrival of the Armada in the summer of 1588, bad beer bred infection within the fleet. The brewer responsible for the beer blamed the poor quality on the lack of hops; this explanation is plausible given the prices and dearth of wheat and the Queen's fiscal restraint. While dearth and scale exacerbated the problem, parsimony played a role in the death of thousands.

We have already seen that revictualing while at sea was frequently difficult for seamen in non-naval employment. This is doubly true for those in the Queen's employ, especially when the navy was in enemy waters. Sixteenth-century communications were poor, and precious time was wasted trying to locate the fleet; storms, contrary winds, or a host of other factors could complicate a rendezvous. Attempts to find safe ports to revictual were equally chancy. Even when the navy was in home waters (as it was in 1588), provisioning proved difficult.[66] During the height of the invasion crisis the Lord Admiral pleaded with the Privy Council several times to provide victuals for his men. Although the exact nature of the problem is uncertain, the men were in great need. On May 28 Howard begged Lord Treasurer Burghley,

My good lord there is here the gallantest company of captains, soldiers and mariners that I think ever was seen in England. It were a pity they should lack meat, when they are so desirous to spend their lives in her Majesty's service.

By the end of the campaign, Howard's words became more insistent; on August 8 he wrote to Secretary of State Walsingham, "Sir, if I hear nothing of my victuals and munition this night before here, I will gallop to Dover to see what may be [got] there, or else we shall starve." The English navy could not pursue the Spaniards after the battle of Gravelines in 1588 for want of provisions and ammunition. The men were in such a state of dire need that Howard was reduced to eating beans, and some of the men drank their own urine. Howard warned Burghley that poor victuals "may breed danger and no saving to her [Majesty]." Henry White, an officer who faced the Armada attack, was more vehement in his condemnation of the Crown: "our parsimony at home hath bereaved us of the famousest victory that ever our navy might have had at sea."

Such horror stories are not limited to the campaign of 1588. Returning homeward from the Portugal expedition of 1589, large numbers of seamen starved to death.[67] The fleet was so poorly victualed that "many died for hunger in their way home and more would have done if the wind would have taken them short." During the Cadiz expedition of 1596, seamen made complaints about poor victualing. There was constant tension between those who wanted to return home because of "fear of hunger" and the "better sort" who wanted "farther action to gain more reputation." By the time they did turn for home, the Earl of Essex and his men reportedly had only rainwater to drink and ropes' ends to eat. The common practice on expeditions of cutting the men's allotment in order to preserve provisions was not an agreeable solution to the problem; it caused seamen to dissent (where they might protest openly in civilian service), compromised their caloric intake and led to greater malnutrition. During these expeditions, seamen died from undervictualing, and it presumably endangered the health of countless others.

Given the nature of navy victualing, the only surprising aspect is the relative lack of food-related protests. The absence of documented mutinies, with the exception of 1587, should not be interpreted as a sign of seamen's complacence. Commanders' correspondence reveals an almost omnipresent concern of desertions and insurrection because of poor victualing.[68] In at least some instances, these disturbances had a nutritional basis; those suffering from vitamin deficiency are subject to behavioral alterations. During the Portugal expedition the men had "no victuals to sustain them for such a voyage," which gave rise to "disorders and injuries which be daily done and offered . . . not in a manner as if we were friends but mere enemies." There was a distinct fear of going "to sea without victuals or hope of provision" and "famish[ing] there." Martial law was imposed in port to keep "the people in good obedience."[69] Although little was recorded for posterity, the Privy Councillors investigated reports that the soldiers and seamen of one ship did mutiny during the expedition.[70] The striking lack of mutinies or protests can be explained, in part, by the limited effectiveness of this form of protest when the fleet was far from home.[71] There also seems to have been an awareness that the Lord Admiral and other commanders were actively working to relieve their men. Thus, in the face of a national threat, martial law, and limited naval duty, seamen tried to survive until their end of the campaign.

THE CROWN'S STRUGGLE FOR SOLUTIONS

In spite of its record, the Crown seemed to recognize the need to furnish seamen with sufficient provisions. Darell acknowledged that seamen were willing to submit to rationing in extreme circumstances, but "otherwise the mariners will hardly endure to be abridged of any part of their allowances."[72] Lacking a clear sense of a balanced diet, seamen were very concerned with the quantity of their portions.[73] Very few contemporaries seem to have recognized that seamen's diet was not beneficial in the long term.[74] Stuart Captain Nathaniel Boteler was one of the few who observed that "our much and indeed excessive feeding upon these salt meats at sea cannot but procure much unhealthiness and infection." Although it ultimately contributed to health problems among the men, seamen were creatures of habit; "the difficulty consisteth in that the common seamen . . . are so besotted on their Beef and Pork as they had rather adventure on all the Calentures and Scobots in the world than to be weaned from their Customary Diet." Ignorance, inertia, and custom combined to preserve the staples of seamen's diet throughout Elizabeth's reign.

Naval seamen's diet was partially altered in the 1590s, not to relieve its monotony or to promote a healthier fighting force but as a result of the Crown's search for cheaper foodstuffs. From 1590, bacon, pease, and lings appear regularly in victualing accounts.[75] Pease were used to supplement the diet of the very poor. Normally, they were fed to animals. In 1595 more Mediterranean fare of rice and oil appears along with vinegar and oatmeal for the journey southward. In 1597 pork was substituted for half the beef rations. Thus, by 1600 seamen's diet was more varied,[76] as surveyors were clearly seeking cheaper foodstuffs in an attempt to stay within their budget.[77] The analysis of Quarles's accounts demonstrates that beef was by far the most expensive item in seamen's diet. The navy added pork and bacon as alternatives. Doubtless, it was easier to fill smaller quotas from a greater range of products and to economize with lower-grade foodstuffs. Seamen referred to the dried fish that the Crown supplied them with as "Poore John"; this nickname referred to the price, the segment of society that purchased it, and seamen's opinion of it. Nonetheless, the Surveyors continued to scour England for affordable supplies, which became exceedingly difficult in the 1590s. The desperate surveyors suggested in July 1597 that costs could be kept down if seamen were allowed only two flesh and five fish days in a week, with half the quantity of beer on fish days. Victualing charges in the London area were especially costly.[78] The high price of wheat forced Quarles and Darell to bring it in from Hamburg in January 1597, even though the deteriorating quality of foreign wheat was evident. The Lords of the Privy Council wrote: "wee vnderstand the corne that is come of late oute of the East Cuntries dothe not proue so good as yt hathe done in former yeres."[79] Like most of the population of the late sixteenth century, seamen's diets deteriorated in quality.[80]

Given its provisioning problems, it is understandable that the loss of thousands of pounds in wasted provisions rankled the Crown; it attempted to salvage its precious cargoes at all costs.[81] In 1590 casks of salt beef fell into the bilge water of one of the Queen's ships and became "soe vnsavorye and vnwholsome that the same was not in anie sorte serviceable." However, the Crown ordered the beef to be washed, resalted, and repacked for consumption. In 1588 Darell began experimenting with rebrewing sour beer. It seems unlikely that seamen, accustomed to non-naval service, would have deemed such victuals acceptable or edible despite their impressed status. Only England's most poverty-stricken seamen would have found naval fare an improvement over the victuals affordable within their economic strata.[82]

Richard Hawkins wrote that the "corruption of the victuals, and especially of the bread, is very pernicious" and "in long Voyages can hardly be avoyded."[83] There were, however, some limited means available to ensure preservation of food and drink.[84] Late in the reign there seems to have been a deliberate effort to ensure better-quality beer and biscuit for the entire navy; biscuit was "baked of extraordinary goodnes . . . [in the hope that it would] contynewe serviceable for the tyme of theire vivctuallinges," and beer was "brewed of like extraordinary goodness" for service in Ireland in 1600; however, many opportunities were missed. While Hugh Platt's experimentation into the preservation of food and drink yielded valuable ideas, the Crown failed to utilize them. Platt proposed to John Hawkins and Francis Drake that they carry "a cheape, fresh and lasting victuall, called by the name of *Macaroni* amongst the Italians," which could be used when provisions ran out. It seems that Hawkins and Drake took macaroni along on their ill-fated and last voyage in 1595. It is impossible to say why macaroni was not adopted by the navy. The death of Hawkins at this juncture, the single greatest innovator in regard to shipboard cleanliness and seamen's health, might have played a role in ending such experimentation. Seamen's conservative nature regarding their diet may have acted against macaroni's adoption. Whatever the reason, seamen would have benefited from this excellent source of carbohydrates, which was one of the few items in the sixteenth century that could be preserved on long voyages. Platt's ideas regarding powders to preserve victuals were also resourceful. However, the Crown failed to act on Platt's suggestions. It is unclear why. Was it simply the Crown's inertia?

In addition to limited attempts to preserve naval beer and biscuit, there was a more serious effort to monitor the quality of victuals as the war dragged on.[85] On Drake and Norris's Portugal expedition, officers in charge of rations were to be examined under oath regarding the state and quantity of the provisions. In 1596 the Crown hired three men "to suruey the goodness and quantetie of all the victuelles prouided for this seruice." The following year the Privy Council resolved that frauds within the naval bureaucracy "for . . . privatt gayne are nowe to bee more strictly looked vnto." In 1597 bakers were ordered to assist Quarles and Darell in viewing wheat. The Crown also requested that a group of officers from each ship be present to receive their provisions "And findinge any thinge . . . not to be sweete and fitt for men to eate to refuze yt."[86]

Once on board, some attempt was made to improve the storage areas for victuals and to protect them from shipboard dangers.[87] In an effort to diminish the rodent population, cats were welcomed on shipboard. Richard Hawkins explained that,

although I propounded a reward for every Ratt which was taken, and sought meanes by poyson, and other inventions to consume them, yet their increase being so ordinary and many; wee were not able to cleare our selues of them.

Navy Board member Sir William Winter recognized a connection between disease and filthy ballast in 1578. It is unclear if Winter's views influenced Sir John Hawkins or if Hawkins came to the realization himself; Hawkins moved the cookroom of his warship, the *Mary Rose*, to the upper deck for better ventilation in 1590, "as well for the better stowinge of her victualles as also for better preserving her whole companie in health." A younger contemporary of Hawkins, William Monson, maintained that the cookroom's proximity to the ballast and provisions "begets sickness." The idea did not seem to disseminate widely among other commanders or shipbuild-ers.[88]

Despite these measures, navy victuals remained one of the leading causes of discontent among seamen, and the health problems caused by their diet endured well past the sixteenth century. Although it might have done more to minimize problems, the Crown was unable to eradicate the problem, the consequences, or the civilian maritime tradition that validated seamen's protests over their provisioning.[89] The Crown made some concessions for this. While it halted well short of sanctioning work stoppage, the naval seamen were allowed to voice their displeasure regarding their victuals "in a civil manner," which, at the very least, granted them an outlet for their frustration. Conversely, a seaman who created "a mutiny for his victuals" was to be tied to the mainmast and punished if it could be proved he had sufficient provisions. Given the absence of a naval caste of seamen, it was not always possible to silence seamen's voices or to make them serve when they had determined that the risks to their own welfare were too great. The Crown, demonstrating an accepted recognition of "subsistence issues" as a cause of unrest, dictated in 1589 that desertion should "be severely punished, unless it shall appear by due proof upon examination that the said parties were indeed constrained through mere necessity for lack of victual to withdraw themselves." In this way, the Crown accommodated, to a limited extent, the intractable maritime custom and expectation of its impressed seamen to voice their opinions about poor provisioning and, in the most extreme cases, to act to preserve their health.

MORBIDITY AND MORTALITY AT SEA: AN OVERVIEW OF THE PROBLEM

Hakluyt observed that "of so many [seamen], so few grow to gray heires."[90] While the Tudor populace in general was accustomed to high morbidity and mortality levels as facts of life, seamen were vulnerable to the traditional ailments of the land population as well as a host of problems particular to seafarers. Seamen's health has always been compromised by numerous seafaring hazards such as shipwrecks, storms, calms, leaks, and job-related accidents and injuries. Long-distance voyagers were especially susceptible to mysterious new illnesses that claimed numerous seamen in Elizabeth's reign alone.

Overall rates of morbidity and mortality varied according to the type and duration of the journey. A crew greatly diminished by death or disease rarely brought its voyage to a successful end, whether that was a naval goal or trading venture. While shipboard conditions played a role in seamen's morbidity, destination and duration of the voyage appeared to have been greater determinants.

It is impossible to analyze the numbers of seamen lost overall in Elizabeth's reign,[91] let alone to assess morbidity and mortality rates of the various maritime sectors or for specific diseases. Anecdotal evidence and general figures for known voyages provide some sense of morbidity and mortality in the maritime community, but most of this evidence refers to specific voyages and is predominantly for long-distance voyages. It is reasonable to assume that, overall, numbers of those who capitulated to disease and death were much lower on vessels employed on short-distance merchant voyages along established routes, on coasters, and on pirate vessels that haunted local waters. In all three cases there were other hazards to contend with but none so daunting as starvation, tropical diseases, and ailments associated with the corruption of victuals and prolonged vitamin deficiency. Manning rates on short-distance voyages (such as coasters) tended to be much lower than on warships, so infection did not spread as readily. While pirate ships carried greater numbers aboard, many had the luxury of frequenting local waters and appropriating cargoes from those who had made the extended journeys, thereby eliminating many of the hazards associated with long-distance oceanic travel such as acute vitamin deficiency and tropical maladies.

While it is true that long-distance voyages were the most hazardous to seamen, certain routes posed greater health risks than others. Voyages of exploration such as Drake and Cavendish's circumnavigations were particularly arduous. Hair and Alsop's study of the Guinea trade demonstrates that while mortality could vary widely from voyage to voyage, overall mortality was considerable. The first voyage in 1553 had an extremely high mortality rate of about 70 percent, but mortality decreased on subsequent journeys.[92] Similarly, the East Indies trade claimed large numbers of seamen; the huge increase in seamen's wills in the Prerogative Court of Canterbury in 1603 with the return of the first voyage of the East India Company's fleet provides convincing evidence of this. One has simply to read the history of European expansion to learn of the costs in terms of human life and suffering; the price was paid in human currency.

DISEASES

Seamen had to contend with many diseases caused by their diet. Scurvy, an ailment "so ordinary at Sea," was the greatest killer.[93] Richard Hawkins estimated that over 10,000 men had died of it during a 20-year period: "it is the plague of the Sea, and the spoyle of Mariners." As we have seen, vegetables and fruit were not a customary part of the seamen's diet in any facet of maritime employment, which meant that seamen's meals were woefully deficient in vitamins B and C.[94] The cause of scurvy remained largely a mystery.[95] Scurvy usually took one or two months to appear, with the gradual depletion of seamen's vitamin C stores:

it possesseth all those of which it taketh hold, with a loathsome sloathfulnesse, even to eate: they would be content to change their sleepe and rest, which is the most pernicious Enemie in this sicknesse, that is knowne. It bringeth with it a great desire to drinke, and causeth a generall swelling of all parts of the body, especially of the legs and gums, and many times the teeth fall out of the iawes.[96]

The lack of vitamin B in seamen's diet could lead to a loss of vigilance and depression. Mental disorders and paralysis resulted from a prolonged shortage of vitamin B.[97] Such deficiencies were particularly acute on long voyages of circumnavigation, but they also appear in shorter voyages as well. Vitamin B deficiency was a problem during Drake's West Indian voyage of 1585–86: "yea many of them [seamen] were much decayed in their memorie." Richard Hawkins also speaks of some of his men "possest with frensie." Because vitamin A was also wanting in their diet, seamen must have experienced a loss of their night vision.[98] This was an obvious disadvantage to those on watch and, thus, to the crews aboard. Beriberi was a deficiency disease caused by lack of thiamine, which ultimately led to paralysis and death.[99] Since thiamine could be found in several items in the seamen's diet, beriberi almost certainly appeared only when provisions were very low.

Dysentery, known to contemporaries as the "bloody flux," was a recognized part of shipboard life and a problem that subsequently claimed many seamen:[100] one-fifth of the Queen's 2,500 seamen reportedly died of dysentery during the West Indies voyage of 1595. Francis Drake and John Hawkins, two of the finest seamen of their day, were among the victims. Although it was said to have "diuers causes," at least some contemporaries believed that certain fresh fruits induced the flux, leading medical opinion to advise against consumption of the rich source of vitamin C. Seamen were also susceptible to typhus or "ship fever," a common aspect of filthy, louse- and flea-ridden environments. Typhus so afflicted the men of the Portugal expedition in 1589 that many of the crews were useless to carry out their assigned functions.[101]

Elizabethan seamen also had to contend with food poisoning, particularly acute during the armada crisis.[102] The Lord Admiral observed, "It is a thing that ever followeth such great service," and the combination of food poisoning and dysentery nearly crippled the English fleet in the summer of 1588. Howard observed that "those [recruits] that come in fresh are soonest infected; they sicken the one day and die the next" and that the unidentified infection was "thought to be a very plague."[103] This affliction baffled surgeons and physicians in regard to both its source and a remedy. The seamen, vigilant in matters of their own health, ultimately recognized that the mysterious ailment was related to their diet; in 1588 the Lord Admiral reported that the seamen "have a conceit . . . that sour drink hath been a great cause of infection amongst us."[104]

Seamen in transoceanic voyages had to struggle against tropical maladies unknown in England, most notably, malaria and yellow fever.[105] These ailments were often confused and were referred to as "calenture" or "calentour," an adaptation of the Spanish word for "burning ague." At least 300 of the 1,580 men on Drake's 1585 voyage to the West Indies died of malaria or yellow fever (possibly in combination). Those who survived suffered "great alteration and decay of their wittes and strength for a long time after."[106] George Watson's treatise of 1598 on the causes and cures for diseases particular to foreign lands and climates—a pioneering study—illustrates the great degree to which contemporaries were grasping at straws as to the causes and cures of these tropical maladies.

Seamen also had to contend with traditional illnesses that afflicted the land population. Tudor seamen were particularly vulnerable to the Black Death because of its association with the fleas on the black rat that infested ships and ports. Fortunately for the navy, the most vicious outbreaks of plague in Elizabeth's reign were not years of major campaigns.[107]

Many of the impressed men—those termed "the scum and dregs of the country"—and the lower echelon of the maritime community were malnourished or diseased before they set foot on board. Malnutrition reduced their immunity to disease and infection, making these men very susceptible to any number of shipboard afflictions.[108] Given the crowded conditions on most Tudor vessels, this was bound to affect the health of the rest of the crew.

While precise numbers of sick and dead seamen elude us, we are on safer ground in discussing the consequences of shipboard disease. Maritime objectives could not be accomplished when manpower was compromised by sickness and death.[109] Drake was forced to alter his plans in 1585–86 because "of the sclenderness of our strength"; due to the "inconuenience of continuall mortality, we were forced to giue ouer our intended enterprise." A commander would rarely hazard his ship and crew in an attack if a significant number of his men were in poor health. Furthermore, it made even the most peace-loving crew and their ship and cargo easy targets for predators. On a Guinea trading voyage of 1556–57, participant William Towerson recorded that an enemy vessel approached his ship having "perceiued that we had bene upon a long voyage, and iudging us to be weake, as indeed we were." Mortality severely reduced the manpower of the privateering vessel *Jaquet* of Falmouth in 1586; the few survivors of the original 82-man crew were helpless to sail their vessel home. Of the twelve or thirteen ships that made nine round trips to Guinea between 1553 and 1565, four or five ships were lost along with several pinnaces. Most were abandoned because of lack of men to sail them.

PREVENTION AND CONTAINMENT OF DISEASE

To a large extent, health risks and harsh shipboard conditions were seen as inherent to seafaring. Captain Luke Foxe wrote:

for to keepe a warme Cabbin & lye in sheets is the most ignoble part of a Sea man, but to endure and suffer; as a hard Cabbin, cold and salt Meate, broken sleepes, mouldy bread, dead beere, wet cloathes, want of fire, all these are within board.[110]

Despite the general acceptance that "the winges of man's life are plumed with the feathers of death,"[111] some prudent seamen attempted to improve the lot of men at sea, which had rapidly deteriorated in the age of expansion. This impetus came principally from the private sector, usually high-ranking seamen who undertook to lower morbidity and mortality not only for reasons of compassion but to solve manning problems and improve the prospects of having successful voyages.

Contemporaries believed that seamen's lack of clothing was a contributing factor to their high rate of sickness.[112] Richard Hawkins observed that it was "a common calamitie amongst the ordinary sort of Mariners, to spend their thrift on the shore, and to bring to Sea no more Cloaths then they haue backes." Although the evidence of seamen's wills suggests that even the less affluent seamen brought more than one shift of apparel,[113] there are frequent complaints from those in authority about the lack of seamen's clothing. Given that the shipboard duties of the majority of the crew were labor-intensive, seamen's clothing underwent a great deal of wear and tear. Raleigh estimated that a suit of apparel would be worn to shreds within six months at sea. Richard Hawkins maintained that wearing scant, wet, and salt-encrusted clothing was bound to upset the humors. Both he and John Hawkins provided clothing for their seamen, but seamen on expeditions to locate the Northwest Passage had to wait until 1602 to receive the first "Arctic kit," provided by the sponsor, the East India Company: leather mittens, leather breeches with fur, woolen hose and stockings, furred cassocks with hoods, and leather boots. Not until the opening years of the seventeenth century did merchant companies and the navy begin to recognize the need for improved measures.

Earlier in the sixteenth century the state provided clothing for naval seamen. The men in Henry VIII's navy were allotted green and white coats at a cost of 34 pence each. This practice was discontinued in 1560.[114] Unlike the men of the Elizabethan army who received both summer and winter issue at the joint expense of the Crown and the county,[115] the Elizabethan navy granted its impressed seamen only a small sum as "coat and conduct" money. These funds were to be put toward travel costs and to buy apparel.[116] It seems unlikely that money not eaten up in travel costs secured much protection against the elements. Richard Hawkins noted,

That money which is wont to be cast away in Imprestes [cash advances on wages] might be imployed in apparel, and necessaries at the sea, and given to those that haue need, at the price it was bought, to be deducted out of their shares or wages at their returne.

The Lord Admiral recognized the association between clothing and the health of the men under his command:

It is like enough that the like infection will grow throughout the most part of our fleet; for they have been so long at sea and have so little shift of apparel, and so [few] places to provide them of such wants, and no money wherewith to buy it, for some have been—yea the most part—these eight months at sea. My Lord, I would think it is a marvellous good way that there were a thousand pounds worth or two thousand marks worth of hose, doublets, shirts, shoes and such like, sent down; and I think your Lordship [Lord Burghley] might use . . . all expedition for the providing and sending away of such things; for else, in very short time I look to see most of the mariners go naked.[117]

Although the ongoing need was acknowledged, it was rarely met. As in most things, the Crown provided for naval seamen only when the most dire of circumstances compelled it to act. As always, relief was sporadic[118]; these ad hoc measures did not result in a comprehensive plan to improve the condition of seamen employed in the service of their sovereign. In general, if naval seamen were in need of clothing, they did without or fell prey to some enterprising official contractor, landlady, or fellow seamen who sold them overpriced apparel on credit.[119] Not until the closing years of the war (when the period of greatest naval activity was past) do navy accounts show that the Crown made its most benevolent gesture; in 1602 canvas shirts, cotton waistcoats, caps, hose, and "rugge" to make gowns were ordered.[120] Was this merely a case of the Crown's agreeing to what John and Richard Hawkins and Howard had long advocated? It is significant that such measures were not undertaken until the final years of the war.

Some advances were made in the area of shipboard and personal hygiene. The official orders show that the regulation of hygienic conditions (relative to the standards of the day) was instituted much earlier for private expeditions than in naval service.[121] Sebastian Cabot's orders for the Company of Merchant Adventurers (1553) stressed the need for cleanliness throughout the ship "for the better health of the companie." The 1557 instructions of a merchant fleet to Russia show a similar emphasis:

no beere nor broth, or other liquor be spilt vpon the balast or other place of the shippe, whereby any anoyance, stinke or other vnsauorines shall grow in the shippe to the infection or hurt of the persons in the same.

Richard Hawkins maintained that a sanitary shipboard environment was a necessity: "the best prevention for this disease [scurvy] . . . is to keepe cleane the Shippe, to . . . sprinkle her ordinarily with Vinegar, or to burne Tarre, and some sweet savours." In the navy, however, orders specifically stating that warships should be cleaned and washed do not appear until 1596, "which, with God's favour shall preserve from sickness and avoid inconvenience." In 1597 the navy officially sanctioned hammocks, as cabins were thought to be "sluttish dens that breed sickness . . . and in fight are dangerous to tear men with their splinters." The Crown paid £300 for canvas to make "Hamacas or Brasill beds" as part of the outfitting of the Cadiz expedition under the Earl of Essex. These "hanging cabones" were thought to decrease the chance of fire on board as well as created a more sanitary shipboard environment.

Some masters and captains, even on privateering vessels, encouraged sanitary habits[122] and personal tidiness by carrying soap and needles and thread for their men to wash and repair their clothes. Among the artifacts salvaged from the *Mary Rose* were combs and ear-scoops. Soap was carried aboard the early Elizabethan voyages to West Africa. As we have already seen, even sixteenth-century seamen had limits of tolerance. The crew of the *True Love* approached their master about the "stinche" of his apprentice which "greeved, troubled and annoyed" them. The offending boy was dunked into the sea and given a new suit of clothes.

Alongside concern for the shipboard environment, it was a commonly held view that, whenever possible, seamen should be put ashore to refresh themselves; contemporaries thought this was a particularly effective treatment both to maintain and revive seamen.[123] In addition to giving his men a respite from their shipboard existence, Richard Hawkins put great faith in the power of exercise to ward off ill health. For the purposes of containment and treatment, the most common solution was to put the sick ashore if possible. During the West Indies expedition in 1585–86 the naval fleet was so debilitated by sickness that they spent Christmas ashore at St. Christopher's to rest the men and air the ships. Sickness broke out among a contingent of ships during a voyage of 1590–91, "and soe they sayled to an Island called Trinadatho . . . here they remayned a tyme to recover theire healthes." When sickness appeared aboard the *William* of Ipswich during a voyage in the late 1580s, the crew "wente to panerchia while the wounded & diseased people the better to gett theire health were sente a shore and the said Barnes [the surgeon] appoyneted to goe with them." When numbers and circumstances warranted, the sick were transported home. During Humphrey Gilbert's 1583 voyage to Newfoundland, so many men were paralyzed with the flux that "it seemed good therefore vnto the Generall to leaue the *Swallow* with such prouision as might be spared for transporting home the sicke people."[124]

In the most extreme outbreaks, the ships would be vacated and the men put ashore while the ships were cleaned. When the situation permitted, ships were "rummaged"; that is, the filthy ballast was changed, and the ship was scrubbed in an effort to provide a healthier atmosphere for all. In cases of epidemics, this did little to alleviate the situation. The ill-fated *Elizabeth Jonas* in 1588 provides an apt illustration:

The *Elizabeth Jonas*, which hath done so very well as ever a ship did in service, hath had a great infection in her from the beginning, so as of the 500 men which she carried out, by the time we had been in Plymouth three weeks or a month, there were dead of them 200 or above; so I [the Lord Admiral] was driven to set all the rest of her men ashore, to take out her ballast, and to make fires in her of wet broom, three or four days together; and so hoped thereby to have cleansed her of her infection; and thereupon got new men, very tall and able as ever I saw, and put them into her. Now the infection is broken out in greater extremity than ever it did before, and [the men] die and sicken faster than ever they did.[125]

While the Lord Admiral's compassion for his men is readily apparent in his letters and his actions, his primary concern was to relieve immediate suffering. There is no evidence to suggest that Howard sought permanent reform in the navy. The changes that were instituted were brought in at the behest of John Hawkins, who worked to improve the lot of seamen and lessen the virulence of epidemics in the fleet. Hawkins's recommendation to man warships at a lower rate shortly before the coming of the first armada was an attempt to relieve some of the overcrowding and lessen the spread of disease.[126] The impressment of the "tag and rag,"[127] the lowest element of society, for naval duty meant that those men forced aboard to labor were often very susceptible to infection or brought disease with them. The Crown approved a pay increase for seamen in 1585 after listening to John Hawkins's argument that higher wages would attract a better quality of seamen to naval service:

By this meane, her Maiesties shippes wolde be ffurnyshed with able men suche as can make shyfte for themselves, kepe themselves clene withoute vermyne and noysomeness which bredeth sycknes and mortalletye.[128]

Given the frugal nature of the Elizabethan Crown, this pay increase was made possible only by the decrease in numbers resulting from Hawkins's new manning rate.

The impetus for change within the maritime community came largely from the civilian sector or from career seamen such as Richard Hawkins. Had the Crown capitalized upon the ingenuity of such men and adopted their solutions, undoubtedly a great deal of human suffering could have been avoided. The Crown, however, was generally reluctant to break new ground. While officials complained throughout the war years of the endless search for seamen for the navy, the Crown did not actively seek new means to keep the men whom it had in fighting form. Awareness of the health problems originating in England's first large-scale, naval war came slowly to the Privy Council, few of whose members had any experience of naval warfare. Overall, the state did little to improve conditions and offer incentives to draw men into service in the navy.

While there were attempts to prevent and contain disease within the maritime community, high levels of morbidity and mortality remained. Although Dr. James Lind wrote of the period of the Seven Years' War, 1756–63, his analysis is true of the Elizabethan period as well:

the number of seamen in time of war who died by shipwreck, capture, famine, fire or sword are but inconsiderable in respect of such as are destroyed by the ship diseases and the usual maladies of intemperate climates.[129]

Although it ultimately had little success during this period, the search for solutions and the attempt to improve the lot of seamen in order to preserve manpower and ensure the success of the voyage were nonetheless valuable pursuits; the active quest to lower mortality at sea recognized that the status quo—at least to those in the private sector—was not an acceptable one. Because impressment freed the Crown from having to compete for manpower on the open market, it had much less incentive to implement and bear the cost of improved health measures for its seamen.

SEAFARING HAZARDS, INJURIES, AND FATALITIES

In addition to the numerous health problems already mentioned, seamen had to contend with diverse other dangers. Storms and calms aggravated the weaknesses of sixteenth-century vessels.[130] Methods of navigation were imperfect. While advances were being made, sixteenth-century ships were hampered by their limited maneuverability; they lacked the ability to tack close to the wind, which could drive ships ashore in blustery weather. In 1593 the *Toby* of London encountered a storm in its approach to the Strait of Gibraltar and was driven onto the African coast. Mariner Silvester Scriven, a survivor, testified that many of the crew were swept off the deck during the storm, and "all the company perished with the shippe savinge twelv persons that by swiminge & han[g]inge to tymbers of the shipp were caste to the shore whereof this examinante was one." Even the most routine voyages placed a great deal of wear and tear on ships; seams worked under the strain of sail, combat, and storms, and caulking had a tendency to give way. Chain pumps were effective only for minor leaks. Anchors were often too light and their cables too weak so that both were frequently lost. Rudders and tall masts were vulnerable to the weather. While testifying before the Admiralty Court, Thomas Chartham declared himself to be a "sea man and *thereby* knowinge such misfortunes are incidente oftentymes at sea."[131] Although there were improvements to pumps, capstans, log-lines, studding, and sails, creative ideas could not overcome some of the most routine problems of sixteenth-century seafaring. While some of these hazards were "acts of God," others could be minimized by careful maintenance of the ship.[132] Discontented crews could refuse employment or, if they were already employed, refuse to sail. Shipmaster Cutbert Gripe, part-owner of the *Fortune*, was forced to sell the ship at Legorne when his company was hesitant to make the return journey in the ship; they feared she would split on the voyage homeward because she was rotten and "sore bruscd with stormes."[133]

Because of the nature of their working environment, drownings among seamen were common. Certainly, some job-related injuries and fatalities were to be expected.[134] Nicholas Turning and Nicholas Curnaby of the *John Bonaventure* of London were drowned in May 1603, when the rope gave way as they were coming aboard. In December 1597 Alexander Gibbons was commanded to go up and let out the foresail. He lost his footing on frost "& he fell downe on his heade and brake out his braynes." Other fatalities can be attributed to sheer negligence.[135] A battle between an English vessel and the *Galleon Lombardo* in the mid-1580s resulted in the galleon's being "fired by her owne powder and negligence of her owne men." John Darnbye and Henry Prentisse of the *Swallow* of Harwich capsized the ship's boat in the Thames in 1584, when they both stood on the same side while working with a cable, "and soe by theire owne unskilfulnes they were drowned." In 1579 the men of the *Parnell* left the portholes of the ship open at night; a great tempest arose suddenly "whiche greatly tossed the said shippe," and "the water yssued in [the portholes] in great abundance." The crew did not awaken "vntill the water was come in in suche abondance that all hope of recoverye was paste and that she [the *Parnell*] sanke presentlye downe." Alcohol consumption was an important part of every seaman's diet, and many accidents and injuries were alcohol-related.[136] William Trewneck, the master of the *May Flower*, was drunk when he rose from his bed "to do his business in the night"; he fell overboard and drowned. Shipboard brawls happened all too frequently, with or without alcohol. In 1604 John Magnes and John Ivington, friends and shipmates aboard the *John and Frances* of London, had a violent fight, which ended in Magnes's death. Similarly, an argument broke out between Robert Noble of Suffolk, the master's mate of the *Primrose*, and Thomas Cambridge, master of the *Fox*, over docking of the latter's vessel; words were exchanged, a hatchet was thrown, and Noble struck Cambridge with an oar, knocking him into the Thames to his death.[137]

The shipboard environment and journeys by sea were dangerous not only by virtue of the relationships between those aboard and the hazards inherent in seafaring; sailor Thomas Basset maintained that the late sixteenth century was a difficult time to be a seaman, given the increasing duration of many voyages, the subsequent problems with manpower and provisioning, and "the dangerousnes of the tyme."[138] English seamen, as we have seen, could not remain aloof from the political, commercial, and religious tensions with Spain. Barber-surgeon Arthur Dowton told the Admiralty Court in 1595 that "it is very notoriouse that the articulate kinge of Spayne is an open enimy to this Realme of England and all th' inhabitantes ther of whereof noe man can be ignorante."[139] The hostility between Spain and England had very real consequences for seafarers. In February 1591 the Lord Admiral wrote to Julius Caesar, judge of the Admiralty, that "there are manie Englishmen kepte prisoners in Spaine whose freindes are not hable to redeme them oute of captivitie."[140] Falling into the hands of the enemy meant that seamen were given over to the Inquisition and frequent torture, like many of those who sailed on Drake and Hawkins's ill-fated trading voyage of 1567, some of the participants of John Hawkins's third slaving voyage of 1568, and John Oxenham's crew in 1576. The *Gillian* of London was one of several English vessels caught in Spain's embargo of 1585. Many of the crew were imprisoned, and "fyve of the company died for honger."[141] One's punishment was meted out according to the intensity of one's "heretical" convictions.[142] In extreme examples, Englishmen were executed. Most were given sentences as galley slaves.[143] Elsewhere, the men who survived the shipwreck of the *Toby* in 1593 were captured by the Moors, presented to their king, and then imprisoned; they were "kepte with water & barly breade vntill they were redeemed & boughte by englishe marchantes there residente."[144] For the minority who made it back to England from foreign captivity, there existed a real risk of additional health problems as a consequence of imprisonment.

Pirates were a perennial threat to seamen, but the problem was very pronounced in the late sixteenth century. Despite the Admiralty's efforts to bring pirates before the court and curb lawlessness at sea, the Crown acknowledged in the 1590s that maritime violence was escalating.[145] The maritime community in its entirety was mobilized for war—for defense if not for offense. Since no ship was afforded the luxury of a nonpartisan stance, even fishermen using the Grand Banks off Newfoundland had to be armed out of necessity. Given the internal conflicts within France and the Low Countries, it was difficult (if not impossible) once at sea for Englishmen to discern the political and religious convictions of many foreign ships and thus gauge their intent. Mariner Richard Elforde of Plymouth served for nine months aboard a ship of a French governor called the *Harry*. Elforde testified before the Admiralty Court that the Frenchmen commonly threw captured Englishmen overboard to their deaths. Elforde claimed that the governor had ordered a "zero tolerance" policy toward Englishmen; their commission reportedly directed them to "spare none, take all that you may come by."[146] Similarly, Dunkirk seamen "threatened they would send a diving as many englishe men as they should meete &

overcome and that they looked for Englishmen."[147] Undoubtedly, ships were dangerous work environments, a point proven by large numbers of unfortunate and negligent seamen at great personal cost. Anecdotal evidence suggests that friction between crewmates was not uncommon. Long, dangerous voyages kept stress levels high and men at close quarters. Growing levels of shipboard illness, vitamin deficiency, and malnutrition led to carelessness and injuries in the work environment. Such incidents, although not uncommon, paled in comparison to the overwhelming dangers posed by hostile forces within the international maritime community and the growing violence at sea. Therefore, the growth in disease and vitamin deficiency at sea had a parallel in terms of dangers posed by escalating maritime brutality.

HEALTH CARE AFLOAT

Although at least some seamen took responsibility for the maintenance of their health, the sick and injured were usually given some form of health care afloat or on land. The Laws of Oléron stipulated that employers had health care responsibilities for their ill and wounded employees. Although it was usually recommended that the sick and injured be cared for ashore rather than on shipboard, charges were still to be absorbed by the employer(s).[148] When men were kept on shipboard, the onus of fighting morbidity and treating injuries was shared by officers, seamen, and, when present, barber-surgeons. The introduction of longer-distance naval and commercial voyaging and the contemporary interest in lowering incapacitation rates at sea led to a growth in medical personnel on shipboard. Physicians would have been a logical choice to serve on ships because they were highly educated by the standards of the day, and their expertise centered on internal ailments, the greatest killers of seamen. The barber-surgeon's practice focused on external problems such as fractures, battle wounds, and venereal diseases and was a trade learned through apprenticeship.[149] Despite the fact that apothecaries, physicians, and surgeons had separate functions within the field of medicine, there was a great deal of overlap in practice. As in the case of medical practitioners on land, Tudor army and sea surgeons would have had to employ a variety of techniques that were, strictly speaking, outside the surgeons' expertise. Judging from the items in the barber-surgeon's chest found aboard the *Mary Rose*, the ship's surgeons trespassed into the physicians' and apothecaries' domains. There are examples of ship's surgeons like Ralph Rowland who treated a sick seaman who was "sometymes verey hott and somctymes extreame coulde"; Rowland prescribed purgative pills for his patient. Monson's *Naval Tracts* recommended that the surgeon's chest "must be well furnished both for physic and surgery."[150]

Throughout the war years naval seamen became more and more accustomed to having surgeons aboard.[151] By the time of King Charles I, all warships in royal service had a surgeon, and the Crown provided medical practitioners with money to furnish their medical chests with supplies. By the early Stuart period, it was accepted that seamen "will do nothing without a chirugeon, for that it puts them out of heart" and that the lack of a surgeon "is a great discouragement to our men." Monson wrote that the surgeon should be placed in the hold "where he should be in no danger of shot; for there cannot be a greater disheartening of the company than in his miscarrying, whereby they will be deprived of all help for hurt and wounded men." Although many private voyages were not documented, it appears that the most needy areas of the private sector also experienced the growing presence of surgeons during the late sixteenth century. Surgeons and their mates were carried aboard all the ships of the East India Company from its inception in 1600, an employer well known for its concern for shipboard conditions and the health of its seamen.

The Elizabethan navy offered little in the way of incentives to medical personnel through pay or conditions. As in the case of able seamen, the most talented surgeons usually managed to escape naval duty.[152] Surgeon William Clowes wrote:

And what shall be sayd of some which had not long since have been commanded to prepare themselves, and with all speede to serve their Maiesty in the Warres, then presently with many solemne circumstances, did desire to be excused, protesting, that they had no knowledge in surgery, but onely, for the drawing, and stopping of a tooth, letting of bloud, or the cure of the french Pocks.

While such protestations were probably made in order to seek exemptions from naval service, there were a sizable number of substandard surgeons sent to sea. Clowes maintained that a large number of supposed surgeons, "uncleane birds," were "altogither ignorant in the art." Some ships employed apprentices, journeymen, those holding licenses to practice as midwives, oculists, couchers for cataracts, dentists, bone-setters, venereal disease specialists, or those who treated hernias or harelip. When the surgeon died at sea or was injured, his mate was usually thrust into his position whether he was qualified or not. When the surgeon died in 1578 during Drake's voyage of circumnavigation, his mate, "a boy, whose good will was more than any skill hee had," was promoted. Given these conditions, many of the more affluent or cautious members of the seafaring community made their own arrangements for health care afloat.[153]

Although there were numerous complaints about the quality and competence of "sory surgeons" in the navy, we hear remarkably little criticism of non-naval surgeons.[154] The Admiralty depositions contain seamen's grumblings on all manner of grievances; however, ships' surgeons seldom appear in a negative context. Pay was considerably higher in the merchant service and aboard privateers. It is possible that, as in the case of experienced seamen, the lure of profits associated with privateering expeditions attracted skilled medical personnel. Roger Crosse appeared repeatedly before the Admiralty Court as the surgeon for various privateering vessels.[155] Although quartermaster John Godfrey of the *Salamander* died of his battle wounds in the late 1580s, he bequeathed his sea chest, his apparel, and his four shares in the voyage to Crosse, who took "great Paynes aboute the curinge of him." In 1589 a crewmate maintained that Thomas Barnes of the *William* of Ipswich was "accompted a good surgeon" and cured several injured seamen, which he "would not haue donn yf he had [not been] skilfull in his arte."[156] Such bequests suggest that seamen appreciated the attentions of surgeons. In several cases we can distinguish between those seamen who owed a monetary debt to a surgeon and those who wished to show their gratitude for care.

THE EFFICACY OF PROACTIVE TREATMENT

High morbidity and mortality continued despite the presence of surgeons. On limited occasions when the Crown called upon the "skillful phisicions"[157] of the realm (as it did in 1588) "for remedie of the dyseased and for staie of further contagion" in the fleet, the measure proved futile. The sum of £253 was spent for "Phisions and Surgeons" for Drake's Portugal expedition of 1589, but under half the men who left England returned. Whether they were trained specifically for the treatment of internal ailments, even the most celebrated surgeons and physicians were of little use in the war against morbidity.[158] In part, we can account for the failure of the medical profession in that maritime medicine was still in its infancy, and medical practitioners attempted to apply traditional and largely ineffectual cures and treatments used on the land population to all manner of seafaring diseases and injuries. Even the eminent William Clowes, the Lord Admiral's personal surgeon, was perplexed by seafaring maladies; he recommended established techniques, such as bloodletting, to treat scurvy.[159] Men of lesser reputations followed his example. When widespread infection devastated the English fleet, as it did time and time again, "for the sooner recoverye of theyr [the seamen] healthes" it was "thowght . . . good to lett them blood." Given this approach, maritime medicine proved woefully inadequate.

Tudor surgeons suffered their greatest failure in their efforts to combat disease, the primary cause of death at sea. They were somewhat more successful in treating external problems, although it can be argued that seamen were best served by medical personnel in the last years of the war. In the opening years of the war, Colonel Anthony Wingfield stated that "our English surgeons be unexperienced in hurts that come by shot; because England hath not known wars but of late, from whose ignorance proceeded this discomfort."[160] Given the length of the war, at least some surgeons gained expertise treating battle wounds. Yet a number of seamen perished largely because of medical attention; Martin Frobisher died as a result of a surgeon's treatment of a slight wound from a Spanish musket ball. What should have been a routine procedure of an inconsequential wound claimed the life of one of the era's greatest seamen.[161]

When they did occur, successes and advances rarely came from the medical community; most breakthroughs can be credited to experienced seamen who were actively looking for solutions.[162] For instance, observant seamen recognized the power of fruit to eliminate scurvy. J. D. Alsop has noted that there are references to antiscorbutics among Guinea seamen as early as 1562. Richard Hawkins also recognized the connection between fruit and scurvy: "That which I haue seene most fruitfull for this sicknesses, is sower Oranges and Lemmons." He wrote, "This is a wonderfull secret of the power and wisedome of God, that hath hidden so great and vnknowne vertue in this fruit, to be a certaine remedie for this infirmitie." Scurvy grass was sometimes employed as a means of preventing the disease; one master had it pressed and the juice put "into a Hogshead of strong Beare, with command that every one that would should have a pint to his mornings draught, but none would taste it untill it was past time, and themselves almost past meanes." In 1601, after four and a half months at sea, the men of the first East India Company voyage showed serious signs of vitamin deficiency and "could hardly handle the sayles." Until his supply ran out, Commander James Lancaster gave his men the lemon juice that he had brought to sea, "three spoonfuls every morning," which helped to restore their healths. These empirical seamen discerned effective treatments. Dr. John Woodall, Surgeon-General of the East India Company, finally recommended in *The Surgeon's Mate* (1617) that seamen be given a dosage of lime juice when they returned to port. Although this treatise was insightful when compared to the views of other medical practitioners of the day, Woodall would have benefited from closer consultation with men such as Lancaster. It is difficult to surmise whether even Lancaster recognized the fact that lemon juice was a much more effective antiscorbutic than lime juice. The Company, however, complied with Woodall's advice and not Lancaster's example; lime juice, the less effective treatment, was recommended to East India seamen. It was the tragedy of the age of expansion that the hard-won lessons of maritime medicine were rarely applied. Lemon juice and fruit as treatments for scurvy would not be officially sanctioned by the Admiralty Board until 1795.[163] Perhaps if medical authorities had been the originators of these solutions, they would have been disseminated more thoroughly and at an earlier date.

Although most medical practitioners failed to pinpoint the exact connection between the seamen's diet and scurvy, ailing seamen aboard all types of vessels were given a special diet whenever such items were available. Dietetics was viewed by contemporaries as an essential part of medical treatment.[164] It was believed that salted foods should be avoided because they taxed the fragile constitution of the sick. In 1586 the commander of the privateering vessel, *Golden Noble*, went ashore in Barbary, "where much money was consumed in providing fresh victualls for the company whoe were greatly infected with sicknes." In the case of the navy, commanders sometimes ordered wine and arrowroot for the sick. In 1588 Howard requested wine, cider, sugar, oil, and fish for the sick at Plymouth "to relieve such men withal as by reason of sickness or being hurt in fight should not be able to digest the salt meats at sea." In addition, the Lord Admiral ordered extra beer and wine for the men at his own expense. He later impounded a cargo of rice from the *Mary* of Hamburg for the sick.[165] In 1595 the Crown reimbursed Robert Cross, captain of the *Swiftsure*, for victuals for the "releive the sicke men whoe could no longer endure to feede on saulte meates." In 1599 the "sycke diseased & impotente" naval seamen were given special victuals, although accounts do not specify what foodstuffs the men received. Although commendable, these occasional measures pale in comparison to the Spanish navy's arrangements for the dietary needs of its sick men. The Spaniards carried livestock aboard their ships to be slaughtered for the ill and wounded. The *Nuestra Senora del Rosario* alone had three calves and 50 sheep for the sick. Eggs or fish was supplied on fast days instead of fresh meat. Nuts, raisins, and preserves were also dispensed, as they were highly regarded for their curative qualities.[166]

While it is difficult to compare provisions consumed in the civilian sector of the English and Spanish maritime communities, clearly, the English navy's ad hoc method of providing for its sick and injured men left much to be desired. When special victuals were ordered, it was almost always at the behest of a captain or commander—the Crown did not take the initiative to provide for its seamen. On the other hand, the Spanish navy made superior preparations for their debilitated men before leaving port.[167] This extended well beyond diet for the sick. Spanish navies included hospital ships within the fleets, while sick and injured English seamen were kept in the gunner's room or on the ballast.[168] Such arrangements show the great disparity between the health provisions made for the respective navies. Spanish maritime expansion had been under way for much longer than its English equivalent, and during the sixteenth century, Spain developed a policy of care for its seamen. In addition to hospital ships, Spanish religious orders tended sick seamen who were landed in port.[169]

NURSING CARE

Although their numbers were increasing, many ships, particularly those in the private sector, did not have medical personnel aboard. In the absence of surgeons, seamen cared for their shipmates.[170] When violence broke out aboard the *Examiner* in 1588, the master's mate dressed the captain's wound. Like the community on land, the practice of medicine was not limited to the "professional" healers.[171] For instance, Sir Francis Drake and his officers were reputed to be knowledgeable of "lotions, emplaisters and unquents."

While many career seamen would have garnered some rudimentary knowledge of first aid, crewmates were very important for moral support and as caregivers. Most health care at sea was essentially palliative regardless of the qualifications of the caregiver; nursing, as opposed to proactive treatment like surgery, was vital. One might well argue that this was the most successful aspect of health care at sea. Even in those cases in which a surgeon was present, crew members were frequently involved in the caring of the sick and injured.[172] The articles of the Company of Merchant Adventurers (1553) provided for this: "the sicke, diseased, weake, and visited person within boord, to be tendred, relieved, comforted, and holpen in the time of his infirmitie, and every maner of person, without respect, to beare anothers burden." Among the general population, tending and visiting the sick were a social and religious duty that involved much of the community.[173] These duties were taken very seriously by the maritime community as well. There are numerous examples of compassion and tenderness between seamen and their ill crewmates. Mariner Richard Clerk lay on his deathbed with a burning fever, and gunner John Marsh remained by his side "vntill he yelded vppe." In addition to ships' surgeons, seamen's shipboard wills habitually contain bequests to crewmates who helped to nurse the dying men.[174] Although seaman Thomas Mudge gave the ship's surgeon a quantity of pepper for his services, he also left many of his possessions to swabber John Collins for his attention during Mudge's illness. Sailor John Fry remembered a crewmate in his will "for his paynes taken with mee in my sickness." As in the case of sickness among the land population, professional medical practitioners were not usually the principal caregivers, especially if patients were deemed to be on their deathbed.[175]

HEALTH CARE ASHORE, RELIEF, AND CHARITY

Shipboard health care was an established shipboard practice, whether palliative or proactive, given by a professional healer or a crewmate. The Laws of Oléron are much more specific about the seamen's entitlement to care ashore than afloat, but they indicate that shipowners were bound to provide medical care for their seamen.[176] Article 7 dictates:

If it chaunce that any maryner be taken with sekenesse in the ship doyng service there to be belongyng, the maister ought to set hym out of the shyp, and seke lodgynge for hym, And ought for to fynde hym lyght, as talowe or candell, and to gyve hym a lad of the shyp for to take hede of hym, or hyre a woman to kepe hym; and ought to purvey hym suche meat as is used in the shyp, that is to wyte, as moche as he toke whan he was in helth, and no more, but yf the mayster wyll And yf he wyl have deyntyer meates, the mayster is not bounde to gete hym any, but to be at his costes.

Custom decreed that those seamen who were taken ashore for care were still entitled to their wages:

yf the shyppe be redy to departe, it ought not to tarry for hym, and yf he recover, to have his hyre in payinge and rebatynge that the mayster layde out for him. And if he dye his wyfe or next kynne or frende oughte to have it for hym.

This medieval model afforded care and wages for sick and injured seamen as part of the conditions of their employment. This was not unlike the bonds of responsibility between other laborers and employers. In husbandry, the law dictated that "if a servant retained for the year falls sick, or is hurt or disabled, by act of God or the master's business, he is not to be put away nor his wages to be abated."[177]

Shipmasters in the civilian sector of the maritime community seem to have lived up to their traditional obligations to their employees. In the Admiralty depositions, seamen mention that they or their shipmates were taken ashore for care as a matter of course. Shortly after he was hired to sail on the *Mary Gallant* in 1590, James Waldon fell sick while the ship was still anchored at Lee. Master John Harris promised Waldon that he would have good broth and care ashore. He was later rowed into port and carried ashore. Michael Nerial, mariner and captain of the *Anne Clair*, hired quartermaster John Foster to sail to Melvyn. Foster contracted the plague while he was ashore, so Nerial arranged for him to be cared for in a local hospital. When Foster died a few days later, all his shipmates were in attendance at his funeral at the hospital's churchyard. Nerial claimed that he had disbursed five pounds on Foster's care and burial.[178]

Without question, care for the sick could be costly. The charges incurred by seaman Thomas Onyon's two-month sickness proved expensive indeed; Onyon's lodging, diet, nursing, and laundry cost £17 11s. 8d. Onyon made £3 per annum as a seaman.[179] Other masters resented being saddled with the responsibility for a sick seaman.[180] Sailor Cutbert Richardson of Suffolk fell sick shortly after he was hired to sail to France in the late 1570s. Shipmaster Michael Cooper would not release him from the ship and compelled him to work the voyage. In 1601 mariner Samuel Lowell of Limehouse came down with the flux aboard the *Moonshine*. Master Thomas Pyn did not believe that the man was genuinely ill, although master's mate William Bateson was convinced of the authenticity of Lowell's condition. Pyn beat the sick seaman routinely throughout the voyage with a rope's end, "callinge him roage villaine, rascall, & that it were a good deed to kill such a viallaine as would not worcke." When Lowell took to his cabin, Pyn ordered one of the crew to drag him from his sickbed; the master had him beaten again, ordering him to "stand vpp you ill lookeinge slave." Lowell died aboard the *Moonshine* three weeks later off the coast of Scotland. Whether he died as a result of his sickness or the injuries he sustained is uncertain. Pyn's treatment of Lowell is the most glaring example of dereliction of care for the sick that appears in the Admiralty depositions for the late Elizabethan era. Surely, seamen who were so forthcoming with their criticisms on other subjects would have regaled the Admiralty Court if such abuses were common. Instead, there was an expectation of some form of care.

The weight of existing evidence suggests that most ill and injured seamen received compassionate treatment from their crewmates. Shipmates routinely took an active interest in their colleagues even when responsibility had been transferred to a caregiver ashore. At the turn of the century, William Thompson "was a goode Lustye man of some twentye yeares oulde . . . and a pretty maryner" before he took sick aboard the *Mistress* of London. Treated by the ship's surgeon in the gunner's room of the ship for a time, Thompson was eventually taken ashore in France, and a local woman was hired to take care of him. While the ship was in port, his crewmates came to visit him regularly during his sickness. The boatswain of the *Mistress* chided the cook, Edward Baker, for not calling on Thompson.[181] The sick man repeatedly told his shipmates that he wanted to see Baker and that the slight "had brock his harte." Typical of Tudor society, illness and dying were community experiences.[182] In the geographically mobile maritime community, the sick, injured, and dying were surrounded by fellow seafarers rather than their kin or neighbors. The duty to visit the sick and comfort the dying extended to those seamen on and off shipboard and is a testament to the cohesion of the maritime community.

While the non-naval sector of the maritime community seems to have operated according to the Laws of Oléron, the Crown often ignored its responsibilities to seamen. Although it did provide medical care for its seamen afloat, the Crown generally absolved itself of responsibility once they were ashore. When the navy was fighting in home waters in 1588, thousands of men were discharged in a debilitated state. The fleet had been ravaged by infection before it had ever left port, and this same infection plagued the English navy throughout the summer. The problem was exacerbated by the demobilization of the fleet in late summer. Howard writes to Lord Burghley on August 10, 1588:

My good Lord:-Sickness and morality begins wonderfully to grow amongst us; and it is a most pitiful sight to see, here at Margate, how the men, having no place to receive them into here, die in the streets. I am driven myself, of force, to come a-land, to see them bestowed in some lodging; and the best I can get is barns and such outhouses; and the relief is small that I can provide for them here. It would grieve any man's heart to see them that have served so valiantly to die so miserably.[183]

The needs of the men of the navy were virtually ignored by the Crown, and any aid that seamen received was the result of the compassion and initiative of individuals like the Lord Admiral or of extraordinary circumstances. Following the Portugal expedition of 1589, the Crown, fearful that the men had the plague, ordered officials to build and absorb the costs of cabins for the sick.[184] It took this threat to the larger population to prod the Crown into taking such measures. The explanation of the Lord Admiral's actions and the Crown's inertia is fairly easy to comprehend; Howard had retained the early Tudor ethos, which dictated that commanders had the paternalistic responsibility for the men under their command, while the Crown clung to an outmoded notion that it was not responsible for the men in its employ.[185]

While Hawkins acknowledged that the fleet had been decimated by illness and was "utterly unfitted and unmeet to follow any enterprise" in 1588, there is no evidence that the Crown approached the London Company of Barber-Surgeons for help in tending the sick and wounded who came ashore, as it would later do under Stuart monarchs.[186] Of the thousands of men who were sick and injured during the summer of 1588, the Crown gave a donation of £80 to be split among the injured seamen of the fleet and a single bequest of £7 to the hundreds of sick men of the *Elizabeth Jonas*.[187] The vast majority of seamen were obliged to furnish their own medical care and maintenance during their time of infirmity. In theory, those seamen who showed promising signs of recovery might hope to be retained and be paid their wages until they returned to duty.[188] As the Crown was verging on insolvency (or believed itself to be), it seems unlikely that many seamen were retained or ever received their wages. Evidence points toward the quick discharge of sick and disabled seamen.[189] Undeniably, many disabled seamen who had fought for the Queen were reduced to an indigent state attempting to pay for their own medical care.[190] Sailor John Steele petitioned the Crown for a begging license on the grounds that he had served the Queen for many years at sea. His last recorded voyage was the Cadiz expedition under the Earl of Essex; as a result of his service, Steele "hath bin inforced to accepte much phisick" and owed surgeons the large sum of £30. John Arnold served aboard the *Jonas* of Bristol against the Spaniards in the Narrow Seas. He had his arm struck off in battle, and medical care had consumed his resources, "whearof he is Lame impotente and vnfitt for service or Laibour and in moste poore and distressed estate." The London parish records of St. Botolph Aldgate show that a collection was taken up for ship carpenter John Babbs in 1590. Babbs had obtained a license to beg, as his leg had been maimed during his naval service, and he was greatly indebted to his surgeons. Gunner Ralph Brown had served in the navy and had been shot several times. He petitioned the Crown in 1589 for a six-month license to collect benevolences in Surrey and Kent in order to repay his surgeons.

Lacking money for maintenance or travel, injured or diseased seamen might obtain a begging license from the Crown to see them to their home parish, where they could seek parish and possibly familial aid. Given the growing problem of vagabondage during Elizabeth's reign, parishes were likely to give an unauthorized beggar an icy reception.[191] The State Papers for 1589 show that the Crown authorized the Lord Lieutenants of the shires to appoint provost marshals for apprehension and punishment of soldiers, mariners, and other vagrants, masterless men, and sturdy vagabonds. Following their service on one of the Queen's ships in 1589, ship's carpenter Humphrey Green and sailor Henry Clark had to petition Julius Caesar, the Judge of the Admiralty Court, for a passport to travel to Norfolk, where they had been born and lived; both were "maymed to their vtter vndoinges" and hoped to seek relief in their own parish. Having lost the use of his limbs permanently from naval service, John Calloway of Cornwall also petitioned Dr. Julius Caesar in 1590 for a license to travel with his wife and children to his friends and seek relief along the way. The need was such that Drake and Hawkins, moved by the plight of their fellow seamen after the campaigns of the 1580s, established the Chatham Chest in 1590 to furnish at least some disabled seamen with small pensions. Each mariner was to pay sixpence into a fund every month from their wages. Unfortunately for seamen, few of these measures were fully realized. These institutions and schemes were designed to handle a small number of poor and disabled; they were not equipped to cope with the thousands of incapacitated veterans who resulted from a prolonged naval war. These funds assisted only a small number of such men, those who had the foresight and wherewithal to contribute, a "drop in the ocean" when compared to those who were in need.[192]

Not until the second half of the war did the Crown begin to look to the long-term needs of its debilitated seamen. Until that point the Crown, as in the past, discharged its responsibility by issuing occasional grants of money.[193] Around the time of the halfway mark of the war, legislation was passed to assist disabled seamen. The 1593 statute imposed a rate for relief of the disabled veterans:

noe Parishe be rated above the somme of sixe Penc nor under the somme of One Penny weekely to be paid, and soe as the totall somme of suche Taxacion of the Parishes in anye Countie where there shalbe above Fyftie Parishes amounte not above the Rate of Two Pence for everie Parishe.[194]

The legislation of 1593, 1598, and 1601 finally provided some limited provision for sick and disabled naval seamen. Although there was no specific provision for health care, relief was to be afforded to men who could give documentary proof of their service by virtue of legislation 35 Eliz. c.4, an act for the relief of sick and diseased soldiers and mariners; 39 Eliz. c. 21 and 43 Eliz. c. 3 confirmed the earlier act.[195] Given the Crown's abhorrence of vagabondage, seamen were obliged to return to their home parish to obtain relief from local authorities. This stipulation presented difficulties for sick and injured seamen who were not resident in the port where they were discharged. The statute of 1593 acknowledged that "manye of suche hurte and maymed souldyours and Marriners doe arrive in partes and places, farre remote from the[ir] Counties" of origin.[196] Prior to 1593 seamen had to make their own arrangements and afterward, the Crown allowed for a small stipend to assist those men who were obliged to travel to their home parishes if they could document their service and present it to the appropriate officials. It would seem that itinerant seamen who lacked a fixed dwelling had no parish to prevail upon[197] and thus fell through the cracks of this limited safety net.

Even for those who had roots in a particular parish, travel posed considerable hardships for the sick and injured. Although parishes might provide medical care for its own indigent residents, sick and impoverished strangers were relegated to the parish cage, a covered pen where care consisted of furnishing bales of hay for bedding.[198] Monson claimed that "if they [discharged seamen] arrive sick from any voyage, such is the charity of people ashore that they shall sooner die then find pity, unless they bring money with them."[199] While some seamen obtained travel money subsequent to the 1593 statute, others probably failed to go through the correct channels to obtain money for their journey. Such seamen were among those who found themselves in the cage of a strange parish.

Given that the disabled, sick, and injured normally had to travel to seek relief in their own parishes, that only those with licenses could beg for alms, that many lacked a fixed dwelling, and that the climate of the countryside was such that strangers and vagabonds were seen as an unwelcome imposition upon the parishioners, counterfeit or secondhand licenses were sought after by all manner of needy persons, including legitimate veterans who had not be able to secure licenses. The Crown repeatedly attempted to prosecute those who were pretending to be disabled seamen and soldiers.[200] One of many proclamations against such fraud was issued in 1598:

multitudes of able men neither impotent nor Lame, exacting money contynually vpon pretence of service in the warres without relief whereas manie of them neuer did serue and yet such as haue serued, yf they were maymed of Lamed by seruice, are provyded for in the Countries by order of sondry good Lawes and Statutes in that behalf and provyded.

Robert Stacy of London testified that he had purchased a begging license signed by the Lord Admiral for 20 shillings. Stacy claimed he had returned from Spain "poore & in wante" and had bought the license from one Thomas Straden, who had collected 26s. 8d. with it. John Seymour sold Henry Jones, a Somersetshire tinker, a license to collect benevolences, "which would be verey gainfull for him." Jones was apprehended with Seymour for their illegal activities, sent to prison in Gloucester for 12 weeks, whipped about the city, and then confined in the Marshalsea prison for 15 weeks. Jones testified that Seymour had sold licenses to other poor men at fairs and market towns. Sailor John Scinnor confessed in 1597 that he had manufactured eight or nine seals of the Admiralty and had forged 40 licenses.

Even for those men who had been disabled during naval service, had a fixed address, and succeeded in returning there, pensions were difficult to access. The recent work of Geoffrey Hudson has demonstrated this persuasively.[201] Late in the period, a number of soldiers who were also beneficiaries of the new legislation protested that the pension scheme was not being administered properly. Although disabled veterans were entitled to several pounds per annum,[202] few received anything close to these amounts.

While the existence of the pension scheme signifies a new relationship between the Crown and its seamen, the ethos of the maritime community had long acknowledged that disabled seamen were entitled not only to care but to compensation whenever circumstances permitted.[203] The crew of the privateering vessel *Affection* voted to give Corporal John Stone of Plymouth an additional two shares for the loss of his right leg, which had been maimed in a fight with the Spaniards. When the crew of the *Prosperous* petitioned the Crown in 1598 for the payment of their wages for service on the Cadiz expedition under the Earl of Essex, they included their request for special relief for 13 of the crew who had been maimed.

After 1593, in theory anyway, maimed naval veterans were among the more fortunate members of the "deserving poor" because they had access to long-term benefits; this was some measure of compensation for depriving them of their customary right to weigh remuneration against employment risks. The civilian maritime community had only the Laws of Oléron to provide short-term medical care for the sick and disabled; it had neither the infrastructure nor the resources to provide long-term maintenance for its needy members. Donations and licenses were only temporary solutions; they did not furnish the disabled with the long-term support that they required. There were few charities in place for seamen that met this need. The charters of the Trinity Houses granted them permission to run almshouses. Thames pilots were to pay the guild part of their lodesmanage, and ordinary seamen were to give their primage money to finance the almshouses.[204] The Deptford Trinity House charter dictated that masters of naval ships were to collect one penny from every seaman each month to provide for the disabled:

yf any Maryners happen to be maymed, hurte or fawle sycke and be not able to releefe hymself of his owne propre goods, that then it shall be lefull for the said Maister of the same Shippe to present any suche Marynor so beyng maymed, hurt or syke to the Maister iiij Wardeyns and viij Assistantes of the seid almeshowse, and there he to have releffe as shall be thought by them resonable, provyded alway[s] that yf the Maister of evry suche shipp and his Company do pay theire Dewties to the said Almyshowse and other wyse not.[205]

In addition to the Trinity Houses, Henry VIII had granted a charter to the Newcastle Company of Masters and Mariners in 1534 to support 12 poor brethren, their wives, or shipwrecked mariners.[206] The Crown was eager to grant charters to men like John Hawkins, who sought to erect a hospital at Chatham, Kent, in 1594 for relief of 10 or more poor mariners and shipwrights.[207] It was also willing to encourage existing establishments that had fallen into decay. The Privy Council wrote to the mayor and aldermen of Bristol in 1595 suggesting that the city reestablish an almshouse for aged and impotent sailors; 1½ pence of every ton's lading of merchants' goods in the city and a penny from every pound out of each sailor's wages were to be collected for the maintenance of disabled seafarers.[208] Yet these measures provided only for a small number of unfortunates; the absence of a nationwide guild meant that the established forms of relief were localized and were wholly inadequate by the late 1580s.

It has been argued by C. H. Dixon that

state concern for the welfare of merchant seamen may fairly be said to spring from the repulse of the Spanish Armada in 1588, for at that turning point in British history it was the merchant seamen who provided the bulk of the sea defence forces.[209]

It is certainly true that the navy was manned by merchant seamen in 1588. The impetus to provide for seamen seems to have come not from the Crown, as Dixon argues, but from leading seamen in the maritime community, such as Hawkins[210] and the Lord Admiral, who individually sought to relieve their men and, along with Drake, began the Chatham Chest, which predates the Crown's pension scheme. Although the Chatham Chest was a contributory scheme, this was the only possible method to provide for seamen without the Crown's resources. Its significance lies in the fact that its founders recognized and acted to fill a need and an obligation earlier than the Crown. As for the Crown's motivations, it is more probable that the sheer scope of the problem of disabled veterans in relation to the late Tudor crisis of poverty and vagabondage had more to do with the Crown's legislation than a recognition of a welfare commitment or the lobbying of naval commanders. If the Crown was bent on acknowledging its obligations to seamen, would not this legislation have come in the 1580s during the most continuous period of naval activity? If the Crown was concerned about the men of the navy, why was so little done during the 1580s and early 1590s?[211] Even basic medical attention ashore, provided for civilian seamen by their employers, was denied naval seamen. This fact suggests that the Crown was consumed by issues other than the recovery of the sick and disabled seafarers in its employ. The Crown began to introduce legislation to assist seamen only in 1593. Related legislation was passed throughout the closing years of the decade and the opening years of the century; these measures coincide with the period of extreme economic hardship experienced by the Tudor populace in the 1590s. Thus, the Crown's legislation for veterans should not necessarily be seen as late recognition of its responsibilities dictated by both the Laws of Oléron and the rhetoric of sixteenth-century paternalism. Ultimately, the Crown acted as a result of fear for its own security; it knew that disgruntled and impoverished seamen posed a threat. This legislation was designed as a measure to reduce the numbers of vagabonds and beggars to ensure the maintenance of law and order—overwhelming concerns for Elizabethans as well as all Europeans in the sixteenth century.[212] In general, the Crown was content to rely on the existing medieval structures and the goodwill and energy of reformers like John Hawkins to provide benevolences and care for veterans of its naval wars. Only when the problem proved to be both overwhelming when combined with the overall crisis of poverty, population growth, and unemployment and also intractable (given the duration of the war) was the Crown forced to introduce and implement legislation to care for some of its disabled veterans. Therefore, demographic and economic crisis helped pressure the Crown into a new and uneasy relationship with its seamen.

CONCLUSION

Although sixteenth-century seamen faced a myriad of hazards, disease was the most lethal foe. The terror of sickness in the Lord Admiral's letters to the Privy Council is almost tangible: "God of his mercy keep us from the sickness, for we fear that more than any hurt that the Spaniards will do."[213] Given its continual battle to man its warships, one would think that the Crown would have made more efforts to furnish the basic needs of its seamen so that naval duty was more palatable[214] and to lower the risk of illness, injury, and fatality. This was rarely the case. While some allowances must surely be made for the limited nature of Tudor bureaucracy and its inherent inertia, it is apparent that the Crown made little effort to be a conscientious employer or administer to its seamen in a paternalistic fashion, despite the concerns of those within the naval administration. This is particularly true of the period 1585–93. Inattention to many features of naval life, failure to install the measures recommended by prudent seamen, and parsimony increased misery and mortality. For the most part, the

Crown opted to save money and rely on its ancient right to compel men to serve regardless of the human costs. The Crown took little notice of important discoveries (the use of antiscourbutics for instance) that stood to lower shipboard mortality significantly. While we cannot expect the Crown to have conquered the high mortality on naval expeditions, it had the means at its disposal to combat the menace. Those within the naval bureaucracy recognized that consumable provisions, relatively clean vessels, and appropriate apparel would help to stave off sickness. Such advocates were largely ignored, however.

For the greater part of the war, issuing clothing to seamen, finding alternative provisions for the sick and wounded, and donating sums for the relief of the disabled naval veterans were undertaken by the Crown haltingly and capriciously. When assistance was given, Elizabeth and her councillors designed temporary measures for long-term problems. The Crown's insistence on adhering to a piecemeal approach to situations also led to greater suffering as the same problems recurred throughout the war. When the Crown did respond to the needs of the navy, it was often a case of "too little, too late." The Crown attempted to meet unprecedented need and demands with age-old solutions and institutions. The inattention of the Crown is in stark contrast to efforts made by men like the Lord Admiral and the Hawkins family. It could be argued that Howard was essentially a "troubleshooter" who focused on individual crises as they arose and was motivated by early Tudor paternalism, while John Hawkins, motivated by the obligations dictated within the maritime community, was more visionary in that he worked for permanent change in the navy. Yet there was a commonality here; Howard and Hawkins recognized that men would not serve the realm without some financial incentive, improved shipboard conditions, and some measure of health care during and after the voyage. The Crown's frugality and inertia were largely resistant to John Hawkins's innovations or measures undertaken as a result of Howard's compassion and paternalism. Nevertheless, changes did take place. The pension scheme, for instance, although not very accessible to most seamen during Elizabeth's reign, was a very significant piece of legislation for future naval seamen.

Individuals and merchant companies within the non-naval sector of the maritime community led the way in seeking and implementing measures to improve the working environment of seamen. Although mortality rates remained significantly high on long-distance journeys, important knowledge was gained through experience, and subsequent voyages often showed a decrease in shipboard deaths. Merchant companies like the East India Company realized that while mortality was frequently high on their voyages, attempts to improve shipboard conditions and provide for their seamen were, at the very least, appealing to seamen seeking employment. No doubt mortality would have been greater if the Company not been so attentive to the needs of its seamen. Later naval medical practices found their origins in the policies and orders of the Merchant Adventurers and the East India Company.[215]

Evidence indicates that most masters and shipowners adhered to their medieval obligations and provided some health care for the seamen in their employ. Although conditions were far from pleasant aboard sixteenth-century vessels, seamen expected basic criteria to be met: sufficient provisions, health care (if required), and the freedom to assess their own risks. In the interest of shipboard harmony and profit, shipmasters tried to accommodate the needs of the crew. The Crown attempted to circumvent the customs of the maritime community and ignore its medieval obligations in order to conduct war on a shoestring budget. Although many seamen served grudgingly, the lack of widespread mutiny in the navy suggests that most seamen dutifully performed their traditional obligation to their sovereign in time of war. However, desertions and the commanders' awareness that mutiny was on the horizon suggest that impressed seamen were not docile employees who accepted poor conditions and greater health risks willingly. To some degree the general unhappiness with conditions was offset by compassion of individual commanders who were seen to be working for the good of the men and making an attempt to uphold their side of the paternalistic, employer–employee relationship that seamen were accustomed to in other forms of maritime employment. Such efforts bolstered the overwrought ties between seamen and their Queen and kept them from unraveling. Yet, in the most desperate of circumstances, seamen were capable of sweeping condemnation of the Crown: "Wee were preste by her Majesties presse to have her allowaunce, and not to be thus, dealt withall, you make no men of us, but beastes."[216]

While the Crown's social policy normally functioned according to the "carrot and stick" approach,[217] its treatment of naval seamen demonstrates that there was little in the way of reciprocity inherent in the deferential model of early modern society. Despite the recommendations of the Lord Admiral, who advised that "men kindly handled will bear want and run through fire and water," the Crown thought primarily of its financial limitations. Although the relationship began to change after 1593, the Crown attempted to pressure seamen with a stick while neglecting to offer them the carrot.

NOTES

1. *Starving Sailors: The Influence of Nutrition upon Naval and Maritime History*, ed. J. Watt, E. J. Freeman, and W. F. Bynum (Greenwich U.K.: National Maritime Museum, 1981), Appendix 1, 199.

2. Keevil, *Medicine and the Navy*, 44–144.

3. Contemporary wisdom had it that "nothing could poison a sailor." Capp, *Cromwell's Navy*, 244.

4. William Clowes, *A Profitable and Necessarie Booke of Obseruations, for All Those That Are Burned with the Flame of Gun Powder, &c. and Also for Curing of Wounds Made by Musket and Caliuershot, and Other Weapons of War Commonly Vsed at This Day both by Sea and Land, as Heerafter Shall Be Declared* (London: Edm. Bollifant, 1596), 40.

5. PRO E 351/2379; Oppenheim, *The Administration of the Royal Navy, 1509–1660*, 140. D. M. Loades has estimated that over half of the stowage space of a warship would be used to store three months' worth of provisions. David M. Loades, *The Tudor Navy: An Administrative, Political and Military History* (Aldershot, U.K.: Scolar Press, 1992), 207.

6. PRO HCA, 1/45/171, 1/45/175v, 13/30/214–15.

7. PRO HCA, 1/45/173, 1/44/126v, 1/44/67v, 1/41/78–79v; Hair and Alsop, *English Seamen and Traders*, 138; G. J. Milton-Thompson, "Two Hundred Years of the Sailor's Diet," in *Starving Sailors*, 29. Because officers usually ate better than the men under their command, a disproportionate amount of this fresh meat probably ended up on the officers' plates.

8. James Cook, *A Voyage towards the South Pole and Round the World (1772–1775)*, vol. I (London: W. Strahan and T. Cadell, 1777), 137. In the late eighteenth century, Captain Cook had to flog two of his men for refusing to eat the fresh meat that he had provided. Milton-Thompson, "Two Hundred Years of the Sailor's Diet," 29. Christopher Lloyd, "Victualling of the Fleet in the Eighteenth and Nineteenth Centuries," in *Starving Sailors*, 9. If this is true, the common seamen might not have envied their superiors' their fresh meat.

9. Lloyd, "Victualling of the Fleet," 11.

10. Milton-Thompson, "Two Hundred Years of the Sailor's Diet," 29.

11. *Starving Sailors*, Appendix 1, 199. The general population seems to have suffered from malnutrition at the end of each winter. W.S.C. Copeman, *Doctors and Disease in Tudor Times* (London: Dawson's of Pall Mall, 1960), 157.

12. PRO HCA 13/24/193–97v; Hale, *Renaissance Exploration*, 93; Foxe, *North-West Fox or Fox from the North-West Passage*, 102–3.

13. PRO HCA, 13/24/205–6, 13/25/107v–9; Appleby, "A Nursery of Pirates," 16–17.

14. PRO HCA, 13/33/35v–36, 13/33/42–43.

15. PRO HCA, 13/36/53, 13/30/214–15.

16. PRO HCA 1/42/11v.

17. PRO HCA 1/42/3.

18. PRO HCA 1/22/183.

19. PRO HCA, 13/28/28–29, 13/28/302-v; Keevil, *Medicine and the Navy*, 103.

20. PRO HCA, 13/27/395–96v, 13/32/306v–7v, 13/33/67, 13/24/221–22, 13/24/169–171v, 13/24/172v.

21. L. A. Clarkson, *The Pre-Industrial Economy in England 1500–1750* (New York: Schocken Books, 1972), 212.

22. A. B. Appleby, "Diet in Sixteenth-Century England: Sources, Problems, Possibilities," in *Health, Medicine and Mortality in the Sixteenth Century*, ed. C. Webster (Cambridge: Cambridge University Press, 1979), 97–116; this sentiment was expressed by contemporaries as well. See *A Discourse of the Commonweal of This Realm of England*, Attributed to Sir Thomas Smith, ed. Mary Dewar (Charlottesville: Folger Shakespeare Library, 1969), passim.

23. PRO HCA, 13/36/304, 13/30/247v–48, 13/24/232, 13/24/222-v, 13/32/ 35v, 13/24/231v. See also PRO HCA 13/33/71–72.

24. PRO HCA 13/31/123-v.

25. Alsop, "Sea Surgeons, Health and England's Maritime Expansion," 219; Hair and Alsop, *English Seamen and Traders*, 304–5, 137, 139.

26. PRO HCA, 13/33/35v–36, 13/33/42–43.

27. PRO HCA, 13/27/199–200, 13/25/420, 1/44/223. Because rats cause leaks in casks, cats, dogs, and an occasional weasel were kept on board. The danger was not just to the victuals. Richard Hawkins wrote that "besides that which they [rats] consume of the best victuals, they eate the sayles; and neither packe, nor chest is free from their surprises." Hawkins, *Observations*, 91.

28. Williams, *The Sea Dogs*, 210.

29. Keevil, *Medicine and the Navy*, 103. The Spaniards were probably responsible for the discovery of distilled water c. 1566. *Starving Sailors*, Appendix 1, 199. Long-term use was found to create health problems, but in the short term it was an acceptable risk.

30. Keevil, *Medicine and the Navy*, 103. Keevil is wrong to say that it was lost—it was abandoned during the sixteenth and seventeenth centuries.

31. Milton-Thompson, "Two Hundred Years of the Sailor's Diet," 30; Keevil, *Medicine and the Navy*, 98; Williams, *The Sea Dogs*, 185; Hair and Alsop, *English Seamen and Traders*, 139; PRO HCA 1/44/124v–25; Hakluyt, *The Principall Navigations*, 188.

32. PRO HCA, 13/26/9-v, 1/41/185–86, 1/43/7, 1/43/125, 1/42/77v, 13/24/ 193–94, 13/32/356-v.

33. PRO HCA, 1/43/188-v, 1/41/20–21v, 1/41/46, 1/4/168v–71, 1/42/30; *Sir Francis Drake's West Indian Voyage 1585–6*, ed. Mary Frear Keeler (London: Hakluyt Society, 1981), 108; PRO HCA 13/32/25v–26. See also PRO HCA, 1/43/160v, 1/41/102, 1/43/150v.

34. Outhwaite, "Dearth, the English Crown and the 'Crisis of the 1590s,' " 23–43.

35. In the first half of the sixteenth century, pursers seem to have made greater use of their discretionary funds for additional food items. After the midcentury mark, this becomes more difficult. Loades, *The Tudor Navy*, 208. Remains found aboard the king's warship *Mary Rose* show that at least some of the men aboard enjoyed a wide range of foodstuffs. Carcasses indicate that fresh pork and fish were available as well as fresh peas in the pod. Stones from plums or prunes were found throughout the ship. Venison, beef, and mutton bones were also present. Work continues on other remains that have yet to be identified. Rule, *The Mary Rose*, 197. It is difficult to say if the fresh food was intended exclusively for officers.

36. Cruickshank, *Elizabeth's Army*, 82.

37. Ibid., 76.

38. PRO SP 12/30/43; Boteler, *Dialogues*, 56.

39. Loades, *The Tudor Navy*, 206–7. See also n. 9.

40. Quoted in R. C. Holmes, "Sea Fare," *Mariner's Mirror* 35 (1949), 140.

41. *State Papers*, vol. I., 198, 148–49; Oppenheim, *The Administration of the Royal Navy, 1509–1660*, 384.

42. This paternalistic ideal can be expressed in an alternate form from on high. In the seventeenth century Nathaniel Boteler claimed that seamen "should be used

like little Children, or peevish Patients and made to keep a good Diet whether they will or no." N. Boteler, *Six Dialogues about Sea-Services* (London: Moses Pitt, 1685), 86. Dr. Thomas Trotter, a naval physician during the eighteenth century, maintained that seamen in naval service were neglectful of their own needs, and, hence, their service entitled them to "parental tenderness and attention from the state they protect and the officers they obey." Trotter, quoted in *The Health of Seamen: Selections from the Works of Dr. James Lind, Sir Gilbert Blane and Dr. Thomas Trotter*, ed. Christopher Lloyd (London: Navy Records Society, 1965), 167. Sea-surgeon John Clark commented, "The common sailors have it not in their power to provide themselves such necessaries [healthy foodstuffs]; it is, therefore, certainly the duty of their employers to make some allowance of this kind." John Clark, *Observations on the Diseases in Long Voyages to Hot Countries, and Particularly on Those Which Prevail in the East Indies* (London: D. Wilson and G. Nicol, 1773), 338.

43. Monson, *Naval Tracts*, vol. I, 175.

44. Oppenheim, "The Royal and Merchant Navy under Elizabeth," 488; Oppenheim, *The Administration of the Royal Navy, 1509–1660*, 142; Monson, *Naval Tracts*, vol. I, 175; Clowes, "The Elizabethan Navy," 470; Richmond, *The Navy as an Instrument of Policy 1558–1727*, 27, 35, 42.

45. *The Defeat of the Spanish Armada*, vol. I, lvii–lviii; Pollit, "Bureaucracy and the Armada," 119–32. This theory is argued convincingly by R. B. Outhwaite in "Dearth, the English Crown and the 'Crisis of the 1590s'," 23–43.

46. A. P. McGowan, ed., *The Jacobean Commissions of Enquiry 1608 and 1618* (London: Navy Record Society, 1971), xiii; G. J. Marcus, *A Naval History of England*, vol. I (London: Longmans, Green, and Co., 1961), 82. For a detailed discussion of Hawkins's guilt or innocence, see Oppenheim, *The Administration of the Royal Navy, 1509–1660*, 392–97; Raleigh, *Judicious and Select Essayes and Observations*, 30; Boteler, *Boteler's Dialogues*, 56–57.

47. Appleby, "Diet in Sixteenth-Century England," 97, 105, 110.

48. After operating in debt in 1569, the Crown advanced Baeshe £1,000 and raised his allowance (1565) from 4½d. per man per day in harbor and 5d. at sea to 5½d. and 6d. in 1573. In 1586 the rates were increased again. Loades, *The Tudor Navy*, 203–6; PRO E 351/2384. For a detailed account of the escalation in prices of individual items during Baeshe's term, see Keevil, *Medicine and the Navy*, 66–67.

49. In 1586–87 the Crown granted the surveyor an increase in rates from 5½d. per man in harbor and 6d. at sea to 6½d. and 7d., respectively, "by reason of the greate dearth and scarcitye of victualles." PRO E 351/2383.

50. Bodleian Library, Rawlinson Ms. C. 340/14v–15.

51. PRO SP 12/266/90. For a description of how prices had increased from the time of Baeshe's tenure to Quarles's in 1587, see *Papers Relating to the Navy during the Spanish War, 1585–87*, vol. I, ed. Julian Corbett (London: Navy Records Society, 1898), 54.

52. Although Clarkson states that the early 1590s was a period of abundant harvests, victualing records suggest that the prices of foodstuffs were escalating and, as such, were a cause for complaint and concern among the victualers. Clarkson, *The Pre-Industrial Economy*, 212; PRO E 351/2389.

53. It was possible to speak of "dearth of all things though there be scarcity

of nothing." *The Discourse of the Commonweal of This Realm of England*, xiii, 37.

54. Bodleian Library, Rawlinson Ms. C. 340/15.

55. Clarkson, *The Pre-Industrial Economy*, 33; *Discourse of the Commonweal*, ix.

56. PRO SP 12/273/40.

57. Harbor allowance was raised to 6½d. per man, and sea allowance was increased to 7d. PRO E 351/2399; Loades, *The Tudor Navy*, 277–78.

58. *Sir Francis Drake's West Indian Voyage 1585-6*, 18–19; Corbett, *Drake and the Tudor Navy*, vol. II, 9, 71, 299; Loades, *The Tudor Navy*, 206–7; PRO E 351/2401; Bodleian Library, Rawlinson Ms., A. 204/196, A. 204/206v; PRO, E 351/2382, E 351/2383, E 351/2392, E 351/2402, E 351/2400. See n. 84.

59. PRO E, 351/2383, 351/2388; Bodleian Library, Rawlinson Ms. C. 340/14v.

60. Oppenheim, *The Administration of the Royal Navy, 1509–1660*, 141.

61. In 1590 victuals were being loaded on the *Tramontana* and "by Casualtie in hoysinge vp oute of the hoye fell shorte of the shippe into the sea." PRO, E 351/2388, E 351/2396, E 351/2397. In 1602 a storm ruined 460 pounds of biscuit as it sat at Tower Wharf waiting to be loaded on the Queen's ship, the *Advantage*. PRO HCA 13/35/402. Occasionally, entire cargoes were lost in conveyance. In 1597 a hoy loaded with naval provisions sank with over £1,564 worth of victuals. PRO E 351/2395. The following year the *Marigold* of London was carrying naval provisions and was cast ashore in a storm; only some of the lading was salvaged. PRO E 351/2397. Storehouses were also vulnerable to storms, accidents, and theft. Damage to the Rochester buildings in 1594 ruined a considerable store of naval victuals. PRO E 351/2392. See also PRO E 351/2385. In addition, charges of "lewde persons" embezzling away goods from the storehouses were leveled from time to time. PRO E, 351/2392, 351/2393, 351/2396, 351/2390, 351/2387, 351/2389, 351/2390, 351/2391, 351/2379; Raleigh, *Judicious and Select Essayes and Observations*, 33; Keevil, *Medicine and the Navy*, 72.

62. Hawkins, *Observations*, 9.

63. Berckman, *The Hidden Navy* (London: Hamish Hamilton, 1973), 89–90; Raleigh, *Judicious and Select Essayes and Observations*, 31; Boteler, *Dialogues*, 58.

64. Watt, "Some Consequences of Nutritional Disorders in Eighteenth-Century British Circumnavigations," 68.

65. *State Papers*, vol. II, 159; Keevil, *Medicine and the Navy*, 71, 74, 76, 159.

66. Monson, *Naval Tracts*, vol. I, 190; vol. II, 62, 95; vol. I, 220; vol. II, 65.

67. Keevil, *Medicine and the Navy*, 78; Monson, *Naval Tracts*, vol. I, 179, 354; vol. II, 78.

68. *State Papers Relating to the Defeat of the Spanish Armada*, vol. I, 198; *Starving Sailors*, Appendix 1, 199–202; William Gooddy, "Neurological Factors in Decision-Making," in *Starving Sailors*, 187–98; Monson, *Naval Tracts*, vol. I, 193–94.

69. Monson, *Naval Tracts*, vol. I, 193–94.

70. *The Expedition of Sir John Norris and Sir Francis Drake to Spain and Portugal, 1589*, 172.

71. Similarly, most seventeenth-century naval mutinies and protests occurred

when the fleet was in harbor; mutinies aimed at officers at sea were very unusual. Capp, *Cromwell's Navy*, 286.

72. *State Papers*, vol. I, 295.

73. English seamen had a reputation for being large eaters. Since ration sizes in the Spanish navy were significantly smaller, provisions lasted much longer; this was a crucial advantage in naval campaigns. Fernandez-Armesto, *The Spanish Armada*, 67. Mendoza, the Spanish ambassador, remarked that English ships were "loaded with victualls, considering the way Englishmen eat." Florence Dyer, "The Elizabethan Sailorman," 136.

74. Boteler, *Dialogues*, 65; Dyer, "The Elizabethan Sailorman," 137.

75. Andrew B. Appleby, "Nutrition and Disease: The Case of London, 1550–1750," *Journal of Interdisciplinary History* 6 (1975), 108; PRO E, 351, 2388, 2392, 2393, 2401, 2397 2498, 2499, 2393, 2400.

76. Bodleian Library, Rawlinson Ms. C. 340/44. Every seaman was still entitled to one pound of biscuit and a gallon of beer per day. Each man's allowance consisted of four flesh days in a week; he received two pounds of salted beef twice a week and one pound of pork or bacon with a pint of pease on the other two days. On the three fish days he received ½ a quarter of lings or ¼ of stockfish, ½ or ¼ pound of butter, ¼ pound of cheese. For want of fish, double quotas of cheese and butter were substituted.

77. *State Papers Relating to the Defeat of the Spanish Armada*, vol. I, 53; Keevil, *Medicine and the Navy*, 109; PRO SP 12/264/24.

78. *State Papers Relating to the Defeat of the Spanish Armada*, vol. I, 293. London's costs were customarily high. In 1593 Richard Hawkins victualed his ships in the West Country, "which are better cheape in those parts then in London." Keevil, *Medicine and the Navy*, 100.

79. Bodleian Library, Rawlinson Ms. C. 340/5.

80. Appleby, "Diet in Sixteenth-Century England," 110.

81. PRO E 351/2388; *State Papers Relating to the Defeat of the Spanish Armada*, vol. II, 160.

82. It is a testament to the desperation both of the Crown and of the Elizabethan poor that corrupt naval provisions could be sold. In 1602 bacon stores were observed to be "mouldy slymy and vnserviceable . . . and for the most parte not to be eaten by any man yet [they were] sould." PRO E 351/2401.

83. Hawkins, *Observations*, 41.

84. PRO E 351/2399. It has been suggested that John Hawkins was the originator of these practices. Oppenheim, *The Administration of the Royal Navy*, 134; Keevil, *Medicine and the Navy*, 108–9.

85. *Expedition of Sir John Norris and Sir Francis Drake to Spain and Portugal, 1589*, 170; PRO E 351/2499; Bodleian Library, Rawlinson Ms. C 340/5.

86. Bodleian Library, Rawlinson Ms. C 340/72.

87. Hawkins, *Observations*, 91; Monson, *Naval Tracts*, vol. IV, 65.

88. Keevil, *Medicine and the Navy*, 115–16.

89. Monson, *Naval Tracts*, 197, 201; *Expedition of Sir John Norris and Sir Francis Drake*, 169–70. See Chapter 2 for additional information.

90. Quoted in Andrews, *Trade, Plunder and Settlement*, 26.

91. We know more about the navy's figures because of fairly abundant records.

92. Hair and Alsop, *English Seamen and Traders*, 10, 16, 24, 33, 37, 38, 47.

93. George Watson, *The Cures of the Diseased in Forraine Attempts of the English Nation*, ed. Charles Singer (1598; Oxford, 1915), 21; Hawkins, *Observations*, 42.

94. Appleby, "Nutrition and Disease," 6. This was typical of the Tudor population at large.

95. There were, however, a number of incorrect theories proffered. Watson, *The Cures of the Diseased*, 21; Keevil, *Medicine and the Navy*, 133.

96. Hawkins, *Observations*, 40.

97. *Starving Sailors*, Appendix 1, 199. See James Watt, "Some Consequences of Nutritional Disorders in Eighteenth Century British Circumnavigations," *Starving Sailors*, 54–59; *Sir Francis Drake's West Indian Voyage*, 254; Hawkins, *Observations*, 33.

98. For animal and vegetable sources of vitamin A, see Ivan M. Sharman, "Vitamin Requirements of the Human Body," in *Starving Sailors*, 21.

99. *Starving Sailors*, Appendix 1, 199–200; Sharman, "Vitamin Requirements of the Human Body," in *Starving Sailors*, 17–22.

100. J. L. Cloudsley-Thompson, *Insects and History* (London: Weidenfeld and Nicholson, 1978), 138–39; Watson, *The Cures of the Diseased*, 15.

101. Keevil, *Medicine and the Navy*, 77–78.

102. *State Papers Relating to the Defeat of the Spanish Armada*, vol. II, 138–39.

103. Ibid., 138–40. There is a likelihood that the new recruits were more susceptible to food poisoning than the veteran seamen, who had built up a type of resistance to the microorganisms in the decaying food. Cloudsley-Thompson, *Insects and History*, 31.

104. *State Papers*, vol. II, 159.

105. *Sir Francis Drake's West Indian Voyage*, 254; Watson, *The Cures of the Diseased*, 7–8; Cloudsley-Thompson, *Insects and History*, 168.

106. This description suggests that vitamin B deficiency may have also been present. *Sir Francis Drake's West Indian Voyage*, 236.

107. The major plague epidemics for this period occurred in 1563–64, 1592, 1602, and 1603. S. T. Bindoff, *Tudor England* (1950; rpt. Middlesex, U.K.: Penguin Books, 1983), 283. In 1580 the mayor of London prohibited seamen who were believed to have come in contact with the plague to disembark. *A.P.C.* vol. XII, 61. A royal proclamation issued in July 1589 banned mariners from coming near the court because it was believed that many of the men discharged from the Portugal expedition carried the plague. *Tudor Royal Proclamations*, vol. III, 39. Parish records show that many of Elizabethan London's most prominent seamen died of the plague in 1603. Whether it was contracted ashore or afloat is not apparent in most cases, but overall London lost between one-quarter and one-fifth of its population.

108. Charles Webster, "Mortality Crises and Epidemic Disease in England 1485–1610," in *Health, Medicine and Mortality in the Sixteenth Century*, ed. Charles Webster (Cambridge: Cambridge University Press, 1979), 38.

109. *Sir Francis Drake's West Indian Voyage 1585–6*, 171, 254; Hair and Alsop, *English Seamen and Traders*, 22; PRO HCA 13/26/241-v; K. R. Andrews, "The Voyage of the *Jaquet* of Falmouth to the West Indies and Newfoundland 1585–

86," *Mariner's Mirror* 59 (1973), 101–3; Hair and Alsop, *English Seamen and Traders*, 47, 23, 26, 45.

110. Foxe, *North-West Fox or Fox From the North-West Passage*, VI.

111. This is the assessment of one sea captain in 1577. Keevil, *Medicine and the Navy*, 76.

112. Hawkins, *Observations*, 41. Boteler complained that "these lads are generally known to make more of their bellies than their backs." Boteler, *Dialogues*, 36; Raleigh, *The Last Fight of the Revenge*, 111; Keevil, *Medicine and the Navy*, 99, 102; Manwaring, "The Dress of the British Seaman," 164.

113. Hair and Alsop, *English Seamen and Traders*, 135. My own findings support Hair and Alsop's research.

114. Rule, *The Mary Rose*, 201; Loades, *The Tudor Navy*, 202. It is unclear why this was the case. Economy was probably the most significant factor.

115. Cruickshank, *Elizabeth's Army*, 91–92.

116. PRO SP, 12/29/7, 12/27/137, 12/264/112, 12/226/73; Hawkins, *Observations*, 22. Merchant companies already provided imprests in kind for needy seamen in the form of cloth from which to fashion clothing. Hair and Alsop, *English Seamen and Traders*, 12, 20, 33.

117. *State Papers*, vol. II, 97.

118. In 1580 the Crown ordered £310 10s. worth of clothes for seamen and deducted the money out of their wages. *A.P.C.*, vol. XII, 154.

119. Keevil, *Medicine and the Navy*, 68.

120. Manwaring, "The Dress of the British Seaman," 165.

121. Keevil, *Medicine and the Navy*, 113–15; Hakluyt, *Principall Navigations*, 332; Hawkins, *Observations*, 41; Lloyd, *The British Seaman 1200–1860*, 33; PRO SP 12/263 (June 23, 1597).

122. PRO HCA, 13/30/26-v, 13/27/394–96v; Hair and Alsop, *English Seamen and Traders*, 305; PRO HCA 1/46/3v–4.

123. Hawkins, *Observations*, 84; *Sir Francis Drake's West Indian Voyage*, 29; PRO HCA, 13/28/298, 13/28/70–71v.

124. Hakluyt, *Principall Navigations*, 690.

125. *State Papers*, vol. II, 96.

126. Marcus, *A Naval History of England*, 88.

127. Corbett, *Drake and the Tudor Navy*, vol. I, 383.

128. PRO SP 12/185/33; Keevil, *Medicine and the Navy*, 100.

129. *The Health of Seamen*, 3. During the course of the Seven Years' War 133, 708 men were lost to service by disease and desertion, and 1,512 were killed in action.

130. J. H. Parry, *The Age of Reconnaissance*, 2nd ed. (London: Weidenfeld and Nicholson, 1966), 75–97; PRO HCA 13/31/4v.

131. PRO HCA 13/26/60; emphasis added.

132. Although the navy lost few ships to these hazards during the war years, respected shipwright Richard Adams believed the queen's warships were very poorly maintained. PRO HCA 13/25/281v–82. Adams's ability as a shipwright was well respected. The Crown frequently used him as an appraiser for the Admiralty Court. PRO HCA, 14/29/113, 24/51/3, 24/51/28, 24/52/61, 24/52/114.

133. PRO HCA 1/44/124–25.

134. PRO HCA, 1/81/161, 1/81/185. Of the 9,761 extant records of late

eighteenth-century and early nineteenth-century American seamen, Simon P. Newman noted that 86 percent of these men were scarred or disfigured in some way. Most of the injuries were to the extremities. See Simon P. Newman, "Reading the Bodies of Early American Seafarers," *The William and Mary Quarterly* 55 (January 1998), 67.

135. PRO HCA, 13/25/436v–37, 13/25/70v, 13/24/185-v.

136. PRO HCA, 1/46/140, 1/35/145, 1/81/164, 1/80/85, 1/44/174v, 1/46/139v–40, 1/81/113, 1/46/132v–35v.

137. PRO HCA 1/42/185–88v.

138. PRO HCA 13/26/269.

139. PRO HCA 13/31/220v.

140. Friends and family did send petitions to the Crown for assistance freeing captive seamen. Although its powers were limited, the Crown did attempt to organize prisoner exchanges from time to time. Some loved ones were allowed to collect alms to pay ransoms. Most captives probably died as prisoners, served their time, or secured freedom without the Crown. PRO HCA 14/28/48. See also *A.P.C.*, vol. XV, 50.

141. PRO HCA 13/27/231.

142. John Frampton's firsthand account of his own treatment and that of other English merchants and seamen illustrates the diversity of judgments. B.L., Lansdowne Ms. 389/327/331v.

143. For instance, the Crown received a petition in 1592 from 30 women whose husbands "att this instante are remayninge in moste grevouse slavery and boundage in the Galleys." PRO HCA 14/28/219. For conditions, see Ruth Pike, "Penal Servitude in Early Modern Spain: The Galleys," *Journal of Economic History* 11 (1982), 199–208.

144. PRO HCA 13/31/4v. See also PRO HCA 13/24/254v–55v.

145. PRO HCA 14/30/85.

146. PRO HCA 13/30/27-v.

147. PRO HCA 13/27/381v. See also PRO HCA, 13/31/127, 1/35/438.

148. PRO HCA, 50/1/6, 50/1/192–93.

149. R. S. Roberts, "The Personnel and Practice of Medicine in Tudor and Stuart England, Part II," *Medical History* 8 (1964), 217–19.

150. Monson, *Naval Tracts*, vol. IV, 57.

151. Boteler, *Dialogues*, 64; Clowes, *Booke of Observations*, 105; Isobell G. Powell, "Early Ship Surgeons," *Mariner's Mirror* 9 (1923), 11, 15; Monson, *Naval Tracts*, vol. IV, 57–58; Keevil, *Medicine and the Navy*, 110–13.

152. Keevil, *Medicine and the Navy*, 90, 140–41; Clowes, *A Profitable and Necessarie Booke of Observations*, 5, 104–6.

153. Keevil, *Medicine and the Navy*, 65.

154. The expression was William Clowes'. Keevil, *Medicine and the Navy*, 140.

155. PRO HCA, 13/28/302v, 13/30/68v, 13/30/76v–77v, 13/30/277v, 13/31/215v–16v, 13/31/292v–94v, 13/28/13–13v. Experienced men like Crosse would have had a great advantage over novices like Christopher Newchurch, a surgeon during the first East India Company voyage. Newchurch found his training at the Barber-Surgeons' Hall to be so ineffectual that he attempted suicide during the voyage. Over half of the 480 men died during the voyage of 1601–3. Keevil, *Medicine and the Navy*, 112–13.

156. PRO HCA 13/28/70–71v.

157. Keevil, *Medicine and the Navy*, 69, 77, 79.

158. Roberts, "Personnel and Practice," 219; Alsop, "Sea Surgeons, Health and England's Maritime Expansion," 219; Rule, *The Mary Rose*, 188–89; PRO HCA 1/44/171v; Monson, *Naval Tracts*, vol. IV, 57.

159. Clowes, *A Profitable and Necessarie Booke of Observations*, 40–43. For scurvy, Clowes recommended a number of treatments such as bloodletting, purgation, baths, unguents, plasters, and a special drink that, among other ingredients, included scurvy grass. The healing properties of scurvy grass were discovered by mariners and were starting to gain acceptance. This was the only one of Clowes' recommendations to have any merit in the curing of vitamin C deficiency. *Sir Francis Drake's West Indian Voyage*, 99.

160. Quoted in Keevil, *Medicine and the Navy*, 78.

161. Ibid., 79.

162. Alsop, "Sea Surgeons, Health and England's Maritime Expansion," 219; Hawkins, *Observations*, 42, 56; Foxe, *North-West Fox or Fox From The North-West Paasage*, 226; David W. Waters, "Limes, Lemons and Scurvy in Elizabethan and Early Stuart Times," *Mariner's Mirror* 41 (1955), 167–86.

163. Milton-Thompson, "Two Hundred Years of the Sailor's Diet," 27.

164. Copeman, *Doctors and Disease in Tudor Times*, 155, 160. It was believed that therapeutic diets could restore the balance of the humors. PRO HCA 13/27/395; Keevil, *Medicine and the Navy*, 74–75; Bodleian Library, Rawlinson Ms. A. 204/150.

165. These items strongly suggest that the English thought that Mediterranean fare was healthier. Fernandez-Armesto, *The Spanish Armada*, 70–71; PRO E, 351/2393, 351/2398; Keevil, *Medicine and the Navy*, 109.

166. Fernandez-Armesto, *The Spanish Armada*, 70.

167. Ibid., 70–71.

168. Ibid., 70; PRO HCA 13/28/77v–78v. Judging from the size of the surgeon's work space aboard the *Mary Rose*, medical men practiced in confined spaces.

169. It has been said that Spain had the most extensive network of hospitals for its veterans in Europe. Geoffrey Parker, *The Army of Flanders and the Spanish Road 1567–1659* (Cambridge: Cambridge University Press, 1972), 167, 169; Hudson, "The Origins of State Benefits for Ex-servicemen in Elizabethan England" 12. England began to use a hospital ship in its naval fleet during the reign of King Charles I. Captain Nathaniel Boteler was one of the greatest proponents of their use. Keevil, *Medicine and the Navy*, 156–57, 196–97.

170. PRO HCA 13/27/263; Keevil, *Medicine and the Navy*, 90.

171. Roy Porter, "The Patient's View: Doing Medical History from Below," *Theory and Society* 14 (1985), 194.

172. Alsop, "Sea-Surgeons, Health and England's Maritime Expansion," 221; Keevil, *Medicine and the Navy*, 113–14; PRO HCA 1/44/169v–71.

173. Houlbrooke, "Death, Church, and Family in England between the Late Fifteenth and the Early Eighteenth Centuries," 28–29; Beier, "The Good Death," 44.

174. Guildhall Ms., 9171/22/399-v, 9171/20/178v. There are numerous bequests to crewmates who acted as nurses. Unless specified, it is difficult to know whether these men were surgeons or fellow seamen. See PRO PROB 11/102/109v.

175. Porter, "The Patient's View," 194; Beier, "The Good Death," 53.

176. Keevil, *Medicine and the Navy*, Appendix, 1–3. The exception was seamen who were injured as the result of drunkenness or fighting with their shipmates.

177. Kassmaul, *Servants in Husbandry in Early Modern England*, 32.

178. PRO HCA, 13/36/3–3v, 1/44/33.

179. PRO HCA 14/36/67.

180. PRO HCA, 14/20/15, 1/46/2–3.

181. Baker and Thompson had quarreled prior to this over a piece of beef. PRO HCA 1/45/170–75v.

182. Porter, "The Patient's View," 194; Houlbrooke, "Death, Church, and Family," 28–29.

183. *State Papers*, vol. II, 96.

184. *The Expedition of Sir John Norris and Sir Francis Drake to Spain and Portugal, 1589*, 209–10.

185. Under early Tudor "bastard feudalism," the Crown contracted with army and naval commanders, at a fixed price, to provide and equip forces, including provision of clothing, food, and health care. From 1540 onward England moved away from this system. The Crown was obviously very slow to understand or accept the consequences of the move to nationwide direct recruitment. As a result, commanders like Howard continued to feel personal paternalistic responsibilities in some circumstances, while, in other cases, men fell between the cracks.

186. Keevil, *Medicine and the Navy*, 68, 76.

187. Ibid., 74, 76.

188. Loades, *The Tudor Navy*, 202.

189. Corbett, *Drake and the Tudor Navy*, vol. II, 165, 168; PRO SP, 12/211/145, 12/215/66, 12/272/13.

190. PRO HCA, 14/30/136, 14/28/122; Guildhall Ms. 9234/3/85; PRO HCA 14/26/55. See also PRO HCA, 14/28/125, 14/26/55.

191. PRO SP, 12/228/10, 12/228/17, 12/240/60; 39 Eliz. c.4 provided for the punishment of rogues, vagabonds, and sturdy beggars. *The Statutes of the Realm*, vol. IV, part II, 855. The acts of the Privy Council also show that this remained a concern for the duration of the war. PRO HCA, 14/27/144, 14/27/198.

192. Loades, *The Tudor Navy*, 280.

193. Keevil, *Medicine and the Navy*, 76; Oppenheim, *The Administration of the Royal Navy, 1509–1660*, 135.

194. 35 Eliz. c.4, *Statutes of the Realm*, vol. IV, part II, 847.

195. 35 Eliz. c.4, 39 Eliz. c.21, 43. Eliz. c.3., *Statutes of the Realm*, vol. IV, part II, 847–48, 923, 966.

196. 35 Eliz. c.4, *Statutes of the Realm*, vol. IV, part II, 848.

197. See next chapter for the connection between bachelorhood and itineracy.

198. Andrew Wear, "Caring for the Sick Poor in St. Bartholomew's Exchange: 1580–1676," in *Living and Dying in London* ed. W. F. Bynum and Roy Porter (London: Wellcome Institute for the History of Medicine, 1991), 50–52.

199. Monson, *Naval Tracts*, vol. II, 244.

200. 39 Eliz. c.17 *The Statutes of the Realm*, vol. IV, part II, 915; PRO, SP 12/268/54, HCA 1/44/186, HCA 1/44/131v–32v, HCA 1/44/202-v. See also PRO HCA 1/44/90–94.

201. Geoffrey L. Hudson, "Ex-Servicemen, War Widows and the English County

Pension Scheme, 1593–1679" (Ph.D. diss., Oxford University, 1995), 59–64; Hudson, "The Origins of State Benefits for Ex-Servicemen in Elizabethan England," 1–17; Geoffrey L. Hudson, "Negotiating for Relief: Strategies Used by Victims of War in Early Seventeenth Century England," 1–30.

202. Parishes were to pay disabled mariners up to £10 per annum and officers up to £20. Lloyd, *The British Seaman*, 47; Cruickshank, *Elizabeth's Army*, 184.

203. PRO, HCA 13/36/217v–18, SP 12/268/52.

204. Lodesmanage was the payment that pilots received for guiding ships safely into harbor, and primage was allotted to seamen who helped load and unload ship's cargo. Ruddock, "The Trinity House at Deptford in the Sixteenth Century," 465–66.

205. Ibid., 466.

206. Keevil, *Medicine and the Navy*, 51.

207. PRO SP 12/249/525.

208. PRO SP 12/254/6.

209. Dixon, "Seamen and the Law," 11.

210. Hawkins's seamen were very loyal to him in return. One sailor was still defending Hawkins's honor to the Holy Office in Sierra Leone six years after his capture:

[H]e said that they had never captured any ship, and had never even dreamt of doing harm to anybody, and that when John Hawkins took anything, even if it were only a shirt, he paid for it . . . [and] although he could not know the inmost workings of Hawkins's heart, he could judge of them by his acts, which God knew were good. (Hair, "Protestants as Pirates," 208)

211. Prior to the 1593 statute, only the exceptional seamen received pensions. Those who were singled out for royal pensions had clearly earned their reward; a gunner was given a royal pension in 1595 as he had served the Tudor monarchs for 39 years on land and at sea. He had lost his sight during service at Brest and was "poor, aged, and impotent." PRO SP 12/255/42.

212. Robert Jutte, "Poor Relief and Social Discipline in Sixteenth-Century Europe," *European Studies Review* 11 (1981), 25.

213. Keevil, *Medicine and the Navy*, 72.

214. The Lord Admiral wrote to Walsingham in 1588,

I would rather open the Queen's Majesty's purse something to relieve them [seamen], than they should be in that extremity; for we are to look to have more of these services; and if men should not be cared for better than to let them starve and die miserably, we should very hardly get men to serve. (*State Papers*, vol. II, 183)

215. Keevil, *Medicine and the Navy*, 113.

216. These words are taken from the petition of the mutinous men of the *Golden Lion*. Oppenheim, *The Administration of the Royal Navy, 1509–1660*, 384.

217. Paul Slack, "Book of Orders: The Making of English Social Policy, 1577–1631,"*Transactions of the Royal Historical Society* 30 (1980), 17.

Chapter 5

Life Ashore

The examination of seamen's occupational lives has uncovered a relatively comprehensive picture of their time at sea. We turn next to a discussion of a neglected topic: seamen's lives ashore. It is not difficult to understand why the subject has been disregarded: information concerning the lives of seamen's families and activities ashore is sketchy at best. While we can glean information on seamen's careers and their lives afloat from official documents such as Admiralty Court records, State Papers, or documents relating to the Trinity House at Deptford, these sources reveal little about seamen's time ashore. Through the analysis of the official records in conjunction with seamen's wills, those of their widows and children, and parish records, we can draw some conclusions about the nature of bachelor seamen's existence ashore as well as the family lives of those associated with seafaring. First, we must explore the image of "Jack Tar ashore." Seafarers have long been tarred by the same brush; well before the sixteenth century they were considered debauched drunkards and ne'er-do-wells by mainstream society. One can understand why landsmen who witnessed seamen in taverns engaging in postvoyage revelry did not have a high regard for them. While there is plenty of anecdotal evidence to support the view that seamen were carousers, this is only a partial picture of their time on land. As we shall see, there is truth in the image of "bachelor Jack" just as there is truth in the stereotype of the drunken seaman ashore. The majority of Elizabethan seamen led a roving existence without deep ties to a particular parish or place. In most cases these men were common and semiskilled seamen with limited earning power. Few men had the wherewithal to marry even if they wanted to. Skilled seamen who could support a wife and children usually elected to do so. Not surprisingly, married men exhibited much greater bonds to the land community. In contrast with the single seamen with no fixed abode, "family men" show a much greater tendency to become involved in parish affairs and guildlike organizations. They left a paper trail for historians that the rootless, poorer bachelors seldom did. We are on much firmer ground in discussing the private and public lives of the prominent and affluent seamen, whose families and careers are more readily reconstructed. Hence, the following analysis is weighted in favor of the family lives of seamen rather than the nature of bachelorhood. There is a geographical bias as well; much of the information gathered on seamen's families and lives ashore is based upon family reconstruction and parish records of those living in or near London.

Even more elusive than information on the lives of seamen ashore is information on their wives and widows. While frequently alluded to, it was not unusual for parish records and wills to omit the given names of wives and widows. In some wills, testators refer only to "my wife." Thus, numerous women remain nameless and obscure. Among the lower echelons of society, most wives who predeceased their husbands remain in the shadows. We can collect some information about wives and the nature of Tudor marriages from wills, but this is not abundant. Widows who remarried can be difficult to trace, especially if their second husbands did not leave wills or the couple moved from the parish. Other than wills, there are few sources where we can "meet" seamen's wives. The wealthiest widows usually left more information on their lives and estates than their poorer counterparts did. Occasionally, wives and widows appear in official documents, petitioning the Crown for redress on behalf of their husbands or their families or bringing suits in the Admiralty Court. Therefore, the examination of seamen's wives and widows is limited.

While we must acknowledge that seamen's occupational lives were different in a number of respects from those in the land trades, were seamen's lives ashore any different from landsmen's? How did seamen spend their leisure time? What proportion of seamen eventually married and settled down? Do seamen's families have their own dynamics and demographic patterns, or were their families typical of Tudor society? What role did seamen's wives play in the household, given the repeated and lengthy absences of their spouses? Although seamen were immersed in the maritime subculture, did this produce a distinctive way of life? Did the realities of family life change for seamen during wartime? From the limited sources that we do have, we attempt to answer these questions.

JACK IN PORT

Upon returning to port, seamen were keen to relax and enjoy some of the profits of their time at sea. Seamen have long possessed a reputation for making the most of their shore leave.[1] In many instances, they lived up to this image. Whether they were in their home port or a foreign one, seamen spent much of their time drinking and loitering at inns, taverns, and alehouses. Their behavior not infrequently led to trouble with fellow tavern haunters and local authorities. The High Court of the Admiralty depositions provide copious evidence regarding the connection between alcohol, shore leave, and misfortune.[2] In 1597 sailor Thomas Smith alias Tucker paid dearly for imbibing at the Queen's Arms on St. Mary Hill, London. The sailor's drinking companions abandoned him, leaving him with their bill, which he was unable to pay. Sailor John Curtis was imprisoned in 1604 after his drinking companion, Robert Jones alias Gunner, ran away from their bill at a Whitechapel alehouse. In general, returning seamen who had survived their voyage unscathed and had money in their pockets were inclined to celebrate. In some circumstances personal injury or death resulted from drunkenness and shore leave. The crew of the *William* was commanded to appear before the Admiralty Court in 1604 to be questioned about the death of their master after they had been ashore all day and by their own admission, "were farre spente with drinck." Drunken seamen often became argumentative and violent. Fighting, like drinking, was a habitual activity.[3] Barring serious injury, this could be excused by authorities. However, fighting routinely led to other trouble. The men of the *May Flower* were grilled by Admiralty officials in 1602 regarding a fight and robbery. After drinking ashore in London, the crew of the English ship began to tussle with a French crew who were also in port. During the fight, one or some of the English seamen stole the French shipmaster's cloak and money. A tragic, alcohol-related episode occurred in 1604, when John Magnes and John Ivington, two friends and crewmates, began to argue over whether it was better to have sons or daughters. Predictably, the disagreement broke out after a day of drinking ashore. It began innocently enough; Magnes and Ivington and their crewmates from the *John and Frances* were discussing their children and news from home. Observers were astounded when the disagreement turned violent, and Magnes was killed in the ensuing fight. One crewmate testified that the two "aggreed togeather as brothers but beinge somewhat over seem with drinck they fell to wordes." Ivington, the seaman who survived the fight, was charged with Magnes's murder; he acknowledged that the two "were good frendes ever before." What started out as a harmless bout of drinking deprived two men of their lives (Magnes died as the result of his injuries, and Ivington was hanged) and at least one family (Ivington's) of its breadwinner. Incidents like this one were not uncommon.

Although not all seamen found themselves in such dire predicaments as a result of their time ashore, the reckless abandon that accompanied shore leave frequently complicated seamen's lives. This was not lost on sixteenth-century commanders and observers.[4] Richard Madox, an Elizabethan chaplain who served afloat, remarked:

I perceaved that it is nether good that saylers shold be suffered to go ashore when they lye in harboroe, nether that strong drink shold be suffered in haven towns, for thro lyberty on the one syde and temptation on the other syde . . . much disorder both in ship and town [is] commytted and more chardges both to owner and sayler than is needful.

This opinion was not particular to Madox or the sixteenth century. In 1740 another observer commented:

All good qualities, however, they [seamen] always leave behind them on shipboard: the sailor out of water is, indeed, as wretched an animal as the fish out of water; for though the former hath, in common with amphibious animals, the bare power of existing on land, yet if he be kept there any time, he never fails to become a nuisance.

As this quotation demonstrates, such criticisms are not unique to Elizabethan seamen. There is a timelessness about seamen, trouble, and shore leave.

For the most part, commanders could accept that their men needed to blow off steam after being contained on a ship for months at a time, but officers resented the fact that shore leave might well interfere with shipboard affairs.[5] Sir Richard Hawkins wrote:

And so [I] began to gather my companie aboord, which occupied my good friends, and the Iustices of the Towne two dayes, and forced vs to search all Lodgings, Tavernes, and Ale-houses . . . some drinke themselues so drunke, that except they were carried aboord, they of themselues were not able to goe one steppe . . . others . . . [were or fayned themselves] indebted to their Hostes, and forced me to ransome them.

Many seamen were reluctant to leave the pleasures of port life. Madox's criticisms mirror Hawkins's:

we cold have wayd [anchor] betymes but our men were ashore, some drunk and some in dette. Hear lost we agayn our tynker and a carpenter and I knoe not whom els, so that I muse why the masters that with such feloes have oft byn synged wil suffer any to go ashore.

Madox's query is an understandable one. The truth of the matter was that while some measures were taken to keep seamen orderly, they were largely useless. The custom and expectation of making the most of one's time ashore were too engrained. Elizabethan and Jacobean admiral William Monson explains:

Whether it is the sea that works contrary effects to the land, or whether it be a liberty you feel ashore after you have been penned up in a ship like birds in a cage, or untamed horses when they are let loose; certain it is neither birds nor horses can . show more extravagant lewdness, more dissolate wildness, and less fear of God, than your carriage discovers when you come ashore and cast off the command of your superior officers at sea had over you. . . . He that could as easily reduce the ordinary seamen to civility and good behaviour ashore . . . were more than a man.[6]

The attempted solution lay in efforts to ban shore leave.[7] In some cases seamen in the merchant marine were dismissed for spending time ashore. Naval seamen saw little, if any, unsupervised shore leave; captains did not allow them to go ashore without permission. When supplies were needed, the boatswain or the quartermaster led a small contingent of men "of good rule" ashore. They were ordered not to tarry.

Drunkenness, brawling, wenching, gaming, and debt were routine parts of shore leave. These activities were usually done in the company of crewmates or fellow seamen. Alehouses and taverns were important, as seamen frequented such establishments to seek out "their own kind" for companionship in revelry as well as for business and trading contacts and employment news.[8] The fact that most seamen were recognizable by their distinctive apparel helped to single them out to other seafarers in these establishments. This type of visual recognition routinely led to conversations and acquaintanceship. Barring visual identification, seamen were recognized by their speech. They were clearly more at home with other seafarers; accounts often mention seamen (who may or may not have been their crewmates) sharing lodging and leisure time while ashore.

Seamen found it more economical to bunk together ashore. Pirates frequently traveled together ashore for protection.[9] This was true of English seamen in foreign ports as well. Whenever possible, seamen away from home hoped to avail themselves of the hospitality of those who lived there. Others with local dwellings and kinship connections were particularly useful in such situations. When in London, sailor John Wells of Aldeburgh bided his time between his brother's house in nearby Gravesend and the house of a local waterman. In his will of 1580 sailor John Young gave all his possessions and wages to his kinsman John Smith, who had repeatedly given him board and lent him money. Richard Paine alias Allen spent several months ashore at his mother's house in Wapping, where she took care of him.[10]

It was not unusual for seamen to lack a fixed abode. Some formed bonds with their host and hostesses, who provided them with lodging. If they were happy with their accommodations, seamen would return to the same hostelry whenever they were in a given port. They often remembered hosts and hostesses in wills, especially those in major ports like London.[11] In his will of 1558 master's mate Thomas Carter named his host, Thomas Caroe of St. Katherine's by the Tower, as his sole executor in preference over his brother or sisters. Their relationship must have been close; Carter was the godfather of Caroe's son. In many cases, the bond between seaman and host was such that seamen entrusted their host or hostess to keep money and property until they returned. Seaman George Hancock left a chest and the large sum of £45 with his host in Southwark when he went on a voyage to Barbary. Mariner Henry Badcock left the shares of his last voyage to his hostess "for that (as he affirmed) she had ben greatlye his freind and had vsed hym very well." Mariner Thomas Pincheback willed all his possessions to his loving host, waterman John Overs of Ratcliffe. Many seamen formed long-term associations with those who provided them with a "home" ashore.

There does not seem to have been a shortage of women who were willing to provide companionship for Jack Tar when he was ashore. Parish records for London and its surrounding area show that a number of seamen had illegitimate children.[12] While some of these were the consequence of illicit affairs, most were likely the product of committed relationships. Premarital relations, even when they resulted in pregnancy, were considered acceptable when couples were betrothed.[13] In many cases illegitimate births resulted from unfulfilled marriage plans; illegitimacy rates were particularly high during times of economic hardship such as the 1590s and 1600s.[14] Seamen were prone to have illegitimate children, as many left port without knowing that their sweethearts were pregnant, and women who had fiancés in land-based trades had a greater chance of prompt marriage following the discovery of pregnancy since seamen spent so much of their time away from home. Nonetheless, at the lower levels of society there seems to have been little stigma attached to an illegitimate birth provided the couple solemnized the marriage and avoided burdening the parish. In 1588 parish records of St. Botolph Aldgate in London list the burial of a stillborn baby born to a sailor and his (as yet unmarried) wife.[15] This is one example of a larger phenomenon; most unwed mothers or mothers-to-be were in committed relationships. Undoubtedly, there were several bastards who were later legitimated following their fathers' return from sea and the consequent marriage of the parents. Conversely, the child might never be legitimated if its father died during his voyage.[16] This was a risk that at least some seamen were prepared to take.

Jack Tar's boisterous shore leave often had unpleasant consequences. Some shipmasters made futile attempts to limit the seamen's time ashore to avoid trouble and inconvenience. Local officials routinely arrested seamen for unpaid debts at alehouses and for brawling. Occasionally, alcohol consumption led to more serious crimes. In addition to problems with employers and run-ins with the law, shore leave could lead to illegitimate children; public opinion pressured couples to get married in these circumstances, lest the local parish have to bear the financial responsibility of the bastard child. Yet, after months of subjection to the shipmaster's authority, held in check by the confines of the all-male wooden world of a ship, and exposed to numerous hazards, seamen were determined to live it up when on shore. Hence, the wrath of local officials, public opinion, and employers was of secondary importance to the much-needed "release" at the end of the voyage.

BACHELORHOOD

Many seamen led a truly itinerant life. While we do not have accurate estimates for the number of seamen who remained unmarried during this period, figures for later periods demonstrate that there was a high degree of truth in the image of "bachelor Jack."[17] While some gloried in their lack of roots and obligations, others simply lacked the wherewithal to marry. Marriage during the sixteenth century was not simply a matter of finding a compatible mate; marriage was "built on material foundations." In order to marry, couples had to accumulate the necessary resources to establish their own independent households.[18] This was increasingly difficult to do during the Elizabethan period, as real wages declined sharply. The marriage rate fell sharply in response, and the proportion remaining unmarried might have been as high as a quarter of the adult population.[19] Doubtless, the figures were substantially higher for seamen. Of the 89 English seamen and merchants connected with the early years of the Guinea trade who left recoverable wills, only 20 had been or were married. Another 4 were betrothed.[20] Certainly, this sample is biased in favor of young and single men who signed up for this treacherous commerce; long voyages with such high mortality probably appealed more to the adventurous and the unattached. In all likelihood many of these men had not yet reached the mean age of marriage, and, therefore, at least some of them were in the process of amassing the collateral needed for marriage. Undoubtedly, many never did marry. Common seamen were in an especially precarious financial position and were less likely to marry. Because the majority of men in this category descended into penury when they were idle for even short periods ashore, and many were said to live in "shiftinge maner,"[21] long-term commitments were problematic. Furthermore, given that common seamen were usually drawn from the poorer segments of society, few could count on an inheritance to provide sufficient funds for them to marry. For a number of these men, their best hope for marriage was a long shot; they could go to sea on hazardous privateering voyages or pirate expeditions and gamble on a safe, profitable return.

Because their limited finances virtually destined them to itinerant bachelorhood, many formed their closest and most enduring relationships within the male-dominated world of seamen. Evidence from wills suggests that unmarried seamen were likely to develop their most significant ties with other seamen or crewmates.[22] There were several men like Thomas Burges, who died aboard the East India ship *Hector* and left all his worldly goods and wages to a fellow seaman. When mariner Henry Preston fell ill aboard the *Ascension* in 1598, he willed all his goods to the master, William Winter, whom he called "Brother Winter," and the master's mate, George Frude, because of the "affection he bare him he had longe tyme before and so still did call [him] Brother." Predominantly, single deep-sea seamen show enduring ties to their crewmates and fellow seamen; many of their strongest attachments were to men in the maritime community.

Those seamen without families often lacked an anchor to moor them to a specific place. Consequently, the wills of single seamen have a tendency to indicate a "cultural detachment" from their "homes." In a number of cases, this detachment resulted in a marked disinterest in the goings-on of their native parishes. This is illustrated by the fact that, although several bachelors were eager to give bequests to the poor in their wills, many did not care to specify which parish the money should be given to.[23] Conversely, married seamen who gave money to the poor always specified that the money should go to their home parish. Seamen who were without spouses or children and who died at sea show a propensity to leave the bulk of their property to their crewmates who surrounded them at the time of their demise. The pattern can be interpreted in various ways. Lengthy and dangerous voyages were bound to foster camaraderie. Dying seamen were quick to remember those shipmates who had tended them during a period of illness. Sometimes goods were given in thanks for care during a shipboard illness or in payment of debts, which were such an important part of the maritime economy. An effective way to ensure that survivors probated one's will and carried out the testator's wishes was to remember them in the will; goods might be given in return for seamen's acting as witnesses or overseers. There is another possibility as well: those around the dying seaman loomed large in his mind, indicating an absence of more enduring family relationships. Whether dying seamen left bequests to old friends or new ones, one fact is clear. In the absence of wives and children, seamen overwhelmingly bequeathed their often meager possessions to those with whom they sailed and drank, those who were tied to them by friendship, shared experiences, debt and business interests, and a common subculture.

This is not to say that there were not more transient relationships in seamen's lives, especially those of a sexual nature. Although they probably served both married and unmarried clients who had long been deprived of female companionship, prostitutes were especially important to the "nubile unmarrieds," those young men who were not in a position to marry. While specific information on seamen and prostitution remains thin for this period, we know that such women found their way onto ships and frequented ports, where they probably did considerable business. In the late seventeenth century Richard Gibson, a clerk in the Navy Office, petitioned the king to redress abuses in the fleet, principally seamen's sexual liaisons with prostitutes, which led to sexually transmitted diseases; Gibson referred to the fact that many naval seamen engaged in "all manner of debauchery . . . which proves the parent of great sickness and mortality; occasioning thousands of your seamen to do little service by their going ashoar for a cure." In the eighteenth century Robert Park commented that sailors were "devoted to Bacchus and Venus."[24]

Seamen hoping for sexual encounters or relationships were not limited to the female sex. Buggery and other homosexual acts have long been associated with life afloat (and other all-male environments). Although he never addressed the issue directly, Sir Walter Raleigh wrote that "the Marriners doe covet store of Cabbins, yet indeed they are but sluttish Dens . . . serving to cover stealths."[25] Such actions were considered morally reprehensible as well as felonious.[26] During Drake's 1585–86 voyage to the West Indies, for example, Thomas Ogle, steward of the *Talbot*, was "hanged for commyttyng Sodomy"; Ogle confessed his deed "and died very penetently."[27] Doubtless, Ogle was not the only man who indulged in what would later become known as "uncleanliness."[28] We may, however, make a distinction between homosexual acts and homosexual preferences. Very few ascertained cases of homosexual activity took place at sea. Even among the homosexual seafaring population, there is no way of knowing how many were celibate, how many lived a predominantly promiscuous existence, or how many were monogamous. While there is abundant evidence of long-term and extremely close relationships between seamen, we cannot surmise how many of these may have been romantic in nature. All of those testators who left their bequests or estates to male friends had some type of emotional ties; whether these feelings led to a physical relationship is unknown.

MARRIAGE

While many seamen remained single by choice or necessity, others elected to marry and start a family, thereby strengthening their connections with the land population. Family ties were a bridge that connected the population afloat to that ashore. Those with the wherewithal to enter into the married state often elected to do so. While common seamen were almost always in a precarious financial position, officers, especially those in the upper ranks, would normally have the income to support a wife and family. However, even these men would have to wait until their late 20s to choose a bride. There were specific reasons for this. Young adults needed a period of time in service or apprenticeship to obtain proficiency in a trade and to accumulate the finances necessary for marriage. Many of the more skilled members of the maritime community had undergone a period of training that resembled or constituted formal apprenticeship. Training ordinarily lasted anywhere from seven to ten years. Since apprentices were forbidden by the terms of their indenture to marry during their time of service, young men had to wait until their education was ended and they had obtained the necessary resources to establish and sustain an independent household.

Irrefutably, many apprentices were in a very vulnerable financial position. As apprentices, their wages were the property of their masters. When asked his worth by Admiralty officials, 20-year-old Henry Rickman, a young seaman who was one of his father's crew at the time (and probably apprenticed to him), told the Admiralty Court that his only income was what his father bestowed upon him.[29] Such youths were hardly able to support themselves, let alone a wife and children. Furthermore, contemporary wisdom frowned on young men's marrying before their mid-20s. The Statute of Apprentices imposed an age guideline for inhabitants of all cities and corporate towns in 1563; apprentices were not to be released until they were 24 years of age or older. In part, this restriction was designed to prevent "ouerhastie maryages and over sone settyng upp of householdes of and by youthe."[30] Apprenticeship and training then acted as a deterrent to early marriages.[31] While contemporaries might bemoan the rashness of youth in regard to premature marriage, statistics concerning age at first marriage and those who never married are revealing. A sizable number never married at all, and while there were variations based on location and order in society, most men tended to marry in their mid- to late 20s. Their partners were slightly younger.[32] Marriage allegations and family reconstruction for seamen in the London area support the notion that seamen generally followed the same pattern as the larger population. From her study of London marriage allegations, Vivien Brodsky Elliot has postulated that London mariners, as lower-status craftsmen, fell into a pattern of slightly earlier marriages than higher-status craftsmen.[33] Nonetheless, this still points to the fact that most seamen married in their late 20s.

Despite the church's long battle against common-law marriages, it had not succeeded in eliminating them. It is not unusual to find phrases such as the "the unmaryed wyfe of . . ." in parish records in the London area. In 1588 the records of St. Botolph Aldgate in London mention Alice Kemp, who was sailor J. Johnson's wife, as yet unmarried.[34] Many wills, especially nuncupative ones, illustrate that couples considered themselves man and wife following betrothal.[35] Before he went to sea, sailor Richard Morris set his affairs in order, telling his fiancée, widow Margery Graves, and witnesses that

it is not vnknowne to your neighboures but that yowe and I be assured togethers [*sic*] in matrymony and therfore counted man and wife before god. And for that I am nowe presently bound in a voyage to Burdeaux and cannot staye to solemnize the marriage betwene youe and me.

In the presence of diverse people seaman Aron Leedes

required them all to beare witnes That he and Armonelle Tayler there present weare mann and wiffe, Than he declared before them that he was to take his voyage to the Sea, And that yf god shoulde call him before he came home againe from the sea, he desired them to beare witness [that she should inherit his goods].

While these wills illustrate that the testators believed themselves to be married in the eyes of their community and God, the very existence of these statements in the wills speaks to the fact that the seamen were concerned that the courts would not necessarily acknowledge the bond. Despite promises to the contrary, sometimes betrothed couples postponed their marriages or canceled their plans altogether. In 1593 Joan Parkins, a London girl, was a victim of one man's short-term ardor.[36] A Hamburg seaman, known around St. Katherine's Dock as "Peter the Dutchman," spent much of his time drinking in taverns along the Thames. Joan, whose reputation does not seem to have been pristine, believed that she was contracted to Peter and maintained that "noe man shoulde knowe her but Peter." They obtained a bed for the night at a Tower Hill victualing house by claiming "they were man & wiffe." Peter's affections cooled considerably after this, and he denied ever promising her marriage. Joan harassed Peter until she wrung from him an assurance that he would marry her when he returned from Hamburg. Doubtless, many seamen, like Peter the Dutchman, made elaborate promises that they never kept.

Given their itinerant existence, some seamen worried that their sweethearts had found others during their absences[37] and that their engagements had been broken. Long periods at sea probably put a damper on a number of courtships. In his will of 1590 mariner Robert Rickman promised Alice Hutchen who "shoulde have ben my wyfe" four pounds

yf she have kepte her selfe only for me and haue not dyshonested her bodie and be vnmarried and vnbetrothed to anie other mann when our Shipp cometh home but yf she have broken anie of theis Articles then I will that her porcion shalbe equallie devided betwene my brothers and Systers.

Sailor Thomas Baylye was eager that his intended, Joan Wood, receive all his goods provided "she be not contracted to anie other man then myselfe which I do not think she is."

There were many reasons for unfulfilled marriage plans. Sometimes death intervened or occupational demands interfered with marriage plans. As in the case of Richard Morris and Margery Graves mentioned previously, the church service was postponed because of a voyage. Since the male was the principal or sole breadwinner, his employment determined the rhythms of marital life.[38] The completion of a successful voyage could mean the making of a marriage or, at the very least, give the couple additional funds to start their new life together. In this sense seamen were similar to agricultural workers who depended on a good harvest in order to fulfill their marriage plans.[39]

In any marriage the choice of a mate is an all-important one. Members of the lower orders of sixteenth-century society normally had a high degree of freedom in selecting a spouse, but there were parameters. While a parental blessing was important for emotional reasons, it could also be important for economic ones; parents usually helped equip their children with some of the goods necessary for marriage. The evidence from wills suggests that parents were more likely to exert pressure on young women to choose a mate approved by the parents. Sons at this level of society seem to have been left to their own discretion.

Some parents (both male and female) attempted to exercise control from the grave in regard to their children's marriages.[40] The will of Captain Christopher Newport stipulated that one of his daughters would inherit £400 if she married with her mother's approval. This was a powerful incentive to obtain maternal consent. Newport's inducements were not to be taken lightly. He bequeathed only £5 to his other daughter "in regard of many [of] her greate disobediences . . . to my greate hartes greife [she] shall not haue anie right title or interest to clayme receaue or enioye anie more of my goodes landes or Chattels." Although Gillian Estis, widow of mariner John Estis, left much of their considerable estate to the children of shipmaster Nicholas Diggens [Dickens] when she died in 1595, she was neither a parent nor a guardian to the children. She was particularly concerned about the future of the Diggens/Dickens's daughter, Estis (no doubt named for Gillian). The widow inserted an important proviso in her will:

Provided allwayes and my expresse mynde and will is that yf the aforesaid Estis Dickens doughter of the said Nicholas Dickens and Jelian his wief shall not be ruled and gouerned by her said Father and mother in bestowinge her self in marriage they or either of them beinge ther lyvinge that then all . . . the former gyftes . . . by me to her hereby bequeathed shall . . . be vtterlie void.

Katherine Rickman, widow of mariner Thomas Rickman, left most of her goods to spinster Dorothy Harrison provided that Dorothy marry with the goodwill and consent of Katherine's overseers. Thus, Katherine's friend and kinswoman, Thomasin Rickman, wife of mariner Robert Rickman, and Margaret Cook, wife of mariner Walter Cook, were to oversee Dorothy's choice. There are no such provisions for young bachelors.

It is apparent that male suitors had to court not only the women but their parents or guardians as well. The father (or father figure) frequently played a critical role in engineering the marriage of his daughter, not only arranging a dowry but introducing his daughter to suitable young men.[41] Fathers and guardians often relied on kinship ties and occupational and business connections when seeking appropriate mates for their daughters. Discerning seafarers had to look for other qualities in potential spouses as well. While the ideal Tudor marriage consisted of two helpmates who worked together for the welfare of the family unit,[42] a seafaring husband was absent a great deal of the time. Although the wife was seen as the subordinate partner both by custom and in the law, her role was vital. Often she was called on to head the family and raise the children for months or even years at a time. Shipmaster William Ingatt, for instance, could not give the Admiralty Court details regarding his income or his taxes; he stated that his wife took care of his financial matters.[43] Therefore, many seamen picked brides whose fathers, brothers, or deceased husbands were part of the maritime community. Since seamen circulated within the confines of their own community to a great extent, in the course of their lives ashore they met women whose brothers, fathers, and husbands were seamen or practitioners of related trades such as ship carpentry or sailmaking. The maritime elite tended to marry women connected with shipmasters, owners, and merchants. In theory at least, these women would be prepared for the roles that they would have to play; their expectations of marriage would be conditioned by their experiences and would be somewhat different from the expectations of the daughters, sisters, and widows of landsmen.

There existed a complex network of intermarriage among the most skilled English seamen.[44] The Brethren of the Trinity House of Deptford provide an outstanding example. They married each other's widows, daughters, and sisters for generations and by so doing formed a prestigious cartel with extensive connections in London and its environs. Many of the same surnames survive for generations in the ranks of England's elite mariners and as members of Trinity House. Several formidable seafaring dynasties were formed by seafaring fathers whose sons followed in their footsteps and whose daughters and widows married other eminent mariners. The Goodlad family of Leigh, Essex (and later Stepney parish outside of London), contained many seamen. Goodlad men held a prominent place within the maritime community during the Elizabethan and Stuart periods. The Goodlads also had a long affiliation with the Trinity House at Deptford. G. G. Harris has noted that by the early seventeenth century the Goodlads were connected by marriage to the Best, Bower, Harris, Moyer, and Salmon families. To this list we may also add the Breadcake family of Leigh, who were also very well respected during this period. While some of their success can be attributed to the production of healthy and skilled sons, the Goodlads owed much to their connections and wealth gained through intermarriage with other prominent seafaring families. These men were joined by kinship ties, business ties, and ownership of vessels. The Goodlads, the Breadcakes, and the Harrises built at least three ships together. The interconnected families continued to prosper and expand in the seventeenth century.[45]

The Rickman family is another excellent example of the high degree of intermarriage among the upper echelon of seamen.[46] Most, if not all, of the children of shipmaster Robert Rickman selected mates who were mariners or related to mariners from within Stepney parish. Rickman's daughter Katherine married at least twice, choosing local shipmasters on both occasions. Her brother, mariner Thomas Rickman, married the daughter of a seaman in 1601. Their brother, mariner Robert Rickman Jr., married the daughter of a mariner in 1603. Brother Henry Rickman, also a seaman, married the widow of a Ratcliffe sailor in 1610.

To appreciate the high degree of intermarriage among prominent seafaring families, one has only to look at the maritime leadership of England during the Elizabethan period.[47] Sir John Hawkins, the architect of the Elizabethan navy, married Katherine Gonson, daughter of Benjamin Gonson, Treasurer of the Navy. John Hawkins later succeeded his father-in-law in the position. Gonson had secured the post from his father, William Gonson, who had played a critical role in forming the Navy Board under Henry VIII. His Gonson relatives provided Hawkins with a means to enter into the inner circle of the Elizabethan naval bureaucracy. Benjamin Gonson was married to Ursula Hussey, daughter of the second governor of the Russia Company. Hawkins was related to another naval commander, Thomas Fleming, through the Gonsons. Fleming frequently captained the Queen's ships and participated in several of the Earl of Cumberland's expeditions. The Gonson family also connected Hawkins with lesser but still well respected shipmasters such as Thomas White and the Upgrave family. Hawkins's brother-in-law was Edward Fenton, a prominent naval commander who sought the Northwest Passage and was a veteran of the Armada campaign. Hawkins's most famous kinsman was Sir Francis Drake. With such powerful connections and kinsmen it is not surprising that Hawkins's son Richard carried on the family's seafaring tradition.

FAMILY AND COMMUNITY LIFE

Marriage generally meant that the couple had established their own independent home and were an autonomous economic unit. This did not necessarily mean that they could afford to purchase or even rent their own house and property. In fact, only a small number of seamen bequeathed property and leases in their wills, indicating that these few were privileged indeed. Those who were in this group were established and prominent shipmasters who frequently owned shares in shipping as well. They were the elite of the maritime hierarchy.[48] Those seamen who did own or lease property often had sizable holdings, sometimes in more than one county. Shipmaster Cuthbert Carr, for instance, owned property in Ratcliffe in Middlesex, Rye in Sussex, and near Newcastle upon Tyne.[49]

Prosperous seamen who were property owners or tenants who leased property of any size sometimes rented it out to other members of the maritime community. Perhaps some bachelor homeowners rented out their houses when they were at sea.[50] Many seamen who lived in the Thameside parishes of Stepney and Wapping rented out extra houses and properties to fellow seamen, ship's carpenters, and the like.[51] For instance, Stepney seaman Robert Rickman the younger bought a house from his shipmaster grandfather and rented it to a shipwright. Shipmaster Mathew Woodcot had sizable holdings; his tenants consisted of three mariners, a shipwright, and a cooper, all tradesmen associated with the maritime community. To some extent this trend reflects the large numbers of seafaring men living in parishes along the Thames, but it is also evidence of the close-knit nature of the seafaring community ashore. It was convenient to rent to former crewmates and seafaring friends for a number of reasons. Seafaring landlords were probably more understanding of seamen's work and, therefore, payment pattern. Seamen's wives and children could provide assistance to one another when the men were away.

We have little information on what sort of arrangements the less affluent seamen made for their families. We do know that geographic mobility was a feature of most seamen's lives. Whether they were married or not, they sought employment where they could find it, which could lead to enormous variations in work patterns and time spent afloat. Those engaged in coastal trading would be away only for short runs while, at the other extreme, those employed by the East India Company could expect to be away for three years. Seamen's wives, especially spouses of those employed in long-distance voyages, could anticipate that their husbands might be away more than they were at home.[52]

While bachelor seamen were relatively free to roam at will, marriage did not necessarily mean that a seaman and his wife put down deep roots. A seaman would move to another port if he found that it offered better employment or business opportunities. In many cases seamen were drawn to London, long a magnet to Englishmen, Englishwomen, and, in particular, youths.[53] A seaman could contract work on all manner of voyages from this location. As a result, families could suffer dislocation from the support system provided by kin at the same time that the principal breadwinner was absent for extended periods. Little wonder that the members of the maritime community banded together on land. For instance, the wife and three children of captain/pilot John Allen alias Sallowes moved from Surrey to Dunkirk while he went to sea with Dunkirk privateers who made a living capturing and ransoming Englishmen and rifling their cargoes.[54] We can only guess at the impact upon the rest of the family.

Parish records for the London area indicate that a significant number of seamen's wives were seemingly without their husbands and in a parish other than their settled residence at a point of crisis (childbirth or sickness in most cases). While records indicate the nature of the crisis, at whose house the woman was kept, and by whom she was tended, they raise more questions than they answer. Were the women in a predicament because they had just recently arrived in the city, or does this mean that they followed their husbands to ports of embarkation, waiting until their men returned from the sea? Were they so poor that they could not afford to put down roots, or were they merely at a transitional stage? Were those who housed them friends and relations, or were they paid by the parish to care for them?[55] Doubtless, women who were pregnant or sick found it convenient to stay with friends or family while waiting for their husbands' return. This seems to have been the case with the Elsom family. Lucy Elsom, wife of gunner John Elsom, was brought to bed in London, even though the family was said to dwell in the west country.[56] The parish records of St. Botolph Aldgate registered the christening of Robert Etheridge, son of William Etheridge, a Kent sailor, in 1590. The baby was "no parishioner's child" but was christened in St. Botolph Aldgate because William's wife, Frances, had been brought to bed in the parish.[57] Parish records do not outline any charges to the parish, so we may assume that both Lucy Elsom and Frances Etheridge were not thrown on parish relief. A contrasting case is provided by Mary Perry, almost certainly impoverished. Wife of sailor Richard Perry, she became sick in the parish of St. Botolph Aldgate in 1590 and was taken to the house of laborer Reynold Barnett. Perry was not a parishioner. Since Barnett was paid 13 shillings to take care of Perry, we can assume that she was indigent and that Barnett was a poor parishioner paid by the parish to look after her.[58] When Perry's illness worsened, she was taken to the parish cage, where she died. If Perry had belonged to a nearby parish, would not officials have made a concerted effort to return her so as to place the cost and burden of care on the "rightful" parish? Doubtless, she was far from home. Sickness and childbirth were stressful situations experienced by most women, but the trauma was heightened by being alone, being an outsider to the parish at the critical juncture, and lacking sufficient resources to maintain one's self. Geographic mobility intensified the woman's loneliness during periods of separation and lessened access to the vital assistance of accommodating kin and friends, so integral a part of the early modern support system.

Given the hardships of surviving ashore without their mates, it is obvious why some seamen's wives were unable or unwilling to part with their spouses. We have both anecdotal references and reports establishing the presence of women at sea. Females were seen jumping from sinking vessels, and female corpses were observed amid the wreckage of ships.[59] When master shipbuilder Phineas Pett examined the wreckage of the naval ship *Anne Royal* in 1636, he noted that there were "[D]ivers men drowned, and some women." We know that some "public women" did go as guests of seamen. While these women sometimes passed as "wives," there were also some bona fide spouses.[60] Most of the known allusions for the period after 1600 refer to officers' wives at sea. Some English naval commanders unofficially tolerated women on board. The presence of wives was countenanced more in the merchant marine than in the navy. Although they hardly could be said to be present in great numbers, there were women aboard sixteenth-century ships, whether they were wives, sweethearts, prostitutes, or "seamen."

The vast majority of wives who opted to stay ashore felt the loss of their mates in terms of companionship and support. The social problems that stemmed from the nature of seamen's work were enduring and provided long echoes into the seventeenth century. Samuel Pepys, Clerk of the Acts of the Navy, wrote in 1666:

Lord! how some poor women did cry; and in my life I never did see such natural expression of passion as I did hear in some women's bewailing themselves, and running to every parcel of men that were brought, one after another, to look for their husbands, and wept over every vessel that went off, thinking they might be there, and looking after the ship as far as they could by moon-light, that it grieved me to the heart to hear them.[61]

To some extent stresses were mitigated by women's "support networks" of family, neighbors, and members of the maritime community. For instance, when widow Katherine Baynard of Ratcliffe was ill in 1604, her neighbors nursed her on her deathbed. While there were unnamed caregivers present, at least one was wife of a seaman, while another was the daughter of a shipmaster.[62]

Although friends and family were essential for emotional support, they were not always able to help financially, which was one of the biggest problems faced by seamen's wives. Most seamen's families existed primarily on wage labor.[63] The crew of the ship *Margaret and John*, for instance, petitioned the governor of Virginia in 1623 for their wages, arguing that "most of us have wiffe and Children in England whose releife and mantenance onlie [are] depending upon our wages." The seamen of Essex responded angrily to a proclamation of 1590 that ordered them to remain in their home ports (so that they could be available for naval duty on short notice) by arguing that "if they be not shortlie in some sorte eased as they affirme [from the restrictions] they shall not be able to mayntayne themselves, & theire famylles." Seaman Pearse Lemans maintained his daughter and her six children at his "greate chardge" when her husband, mariner

Lucas Harvey, was imprisoned by religious authorities in Spain in 1584. Without this help the Harveys would have been forced to look for parish relief "not beinge other wise able to mayntayne their selves." Harvey's wife was fortunate in that her father was still living and able to support her. While kin and neighbors helped when in a position to do so, most seamen's wives were extremely vulnerable in these situations.

Out of necessity some wives sought employment to supplement their husbands' wages.[64] A common occupation for seamen's wives and widows was working in or owning a victualing house or tavern. Seamen living in rural areas sometimes owned small farms, which were worked by their wives and children. The wives of fishermen impressed for naval duty were called upon to "man" their husbands' boats in order to sustain their families. Others took in washing. Most jobs open to respectable women involved domestic duties. In addition to lawful employment, we must not discount the possibility that the survival strategies of some of these women included illegal activities as well. One eighteenth-century observer claimed that seamen's families were "often driven by Necessity to commit Crimes which Distress alone could force them into against their better Indications." Another commented that seamen "bring such Women as they marry to want, and to make them and their Children as dissolute as themselves."[65]

In lieu of ready money from their husbands' wages or their own paid labor, wives of affluent seamen could often count on income from rented properties or shares in shipping. As in the case of William Ingatt's wife mentioned previously, women entrusted with the care of their husbands' estates had extensive responsibilities. Such arrangements would offer women considerable latitude in decision making, more than in conventional sixteenth-century marriages.

Unlike the majority of seamen's wives, the wives of affluent seamen rarely had to struggle to survive in their husbands' absence. Although such women were more able to exist on credit than their poorer sisters, they ran the danger of overextending themselves, and sometimes it took their husbands a very long time to pay the debts accumulated in their absence.[66] Nonetheless, they, too, must have been burdened by the uncertainty of the bread-winners' return. Unforeseen circumstances such as injury, sickness, capture, or the death of the provider would have dire consequences for every seaman's family. Shipwreck, spoiled cargo, pirates, employer-imposed fines for misbehavior, or an incomplete voyage were all hazards of the trade; even if the seaman survived unscathed, he would stand to "loose his voyage," that is, not be paid for his labor. This is true of the majority of seamen; even some shipmasters would gamble all on the success of a voyage.

There was a great deal of uncertainty regarding each seaman's remuneration. For this reason wealthier seamen did not "put all their eggs in one basket"; they bought shares in several ships and invested in other enterprises. When a seaman diversified his investments, he stood a better chance of reaping some income. This option, however, was normally restricted to the elite members of the maritime community who had larger reserves of currency, goods, and credit. The financial well-being of most seamen and their families was tied to the successful completion of a voyage. Regardless of his skill or wealth, the fate of a seaman's family often rested on the fact that he returned home uninjured, free from disease and ready to go to sea again.

The late sixteenth century was an especially difficult time for seafarers and their families given the international religious and political tensions and the increasing tide of maritime violence. The loss of a voyage and the descent into poverty became even more likely in these circumstances. The career of shipmaster Abraham Lawse provides an apt illustration. Lawse was unfortunate and suffered the loss of his ship or cargo on at least two occasions, once in 1587 and again in 1604. Lawse and his family were reduced to begging on the first occasion because he had been ransomed from the Dunkirkers by merchants after seven months in captivity and was in danger of going to debtor's prison. To exacerbate the situation, Lawse was still a young shipmaster at the time he was captured (approximately 29), a new husband (married for only three years) and a new father. This first incident came relatively early in his lengthy career and at a formative stage in his family life. After his ransoming, Lawse worked as a shipmaster and captain. He managed to keep clear of notable difficulty until 1604, when pirates attacked his ship and took his lading. He weathered the financial loss of the second incident without the help of a begging license. The likelihood is that Lawse had built up more resources by the time of the second attack, helping to cushion the blow. Yet Lawse was fortunate in that he remained healthy, was able to work, and maintained a successful career.[67]

Escalating maritime violence was not the only hazard that characterized the Elizabethan period. With the outbreak of the Anglo-Spanish war the Crown repeatedly scoured the country for experienced seamen to impress. Naval duty was as unwelcome to seamen's families as it was to the men themselves. Aside from the many dangers inherent in naval service, delayed payment or nonpayment of wages was a resented and predictable aspect of duty. This was not particular to Elizabeth's navy. In 1613 the Earl of Northampton wrote that "the [seamen's] pay is so much in arrears that the wives and children of the sailors are hardly kept from making outcry."[68] Consequently, impressment not only caused many seamen's families to look to their parish for relief but also forced seamen to endure hardships that compromised their health.[69]

When a seaman returned home maimed or injured, he and his family were bound to suffer financially. What of those men who were unable to return to the sea? What happened to their families? Those seamen who were rendered unemployable by virtue of sickness or injury had few options. While their immediate concern was survival, members of the "deserving poor" hoped to avoid falling into the ranks of the vagabonds who were feared for both their growing numbers and their association with crime and disease. Maimed and underemployed seamen, bachelors, and married men formed a significant portion of this group. A fortunate few of those who had lost their livelihood because of naval injuries or lost ships to pirates received begging licenses, which granted them permission to travel and collect alms.

Seamen who were granted begging licenses were normally allowed to canvas several parishes and counties. In these situations wives accompanied husbands from parish to parish, presumably with their children. Whether seamen were seeking alms for losses from pirates or similar misfortune at sea or for disability, the presence of hungry wives and children probably induced the good people of England to dig deeper into their pockets to assist them. There were also significant numbers who illegally begged without licenses. Unless they were provided for by their home parish, these people were pariahs in Tudor society. Regardless of whether the poor had obtained licenses from the Crown, these collections provided only a temporary solution. Even those with licenses were given limitations; begging licenses were granted only for finite periods of time, generally three months to a year.

Injured and maimed seamen might hope to find financial assistance besides parish relief, but long-term public assistance was restricted. Hawkins, Howard, and Drake established the Chatham Chest in 1590 to distribute small pensions to those seamen who had paid into the fund. While this has been applauded by historians as the first contributory medical insurance scheme, it is difficult to say if the truly needy ever contributed to the fund. Like the Chatham Chest, assistance from the Trinity House at Deptford was based upon contributions:

yf any Maryners happen to be maymed, hurte or fawle sycke and be not able to releefe hymself of his owne propre goods, that then it shall be lefull for the said Maister of the same shippe to present any suche Marynor so beyng maymed, hurt or syke to the Maister iiij Wardens and viij Assistantes of the seid almeshowse, and there he to have releffe as shall be thought by them resonable, provyded always that yf the Maister of evry suche shipp and his company do pay theire Dewties to the said Almshowse and other wyse not.[70]

The problem with the Trinity House system was threefold. Did the poorer sorts of seamen contribute? How many could the almshouse accommodate? Certainly, it was only a tiny percentage of those in need. Presumably, those who could not find a place at the almshouse were thrown on parish relief. The city of Bristol had one of the most comprehensive programs to assist seamen and their families. It deducted three and a half pence out of every pound value of merchants' goods and a penny from every pound of sailors' wages and established a school for seamen's children as well as an alms-house for aged and maimed seamen.[71] Again, there seems to be no provision for the maintenance of seamen's families, although seamen's widows were given consideration at the almshouse during the seventeenth century, if not before.[72] Following the lead of these benefactors and organizations, the Crown introduced seamen's pensions late in Elizabeth's reign. These were paid by each seaman's parish and were not to exceed £10 per annum for disabled mariners and £20 for officers.[73] However, recent research undertaken by Geoffrey Hudson has shown that the collection of pensions was anything but a straightforward matter.[74] Often it was difficult to collect anything close to the full amount of the pension even when one qualified. In practice, the majority of seamen could expect little by way of compensation. Furthermore, this measure was too late to help many of Elizabeth's seamen who had fought in the first half of the war, the period of greatest naval activity. Only the few who were fortunate enough to receive a pension had some measure of financial security for themselves and their families for the duration of the seamen's lifetime.

Given their limited range of options and fearful of becoming vagabonds, some seamen's wives ultimately sought help from the Crown.[75] While wives and widows never asked for money or pensions directly, they did seek assistance for problems that affected their families' income. In 1592 several wives petitioned the Crown for its help in securing the release of their husbands who were

att this instante ... remayninge in moste grevouse slavery and boundage in the Galleys & other places vnder the spaniardes tiranye to the greate grife and vtter vndoeinge of the said poore plantiffes.

In this case the Crown was sympathetic to the women's petition and tried to arrange a prisoner exchange. Barring help from the Crown, most were unable to pay ransoms for their husbands. When the men of the *George Bonaventure* were captured by the Spaniards in 1596 and sent to the galleys, their ransom was the sizable amount of £15 per man.

Sometimes husbands were detained in England's prisons. The financial consequences could be equally dire. Wives who begged the Crown for clemency did so on the grounds that their husbands were not guilty of any ill intent and that the welfare of the family depended on the seamen's ability to provide for them.[76] For instance, Margaret Man pleaded for the pardon of sailor Anthony Man, her jailed husband, because, she alleged, he was innocent of the charges against him and because she and their children were poverty-stricken as a result of his imprisonment. Similarly, Agnes Cranford petitioned the Crown on her jailed husband's behalf; the unfortunate husband had become embroiled in unspecified trouble when he went on a voyage with seamen who held a commission from the Holland states. Agnes pleaded that Admiralty officials should have mercy on the grounds that her husband was "a poore sea-faring man drawne (against his will) into this trouble, & now [is] wholy vndone thereby" and by virtue of the fact she "hath not the value of one peny to helpe her selfe."

Unquestionably, the existing number of wives' petitions represents only a small portion of those women in need of assistance. Although it would be dangerous to make too many generalizations from such a small sample, one fact is clear. In most cases women petitioned the Crown for a specific remedy: aid in freeing husbands detained abroad; amnesty for those in domestic jails who were innocent; or consideration in a legal suit. These women did not look to the Crown for charity or pensions. Wives wanted their husbands returned. Widows' petitions almost always stem from con- traventions of their "rights," including the customary right to claim their dead husbands' effects and wages if he died on shipboard.[77] In an era when the Crown was begrudgingly moving toward a recognition of obligations toward its veterans, this did not alter the traditional relationship or expec- tations between the Crown and veterans' families. For the most part, wives were not eligible for begging licenses from the Crown. If their husbands returned from the sea, the men petitioned the Crown for begging licenses on the families' behalf. Seamen's organizations and charities make no men- tion of any provision for wives whose seafaring husbands were still living but unable to return home. Therefore, women who could not survive be- cause their husbands were at sea or detained in foreign or domestic jails almost certainly had to look to the parish, other than to the state, in the absence of accommodating kin or friends. Doubtless, there were many women like the wife of mariner Edward Baker. Baker told the Admiralty Court that he was a poor man but had never been on parish relief, although his wife had been on relief when he was away at sea.[78]

THE ESTRANGED

The most vulnerable group of women were those who were in marital limbo. Because there was no divorce in the strict sense, and annulments by the church courts were infrequent, unhappy couples could never fully dis- entangle themselves from their partners. Church courts did recognize adul- tery, cruelty, or continual arguments as grounds for separation, but very few received church sanction to separate.[79] Desertion was an option, es- pecially for seamen who could easily slip away for long periods. Those in common-law marriages were particularly vulnerable to desertion; it was not as difficult to forsake one's partner if the church had not solemnized the "marriage." Deserted wives were hampered because they had no hus- band to provide them with a home, nor did they have the freedom to remarry.[80] During the late Elizabethan period, John Mathews deserted his wife, children, and country to go to Spain for political and religious reasons. Mathews reportedly told English seamen that he would return to his wife and children in England when the Spaniards had set fire to Plymouth, which he expected would happen within a year or two.[81] Thus, Mathews's wife was in a double bind in that she had been deserted and was the wife of a traitor. Seaman Richard Bee had abandoned or been deserted by his wife before his death in 1601. When he was asked by his neighbors on his deathbed if he would leave his goods to his wife, who was evidently not present, he remarked, "no my wief shall haue no penney of them . . . I will dispose [of] them otherwise as I doe thinck good." Instead, Bee gave his possessions to his cousins and the poor of Stepney.[82]

WIDOWHOOD

Although seamen were concerned about providing for their families after their demise, with the exception of the elite of the maritime community, seamen had rather meager possessions to leave their widows and children. What they did have was passed on willingly.[83] Sailor William Lawrence of Wapping lay sick on his deathbed in 1603, and "being demannded by Alice Lawraunce his then wife if he would make his will and give any thinge to his frendes or kinsfolke, he answered no, but all that I haue I giue them vnto thee . . . and I will not giue a pyn from thee." Many seamen expressed regret that they could not leave more to their widows. Mariner Thomas Weller bequeathed "all that I haue I geve to my wiefe appointing her myne Executrix and I am sory that I haue no more to leave her." Seaman Thomas Debnam of Essex expressed a similar sentiment. Debnam left his goods to his wife so that she could provide for herself, their son, and their unborn child. In his will he lamented the amount and quality of his goods, "wishinge the[y] were of better esteeme." Mariner Robert Momford gave his betrothed "wife" what "little goodes that I have." Mariner Humphrey Sallows alias Allen left his goods to his wife, Mary, "for some recompense of her great paines and loveinge care of mee at all tymes . . . which I cannot gratifie according to my desire." Less affluent seamen demonstrated a particular willingness to leave everything to their wives. It was routine for them to bequeath all their goods to their wives, trusting in them to provide for their children. Mariner Peter Vine left all his possession to his wife, Alice, "knoweinge that she wilbe carefull to see my children well brought vp."

Not all husbands were so generous with their widows. Under the Common Law, wives were entitled to only a third of their husbands' estate. By local custom widows were allowed one-half if the husband had no children.[84] Deprived of the breadwinner and his principal asset, skill at his trade, the widow might inherit only part of the estate. Under the terms of his will, mariner William Fettey, for instance, divided all his goods between his wife and William Myson, whose relationship to Fettey is not clear.

While Fettey technically gave his wife her "fair share" under the terms of the Common Law, Fettey's bequest to Myson almost certainly led to a drastic drop in the widow's standard of living.[85] Hence, widowhood frequently brought with it both emotional and financial stresses that compromised any freedom accorded by the status of widow.

In most cases the widow or next of kin could expect some portion of the seaman's wages if he died at sea. Maritime custom is clear on this point:

if any person shal fortune to die, or miscary in the voyage, such apparel, and other goods, as he shall haue at the time of his death, is to be kept by the order of the captaine, and Master of the shippe, and an inuentorie to be made of it, and conserued to the vse of his wife, and children, or otherwise according to his mind, and wil, and the day of his death to be entred in the Marchants and Stewards bookes: to the intent it may be knowen what wages he shall haue deserued to his death, and what shall rest due to him.[86]

This custom was honored on privateering voyages, where widows were to have any plunder or shares of prizes.[87] Legal cases demonstrated the expectation of Elizabethan widows that they were entitled to money from their husbands' last voyage. As in the case of seamen, widows sometimes encountered problems with masters and owners because of verbal employment contracts.[88] A number of widows had to be content with whatever they could get from their dead husbands' employer because they were not always privy to the details of their husbands' employment contracts, and few were in a position to seek redress in the courts. Yet of the small number of women who brought a suit or appeared before the Admiralty Court during the second half of Elizabeth's reign, almost all were widows who sought dead husbands' possessions, which may or may not have included wages. Controversy arose when the husband died at sea, and the widow could not retrieve his effects or believed he had more aboard than she had received. Such complaints also constitute the majority of widows' petitions to the Crown as well. In 1601 Elizabeth Wyndall of Limehouse, widow of seaman Thomas Wyndall, made complaint to the Admiralty Court and petitioned the Crown for help in retrieving her husband's clothes, tools, chest and commodities that were on board the *Violet* of Plymouth when he died.[89] Wyndall claimed that she was very poor and very much in debt. Widow Martha Hook brought a suit in the Admiralty Court to obtain her late husband's shipboard goods. She wanted his clothes "for that his apparel was very good," his sea instruments, and other commodities that he had purchased. Hook's possessions on board the *Gift of God* of London were said to amount to £80.[90] Elizabeth Carr, widow of shipmaster Cuthbert Carr, filed a suit in the Admiralty Court against her husband's business partners. As master and part-owner, Carr had disbursed sums of money for the last voyage of the *Richard* of London before she was cast away in a storm. The widow Carr hoped to recoup that money through her suit in the Admiralty Court.[91]

In the absence of the financial means to take their complaints to court, most widows relied on their husbands' friends to safeguard their possessions until they could claim them. Many seamen who died on shipboard had appointed crewmates to protect their belongings. Fellow seamen were commonly made overseers or guardians of wills. While this is true of men who died on land and those who died at sea, the function of the overseer at sea was crucial to ensure that seamen's effects made it to their widows or next of kin. Sailor Thomas Baylye frequently spoke about his betrothed to his crewmates and made a common request of them as he lay dying: "I praye you all be good to her and her haue my chest and all things deliuered to her."[92] Although seamen recognized the maritime custom that entitled the widow to the dead seaman's effects, only a vigilant guardian could prevent pilfering.

There was another role for the overseers: the wise testator nominated a trusted crewmate or crewmates to take his goods to his widow so that if problems occurred, they could assist the widow in her pursuit of her husband's effects.[93] When such cases were heard in the Admiralty Court, widows routinely had the overseers make their case before officials.[94] When Richard Andrews was slain on board the *Gillian*, his crewmate Robert Hutton (or Hulton) took possession of Andrews's chest and belongings and took them to Andrews's widow. He also spoke on the widow's behalf before the Admiralty Court regarding a discrepancy over Andrews's shipboard belongings. In Martha Hook's suit to retrieve her husband's shipboard possessions, she had Hook's crewmate, mariner Samuel Younge, and Hook's apprentice, William Morrice, speak on her behalf.

In addition to protecting the widow's rights, crewmates had another function: they were useful in selling the dead man's goods or any commodities that he had purchased for the purpose of trading. This was usually done at the mainmast; fellow crewmates normally bid on any sea clothes or goods. In 1604 James Robson requested that two of his friends and crewmates sell all he had on shipboard at the mainmast, including his books.[95] From the widows' perspective, money accruing from these "sales" or auctions was more useful than the possessions themselves.

The income of shipmasters' widows could be fairly lucrative. Many masters purchased shares in a ship or ships, which could be bequeathed to widows.[96] Provided the ship did not meet with misfortune, shipping was a means of generating income. There were a large number of female shipowners, many of whom were widows. Officers and skilled seamen could also provide their widows with another source of income. Because apprentices were bound to both their master and his wife, and many maritime apprentices actually earned wages in sea service, some carried on in the service of their mistress until they fulfilled their term of years, surrendering their wages to her. Indentured servants provided only short-term assistance in that they left their mistresses' home and employ once they concluded their term of years. It is also worth noting that many apprentices were freed from their indentures by their masters in their wills. While both sources of income were a great help to the woman financially during her widowhood, on their own, neither gave the woman financial security.[97] Even in cases where the widow inherited her due from her dead husband's estate, this was rarely sufficient to ensure her economic survival.

A widow's economic security normally had conditions.[98] A number of husbands continued to exercise influence over their wives from the graves. This influence was proportional to the amount of financial leverage that the testator had; those seamen with larger estates were in a position to wield more control. One way to control one's widow was to leave much of the estate to an adult son, entrusting her welfare to him. Master John Salmon bequeathed his lands to his eldest son and namesake when he turned 21, "vppon my blessinge to be good and favorable to his mother." Mariner Robert Osborne left his house with the yard and gardens to his son John, not to his widow, Joan. Osborne's son and daughter-in-law were given the house and were to allow Joan to live with them "vsyng ther mother quietlye." In the event John died, the house was to go to Prudence and Alice, two of Osborne's daughters, thus leaving Joan at the mercy of her children. In cases where widows were deprived of their husbands' estates in favor of grown children, the widows' position and authority within the family unit were severely compromised.[99]

It was quite common for seamen to allow their widows to "use" their land and possessions conditionally. In many cases it was contingent upon the widow's bringing up the children and limited to her widowhood or the minority of her children. In 1604 Thomas Grove, one of the Masters of the Royal Navy, left his vast estate to his wife to provide for their children during their minority. The estate was to pass to Grove's eldest son when he was 21. In the event that Grove's widow remarried, Grove's estate was to pass to Thomas Jr. immediately, despite the fact that he had yet to reach the age of majority.[100]

In most instances, but not all, wives were given custody of the children after their husbands' death. Very young children were almost always left with their mothers. This did not necessarily follow if the children were of an age to be put out to service. Sailor James Thornbush committed his two sons to the care of a friend rather than their mother, who was still alive. Custody of the boys was given to Thornbush's "loving friend M[r.] Francis Foxe of . . . the countye of Suffolke merchant vntyll their age of Twentye and one yeares."[101] Did Thornbush have doubts about his wife's capacity to raise the children, or were the boys to be apprenticed to Foxe? Although his wife, Agnes, was still alive, mariner Thomas Stevyns of Surrey appointed two guardians for his daughter Marie during the time of her minority and to act as executors in her behalf.[102] Mariner Thomas Jennings gave the custody of his son to his wife conditionally: "my will is my wief shall haue the educac[i]on of my sonne, soe longe as she remayneth a widdowe."[103]

More affluent testators frequently requested that bonds be posted to ensure their houses and property be maintained or to guarantee the houses passed on to their children. In 1603 mariner Roger Cooper gave his widow, Susan, his house in Harwich during the time of her widowhood in order to bring up his children. Under the terms of Cooper's will, he allowed her to sell the house if she needed money for the family's maintenance. If she remarried, Cooper insisted that "he that shall marrie her shall putte in bond to my Supervisor of Fortye poundes to keepe and mainetaine the said houses and buyldinges in good needfull & sufficient reparacion."[104] Susan Cooper was fortunate in that she was given control of the house for her lifetime. In their wills seamen almost always specified that the house was to pass to a child or their children (if they had any) after their widows' death. Typically in Tudor society, fortunate widows might enjoy their dead husbands' homes, but these were rarely the widows' to bequeath.

Widows were also circumscribed by the overseers of their husbands' wills.[105] Essex mariner John Benn left most of his estate and shipping to his wife, Joan, in 1575. Although he made her his executrix, he nominated two overseers to help her manage her affairs, requesting that she would always use "the counsaile of my brother Wilson, and my frend Thomas Murfe." Mariner Robert Hollett named his brother-in-law, shipmaster William Bigate, as his overseer in his will. Hollett willed that his wife should "bee ruled by my said Overseer and do nothinge without his consente and well lykinge." By placing constrictions of their widows, male testators hoped to guard their estates for their children. Given the lack of power of women in Tudor society, many men feared that their widows would remarry and that their successors would claim the remains of their estates, depriving their children of their due.[106] In the early 1580s Isabel Frobisher wrote to Secretary Francis Walsingham that Captain Martin Frobisher "whome God forgeve" had spent all the money left to her and her children by her first husband (presumably on the unprofitable voyages to Meta Incognita) and that the family was ready to starve. Those seamen with the most property frequently bound their widows (or their widows' future husbands) to specific agreements and bonds to ensure that they provided for the children, thereby guaranteeing that property and money would be passed on to the rightful heirs. In this way, seamen were acknowledging that many of their wives would remarry; they also sought to guard against undue influence, greed, or poor judgment of their widows' next husbands.

For most seamen's widows in Elizabethan England their husbands' occupation had not provided them with any measure of financial security. Even when widows inherited all their husbands' "moveable and unmovable" goods, it was rarely sufficient to keep the wolf from the door for long, especially if there were children to provide for. Observers in the Admiralty Court during the 1630s remarked on the grim plight of seamen's widows:

miserable is the case of his [the seaman's] wife, children and friends if he die in the voyage, or do not return to demand his own, whereby great number of poor wives and children are left to the parishes.[107]

As mentioned previously, some women had employment that provided income. The family might survive if unmarried children could find employment and were willing to contribute to the family's earnings. A widow might be able to move in with grown, married children if she had them.[108] Hence, independent children could provide a haven for poor widows. Apprentices who were obliged to complete their terms in the service of the widow provided her with a short-term source of money. Overall, a widow's best hope was a diversified income, which few had. Aside from remarriage, which we discuss shortly, the most readily available option to poor widows was parish relief. Along with the elderly and the infirm, widows were regular recipients of relief.

Because most widows were left in a precarious financial state, it is not surprising that the more affluent seamen (especially members of the Trinity House) made bequests to assist such women. In his will, shipmaster Roger Gunston left 40 shillings for the poor almswomen of the Trinity House, most likely mariners' widows, who accompanied his corpse to the funeral and £3 to poor mariners' wives of the younger Brethren of the Trinity House "falne to decaie."[109] Other than bequests in wills, there were probably innumerable donations and loans made (and forgiven) to widows that leave no trace in the records.

REMARRIAGE

Widows and widowers formed a high percentage of the adult population during this period.[110] The probability that one's marriage would be terminated abruptly and unexpectedly was great. In many marriages, partners died in the their middling years, never attaining old age. This is particularly true of seamen. Contemporary observers claimed that few seamen "grew to gray hairs." Although the Admiralty Court depositions demonstrate that there were older men (middle age by our standards) at sea, the vast majority of the men at sea were in their 20s and 30s.[111] Seamen were vulnerable to all manner of hazards, and mortality was high. Even though their husbands were in the prime of life, every seaman's wife faced the very real prospect of widowhood, especially when her husband was away from home.[112]

The incidence of remarriage was so common in Tudor society that many seamen expected their widows would remarry.[113] The will of mariner Thomas White illustrates this point; White bequeathed the sum of five pounds to his niece when his wife remarried. There are not many wills as explicit as White's on this point. However, the expectation that widows would remarry was implicit; most testators' wills contain provisions for this eventuality. Furthermore, some seamen expected that their wives might remarry quickly after their decease. In his will, mariner Roger Cooper directs his wife's future husband to enter into bonds regarding Cooper's property if "my wife happen to marry againe within shorte tyme after my decease."

Remarriage offered much to a widow. For both young and old widows, remarriage could rescue them from poverty and financial insecurity. Those widows in their childbearing years could start a family or have additional children. Furthermore, a widow with a young family needed not only a provider but a partner to help her with raising children.

When looking for new mates, widows and widowers chose them from their own "circle," that is, the same pool of potential spouses from which they chose their previous partner.[114] Many seamen's widows found new husbands within the maritime community. Joan Jones, widow of seaman David Jones, was typical in that she chose another man from the maritime community (a shipwright) as her second husband. Given the tight bonds that existed between the men and women affiliated with the maritime community, it is not surprising that seamen who chose daughters of fellow seamen as their brides would look to seafarers' widows as mates as well.

Because widows were "of their own government," they theoretically had more freedom in the selection of their future husbands than they had had as spinsters. Necessity to marry and obtain a provider (quickly) could intrude on this freedom. Although the mourning period for a spouse was commonly regarded as a year, many remarriages took place within a matter of months. Even in cases where the deceased was a shipmaster (and therefore well off relative to the majority of seamen), widows entered into their next marriage with rapidity.[115]

Such was the fear of the "next husband" that when in a financial position to do so, many seamen set conditions for the widows' inheritance and offered incentives not to remarry.[116] Sailor Alexander Eylmer left his house and tenements to his wife, Margery, with the sum of four pounds per annum if she remained a widow. If she remarried, she was not to have the annual income. Mariner John Grant gave his wife the lease of his house "so longe as she liveth keepinge her self a widdowe." If she remarried, the house was to go to his eldest son. Mariner Steven Upcher promised that his wife could enjoy their "children's portion" during her lifetime if she remained a widow. In his will of 1576, mariner William Lawson guaranteed his wife, Alice, the use of his tenements in the parish of St. Botolph without Aldgate in London as long as she "kept herself a widowe." Sailor John Fowl bequeathed his house to his wife, Joan, during her widowhood; Fowl was uncommonly generous in that he stipulated that Joan was to retain the house if she married "with anie mann of honest Reputacion beinge an Inhabitant within the saide parishe of Leighe." In general, widows of prosperous seamen were not always granted security for their future, nor did most enjoy total independence or freedom of choice.

Wealthier widows had to choose their husbands wisely lest they compromise their economic position. Some women were better off financially by not remarrying. Those who had financial security and were not governed by their husbands' overseers or left in the care of their adult children were in the most advantageous position. In these situations women might elect to remain widows, even though they would be pursued by suitors as desirable matches. Although she remarried after the death of her first husband, shipmaster Thomas Brayford, Bridget (Brayford) White remained a widow after the death of her second spouse, shipmaster John White. Her marriages provided her with two leased homes: a house in Ratcliffe, Middlesex, and one in nearby Limehouse as well as possessions in excess of £100.[117] This wealth gave Bridget White options that many widows did not have. Thus, she decided to live out the rest of her days as a widow.[118] After the death of her spouse, Agnes Salmon remained a widow. Her husband, shipmaster Robert Salmon of Leigh, Essex, predeceased her by five years but left her with a considerable estate. Even after her years of widowhood, Agnes's estate was worth several hundred pounds when she died. She had been left multiple properties, which she bequeathed to her children.[119] Agnes Salmon and Bridget White were the exception rather than the rule.

Doubtless, the existence of kin or friends willing to assist in child raising affected widowers' decision when and if to remarry. While many men hoped to find stepmothers for their young children and compatible companions for themselves, support networks granted them time to seek such a mate for reasons of affection, not desperation. Seamen's wills demonstrate that there were men who remained widowers in spite of the fact that they had young children. They sometimes give us indications of child-care arrangements.[120] Mariner William Motte was fortunate in that his older children could take care of his youngest son (who was under the age of 15). When he went to sea, gunner John Marsh of All Hallows Barking in London entrusted his father-in-law with the considerable sum of £30 and the care of his motherless children, Gyles and Mary. Widower William Rafe left his child Mary in the care of one John Lemon of Greenwich. Mariner Nicholas Webster entrusted the care of his younger daughter, Joan, to his elder daughter Helen or Ellen (Wattes), who had a family of her own. Mariner John Fundall relied on his stepmother, Agnes Fundall, and his brother, Coombes Fundall (who was also a family man), to take care of his children. There was also help for seamen with infants to care for: wet-nursing was a common practice in Tudor England, and fathers with infants could find women willing to suckle their children. In 1587 sailor John

Rising of Tower Wharf had a wet nurse for his young daughter, Margaret. It is apparent that arrangements could be made for children whose sole parent went to sea to earn a living. In the absence of a support network, seamen with young children almost certainly had to remarry quickly.

Generally speaking, widowers had more freedom than widows in matters of remarriage. Widows were at a disadvantage because they outnumbered widowers. Furthermore, widowers tended to control property. Widowers without children or children who had been put out for service had more freedom of choice regarding when and if to remarry than those with young children and "child-care problems." No doubt many seamen with young children avoided quick marriages of convenience because of kin and friends who were obliging enough to take in their children when the fathers were at sea. Whether seafaring widowers sought to remarry or to entrust their children to kin and friends, the death of a wife and mother (although tragic) did not usually lead to a breakup of the household.

FERTILITY

Fecundity varied within each marriage and was affected by such factors as duration of the marriage, age of the woman, diet, health, period of breast-feeding, employment, and working conditions. In the case of seamen and their wives, to some extent fertility must have been affected by periods of abstinence when husbands were away. Again, this would be dependent on individual employment patterns and each couple's fecundity. Even among landsmen's families, there was normally a two-year gap between pregnancies, due in large measure to the contraceptive effect of prolonged breast-feeding. Parish records of Stepney demonstrate that many seamen's wives succeeded in giving birth to several children, placing them well within the national and European average. While most women gave birth to six or eight children, the average size of European families was four to six persons.[121]

Despite the fact that a seaman and his wife conceived, delivered, and baptized several children, this did not mean that all or even some of these children would grow to adulthood. The loss of a child or children was common to most English families. Reconstruction of seamen's families shows that they were typical of the general population. As an illustration, we can examine the family of seaman Israel Clark of Stepney. Clark and his wife had eight children between 1569 and 1583. Between October 1578 and July 1584 Clark buried his entire family, including his wife and a servant before he died the following year.[122] While Clark's story is one of the more tragic examples, it was not unusual.

Among those seamen who made wills, a significant number mention a wife but no children. There are many possible explanations. While some of these couples were infertile, others were recently married. Some seamen might not have had enough time at home to father children when they wrote their wills. We must also take into account that wills are static; they rarely make mention of children who predeceased their parents or parent. Given the high incidence of childhood, especially infant, mortality, many women had experienced repeated pregnancies and yet outlived their progeny. Between 200 and 300 infants per 1,000 died before their first birthday. As a result, a childless marriage did not necessarily mean that the couple was infertile.[123]

Despite the high incidence of childhood mortality, many seamen had a large number of children, many of whom survived to young adulthood at least. Stepney parish records show that several seamen managed to father a large number of children.[124] Shipmaster John Vassell sired twelve children between 1571 and 1602 (including twin sons). When he died in 1625, in his late 70s, eight of his children were still living. Shipmaster Robert Rickman fathered twelve children between 1577 and 1597, most of whom survived to adulthood. Rickman, however, had only one child alive when he died in 1625 in his mid-70s. Shipmaster James Woodcot fathered eight or nine children by two wives between 1572 and 1597. Woodcot lived into his mid-50s and had five surviving children when he wrote his will in 1603.

SEAMEN AND THEIR CHILDREN

Although some argue that the high incidence of infant and childhood mortality led to parents' erecting emotional barricades between themselves and their offspring,[125] wills from the period demonstrate that fathers were deeply concerned with the welfare of their children. While seafaring fathers were routinely absent from the home (although it was common to find fathers and sons or sons-in-law on the same ship), this does not mean that they did not play a role in child-raising. A husband and father had a patriarchal duty as the master of his household. As they did in life, many seamen tried to influence their children after their deaths. Wills provided a final forum for instruction, and many fathers attempted to establish "guidelines" for their children to live by. It was not unusual for fathers to advise, admonish, or, in some cases, threaten their children (particularly eldest sons) to do their duty to their siblings, stepmothers, or mothers.[126] Mariner John Salmon promised his lands to his eldest son and namesake when he turned 21; John the elder also charged his heir "vppon my blessinge to be good and favorable to his mother his brother and Systers." In his will sailor John Fowl beseeched his children not to "vex or trowble the saide Johan my wief for anie thinge during her widdowhood." Seaman Simon Stamford ordered his son Thomas "to abide and continue with his said mother and to obey and serue his said mother as a good and duetiefull child." Property was sometimes used as a weapon to ensure "good behavior." Master William Goodlad wrote in his last testament that my will and mynde is, that if my said sonne william shall not permitt the said Sara my wiefe peaceably to have and enjoye the benefitt of my said house orcharde and landes, duringe the minoritie of the said William . . . then it shalbe lawfull for the said Sara my wife to . . . deducte. . . . Thirtie poundes of lawfull money of England out of his parte and portion.

Wills were occasionally used to castigate disobedient adult children. Given his wealth, mariner Robert Salmon gave modest bequests to his grandchildren, "Beinge sorry that their Mother is the onlie cause that I giue them noe more."

Seafaring fathers showed interest in the educational, financial, and moral well-being of their progeny.[127] In his will of 1601 mariner Robert Eyles gave all his property to his wife, Bridget, "desieringe her of all [the] love that ever hath byn betwixte vs to have a motherly Care and regarde of those Children which god hath given vs." In his will shipwright Nicholas Dorrett granted his wife his tenements so she could bring up his daughter Sarah and his young cousin, Agnes.[128] Dorrett directed his widow to "bringe them vpp in the feare of god and decentlie." Although Dorrett claimed that he trusted his wife to educate the children, he also stipulated that if the girls were "not well and orderlie brought vpp," his friends were to have money and property to raise them. In 1583 mariner William Motte granted the custody of his youngest, son Thomas (still a minor), to his elder sons Robert and William until Thomas turned 15; the elder Mottes were instructed to "keep Thomas with meate drynk & clothing & keping hym to schoole." In his will seaman Richard Wade the elder showed a keen interest in the education of his children; "Richard [the younger] shalbe kepte at the Schole till [he] can write and reade And that Johan and Margaret my daughters shalbe instructed tell they can reade Englishe." Fathers appointed overseers to look after their children, regardless of whether or not their wives were still living. Even if the testator's wife survived him, overseers were expected to act as guardians to look out for the children's welfare. While mariner Samuel Taylor gave the custody of his young children to his wife, he appointed overseers to assist her and the children "desiringe them with good conscyence to defend and regard the fatherless."[129]

Testators were concerned primarily with safeguarding their children's portions from unscrupulous stepfathers or guardians. Bonds were normally requested by all but the poorest seamen. Frequently, they asked friends (often other seamen) to invest money for the children.[130] In his will mariner Richard Cossins requested his friends shipmaster William Boggett (Bigate) and Richard Nottingham, Clerk of the Trinity House, to invest his three children's portions so they might benefit. Cossins was taking no chances; he put his trust in two well-respected and prominent men of the maritime community. Seaman John Godderd of the *Hector* requested that two of his crewmates receive his wages and shares from the East India Company and invest the money for the profit of his sons.

As in the case of widows, testators with property were in a position to exert control over their children even after they were buried. Primogeniture as a principle of inheritance seems to have been followed only when the estate was of a reasonable size and therefore worth preserving intact. Property was not, however, a guarantee that the testator would bequeath his entire estate to a single male heir. Most seamen were eager to provide for all their children. In some cases eldest sons or only sons were favored, but rarely to the exclusion of their sisters or younger brothers. Mariner John Fundall willed his estate to his son John and his daughter Anne, but he stipulated that John Jr. would have twice as much as his sister: "the boye must have ij partes of all my goodes."[131] Fundall probably counted on his young son to use his money to secure a good master and pursue a profitable trade. Girls placed more stock in securing a good marriage to ensure their future rather than in training.

While younger sons normally benefited from their fathers' wills, and many were given equal consideration with their older brothers, younger sons or sons from a second marriage were seldom favored. Mariner Thomas Boyse gave preference to the sons of his first marriage, Thomas and Abraham, over his sons Isaac and Jacob from his second marriage. The two elder sons were to receive £7 each two months after the return of Boyse's ship, the *Swiftsure*, from Barbary. Boyse stipulated that his younger sons were to receive £3 6s. 8d when they came of age.[132] Fisherman and mariner Thomas Okey gave his eldest son, Francis, his vessels and most of his oyster lanes, doling out properties, for the most part, to his younger sons according to seniority. Robert Okey was unfortunate in that he was the youngest of five sons and received nothing except the promise of property if his brothers predeceased him.[133]

Although we can make some generalizations about inheritance practices of the period, ultimately we must allow room for the preferences and partiality of the testator. Parental favoritism did exist,[134] which may or may not have been based upon financial need. Mariner Thomas Stevyns favored his daughter over his three sons, giving them all different amounts of money and goods. Thomas Okey gave his eldest son much of his estate; his fourth son received more than his second and third sons. Okey's two daughters each acquired more than his third or fifth son. His youngest son was given less than his stepchildren.

Unquestionably, wills demonstrate that parents were keen to provide for their children. There was some degree of reciprocity, although many testators had lost one or both parents at the time they made their wills.[135] When adult children predeceased their parents, they were likely to remember them in their wills.[136] Even if they had families of their own, many men felt duty-bound to leave their parent or parents something in their wills.

Although his father was well-off, master's mate Henry Rickman left his father 40 shillings "in token of my Filiall dutie," while his brother mariner William Rickman left their mother some dishes. Since women who had survived their childbearing years often outlived their husbands, mothers figure more prominently in wills than do fathers; it was not uncommon to find references to "lovinge mother[s]." Mariner John Hedley gave his mother (who is described only as the wife of John Coster) all that his deceased father had given him. Mariner John Walker left his mother £30 in his will. Mariner Anthony Cam bequeathed his mother a pound of pepper and a loaf of sugar. If they survived their adult sons, parents stood a good chance of inheriting the seamen's estate if the men had no wives or children.

Parents gained through marriage were also remembered in wills. If a seaman married, he was duty-bound to act as a son to his "other" parents.[137] The testator's spouse's parents are commonly mentioned in wills if they were still alive.[138] Mariner George Wattes left five pounds to his wife's father, mariner Nicholas Webster. Even though he had remarried, sailor Daniel Linche remembered his dead wife's mother in his will.

There is little information on the lot of orphans who had no kin or guardians to take them in. In such cases orphans became wards of their parishes. When he was imprisoned in the Marshalsea prison, the three children of Thomas Morgan, a master's mate accused of piracy, were maintained by his parish.[139] Although orphans could look to their parishes for assistance in the absence of kin or friends, those left to the parish had limited prospects in life. Parishes tried to secure positions for orphans in service or apprenticeship. Those children who had inherited money would be much better off than those with nothing. Even in situations where the children stood to inherit some money or property, without parents or guardians to act as protectors, they were largely defenseless; they were at the mercy of the parish and their masters. They lacked the advantages that were contingent upon having one or both parents alive to provide moral and financial support.

In addition to one's own children, stepchildren, and orphans, skilled seamen might be entrusted with the care of servants and apprentices. As we have seen, the master would be expected to act *in loco parentis* and would be responsible for clothing, feeding, sheltering, training, and disciplining any subordinates under his roof. A few seamen's households in Stepney had black servants as well.[140] Thus, the household unit could be a very complex one.

COMMUNITY INVOLVEMENT AND CAMARADERIE

In general, the assistance of neighbors, friends, and relatives was very important in Tudor society. Seafaring husbands, fathers, and guardians were forced to rely heavily on this network to assist their families when they were away from home. Seamen counted on their colleagues among the maritime community—both on land and at sea. Frequently, the support networks were synonymous; seamen's neighbors, friends, and relatives were associated with seafaring, and crewmates were neighbors and friends. Hence, those who lent and borrowed money and those who were present for births, baptisms, betrothals, marriages, will making, and funerals were often connected within the maritime network. They commonly relied on other seamen to train their sons as apprentices or take in their daughters as servants. Seamen met their sweethearts and future brides through their occupational and social links to other seafarers and their families. They relied on crewmates to safeguard their possessions both during their life and after their death, to invest money for their wives and children, to protect their estates until their children came of age. In many situations seamen cared for their deceased colleagues' loved ones. They were the same men to whom seamen looked for companionship on land and at sea.

One has only to peruse seamen's wills and those of their widows and children to appreciate the degree of solidarity and interconnectedness of the maritime community on land. A number of seamen remembered their godchildren with a small bequest. When they can be identified, these godchildren were frequently sons and daughters of other seamen.[141] Several seamen remembered the widows or children of other seamen (whether deceased or living) in their wills. In their last testaments, widows acknowledge their bonds with other seamen's wives, widows, and children. Seamen's sons or daughters who were in positions to make wills routinely remember the children of other seamen. When she died, Alice Huggett, daughter of shipmaster Bartholomew Hugguett and his principal heir, left Barbarie Ireland, daughter of a local mariner, the large sum of £30.[142]

While the lack of a spouse or children did not necessarily mean that a seaman was divorced from close relationships with those on land, there was, undoubtedly, a connection between familial commitments, attachment to the land community, and parish involvement. The commitment of many seamen to a parish or community was minimal. However, men with property and families within a specific parish had a vested interest in tending to the affairs of the community.

There was a relationship between wealth, occupational skill and status, and leadership in the community. In seaside communities along the Thames the maritime elite provided at least some of the parish leadership on land. Again, the same individuals who could afford to marry and establish an independent household assumed prominent places within their home parishes. Aside from the seamen who served as churchwardens and auditors, some seamen rose to positions of great distinction in their communities. Thomas Grove, for instance, served both Elizabeth and James (briefly) as one of the six masters of the Royal Navy and was also the mayor of Rochester.[143]

Because seamen tended to live in or near ports, we see more seamen involved in dockside communities than in inland parishes. For example, in Stepney almost all the parish officials were shipmasters or prominent shipwrights. The Stepney vestry book for 1579–1662 reads like a "who's who" of London's maritime elite during the Elizabethan and early Stuart periods. They acted as churchwardens and auditors for the parish. Being seafarers, it was normal for a few to be absent from parish meetings. The word "gone" often appears beside the names of the shipwrights and shipmasters in the vestry minutes.[144] The dominance of shipmasters in the parish leadership is not surprising given the numbers of seamen in the parish. While some prominent seamen did live in London proper and took part in parish affairs, parish leadership was in no way dominated by seamen in the same way as Stepney was. However, it seems that most seamen living in London or it environs lived in Stepney, Whitechapel, or across the river in Rotherhithe, Surrey. More research needs to be done on the parish leadership of seaside communities to determine if Thames-side parishes were aberrations or examples of a larger pattern.

Regardless of a seaman's level of involvement with the land community or whether he had a family of his own, seamen remained deeply attached to their seafaring companions. These bonds were clearly expressed in both married and bachelor seamen's wills. Such was their devotion to the sea and their lives afloat that some men requested that they be buried at sea regardless of where or how they died.[145] In his will Master Thomas Rickman specified that he wanted to be buried at sea "accordinge to the manner thereof." Boatswain Richard Brown willed that his body "be howssed according to the Lawe and custome of the see." Mariner John Wardell requested that his crewmates inter his body "after the mariner Custome." This insistence to be buried at sea according to their own rites is evidence of their deep attachments to their fellows and the maritime subculture.

Whether or not they had wives and children, seamen normally made bequests to their seafaring friends. Seafarers frequently received such items as sea clothes, commodities purchased for personal trade, navigational equipment, whistles, and beds from their deceased friends. In addition, some seamen left money for close friends to make rings to remember them by.[146] Master Rowland Jourden left mariner Richard Giles £3 in his will so that Giles could make a ring. Seaman William Feres bequeathed money to his friends (who were also mariners and his business partners) "to make them ringes for a remembraunce of me." James Smith of the *Primrose* left 40 shillings for Thomas Faster, the master of the ship, to make "a ringe to weare for the memorie." It was not unusual for seamen to bequeath money so that their crewmates could have a gathering.[147] This practice was not particular to the more affluent seamen. In 1590 Robert Rickman Jr. be-

queathed 10 shillings to his company "desieringe them that of theire char-
itie they will praie for me that god will forgiue my soule my bodies
mysdee[d]s." John Puett of Bristol, master gunner of the Queen's ship the
Swallow, bequeathed 20 shillings "to make a breakefaste amoungeste the
maister gonners." John Allen alias Sallows was very generous to his crewmates: "I will to be gyven in a banquett to our Shippes Company the
somme of seaven poundes." Rowland Giles gave £6 13s. to the crew of his
ship the *George Bonaventure* to drink with. Mariner Roger Gunston left
£3 for a repast for the masters and wardens of Trinity House and the
Brethren who went to his funeral.

The study of seamen's wills confirms the importance of other seamen
and their families both on land and at sea. While fellow seafarers figure
prominently in their colleagues' wills, they are given a more significant
place in bachelor seamen's wills. Nonetheless, the men of the maritime
community formed deep bonds with those in their occupational group regardless of whether they were married or single; no matter how devoted a
man was to the land community, he remained intimately connected with
his fellow seafarers.

OLD AGE AND RETIREMENT

What happened to old seamen? Was there a point when they "retired"
from the sea? Unfortunately, there is little information to establish firm
conclusions. We know that seafaring was predominantly a young man's
occupation, that most active seamen were under the age of 40 and that
most masters were under 50.[148] This can be explained by many factors.
First were the expansion of long-distance voyages and introduction of impressment as a result of the protracted naval conflict with Spain, which
deprived seamen of their customary right to weigh health risks against possible remuneration. During Elizabeth's reign, seamen were expected to endure greater risks to their health on both naval and non-naval voyages.
While the private sector respected its traditional maritime obligation to
supply health care to injured and ill seamen, those employed by the Crown
seldom were accorded the same attention. Under such circumstances, we
should not wonder that so few seamen lived to advanced ages.

We do occasionally run across aged seamen in the Admiralty Court depositions. These men were usually shipmasters in their 50s, 60s, and, sometimes, their 70s. They were called into court because they were old and
very experienced in the ways of the sea and made useful witnesses regarding
maritime matters. We do not know if they still went to sea to earn a living.
They were unusual within the occupation in that they attained such an
advanced age. The evidence from seamen's wills suggests that few lived to
see their grandchildren. Some of these shipmasters continued to work, although probably in a limited capacity. Those with ability and experience

were always a valuable part of any crew. Men of skill might hope to find positions in the limited naval bureaucracy or in the Queen's dockyards. Thomas Grey held a post as a shipmaster for the Queen's navy until his death in his 70s.[149] Lesser officers and seamen were also hired to work in the Queen's dockyards.[150]

The idea of "retirement" was not an option for most seamen. Some of the maritime elite had made a handsome living and had investments and shares in ships that would provide them with an income in their old age. These men could turn their attention to other concerns. Shipmaster David Carpenter of Ratcliffe seems to have filled his later days with parish affairs. Although he was in his 60s in 1611 and described as old and deaf, he still maintained his position as churchwarden in Stepney parish.[151] Carpenter was in the minority. The realities of seafaring meant that many seamen did not live to old age, thus making the point moot. For those who did survive, they had a limited range of options. Generally speaking, seamen, like many in Tudor society, had few or no provisions for their twilight years.[152] Only a small number were in a position to save money for their old age; doubtless, few believed they would live that long. Most probably worked until they could work no more. Some might prevail upon adult children to support them in their dotage, while others relied upon charity of seamen's organizations or their parishes.[153] Funds like the Chatham Chest and the Trinity House almshouse were open to disabled seamen who had contributed to their funds. Sir John Hawkins established a hospital near Rochester in 1594 specifically for the purpose of supporting 10 aged mariners or shipwrights. Bristol's almshouse was also open to old seamen. Certain individuals might fall upon the parish, especially if they had served the parish. The records of Stepney parish note the burial of Henry Rainsford "an old sailer sometyme beadle of Ratclife and now a pencioner." By and large, those seamen who survived the rigors of their occupation past middle age were a small minority, and an even smaller minority had sufficient means to "retire."

CONCLUSION

Seamen were a diverse bunch. At the broadest level of categorization we can divide seamen into married (which includes widowers) and bachelors. It appears that a large proportion of seafarers were in the latter grouping. This was not particular to Tudor England; preliminary research done on seafarers of later periods indicates that many remained single. Some restless young men gloried in their bachelorhood and were drawn to a seafaring life because they longed for a roving existence. However, many single seamen remained bachelors because they lacked the means to make a marriage. Marriageable or married seamen were frequently skilled or semiskilled mariners. Even among these men, tough economic times and high inflation during the second half of Elizabeth's reign made it more difficult to establish and maintain an independent household. Furthermore, during the war years, impressment intruded upon the careers and earning power of seafarers, affecting their ability to accumulate the financial foundations needed for married life. It is apparent that those men who came of age during the late Elizabethan period were hard put to support a family.

The lack of a wife and children often left the seaman without an anchor to the land community. While they usually retained ties with siblings or parents if they were still alive, in a number of cases seamen without fixed dwellings or families of their own show a detachment from the land community. Some bonded with the hosts and hostesses who lodged them or kinsfolk who would put them up for a time. Nevertheless, their wills show that many formed their closest bonds among their fellows in the normally all-male world of a sailing ship. Men in such circumstances had few reasons to tarry for long periods ashore.

Seamen were unusual in Tudor society in that a very high proportion of their number did not marry. When we consider those who did marry, their households vary little from those of landsmen in terms of composition and size. There were differences that distinguished seamen's households: the degree of autonomy that their wives enjoyed, or endured, and the extended absenteeism of the breadwinner and patriarch. Some shipmasters were atypical in that they had black servants from remote parts of the world in addition to their white servants; doubtless, their presence was still a rarity in sixteenth-century England. Yet these men had much in common with the land population. Seamen tended to marry at roughly the same age as the general population, chose spouses from within their social network, established independent households, and had children, and the elite often became active members of their communities when they were at home. In this sense, their immersion in the maritime subculture relegated them to their own niche within the larger society, but, clearly, it did not produce a wholly distinctive way of life.

Like all Elizabeth's subjects, seamen and their families endured the same crippling inflation, which made it harder for families to survive. Unlike most landsmen, seafarers were burdened by another aspect of the late Elizabethan period: the war with Spain. Because seamen were on the front lines (long before any conflict was openly acknowledged), they and their families were touched in a way that few others were in England. The inevitable offshoot of Tudor naval warfare was impressment; because impressed seamen were deprived of their economic freedom for months or years at a time, some marriages were postponed or made impossible. For those men with dependents, impressment jeopardized their families' financial well-being. Furthermore, the war augmented the hazards at sea and in foreign ports. The rising tide of maritime violence increased the chances that a seaman would lose his voyage, compromise his health, or surrender his life;

any of these eventualities would have drastic consequences for his dependents. Obviously, it was not an easy time to be a seafarer or a member of a seaman's family.

Perhaps this is why seamen chose women associated with the maritime community; such women were ideal mates who had learned to cope with the realities of marriage to a seaman, whether firsthand or by growing up with seafarers in their families. The pattern is unmistakable; just as many chose their crewmates as their most trusted friends, seamen from London and its environs courted and married their colleagues' widows, sisters, and daughters. This trend is particularly pronounced where it can be most readily studied, among the maritime elite. In this way they could recognize friendships, increase their business connections, cement business partnerships, and forge seafaring dynasties.

The high degree of freedom for seamen's wives in household management, relative to most landsmen's wives, could be a blessing or a curse, depending on one's circumstances. For all but the wealthiest, this freedom was circumscribed in that few were free from the omnipresent threat of poverty. Although some seamen's wives were in the paid labor force, they, like other Tudor women, were vulnerable because they lacked real earning power and because they were hampered by the patriarchal views upheld by both the Common Law and the Church. Even in their widowhood few had complete autonomy of their lives or property. Dead husbands routinely limited their widows' control over their estate in favor of their children.

The importance of a solid support network cannot be underestimated when considering the nature of life as a seaman's wife. Without the aid and companionship of neighbors, friends, and kin, life was much more difficult. To this source wives and widows turned when they needed assistance. The women of the maritime community helped one another, not just because their husbands shared the same occupation; they were often related through blood or marriage or lived in the same neighborhood. Similarly, seamen looked after their friends' wives, widows, and children and depended on their fellow seafarers to render assistance when they needed it. The devotion of those connected to the maritime community is evident in the wills of seamen, their widows, and their children.

Some seamen's families lacked a support network, were dislodged from it, or encountered problems that proved too much for their relations, friends, and neighbors. The most insurmountable problems were almost always financial. In these circumstances, seamen's wives and widows had limited options. Those who were eligible looked to seamen's organizations for charity. These private organizations were not plentiful, and those that did exist catered almost exclusively to seamen rather than their dependents. Most, however, relied on their parish for assistance. Given popular opinion and the rules governing almsgiving, those without firm roots in the parish were denied this important source of assistance. Those without options fell into the ranks of the vagabonds. While we have no idea how many met this fate, parish records, Admiralty records, and even the State Papers contain many references to seamen and their families who had fallen on hard economic times. It is apparent that private and public charity geared at helping seamen's wives and widows lagged far behind the need.

Even in periods of economic distress, seamen's wives and widows seldom petitioned the Crown for a remedy. When they did petition the Crown, it was for help in legal or diplomatic matters far outside their control: clemency for an innocent husband fallen into some sort of trouble or aid in freeing captured husbands who languished in foreign prisons or galleys. Like their husbands, seamen's wives were not shy in pursuing their due from employers and the Crown, but it seems that they were very well aware of what their "due" consisted of and did not expect more than what custom dictated. Regardless of their circumstances and the stresses placed on seamen and their families during wartime, these women did not petition the Crown for financial aid, as they had no entitlement to it under maritime custom. Therefore, their focus was on preserving and utilizing custom established by the maritime community and the Crown rather than seeking to expand the boundaries of custom and setting new parameters. These women did not seek special consideration from the Crown even in instances where their husbands fought, were injured or disabled, or died in the Queen's service. In an age when the Crown was begrudgingly forced to offer the unprecedented measure of limited pensions for injured, maimed, and ill naval seamen, their wives and widows did not factor into the Crown's dispensations. While their husbands' sense of entitlement regarding state service was being altered,[154] their wives did not expect anything for their own losses. In other words, pensions were the Crown's to dole out to veterans, but it was not the wives' or widows' place to ask or expect monetary aid. Instead, they relied on their wits to survive and the crutches of their support networks and the parish.

While the responsibilities and stresses were considerable, these women rarely faced the world alone. Whether they were at sea or at home, seamen, as heads of their households, made their opinions known. If their last testaments are any indication, seamen had much to say about the care and conduct of their families and their estates. In their wills, fathers made provision for their children in terms of funding apprenticeships and education and bequeathed their progeny sums of money and property that had a direct bearing on their marriage and life prospects. They appointed overseers to guide their widows and children as they would have done. Even in their widowhood few women had complete autonomy over their lives or property. It seems unlikely that testators who went to such pains to safeguard and counsel their wives and children after their deaths did not do so in life.[155]

Some seamen also found the time for parish involvement when they were home. Many prominent shipwrights and shipmasters played important roles within the parish leadership. While there were exceptions, the connection between skill and reputation within the maritime community, marital status, and parish involvement is an unmistakable one; highly skilled seamen could and did marry (often more than once), and these men who occupied prominent positions at sea who provided the leadership for their parishes on land. Some of these men were affluent enough that they could afford to "retire" in their old age, although few seemed to do so. Many died in the prime of their lives, and those who reached "old age" worked until they could not go to sea any longer. No doubt old sea dogs found the transition to a solely land-based existence a difficult one.

While the historian must often speak in generalities, we must acknowledge that it is difficult to speak of a composite figure known as "Jack Tar." When seamen were ashore, they lived in many different circumstances. Despite the fact that Jack Tar ashore had many faces and circumstances, we can make one generalization about seamen. The most overwhelming theme to emerge from the study of seamen's lives ashore is the strength of their occupational ties when they were on land. Regardless of their ties to a community and marital or occupational status, seamen of all ages and backgrounds looked to those connected with the maritime community as a reference group and a support network and for social interaction when they were on land or at sea. The bonds between crewmates were not limited to shipboard life; they extended to all aspects of a seaman's life. Whether one was looking for a suitable spouse, choosing a master or guardian for one's child, naming an overseer for a will, or finding a compatible business partner, seamen looked to their "own kind" in most cases. Although seamen were a group set apart physically when they were at sea, they were segregated from the land community to some degree by their immersion in their own subculture. While those with families and firm ties to the land population straddled the two communities, those who lacked those ties were more likely to be men separated physically, socially, psychologically, and culturally from the land population.

NOTES

1. Capp, *Cromwell's Navy*, 245, 248–49; B. R. Burg, *Sodomy and the Pirate Tradition: English Sea Rovers in the Seventeenth-Century Caribbean* (New York: New York University Press, 1983), 155–60; Judith Fingard, *Jack in Port* (Toronto: University of Toronto Press, 1982), 126–39.

2. PRO HCA, 1/46/44, 1/46/124v, 1/46/139v–40v, 1/46/44v–45v, 1/46/132v–33, 1/46/135-v. One eighteenth-century observer asserted that seamen needed to be kept "from mispending their leisure Time in Debauches, and other Criminal Exercises, which are too common amongst our Seamen of late." *An Inquiry into the Causes*, 9.

3. White-Patarino claims that most seamen's brawls brought before the court were fought over issues of honor and status. Alcohol was almost always involved. White-Patarino, "Living outside the Ordered Society," 11.

4. Madox, *An Elizabethan in 1582*, 105; Laffin, *Jack Tar*, 11.

5. Hawkins, *Observations*, 20; Madox, *An Elizabethan in 1582*, 131.

6. Monson, *Naval Tracts*, vol. III, 123.

7. Baumber, "An East India Captain," 272; Boteler, *Dialogues*, 42–43; Bodeliean Library, Rawlinson Ms. C.846/179.

8. Seamen were not alone in designating alehouses as the center of community activity. See Keith Wrightson, "Alehouses, Order and Reformation in Rural England, 1590–1660," in *Popular Culture and Class Conflict 1590–1914: Explorations in the History of Labour and Leisure*, ed. Eileen Yeo and Stephen Yeo (Sussex: Harvester Press, 1981), 1–28; PRO HCA, 1/46/148v, 1/46/106.

9. Ewen, "Organized Piracy round England in the Sixteenth Century," 39.

10. PRO HCA 1sh44/210v–11; Guildhall Ms. 9171/10d/78; PRO HCA 1/45/184.

11. Hair and Alsop, *English Seamen and Traders*, 250–51; PRO PROB, 11/83/220, 11/85/36v, 11/102/187. For more examples, see Hair and Alsop, *English Seamen and Traders*, 112, 166, 167, 188, 197, 209, 228, 288; see also PRO PROB, 11/72/283, 11/74/157v, 11/102/179; GLRO, DW/PA/5/1593/188, DW/PA/5/1596; Guildhall Ms., 9172/12b/87, 9171/16/429v, 9171/19/350-v, 9171/19/383v.

12. There were probably many more cases than are listed. Parish records are terribly idiosyncratic; historians owe a great debt to those annalists who recorded essential details. Many, however, did not. Frequently, records of baptisms and burials of illegitimate children did not include the alleged father's name. When the father was named, his occupation is rarely listed in the records. There are undoubtedly many instances of seamen's fathering illegitimate children that were not recorded. The following is a handful of examples where the father was named and was a seaman: GLRO, X24/66/28, X24/66/37, X24/66/40, X24/66/41, X24/70/39v.

13. One-third of Elizabethan brides were pregnant before they reached the altar. Ralph Houlbrooke, "The Making of Marriage in Mid-Tudor England: Evidence from the Records of Matrimonial Contract Litigation," *Journal of Family History* 10 (1985), 345. Of this number, most pregnant brides came from the lower orders of Tudor society, where prenuptial sexual relations were more acceptable. Judges in disputes over matrimonial contracts considered sexual relations as indications of intent. Ibid., 344.

14. These extremely high rates were not duplicated for another 150 years. Ralph Houlbrooke, *The English Family 1450–1700* (London: Longman Group, 1984), 82. One-third of the illegitimate children born in the village of Terling between 1570 and 1699 were conceived between 1597 and 1607. Keith Wrightson and David Levine, *Poverty and Piety in an English Village: Terling, 1525–1700* (London: Academic Press, 1979), 127–32.

15. Guildhall Ms. 9234/1/69.

16. GLRO X24/66/40.

17. Rodger, *The Wooden World*, 78; Valerie Burton, "The Myth of Bachelor Jack: Patriarchy and Seafaring Labour," in *Jack Tar in History: Essays in the His-*

tory of Maritime Life and Labour, ed. Colin Howell and Richard J. Twomey (Fredericton, N.B.: Acadiensis Press, 1991), 187–88.

18. Houlbrooke, *The English Family*, 63, 67.

19. The marriage rate increased during the period 1566–1581, when real wages improved briefly. Ibid., 63, 67.

20. Hair and Alsop, *English Seamen and Traders*, 110–11. These findings are in line with later estimates. Figures do not exist for the eighteenth-century maritime community as a whole, but N.A.M. Rodger postulates that since there were so many young (under 25) seamen in the merchant marine, the vast majority were unmarried, as they had not reached the mean age of marriage for the period. He estimates that roughly one-fifth or a quarter of naval seamen were married. Most of these men were officers, petty officers, and older seamen. Rodger, *The Wooden World*, 78–79. Numbers for the nineteenth century indicate that only two-fifths of merchant seamen were married or widowed. Burton, "The Myth of Bachelor Jack," 187.

21. PRO HCA 13/34/30.

22. Guildhall Ms., 9171/20/195v, 9171/19/88v. See also Guildhall Ms., 9171/20/179v, 9171/20/195v, 9171/13/159v; PRO PROB, 11/102/198, 11/102/220v. White-Patarino's findings support this assertion. Of 100 sixteenth-century wills that he sampled, all the seafaring testators made a bequest to a friend or crewmate aboard their ship. White-Patarino, "Living outside the Ordered Society," 7. This is not to say that married men did not form lasting and affectionate bonds with other members of the maritime community. However, such men were more likely to leave the majority of their goods to their wives and children, while allocating smaller bequests to fellow seamen and crewmates. In several cases, fellow seamen were also entrusted with the care of the widow, children, and estate.

23. Hair and Alsop, *English Seamen and Traders*, 95, 140–41.

24. Berckman, *The Hidden Navy*, 6; Robert Park, *The Art of Sea-Fighting in 5 Parts* (London: Richard Mount and Thomas Page, 1706), preface.

25. Ibid., 5.

26. 5. Eliz. c.5, *Statutes of the Realm*, vol. IV part I (London: Pall Mall, 1963), 447.

27. *Sir Francis Drake's West Indian Voyage 1585–6*, 111, 148, 149. Ogle's case is the only execution for buggery at sea that I have discovered for the Elizabethan period. There is a distinct possibility that Ogle's sin was not buggery per se but engaging in relations with boys. Many of the cases involving sodomites and the death penalty during the seventeenth century involve youths. Burg, *Sodomy and the Pirate Tradition*, 144–49. The records show an absence of cases where consenting adults engaging in buggery were punished by death. White-Patarino's research supports this as well. Of the seventeen cases that he examined from the period 1550–1688 that were brought before the Admiralty Court, most cases involved disparate power relationships. White-Patarino, "Living outside the Ordered Society," 13–14.

28. Arthur N. Gilbert, "Buggery and the British Navy, 1700–1861," *Journal of Social History* 10 (1976), 72.

29. PRO HCA 13/36/310–11v.

30. Houlbrooke, *The English Family*, 67.

31. Vivien Brodsky Elliott, "Single Women in the London Marriage Market:

Age, Status and Mobility, 1598–1619," in *Marriage and Society: Studies in the Social History of Marriage*, ed. R. B. Outhwaite (London: Europa Publications, 1981), 84.

32. E. A. Wrigley, "Family Limitation in Pre-Industrial England," *Economic History Review* 19 (1966), 187; Laslett, *The World We Have Lost*, 101; Elliot, "Single Women in the London Marriage Market," 82–83, 86–89; Houlbrooke, "The Making of Marriage in Mid-Tudor England," 342.

33. Elliot, "Single Women in the London Marriage Market," 83.

34. Guildhall Ms. 9234/1/69.

35. PRO PROB, 11/59/169v–70, 11/67/159v.

36. PRO HCA, 1/44/115–16, 1/45/51–52v.

37. PRO PROB 11/76/296v-1; Guildhall Ms. 9171/17/369.

38. Burton, "The Myth of Bachelor Jack," 193.

39. We can also compare some seamen to agricultural workers in that the timing of their marriages took place during the "off-season." Few seamen who were engaged in seasonal seafaring were married during times of peak employment. In early modern Brighton, for instance, fishermen and those employed on ships engaged in carrying seasonal cargoes frequently married during December, just as agricultural laborers normally married after the harvest was brought in. Houlbrooke, *The English Family*, 85. For more information on seasonal seafaring, see Williams, *The Maritime Trade of the East Anglian Ports, 1550–1590*, 239–42. There does not seem to have been a discernible seasonal marriage pattern among seamen engaged in transoceanic trade or privateering. These seamen were not governed by seasonal employment, and therefore individuals set marriage dates based upon their own employment patterns and the state of their personal resources.

40. PRO 11/132/208–9; Guildhall Ms., 9171/19/94–95, 9171/22/574.

41. Houlbrooke, *The English Family*, 185–87; Elliot, "Single Women in the London Marriage Market," 90–92, 99–100.

42. Gouge, *Of Domesticall Duties*, 209–10.

43. PRO HCA 13/29/197–98v.

44. W. R. Chaplin, "William Rainsborough (1587–1642) and His Associates of the Trinity House," *Mariner's Mirror* 31 (1945), 193–94. Similarly, family reconstruction of London shipwrights demonstrates that they also tended to intermarry, suggesting that occupational bonds were principal determinants; Harris, *The Trinity House of Deptford*, 77; PRO PROB, 11/121/100, 11/121/346v, 11/123/408, 11/142/292v, 11/144/368v, 11/182/299v, 11/388/291v, 11/395/26v; PRO SP 12/248/May 25, 1594.

45. PRO PROB, 11/78/37, 11/88/95v, 11/112/134v, 11/114/462v, 11/154/89. By 1640 Robert Salmon was styling himself "esquire." PRO PROB 11/186/354.

46. *The Marriage Registers of St. Dunstans, Stepney*, vol. I. 1568–1639, ed. Thomas Colyer-Fergusson (Canterbury: Cross and Jackman, 1898–1901), 253, 319; Guildhall Ms., 9171/25/152, 10,091/1/14, 10,091/1/87v; *Allegations for Marriage Licenses Issued by the Bishop of London 1520–1610* vol. I, extracted by Joseph Lemuel Chester, ed. George Armytage (London: Harleian Society, 1887), 264, 276.

47. Ronald Pollit, "John Hawkins's Troublesome Voyages: Merchants, Bureaucrats, and the Origin of the Slave Trade," *Journal of British Studies* 12 (1973),

35–37; PRO PROB 11/102/36-v; David A. Thomas, *The Illustrated Armada Handbook* (London: Harrap, 1988), 22–23.

48. Of the 89 wills examined by Hair and Alsop, only five testators transferred. property. Hair and Alsop, *English Seamen and Traders*, 131. Unlike Hair and Alsop's research, my sample of wills is heavily weighted in favor of skilled seamen. Approximately half of my sample did, or could afford to, own or lease property.

49. Guildhall Ms. 9171/19/453.

50. PRO PROB, 11/102/181v, 11/83/223.

51. Guildhall Ms., 9171/24/361-v, 9171/23/429. For other examples see Guildhall Ms., 9171/29/172v, 9171/17/36v.

52. Seamen's work patterns were not unusual in early modern society. E. P. Thompson postulated that for workers who determined their own work patterns, preindustrial labor rhythms consisted of "an alternation of intensive labour and boisterous relaxation." E. P. Thompson, *The Making of the English Working Class*, 3rd ed. (Middlesex: Penguin Books, 1984), 473; E. P. Thompson, "Time, Work-discipline and Industrial Capitalism," *Past and Present* 38 (1967), 49–50.

53. Despite all the social ills inherent in living in the capital, London was seen as a city of great opportunity. It experienced a threefold increase in its population from the accession of Henry VIII in 1509 to the death of his daughter Elizabeth in 1603. Many of these were young migrants. Rappaport, "Social Structure and Mobility in Sixteenth-Century London: Part I," 109, 114; Majorie McIntosh, "Servants and the Household Unit in an Elizabethan English Community," *Journal of Family History* 9 (1984), 17; Steven R. Smith, "The London Apprentices as Seventeenth-Century Adolescents," *Past and Present* 61 (1973), 149.

54. PRO HCA, 1/46/105, 1/46/104v–10v, 1/46/111v–13, 1/46/115–18v.

55. The husbands of the women in my study were alive; normally, parish records specify if the women were widows. Many parishes paid their own poor to care for sick and distressed "outsiders." Wear, "Caring for the Sick Poor in St. Bartholomew's Exchange 1580–1676," 51.

56. Guildhall Ms. 9234/4/153.

57. Guildhall Ms. 9234/3/113v–14.

58. Wear, "Caring for the Sick Poor in St. Bartholomew's Exchange 1580–1676," 51–52.

59. Berckman, *The Hidden Navy*, 12. There is also reason to believe that three of the skeletons found aboard the ill-fated *Mary Rose* belonged to females. Private communication, Dr. Margaret Rule to author, August 21, 1989.

60. Those women who were hired by officers enjoyed a much more comfortable existence than the "stowaway whore" who was harbored belowdecks by the common seamen. There are allusions to both types on English vessels. While Spanish officials specifically banned prostitutes on board the armada ships, wives were allowed. Berckman, *The Hidden Navy*, 1, 2, 5, 6, 31; Fernandez-Armesto, *The Spanish Armada*, 62. In the Georgian navy wives were permitted on board provided it was peacetime. Rodger, *The Wooden World*, 76.

61. Laffin, *Jack Tar*, 32.

62. PRO HCA 13/36/305v–6v.

63. Carl Bridenbaugh, *Vexed and Troubled Englishmen 1590–1642* (New York: Oxford University Press, 1968), 237; PRO SP 12/231/46; PRO HCA 13/26/232–33.

64. Guildhall Ms. 9222/74; Woodward, "Ships, Masters and Shipowners of the Wirral 1550–1650," 243; Laffin, *Jack Tar*, 31; Hair and Alsop, *English Seamen and Traders*, 247.

65. *A Proposal for the Encouragement of Seamen, &c. to Serve More Readily in His Majesty's Navy, for Preventing of Desertion, Supporting Their Wives and Families, and for the Easier and Quieter Government of His Majesty's Ships* (London: A Millar, 1758), 15–16; *An Inquiry into the Causes*, 7–8.

66. In the seventeenth century, Captain George St. Lo claimed that seamen's wives and children were often "burdensome to parish or if she has credit, perhaps runs her husband in debt more than he can get up in a Year or two." George St. Lo, *England's Safety; Or, a Bridle to the French King* (London: William Miller, 1693), 17.

67. Guildhall Ms. 9234/6/115; PRO HCA, 1/46/203v, 14/25/209, 14/24/181–82; Guildhall Ms. 9234/1/115; PRO HCA 13/27/448v; *Marriage Registers of Stepney Parish*, 16; GLRO X24/66/33v; PRO HCA, 24/2/unfoliated, 25/2/unfoliated, 13/27/448v, 24/68/80, 1/46/203v.

68. He also blamed much of the pilfering that went on in the navy on needy seamen. Laffin, *Jack Tar*, 64.

69. Nicholas Rogers, "Liberty Road: Opposition to Impressment in Britain During the American War of Independence," in *Jack Tar in History*, 54.

70. Ruddock, "The Trinity House at Deptford in the Sixteenth Century," 466.

71. The letter from the Lord Admiral and the Queen's councillors to the mayor and aldermen of Bristol is dated 1595, but the practice of deducting these sums for the maintenance of seamen and their families predates this time. PRO SP 12/254/6. Presumably, "seamen's children" included orphans as well.

72. Patrick McGrath, "Merchant Shipping in the Seventeenth Century": The Evidence of the Bristol Deposition Books," Part II, *Mariner's Mirror* 41 (1955), 37.

73. Lloyd, *The British Seaman*, 47; Cruickshank, *Elizabeth's Army*, 184.

74. Hudson, "Ex-Servicemen, War Widows and the English County Pension Scheme, 1593–1679," 59–64; Hudson, "The Origins of State Benefits for Ex-Servicemen in Elizabethan England," 1–17.

75. PRO HCA, 14/28/219, 1/44/227-v.

76. PRO HCA, 14/33/134, 14/36/44, 14/30/3, 14/30/39, 14/31/93.

77. PRO HCA, 14/34/142, 14/22/90, 1/46/163–64.

78. PRO HCA 1/45/175–76v.

79. Houlbrooke, *The English Family*, 115–18. Unofficial separations were more common and becoming increasingly so toward the end of the sixteenth century. Among the lower orders, men sometimes sold their wives, but few instances of this came to the attention of church officials.

80. Peter Rushton, "Property, Power and Family Networks: The Problem of Disputed Marriage in Early Modern England," *Journal of Family History* 11 (1986), 212.

81. PRO HCA 13/32/163.

82. Guildhall Ms. 9171/19/205v.

83. Guildhall Ms., 9171/19/381, 9171/17/101; PRO PROB 11/97/88v; Guildhall Ms. 9171/10d/132; PRO PROB, 11/149/320v, 11/91/33.

84. Houlbrooke, *The English Family*, 210.

85. In most known cases the widow and any living children inherited the bulk

of the estate. Fettey's will was somewhat unusual in this regard. Did Fettey grant half his estate to Myson as payment for a debt?

86. These are orders compiled by Sabastian Cabot, governor of the Merchant Adventurer's Company in 1553. Hakluyt, *The Principall Navigations*, 236. This custom was also outlined in the Laws of Oléron. PRO HCA 50/1/192–93.

87. PRO HCA 13/30/285v–86v.

88. Bridenbaugh, *Vexed and Troubled Englishmen*, 237.

89. PRO HCA, 14/34/141, 14/34/142.

90. PRO HCA, 13/25/199v–200, 13/25/228v.

91. PRO HCA, 1/46/163, 1/46/177–79. There are indications that Carr's relations with his partners were not the closest. In his will Carr appoints two overseers to assist his wife. It is curious that Carr's business partners were not given these positions. Furthermore, his partners were not mentioned at all in his will. Surely, Robert Carr, one of Cuthbert Carr's business partners and a shareholder in the *Richard*, was a kinsman. Yet Elizabeth Carr had to resort to the courts to reach a settlement. For Cuthbert Carr's will, see Guildhall Ms. 9171/19/453. The records do not specify if Carr died as a result of the casting away of the *Richard*. Carr was buried in his home parish in August 1603. GLRO X24/90/16.

92. Guildhall Ms. 9171/17/369; PRO HCA 13/25/234-v.

93. The necessity of having a shipboard will or, at least, to make known one's intentions to crewmates was very important. The transmission of the dead man's shipboard possessions could be a difficult process; Hair and Alsop have pointed out that the transmission of the seaman's effects often occurred months after his death and that there were frequently geographical obstacles to delivering the effects as well. Hair and Alsop, *English Seamen and Traders*, 96–97; PRO HCA, 13/25/199b–200, 13/25/228v.

94. PRO HCA 13/25/234-v.

95. Robson also mentions that he sold other seamen's goods at the mainmast, which suggests that the practice was widespread. Wills from the Elizabethan period abound with such references. See Hair and Alsop, *English Seamen and Traders*, 99, 342–43.

96. Scammell, "Shipowning in the Economy and Politics of Early Modern England," 397. Shipmasters who engaged in fishing often gave their wives their nets as well. Farrant, "The Rise and Decline of a South Coast Seafaring Town," 64.

97. It is noteworthy that, while affluent seamen almost always entrusted a sum of money to the care of fellow seamen to invest for the testator's children, seamen rarely did this for their widows. As we shall see, most testators were particularly concerned with providing for their children, who were often minors.

98. PRO PROB 11/112/134v; GLRO X/32/31.

99. Keith Thomas, "Age and Authority in Early Modern England," *Proceedings of the British Academy* 62 (1976), 247–48.

100. PRO PROB 11/105/55.

101. PRO PROB 11/98/142v.

102. Stevyns mentions three sons as well. He makes no such provisions for them, although at least two of them were under 21. Were they already in service and thus had guardians?

103. PRO PROB 11/94/250v.

104. PRO PROB 11/101/394.

105. PRO PROB 11/57/270v–71; Guildhall Ms. 9171/20/341.

106. Stephen Collins, "British Stepfamily Relationships, 1500–1800," *Journal of Family History* 16 (1991), 331, 335; PRO SP 12/151/17.

107. Andrews, *Ships, Money and Politics*, 73–74.

108. Elderly widows were much more likely to move in with married children than widowers. Houlbrooke, *English Family*, 191. By virtue of the Poor Law of 1601 adult children were obliged to assist their elderly parents if they could not support themselves. Margaret Pelling, "Old People and Poverty in the Early Modern Towns," *Society for the Social History of Medicine Bulletin* 34 (1984), 3.

109. Guildhall Ms. 9171/24/277–78. See also PRO PROB 11/186/354.

110. It has been estimated that about one-fifth of householders between the late sixteenth and early nineteenth centuries were widowed. Houlbrooke, *The English Family*, 208.

111. See Hair and Alsop, *English Seamen and Traders*, 109–10; Scammell, "Manning the English Merchant Service," 138.

112. Widows constituted a much higher percentage of the population than widowers, particularly among the poor and in the towns. Houlbrooke, *The English Family*, 213.

113. PRO PROB, 11/102/36-v, 11/101/394.

114. Guildhall Ms. 9051/4/169v. Through record linkage it is possible to state that many widows of London shipmasters chose to marry other local shipmasters.

115. This holds true of the general population. Houlbrooke, *The English Family*, 214; Jean-Louis Flandrin, *Families in Former Times: Kinship, Household and Sexuality*, trans. Richard Southern (Cambridge: Cambridge University Press, 1979), 115.

116. This was the case for early modern husbands in general. Houlbrooke, *The English Family*, 211; PRO PROB 11/102/107-v; Guildhall Ms. 9171/19/61-v; PRO PROB, 11/67/153v, 11/57/423v; Guildhall Ms. 9234/1/41; PRO PROB 11/61/54–55.

117. Guildhall Ms., 9171/19/298v–99, 9171/19/161v, 9168/15/210; PRO HCA 25/3/III/83; *Allegations for Marriage Licenses Issued by the Bishop of London 1520–1610*, vol. I, 216.

118. Bridget White, widow, was buried in Stepney in 1602. GLRO X24/70/95. We do not know exactly when John White died. His will was probated by Bridget in 1600. Admiralty Court records tell us that White was in his early 30s when he died. PRO HCA 13/31/192v.

119. PRO PROB, 11/88/95v–96v, 11/78/237–38.

120. Guildhall Ms., 9172/12v/80, 9171/17/36v–37v, 9171/19/181v, 9171/19/30v, 9051/5/Part 2/316, 9171/19/392v, 9231/1/145.

121. Flandrin, *Families in Former Times*, 53–55.

122. Perhaps they had more children. The possibility exists that he and his wife had other children, baptized in a parish other than Stepney. GLRO, X24/66/3, 5v, 7v, 9, 12v, 17, 22, 26, X24/70/18v, 27v, 29v, 33v, 34, 34v, 37. It is possible that Clark's son, his namesake, was the only one who survived. He had two sons named Israel, and only one was buried in the parish.

123. Infants and children were especially vulnerable in their first few years. Infants born to poor couples were more likely to die before adulthood than those born into wealthier families. Infants who lived in towns or the fens were more apt

to die than those who lived in healthier environments. In addition to the hazards inherent in childhood, children were susceptible to the health epidemics that ravaged the adult population. They were also very prone to accidental deaths. Houlbrooke, *The English Family*, 136–38; Flandrin, *Families in Former Times*, 53–55.

124. This investigation is restricted to children who were baptized or buried in the parish. There may have been additional children who were born or baptized in other parishes. PRO, PROB 11/146/279, HCA 13/33/311, HCA 13/25/314; Guildhall Ms. 9171/25/152; PRO PROB 13/30/125; Guildhall Ms. 9171/21/165v; PRO HCA 13/40/139v.

125. Lawrence Stone, *The Family, Sex, and Marriage in England 1500–1800* (New York: Harper & Row, 1977), 105–7.

126. PRO PROB, 11/112/134v, 11/61/54–55; Guildhall Ms. 9171/20/260v; PRO PROB, 11/121/100v, 11/186/354.

127. GLRO X19/15/240; Guildhall Ms. 9171/12b/80; PRO PROB 11/58/28v–29.

128. The term "cousin" often denoted a niece or nephew. Eve McLaughlin, *Wills before 1858* (1979; rpt. Birmingham: Federation of Family History Societies, 1989), 15.

129. Guildhall Ms. 9171/17/174. Such requests were not mere rhetoric. There were cases when overseers defrauded seamen's children of their inheritance. See PRO HCA 14/28/76.

130. For examples, see PRO PROB, 11/102/75-v, 11/102/345.

131. Guildhall Ms. 9051/5/part 2/316.

132. Guildhall Ms. 9171/16/285v–86. According to parish records, Isaac was 5 and Jacob was 2 when their father was buried in November 1576. GLRO, X24/66/4v, X24/66/9, X24/70/15v. In the long run Boyse's second wife, Margaret, ensured that her own sons, the junior sons of Thomas Boyse, benefited. Instead of the £3 6s. 8d. they were to receive under the terms of their father's will, the widow Boyse topped up the amount that Isaac received so he would get £10 at his age of majority. Jacob, the youngest son, was to have 20 marks. Guildhall Ms. 9171/16/385–86. In her will, Boyse's widow, Margaret, however, did not mention her stepsons and left her property to her sons by Boyse and the daughters from her first marriage. Guildhall Ms. 9171/16/385–86. As a result, much of Boyse's estate went to his younger sons and his stepchildren by virtue of his widow's will.

133. Guildhall Ms. 25,626/2/341-v.

134. For examples, see PRO PROB 11/104/219v–20, Guildhall Ms. 25,626/2/341-v.

135. Current estimates suggest that one-half of adults had lost one or both parents by the age of 25. Houlbrooke, "The Making of Marriage," 350.

136. Guildhall Ms., 9171/24/116v, 9171/22/252, 9171/20/46, 9171/17/249, 9171/12b/99, 9172/12b/87-v, 9171/19/19v–20, 9171/21/92v.

137. In the sixteenth century the term "in-law" was usually reserved for stepparents. Fathers and mothers "by marriage" often speak of sons and daughters (i.e., spouses of one's biological offspring) in their wills. Testators commonly made their daughter's husbands overseers or executors along with their natural sons.

138. For examples, see Guildhall Ms., 9171/19/30v, 9171/17/343-v.

139. PRO HCA 1/41/115v.

140. Shipmaster John Paul had a black servant named Agnes. Master Robert

Rickman had a black "more wench." Master Bigate had a black servant called George Fatepoint. Captain Michael Geare had a black woman servant. GLRO, X24/70/part II/13, X24/70/46v, X24/70/46v, X24/70/25.

141. This was typical of the general population as well. Choosing godparents for one's child was a common way of securing or recognizing friendships. Cressy, "Kinship and Kin Interaction in Early Modern England," 66.

142. Guildhall Ms. 9171/19/461-v; GLRO, X24/70/4v, X24/70/12v.

143. PRO PROB 11/105/55.

144. See GLRO P93/Dun/327; *Memorials of Stepney Parish*, ed. G. W. Hill and W. H. Frere (Guildford: Billings and Sons, 1890–91), vii–viii.

145. Guildhall Ms. 9171/19/90; Hair and Alsop, *English Seamen and Traders*, 169, 175; Guildhall Ms. 9171/19/45v–46. Conversely, Jonas Bouchlie, gunner of the *Trinity Burre*, left 20 shillings for his crewmates "so that I maye be buried ashore." Bouchlie's request is an isolated one. Guildhall Ms. 9015/5/part 1/41.

146. PRO PROB, 11/82/325v, 11/57/201v–2; Guildhall Ms. 9172/12a/58. See also GLRO X32/6/293-v; PRO PROB 11/102/322v–23.

147. PRO PROB, 11/76/296v–97, 11/63/4v, 11/113/236v, 11/82/325v; Guildhall Ms. 9171/24/277–78. See also PRO PROB, 11/92/79–80, 11/180/354; GLRO X32/7/631v. Seamen associated with the Trinity House frequently made a bequest to the house; the bequest might consist of money left for a meal for the Brethren or money to the almshouse.

148. Scammell, "Manning the English Merchant Service in the Sixteenth Century," 138, 147.

149. Presumably, Grey did not go to sea much at such an advanced age. PRO HCA 13/28/281v–82.

150. Many of the Queen's ships had skeleton crews assigned to them when they were not involved in active duty. See Tom Glasgow (Jr.), "Viceadmiral Woodhouse and Shipkeeping in the Tudor Navy," *Mariner's Mirror* 63 (1977), 254–62; Isobell G. Powell, " 'Shipkeepers' and Minor Officers Serving at Sea in the Early Stuart Navy," *Mariner's Mirror* 10 (1924), 156–72.

151. *Memorials of Stepney Parish*, 31. While he had a long and distinguished career as a shipmaster, the value of Carpenter's goods was estimated at just over £35 at his death. Guildhall Ms. 9168/17/23.

152. McGrath, "Merchant Shipping in the Seventeenth Century," 37.

153. Ibid., PRO SP 12/249/July 4, 1594; Oppenheim, "The Royal and Merchant Navy under Elizabeth,"484–85; GLRO X24/70/53v. Those who had fallen "to decay in their worke by reason of theyr yeares, weaknesse or infirmities" were considered to be the "deserving poor" and therefore eligible for parish relief in their home parish. The elderly constituted a very high proportion of those on relief rolls relative to their representation in the general population. Pelling, "Old People and Poverty," 39.

154. Hudson, "Ex-Servicemen, War Widows and the English County Pension Scheme, 1593–1679"; Hudson, "Negotiating for Relief," 1–30; Hudson, "The Origins of State Benefits for Ex-Servicemen in Elizabethan England," 1–17.

155. We know that, whenever possible, absent seamen had returning seamen take back messages and letters to their loved ones. PRO HCA, 13/25/304–7, 13/32/125v.

Chapter 6

Conclusion

What picture emerges from this study of the Elizabethan maritime community? To answer this question, let us divide the mural into panels for analysis. We analyze the nature of maritime community at sea and on land and then summarize the main findings concerning the effects of the Anglo-Spanish war on Elizabeth's seamen as individuals and as a group.

THE MARITIME COMMUNITY AT SEA

Although there was specialization among seafarers, there was a high flow of traffic between the various sectors of the maritime community. Naturally, their opportunities and choices were based on, and limited by, the availability of work at any given time. With the exception of indentured apprenticeships and naval service, most training, hiring, trading, and negotiating were sealed with verbal contracts that seamen arranged themselves, within certain parameters established by the custom of the merchant and maritime community. In other words, seamen were "free agents" who operated within a self-regulating system. Except for the Crown's extensive interference during the war years 1585 to 1604, the maritime community was relatively free of regulation, including statutory or guild control. The maritime elite were a rarity among the skilled wage earners of Tudor and early Stuart England, as they were subject to few external or internal formal regulations, while the economic activities of the semiskilled and unskilled paralleled in many aspects those of the mobile groups within the agricultural workforce.

Although there were factors that determined one's earning potential such as skill, experience, reputation, type of voyage undertaken, and the "the going rate," each seaman was ultimately responsible for his own livelihood. Within the limitations noted earlier, he decided the times of his labor and how long he spent on land and at sea. Wages were central to most seamen's earnings, and remuneration was based upon the successful completion of the voyage. Even the "meaner sort" of seamen normally engaged in some sort of trading as a supplement to wages and in an effort to guard against the myriad accidents and hazards that could cause them "to lose" their voyage. In addition to purchasing goods for the purpose of trading, the more affluent of the maritime community diversified their incomes by buying shares in vessels and engaging in various types of enterprises on land and at sea. Nonetheless, there is ample evidence that the poorer sort remained on the brink of destitution, and even the most industrious shipmasters occasionally lost all in unfortunate investments or unlucky voyages.

Career patterns varied enormously; some seamen worked within the confines of a particular type of voyage, sometimes sailing on the same vessel on an established route carrying the same kind of cargo with a large continuity in crewmates. The employment choices of most seamen, however, were more diverse. During peacetime, seamen could find work within the rapidly expanding sectors of English overseas trade. The war provided a greater range of employment prospects for seamen, at the same time as it restricted free choice for many. From the 1580s onward, it was not unusual to find former "pirates" serving in the Queen's fleet; often these same men worked aboard merchant and privateering vessels as well.

Skilled men had the luxury of being more selective in their choice of employment than the common seamen. Because skilled men received higher wages and were better positioned to own shares in vessels and cargo, they could afford to be more selective and, in some cases, remain inactive for longer periods. Unlike their skilled crewmates, common seamen did not have a diversified income. The observation that a "lost" voyage frequently necessitated a serious economic crisis is doubly true for common seamen, and many were caught in a cycle of debt, where present wages and advances went to pay off previous commitments. Even in cases where common seamen had completed successful voyages and had made money from trading and their wages, their money and credit were not sufficient to allow them much time in idleness once they disembarked from their ship, while their work culture encouraged rapid, flamboyant expenditures of accrued wages and profits.

Although it can be stated unequivocally that seamen put their health and their lives in jeopardy virtually every time they set sail, the concept of "unacceptable risks" and "unbearable conditions" did exist and can be documented time and time again. Without a doubt, the sixteenth-century seamen's definition of what constituted unacceptable risks or unbearable conditions was often the bare minimum to sustain life and health. Nevertheless, many shipmasters and captains were forced to halt or alter their voyages because of the crews' grievances. Despite the fact that contemporaries noted that few seamen "grew to grey hairs," seamen had a reputation for being notorious grumblers and difficult employees, bent on preserving their own skins. Such negative portrayals were particularly voluminous from anxious captains and masters, intent to explore unchartered terrain with inadequate supplies, or profit-driven factors determined to press on in the face of extreme adversity. Because a number of these commanders created for themselves considerable reputations, leaving their names and deeds to posterity, historians have been too ready to credit unreservedly their version of events at the dawning of English overseas enterprise. From our vantage point, we can see that seamen (often willingly) withstood extremely harsh conditions aboard early modern vessels and, as their superiors found out, set for themselves limits grounded in common sense and custom; they then utilized their unique work environment to enforce these.

This study of the English maritime community has shown that seamen had a well-developed concept of the value of their own labor and were not afraid to communicate reservations, complaints, advice, or demands to their employers or potential employers. Apparently, seamen did not need a guild or occupational regulations to foster their occupational consciousness. They were ready to uphold their customs and act upon their expectations. Elizabethan seamen emerge as individualists, concerned primarily with their own livelihoods but capable of collective action when their welfare, customs, and incomes were threatened. In many instances the shipboard hierarchy belowdecks was used to express grievances through petty officers; this was not a democracy afloat.

Seamen's subculture was an interesting combination of individuality and group solidarity. They were used to acting in consort in order to complete their voyages; sixteenth-century ships demanded teamwork. Although the master (or captain, if there was one aboard) had the final word in all matters, each seaman had a voice in the major decisions concerning the voyage. Order rested largely on reciprocity and consensus; seamen supported maritime authority in return for the recognition of their "rights." The wise commander ruled but took care not to violate maritime customs or the expectations of its membership. Failure to uphold these customs could result in the breakdown of consensus, which, in some cases, resulted in verbal or written petitions or, in more serious circumstances, took the form of desertion or mutiny. Seamen were certainly capable of banding together to exert pressure on authorities to uphold their understanding of maritime custom, particularly in relation to risk, wages, perquisites, and food. Seamen did not distinguish between their employers; this attitude extended to shipmasters, captains, factors, and the Crown. The demonstrations in London in 1589 and 1592 prove that seamen did not hesitate to protest en masse the Crown's slow payment of their naval wages.

What was it about the work culture and norms of Elizabethan seafaring that enabled seamen to be such difficult employees? We find the answer in perquisites of employment, labor, and the nature of their work. The occupational lives of seamen were quite different from those of their land-based counterparts, and this had an influence on the nature of the shipboard community. Unlike most men in early modern society, seamen's work lives were divorced from their lives ashore. They were dissimilar from disgruntled laborers on land because they were free of impediments; if shipboard conditions were not to their liking and showed no prospects of improving, there was little to prevent seamen from departing. They simply "voted with their feet," without having to pack up their families or disrupt their lives ashore. Dissatisfied seamen then could (and did) abandon their employers and leave their jobs when necessary. Seamen were the most autonomous and mobile members of the early modern workforce.

Seamen's freedom from internal and external constraints naturally had ramifications for the nature of the shipboard community. Given seamen's ability and willingness to disembark when shipboard conditions were not to their liking, shipmasters had to make some concessions to the wishes of their crews. Once at sea, a dissatisfied crew had a great deal of leverage to bargain with the shipmaster or the merchants aboard who were intent on completing the voyage with a minimum of delay or inconvenience. These circumstances probably had much to do with the long-standing tradition of shipboard consultation.

The requirements of their shipboard labor and their customs and expectations were not the only things that bound the men of the maritime community together. The research of P.E.H. Hair and J. D. Alsop on the wills of mid-Tudor seamen engaged in the Guinea trade has revealed the existence of a "shipboard economy." My own research supports their contention that there was a complex system of lending and borrowing on ships and in the maritime community in general. Therefore, seamen at all levels of the hierarchy were connected by debt. Debt was an important facet of the early modern economy; in the case of seamen, it was natural that they would seek out crewmates and friends within their occupational and reference group from whom to borrow money or with whom to form business partnerships. This web of financial dependence created and nurtured a strong sense of solidarity and fellowship based on necessary trust and cooperation.

In part, the solidarity of the men of the maritime community was fostered by their singular existence. As an occupational group seamen were unique, as they were highly mobile, wage-based, and divorced from the land community for long periods. Their experiences were quite different from those of their counterparts on land. This isolation encouraged a distinctive and well-developed subculture. Because of the strength of their subculture and their unusual mode of existence, seamen on land have been compared to fish out of water.

THE MARITIME COMMUNITY ON LAND

I do not suggest that all seamen were ill at ease when on land. Those who had the wherewithal to settle down and start a family invariably did so, forging deep ties to their particular segment of the land community. In most cases, it was skilled seamen who had the means to make marriages. These men tended to enter into their first marriages at roughly the same time in life as those elsewhere in their socioeconomic stratum in late Tudor England. Many seamen courted women from within their reference group, married, and established independent households. The household structure reflected the status of the head of the family; because many married seafarers were men of skill and reputation, a significant number had servants to assist in the day-to-day chores of running their houses. As skilled and experienced practitioners of a maritime trade, mariners had apprentices who joined their masters' households during their period of instruction. In these ways, mariners were much like other "family men" who practiced a respected trade. Nevertheless, it would not be correct to say that seamen's families were the same as those of landsmen. Unlike most other husbands and fathers, seamen were frequently absent from their homes for long periods; thus, household management fell to the wives, relatives, or business associates, who were forced to cope with the absenteeism of the breadwinners for months or—in the case of the rapidly expanding seventeenth-century East Indian commerce—years at a time. These absences could be both a blessing and a curse. Doubtless, some wives enjoyed the autonomy of running their households single-handedly. Seamen's wives had a contemporary reputation for independence, sometimes expressed in the negative association made with loose living and prostitution. Much of the time they functioned as "single mothers" with all the challenges that that role entailed. They were also burdened by the fact that their husbands were in an occupation fraught with dangers; the health of seafaring spouses might be severely compromised, they might be captured by pirates or hostile elements in foreign ports, facing expensive ransoms or lengthy imprisonment, or they might not return at all. An unfortunate voyage could mean financial ruin for a seaman and his family, the dissolution of an independent unit, and/or reduction to parochial charity.

Although the role of the seaman's wife must have been an onerous one, it did not prevent a large number of seamen's widows from remarrying within the maritime community. We are left to conclude that, although it was difficult, either their lot was not altogether unpleasant, or they were so tightly bound to the maritime community—in cultural as well as economic terms—that they had, in effect, no choice or larger perspective. Because many of these women had lived in households connected with the maritime trades prior to their marriages, they were accustomed to the duties and difficulties associated with this mode of existence. At present we know far less than we need to concerning the culture and ethic of seafarers' spouses and children. High rates of remarriage and children's subsequent career choices indicate the presence of strong ties binding this maritime community together.

Despite the fact that seamen were away from their families for long periods of time (or perhaps because of it), their wills indicate that they took great pains to provide for their dependents. In part, this meant that seamen strove to provide financial legacies for their heirs, but it also meant that fathers selected trusted friends to look out for the welfare of their children. Wills reflect the wishes and personality of the testator, and the overriding concern of men with children was the welfare of their offspring, particularly in those all-too-frequent cases where the children had not reached the age of majority. Therefore, we may conclude that, despite long absences from home, seafaring fathers were not apathetic about the upbringing or the well-being of their children. We do not see a hint here of Laurence Stone's nonaffective family.[1] On the contrary, abundant evident proves that testators were consumed with the desire to provide guidance and financial support for their children from beyond the grave.

Seamen with families and firm ties to the land population straddled the physical divide between ship and terra firma. However, this physical divide did not mirror a sociocultural division. Loved ones and responsibilities on land did not limit the meaningful relationships that married seamen shared with their seafaring colleagues. For single seamen, the absence of a nuclear family of one's own meant that there were fewer concrete ties to bind a seaman to the shore. For the unmarried, the discerned connections to parish, siblings, or, in some cases, even parents appear to have been modest and distant. For many testators within this group, the strongest ties expressed were to the hosts or hostesses who stored their modest belongings or to a sweetheart who—had the seaman lived—might have formed the foundation for a nuclear family. Those who lacked wives and children were more likely to be men separated physically, socially, psychologically, and culturally from the land population in general; they tended to be more itinerant, engaged in flamboyant expressions of seafaring culture, and were relegated to the periphery of respectable society.

In the absence of wife and children, many single men looked to other seamen for fellowship. This tendency was reinforced not only by their long absences away from "home" but also by their uneasiness with the larger society of Tudor England. When ashore, those men without concrete ties normally drifted to the margins of mainstream society and immersed themselves in the company of other bachelor seafarers. Given the amount of time spent as part of the exclusively male shipboard community, those who lacked close personal relationships ashore felt, to some extent, alienated from the larger culture; it stands to reason that these same men would feel more comfortable in the company of those who shared their occupation and were products of their unique subculture. While their wills demonstrate that bonds with kin and nonseafaring friends could be important, bachelor seamen frequently left most of their possessions to other seamen, who were often, but not invariably, their crewmates. The evidence is persuasive that married seamen also formed affectionate and lasting friendships with those in their occupational group. Regardless of their marital status, seamen made significant bequests to other seamen; they chose them as executors, overseers, and witnesses to their wills and entrusted them with safeguarding their possessions, investments, and their dependents. While such responsibilities testify to the strong bonds of friendship within their occupational group, we must also note that these occupational ties were reinforced by kinship ties. Seamen showed a propensity to marry women associated with the maritime community; many courted and married daughters, widows, and sisters of their seafaring colleagues.

All these connections were fostered by the tendency of seafarers on land to live and socialize within dockside communities. At least in the London area—the focus for this research—seamen tended to live in the rapidly expanding dockside parishes of the Thames River. Communities like Whitechapel, Ratcliffe, Limehouse, and Rotherhithe were densely populated by seafarers. Thus, we can add another bond that connected those associated with the maritime community: they were neighbors as well. Seamen, their wives and children provided vital support networks for each other. Seamen of all ages looked to those connected with the maritime community as a reference group and a support network for social interaction when they were on land or at sea. The bonds between crewmates were not limited to shipboard life. They extended to all aspects of a seaman's existence; whether one was looking for a suitable spouse, choosing a master or guardian for one's child, appointing an overseer for a will, or finding a business partner, seamen looked to "their own kind" in most cases. It is not an exaggeration to say that, as a result of a web of interdependence based on occupational ties, a shared subculture, kinship, friendship, business connections, and a system of debt, those associated with the maritime crafts formed a community within the larger society. This was presumably most pronounced for those seamen who were engaged in overseas commerce and who developed their careers out of major ports. At the moment we can only guess at the degree of similarity of those engaged in the coastal trade, fishermen, or those who resided in the small, seaside agricultural communities of the south and east coasts.

MARITIME AND LAND COMMUNITIES: AN ANALYSIS OF SOCIAL CONSENSUS

While we cannot underestimate the unity of the Elizabethan maritime community within the larger society, it would be incorrect to say that the two "communities" (to use the contemporary distinction made between seamen and landlubbers) were dissimilar. In fact, the two have some very important similarities. Both were hierarchical. Furthermore, although each had stringent codes that regulated the behavior of its members, those in positions of authority on land or at sea did not have the means to enforce their laws in the face of widespread resistance from the rank and file. Hence, in the maritime hierarchy and the hierarchy of early modern society, order was maintained principally through consensus and reciprocity. This consensus was based upon a shared set of expectations and the fact that those expectations would be met, or at least some remedy sought, by those in authority in return for obedience.

Unfulfilled expectations compromised consensus. It was necessary for those both on land and at sea to have accepted channels for their members to express their dissatisfaction and to seek redress; these "safety valves" were essential to the well-being of the community. The stability of the societies was dependent upon their members working within an established framework and acting in a manner that was sanctioned (or at least tacitly accepted) by the other members of that society. This was the case with the various methods of protest.

Petitions might be made in written or verbal format. Protesters were keen to draw the attention of those in authority to concerns. If those in positions of power did not attempt to address the grievances, protest might take a more menacing form and tone. The land community might resort to riots, while the men of the maritime community could turn to mutiny when at sea or riot if their protest took place on land. Both mutiny and riot stemmed from frustrated expectations on the part of those in subordinate positions in society.

When taken at face value, riot and mutiny seem to be direct challenges to those in authority. Appearances are often deceiving. Rioters and mutineers were almost invariably socially conservative, intent on working within the system. They sought not the overthrow of those in authority; they wanted their grievances addressed. In many cases, riot and mutiny resulted from the failure of authority figures to respond to written or verbal petitions. There was a protocol to riot and mutiny in Tudor and Stuart England; the aggrieved parties normally turned to more dramatic forms of protest only after their earlier efforts had been rebuffed or ignored. Mutiny was the final stage in an escalating process. It was still within the boundaries of loosely acceptable forms of protest, albeit at the end of the gamut. It was a sign of pronounced unrest among the shipboard community and an indication that all prior attempts to rectify grievances had failed. Thus, the bonds between governed and governors were breaking down. Those in authority were seen to have violated the unwritten social contract that dictated that they were to care for those under their control. This dereliction of duty, when not rectified in the face of protest, then relieved subordinates from obedience to their directives. In the most extreme cases, failure to rectify the grievances threatened the consensus that was the bedrock of early modern society at sea and on land. The prospect of the consensus crumbling produced fears of a degeneration into chaos; this was rarely in the interest of the governors or the governed. Therefore, popular protest usually elicited a favorable response from those in authority, and, although authority figures found demonstrations of displeasure frightening, the aggrieved parties rarely stepped outside the boundaries of "accepted" forms of protest. This give-and-take was the essence of the deferential model and the glue that held the societies together.

Just as there was a protocol to protest, there were also concerns deemed more legitimate than others. Subsistence issues, for instance, were recognized as a wholly appropriate basis for protest in both communities. In cases where those in subservient positions resorted to mutiny and riot, authorities acknowledged food shortages as a justifiable catalyst. One need only examine early modern protest on land and at sea to see that desperation for food was the impetus for many disturbances. Inadequate provisions were one of the leading causes of protest and mutiny at sea. Although authorities on land and at sea did not welcome these disturbances, they generally recognized them as an acceptable response to their own inadequacies or the inadequacies of the marketplace.

The similarities between the two "communities" did not end there. Not only was order maintained and renewed in the same way, but the distribution of justice operated according to the same set of assumptions and had similar goals. While those in authority could bluster about harsh penalties for deviations from an established code of behavior, the truth of the matter was that they had limited means to enforce laws and rules on land or at sea. Therefore, law, order, and the justice system relied upon the willingness of all (or at least the majority) to participate. This participation can be easily explained. First, most people believed that their personal well-being and that of their community were best served by the maintenance of order. The enforcement of laws that curtailed and punished actions that threatened the welfare of individuals and the community was in everyone's interest. This does not necessarily mean that this was a conscious decision; for some at least, participation and/or acceptance was simply a habit. It arose, not least, out of two distinctive features of the English criminal justice system: it was participatory, and it was widely believed to be derived from, and tied to, a commonly accepted moral code.

Both the maritime code and the state's laws were equally harsh in theory, but both allowed for a great deal of latitude and mercy in practice. This had much to do with the view that offenders were not necessarily criminals; they were often wayward souls who did not deserve to feel the full weight of the law for their offenses. Furthermore, the early modern justice system functioned in a paternalistic fashion; while there was a strong punitive aspect to the justice system, it was intended, in most cases, to be corrective and to rehabilitate the "sinner." The application of maritime justice afloat and at sea demonstrates that the seafaring community functioned with roughly the same dynamic, parameters, and mechanisms as the land community.

The fact that crew members normally had a voice in the major decisions concerning the ship, the voyage, and the cargo is very revealing about the nature of the shipboard community. The high degree of consultation on matters of import might well be explained by the great need to maintain consensus. One might well argue that, given seamen's mobility and freedom from constraint and the physical separation of a vessel from the coercive powers of state, church, and society, the need for consensus was greater than among the society on land. Those in positions of authority in the shipboard community had little at hand to bolster their authority or to enforce the good behavior of their subordinates. Although shipmasters could rely to some extent on threats of fines or corporal punishments for offenders, they were powerless to prevent defections. Therefore, shipmasters had to be doubly certain that they achieved and maintained consensus. Alternatively, they engaged in the bitter recriminations and fault-finding that we see laced through contemporary commentary on early modern seamen. The systematic venting of anger and/or annoyance was not a normal activity by Tudor and early Stuart elites; its presence in respect to employee–employer maritime relations is a sure sign of elite frustration.

With the advent of war with Spain, the seamen's traditional voice in shipboard affairs was compromised by the needs of the state. The state employed its age-old right of impressment, which forced seamen to serve for low wages in hazardous conditions. While the powers of the early modern state were still relatively weak by modern standards, these powers should not be discounted. Bolstered by the authority of the state and pressed to accomplish much in limited time with modest resources, shipboard commanders in the navy no longer courted consensus like the shipmasters in the peacetime forms of maritime employment. Thus, the war with Spain brought an attack on seamen's traditional customs and practices; the state's needs challenged and altered the nature of the maritime community, although they never destroyed it.

EFFECTS OF WAR ON THE MARITIME COMMUNITY

Although present in the 1570s, the tensions between England and Spain became acute in the 1580s. The cases in the High Court of the Admiralty provide a useful barometer; the tide of maritime violence escalated noticeably from the 1570s onward, reaching a crescendo during the war years. As we have seen, this violence affected all seamen. Many English seamen willingly jumped into the fray in the anticipation of profit (or more lofty motives), thus increasing the level of disorder. Those seamen who endeavored to carry on as they had were plagued by the growing lawlessness on the seas and their increasingly hostile reception in many foreign ports. Indisputably, the late sixteenth century was a very dangerous period for seamen; the seafarers' occupation has always been fraught with hazards, and it became increasingly so during this period of maritime expansion and in light of the Anglo-Spanish war. These circumstances had a significant impact upon English seamen.

From the seaman's perspective, the most problematic aspect of the war of 1585 to 1604 was impressment and naval duty. Impressment deprived seamen of their customary freedom to choose the time and conditions of their employment. As we have seen, state-enforced employment was deeply resented, and not a few seamen tried to evade service through bribery or desertion. The absence of a sizable standing navy meant that there were few career naval seamen in Tudor England. This fact meant that war had a disproportionate impact—frequently negative—upon the maritime community, but it also meant that, for the most part, seafarers viewed naval service as a temporary hardship that was to be endured. They were not to know that this war would become the longest, most strenuously fought contest in England's history and the first where sea power played a prominent role. This explains (in part) why seamen made no effort to negotiate or modify the terms of their employment with the Crown. It was only in March 1590, when the Crown attempted to confine all seamen to their home ports in case they were needed for her Majesty's service, that seamen's outrage forced the Crown to cancel its directive. It is instructive that it took this very extreme measure, one that deprived every seaman of his liberty and livelihood, for seamen to balk en masse at the Crown's orders. This outstanding incident aside, most seafarers performed their obligations to their sovereign; discounting (for the moment) the innumerable men who managed to avoid service, tens of thousands of seamen did serve aboard the Queen's fleet. Their aversion to naval duty did not affect their performance once they were afloat; as a fighting, cooperative force, they were second to none in the Western world during this period.

Their impressive record during the war years does not obscure the fact that seamen did begrudge the conditions of their employment. The most cursory of examinations reveals why naval service caused so much resentment. First, despite John Hawkins's valiant efforts to raise naval wages to a competitive level with the merchant marine, remuneration for serving in the Queen's fleet lagged behind that of other types of maritime employment. Furthermore, state bureaucracy was extremely lax in paying seamen. Complaints were frequent that pay was far in arrears or that they were never paid at all. Impressment could spell financial ruin for those who fought for Queen and country. For those men with dependents, impressment compromised the economic well-being of their families. Just as few seamen could afford to lose their voyages or to remain in idleness for long periods ashore, most could ill afford to devalue the price of their labor by serving in the navy. This must be considered a primary reason for avoidance, absenteeism, and desertion.

Low wages and delayed payment were not the only hazards of naval service. Naval campaigns were certainly more dangerous than the peacetime forms of seafaring. Waging war upon the seas was perilous by its very nature, but the most threatening enemy of sixteenth-century navies was disease. The high morbidity and mortality rates in the Elizabethan navy were a direct result of a state's placing large numbers of men in unsafe, unhygienic conditions with inadequate food for extended periods. No other form of maritime employment rivaled the navy in terms of loss of manpower. It was notoriously difficult to man some risky, deep-sea endeavors, such as innovative voyages of discovery, but no maritime sector compares to the navy's record of overall numbers lost. This can be explained by a number of factors: overcrowded conditions, substandard provisions, impressment officials who "scraped the bottom of the barrel" in order to fill the Queen's ships with men, and the Crown's failure to seize the initiative in regard to "cutting-edge" medical treatment and improvements to shipboard conditions and diet. Efforts were being made by individual seamen and merchant companies to improve shipboard conditions and diet in order to keep their employees healthy. Without a doubt, there was a growing recognition that a successful voyage was contingent upon a healthy crew, and seamen regularly demanded higher wages or turned down employment if the risks were unacceptably high. It was in everyone's best interests to lower shipboard morbidity and mortality rates. The Crown, however, was slow to follow the lead of the civilian sector of the maritime community.

One factor that contributed to high mortality among naval seamen was the inadequate medical care that they received once they left their vessels. Traditionally, employers were morally obliged to provide health care afloat or ashore for their sick or wounded seamen. Although evidence on this issue is meager, it seems that most employers did live up to their obligations in this regard. The Crown was a notable exception; not only did impressment deny seamen their customary right to assess the conditions of their employment, but they received inadequate or no medical care. Although the Crown routinely employed a small number of surgeons for the larger ships in the fleet, seamen were left to their own devices once they were removed from shipboard. In this regard the Crown contravened the maritime custom that dictated that employers were to find and pay caretakers for their ill or injured employees. While we can appreciate that the Crown was heavily burdened financially and otherwise with the task of waging war, the failure to fulfill these traditional responsibilities made naval duty only more hazardous and less welcome to seamen. This contravention of maritime custom was yet another reason that naval service was so distasteful.

Substandard or nonexistent health care was not the only unfortunate by-product of the war years for seamen. The maritime community experienced an influx of landsmen into its ranks, men untutored in the ways and customs of the sea. The more affluent or well-connected novices routinely found places of considerable power within the shipboard hierarchy. This trend was most evident in those semiprivate voyages that had military objectives and, thus, a dual hierarchy of seafaring masters and naval or privateering volunteers and commanders. This displacement of the traditional maritime hierarchy by often unseasoned gentlemen caused many tensions during the war years. This is particularly true of privateering vessels where these gentle-born captains and officers were not bolstered in their often ill-regarded authority by martial law, as they were in the navy. Inexperienced captains and officers, loose discipline, and the lure of plunder were the cause of a great deal of unrest, insubordination, and, in more extreme cases, work stoppage aboard privateering vessels.

The influx of landsmen was not limited to the maritime elite; many "outsiders" took their place alongside the rank and file on privateering vessels. Numbers were an asset on a warship, and because backers were not expected to pay wages in lieu of shares of plunder, landsmen, even unskilled ones, were welcome on privateering voyages. For many seamen, the privateering war against Spain and its allies was one of the few fringe benefits of the war years, and they took part readily in the hope of enriching themselves; having to share their plunder with landsmen who were untutored in the ways of the sea must have been galling. In this sense the seaman's well-established autonomy and freedom from guilds and regulations became a double-edged sword; although it allowed him to be a free agent, the absence of a guild meant that seamen were ill equipped to protect their membership from this intrusion of unskilled labor. The abundance of cheap labour and the lack of protection meant that backers of privateering voyages did not have to offer incentives (for instance, guaranteed wages) to lure men into their employ.

Another negative outcome of the incursion of landsmen into seafaring was that they disrupted the traditional shipboard equilibrium and diminished the seaman's voice in the management of the voyage. The imposition of the dual command structure, the increase in crew sizes, and growing numbers of "outsiders" in the navy, privateering, and "mixed" voyages compromised the status of the seaman within the shipboard community. The new realities of the war years were a setback for those who were accustomed to the more egalitarian traditions of the peacetime forms of employment from which seamen's work culture had sprung. This caused a great deal of shipboard stress between those in authority, particularly those in the military chain of command, who sought to curtail or eradicate these peacetime customs in favor of a new, wartime way of doing things, and seamen who clung tenaciously to the peacetime traditions. In the final analysis, their employment on warships over the course of almost 20 years did not bring about enduring change in seamen's work culture despite the pressure exerted upon it. Seamen chafed at the bit, resistant to the new ways and imbued in the old ways. Seamen's work culture was nothing if not resilient. The centralizing early modern state had met its match.

Undoubtedly, the Crown did impose and intrude upon seamen's work culture, yet its approach to the maritime community overall was an interesting mix of laissez-faire and unabashed interference. First, the Crown promoted the fisheries as a "nursery of seamen" early in Elizabeth's reign, hoping to increase the numbers of skilled seamen who could be impressed into naval service in an emergency. Similarly, the Crown offered bounties to those who built vessels of a certain tonnage that could also be pressed into naval service. The increase in the number of seamen and ships in the late sixteenth century probably owed more to the expansion of the European economy than to the English Crown's encouragement. Nonetheless, the Crown's "blue-water" policy was consistent and deliberate; there is no mistaking its intent.

Although the bounty was given to shipbuilders who built vessels according to the Crown's specifications, there were no such provisions for the caliber of men allowed to practice maritime crafts or, by extension, for those impressed by the Crown. Even when it was apparent that England would go to war with Spain and that the war would be a protracted one, the Crown did not venture into uncharted waters; it made no effort to monitor or improve the quality of those practicing the maritime trades. This is in direct contrast to the Elizabethan state's efforts to begin systematic training of the incipient land forces of the nation. Although the idea had been put forth, the Crown rejected plans for a national training scheme that would ensure that seamen were instructed according to established standards. Instead, the Crown elected to allow the maritime community to train its novices in the ad hoc manner that it had always used. Among experienced seamen, only a tiny proportion had been formally apprenticed; the rest learned and continued to learn through more informal methods of tutelage and "on-the-job" training. While these techniques seem to have served the maritime community fairly well, the Crown had to contend with employees who were accustomed to greater freedoms and looser discipline. If army conscripts of the time could be characterized (with some exaggeration) as cannon fodder and the most expendable elements in society, the naval recruits and conscripts were a trained, integral part of the English economy. This created an almost palpable tension between the Crown as the employer and its employees.

In lieu of a national training program, the Crown could have resorted to training a number of seamen exclusively for careers in the navy. This, of course, implied not only a separate naval caste but a permanent navy as well. Although the idea was put forth, the Crown did not want the long-term responsibility or the financial burden of a large standing navy. While the Crown interfered with seamen's liberties and customs, it hesitated to establish an entirely new relationship with its seamen. Timid of innovation, given to inertia, and fearful of the costs of a permanent navy, the early modern state was willing to rely on the age-old practice of impressment with all the problems that it entailed.

The maritime community was not a force for reform; it, too, shunned change in favor of continuity and did not seek to alter its relationship with the Crown. Naval sea service was to be avoided if possible, but, barring this, seamen submitted to the Crown's terms for their labor. There is no evidence that seamen ever banded together to resist impressment itself. There is, however, ample proof that they did protest when the Crown did not pay them their wages or allow them the essentials to sustain life. Thus, resistance proceeded from situations where the Crown did not live up to its end of the unequal bargain. For the most part, protest was restricted to individuals and relatively small groups (such as a crew). Only in extreme circumstances did seamen band together in larger groups to flex their collective muscle in opposition to the Crown. On these rare occasions seamen formed pressure groups on a temporary basis to draw attention to a specific grievance or set of grievances; they did not form a permanent organization to protect or exert their "rights." Other than those members of the maritime elite who belonged to the Trinity Houses, few seemed to have any interest in establishing a guild or a group that would protect their freedoms and position and monitor their membership. Inertia and a distaste for innovation provide a partial explanation for seamen's reluctance to form some sort of combination; the crux of the matter was that such a group meant unwelcome regulations and encroachment upon their individual liberties. Many seamen were confidently self-assertive in believing that their liberties and customs could be protected without a formal organization constructed for that purpose. Hence, seamen's independence and the strength of their work culture hampered the formation of a trade group, and these fitted nicely into their growing confidence and sense of their own identities.

Several factors defined the seaman's perception of himself. First of all, seamen have always thought of themselves as a group set apart from the land population. It is obvious that they had a very well developed subculture and incredibly strong unifying bonds. Second, the Reformation was a powerful influence. Just as Europe was riven by the splintering of the Roman Catholic Church, so, too, was the European maritime community. Although men of the sea had much in common, religion became a divisive force instead of a unifying one. Protestant seamen sometimes had an ax to grind; as international travelers, a small but sizable number of seamen had been sentenced to death or hard labor by an Inquisition that viewed them as heretics and pirates. This persecution had gone on for many years before the war; open warfare served to bring the rest of England into the seamen's ongoing battle with Counter-Reformation Spain. Although largely economic in nature, this war—as we have seen—had heavy religious overtones for many of the participants. In these circumstances English seamen focused on their differences from Catholic seamen rather than their shared experiences. During the war years, English seamen saw themselves as separate from their land-based countrymen and women, as well as distinct from Catholic seamen, particularly those associated with the Spanish empire, which after 1580 included the two major seafaring nations of Portugal and Spain and all their dependencies. The many successes experienced by English seamen against their enemies fostered a belief that they were not only different but superior.

There is evidence of a strong esprit de corps among the English Protestant maritime community in the late sixteenth century as it confronted a multitude of external challenges. This, I would assert, did not evaporate with the peace settlement of 1604 and the end of both open war with Catholic Europe and state interference. Deep-sea mariners and sailors continued to have a large role in England's prospects in the coming centuries. Furthermore, as Bernard Capp and N.A.M. Rodger have shown, the continuing problems and character of naval seamen's existence did not change dramatically with the passage of time. Even with the introduction of a naval caste and an expanded administration, crew dynamics, authority based on consensus, and seamen's sense of entitlement persisted well past the Elizabethan period.

NOTE

1. Stone, *The Family, Sex and Marriage in England 1500–1800*, 93–119.

Bibliography

MANUSCRIPT SOURCES

Bodleian Library (Oxford). *Rawlinson Ms.* A. 192, A. 171, A. 204 A. 206, C. 340, C. 846

British Library (London). *Lansdowne Ms.* 389

Greater London Record Office (London)

    Archdeaconry Court of Surrey Wills X/32

    Consistory Court of London Wills X/19

    Stepney Parish Baptism Records P93/DUN/X24/66

    Stepney Parish Burial Records P93/DUN/X24/70

    Stepney Parish Marriage Records P93/DUN/X24/68

    Stepney Vestry Book P93/DUN/327

    Whitechapel Burial Records P93/MRY1/X24/90

    Whitechapel Marriage Records P93/MRY1/X24/90

    Whitechapel Parish Baptism Records P93/MRY1/X24/90

    Whitechapel Tithe Collector's Book P93/MRY1/117

    Whitechapel Vestry Memo Book P93/MRY1/90, P93/MRY1/91

Guildhall Library (London).

    Archdeaconry Court of London Wills and Act Books Ms. 9050, 9051

    Boyd's Burial Index (microfilm, Printed Books Reading Room)

    Boyd's Marriage Index (Printed Books Reading Room)

    Commissary Court of London Wills and Act Books Ms. 9171, 9172, 9168

    Dean and Chapter of St. Paul's Wills Ms. 25,626/2, 25,626/3,

    Marriage Licence Allegations in the Registry of the Bishop of London Ms. 10,091/1

St. Botolph Aldgate Baptism and Marriage Records Ms. 9220, 9221, 9223
St. Botolph Aldgate Burial Records Ms. 9222/1
St. Botolph Aldgate Churchwardens' Accounts Ms. 9235/1
St. Botolph Aldgate Parish Clerks' Memo Book Ms. 9234
St. Dunstan's in the East Churchwardens Account Ms. 4887, 4888
St. Dunstan's in the West Churchwardens Account Ms. 2968/1
St. Katherine's by the Tower Baptism, Burial and Marriage Records
Ms. 9659
Public Record Office (London)
Declared Accounts—Pipe Office E 351
High Court of Admiralty (HCA) Acts HCA 3
HCA Copies of Processes HCA 30
HCA Decrees and Sentences HCA 24/52
HCA Examinations HCA 13
HCA Examinations on Commission HCA 13/225
HCA Exemplifications HCA 14
HCA Indictments HCA 1/3
HCA Inquests HCA 1/81
HCA Interrogatories HCA 23
HCA Letters of Marque and Bonds HCA 25
HCA Libels and Miscellaneous HCA 24/51
HCA Miscellanea HCA 30, HCA 1/101
HCA Muniment Books HCA 50
HCA Oyer and Terminer HCA 1
HCA Proceedings HCA 1/4
HCA Prohibitions HCA 30
HCA Vice-Admiralty HCA 49
HCA Warrants HCA 38, 39
King's Rembrances E 101
State Papers (Domestic) Elizabeth I SP 12
Wills from the Prerogative Court of Canterbury PROB 11

PRIMARY SOURCES

An Abstract of All Such Acts of Parliament, Now in Force As Relate to the Admiralty and Navy in England. London: S. Bridge, 1697.
Acts of the Privy Council, vols. XII to XV, ed. John Roche Dasant. Norwich: Her Majesty's Stationery Office, 1899.
Addington, Anthony. *An Essay on Sea-Scurvy.* Reading: C. Micklewright, 1753.
Allegations for Marriage Licences Issued by the Bishop of London 1520–1610, vol. I, extracted by Joseph Lemuel, ed. George Armytage. London: Harleian Society, 1887.
Andrews, Kenneth R., ed. "Appraisements of Elizabethan Privateersmen." *Mariner's Mirror* 37 (1951), 76–79.
———. *English Privateering Voyages to the West Indies 1588–1595.* Cambridge: Cambridge University Press, 1959.
Atkins, John. *The Navy Surgeon.* London: J. Hodges, 1742.

Atkinson, James. *Atkinson's Epitome of the Art of Navigation; or, a Short and Easy Methodical Way to Become a Compleat Navigator*. London, 1714.

Atlas Maritimus & Commercialis; or a General View of the World So Far as It Relates to Trade and Navigation. London: James & John Knapton, William & John Innys, 1728.

Bettesworth, J. *The Seaman's Sure Guide; or, Practical Navigator*. London, 1785.

Blewett, P.R.W. *All Hallows Barking by the Tower—Parish Registers, Baptisms 1558–74*. London: Guildhall Library Printed Books, 1986.

———. *All Hallows Barking by the Tower—Parish Registers, Marriages 1564–74*. London: Guildhall Library Printed Books, 1986.

Bohun, R. *Discourse Concerning the Origine and Properties of Wind*. Oxford: Tho. Bowman, 1671.

Boteler, Nathaniel. *Boteler's Dialogues*, ed. W. G. Perrin. London: Navy Record Society, 1929.

———. *Six Dialogues about Sea-Services*. London: Moses Pitt, 1685.

Camden, William. *William Camden's Annales or the History of the Most Renowned and Victorious Princesse Elizabeth, Late Queen of England*, 3rd ed., trans. R. N. Gent. London: Benjamin Fisher, 1635.

Clark, John. *Observations on the Diseases in Long Voyages to Hot Countries, and Particularly on Those Which Prevail in the East Indies*. London: D. Wilson and G. Nicol, 1773.

Clowes, William. *A Profitable and Necessarie Booke of Obseruations, for all those that are burned with the Flame of Gun Powder, &c. and also for curing of wounds made by Musket and Caliuershot, and other weapons of war commonly vsed at this day both by sea and land, as heerafter shall be declared*. London: Edm. Bollifant, 1596.

———. *A Right Frutefvll and Approved Treatise, for the Artificiall Cure of That Malady Called in Latin Struma, and in English, the Evill, Cured by Kinges and Queenes of England*. London: Edward Allde, 1602.

———. *A Short and Profitable Treatise Touching the Cure of the Diseased Called (Morbus Gallicus), by Vnctions*. London: John Daye, 1579.

A Collection of the Statutes Relating to the Admiralty, Navy, Ships of War, and Incidental Matters; to the 8th Year of King George III. London: Mark Baskett, 1768.

Colson, Nathaniel. *The Mariners New Kalendar*. London: William Mount and Thomas Page, 1741.

Cook, James. *A Voyage towards the South Pole and Round the World (1772–1775)*, vol. I. London: W. Strahan and T. Cadell, 1777.

Crosby, Thomas. *Mariner's Guide: Being a Compleat Treatise of Navigation, Both in Theory and Practice*. London: James Hodges, 1751.

Dalrymple, Alexander. *A Collection of Views of Land in the Indian Navigation—1783*. London: G. Biggs, 1783.

———. *Memoir of a Chart of the East Coast of Arabia*. London: G. Biggs, 1784.

———. *Memoir of the Chart of Natunas, Anambas and Adjacent Islands*. London: G. Biggs, 1786.

Dampier, William. *A Collection of Voyages*. London: James and John Knapton, 1729.

Davis, John. *The Seaman's Secrets (1633)*. New York: Scholars' Facsimiles and
    Reprints, 1992.
The Defeat of the Spanish Armada, vols. I and II, ed. John Knox Laughton. New
    York: Burt Franklin, 1971.
Digges, Thomas. *England's Defence*. London: F. Haley, 1680.
A Discourse of the Commonweal of This Realm of England. Attributed to Sir
    Thomas Smith, ed. Mary Dewar. Charlottesville: Folger Shakespeare Li-
    brary, 1969.
*The Expedition of Sir John Norris and Sir Francis Drake to Spain and Portugal,
    1589*, ed. R. B. Wernham. Aldershot U.K.: Navy Records Society, 1988.
Flavel, John. *Navigation Spiritualized or a New Compass for Seamen, Consisting
    of 32 Points*. Newburyport, Mass.: Edmund M. Blunt, 1796.
Foxe, Luke. *North-West Fox or Fox from the North-West Passage*. London, 1635.
Gouge, William. *Of Domesticall Duties*. London, 1622.
Greenwood, Jonathan. *The Sailing and Fighting Instructions or Signals As They
    Are Observed in the Royal Navy of Great Britain*. London, 1715.
Hakluyt, Richard. *The Principall Navigations, Voyages, and Discoveries of the
    English Nation*, 2 vols. 1589; rpt. London: Hakluyt Society, 1965.
Hanway, Jonas. *A Letter from a Member of the Marine Society Shewing the Gen-
    erosity and Utility of Their Design Addressed to All True Friends of Their
    Country*. London, 1757.
————. *Proposal for County Naval Free Schools, to Be Built on Wastelands*. Lon-
    don, 1783.
————. *The Seaman's Faithful Companion Being Religious and Moral Advice to
    Officers in the Royal Navy, Masters in the Merchant Service, Their Appren-
    tices, and to Seamen in General*. London: John Rivington, 1763.
Hardingham, John. *The Accomplish'd Shipwright and Mariner*. London: John
    Thornton, 1706.
Hardy, John. *A Chronological List of the Captains of His Majesty's Royal Navy
    (1673–1783)*. London: T. Cadell, 1784.
Hawkins, Richard. *The Observations of Sir Richard Hawkins*, ed. James A. Wil-
    liamson. 1622; rpt. London: Argonaut Press, 1933.
*Hawkins' Voyages during the Reigns of Henry VIII, Queen Elizabeth and James
    I*, ed. Clements R. Markham. London: Hakluyt Society, 1878.
*The Health of Seamen: Selections from the Works of Dr. James Lind, Sir Gilbert
    Blane and Dr. Thomas Trotter*, ed. Christopher Lloyd. London: Navy Rec-
    ords Society, 1965.
Hutchinson, William. *A Treatise on Practical Seamanship*. Liverpool: Cowburne,
    1777.
*An Inquiry into the Causes of Our Naval Miscarriages: With Some Thoughts on
    the Interest of This Nation as to a Naval War, and of the Only True Way
    of Manning the Fleet*, 2nd ed. London, 1707.
James, Thomas. *The Strange and Dangerous Voyage of Captain Thomas Iames, in
    His Intended Discouery of the Northwest Passuage into Wherein the Mis-
    eries Indured Both Going, Wintering, Returning, and the Rarities Obserued,
    Both Philosophicall and Mathematicall, Are Related in This Iournall of It*.
    London: Iohn Legatt for John Patridge, 1633.

Kingston upon Thames Register of Apprentices 1563–1713, ed. Anne Daly. Guildford: Surrey Record Society, 1974.

Lind, James. *An Essay on Diseases Incidental to Europeans in Hot Climates with the Method of Preventing Their Fatal Consequences*, 4th ed. London: J. Murray, 1788.

————. *An Essay on the Most Effectual Means of Preserving the Health of Seamen in the Royal Navy and a Dissertation on Fevers and Infection*. London: D. Wilson and G. Nicol, 1774.

Linton, Anthony. *Newes of the Complement of the Art of Navigation and of the Mightie Empire of Cataia*. London: Felix Kyngston, 1609.

London Marriage Licenses 1521–1869, ed. Joseph Foster. London: Bernard Quayvitch, 1887.

Madox, Richard. *An Elizabethan in 1582: The Diary of Richard Madox, Fellow of All Souls*, ed. Elizabeth Story Donno. London: Hakluyt Society, 1976.

The Marriage Registers of St. Dunstan's, Stepney, 3 vols., ed. Thomas Colyer-Fergusson. Canterbury: Cross and Jackman, 1898–1901.

McGowan, A. P. *The Jacobean Commissions of Enquiry 1608 and 1618*, ed. A. P. McGowan. London: Navy Records Society, 1971.

Memorials of Stepney Parish, ed. G. W. Hill and W. H. Frere. Guildford: Billings and Sons, 1890–91.

Millar, John. *Observations on the Management of the Prevailing Diseases in Great Britain*. London: Printed for the author, 1783.

Monson, William. *The Naval Tracts of Sir William Monson*, 6 vols., ed. M. Oppenheim. London: Navy Records Society, 1902–14.

Moore, John Hamilton. *The New Practical Navigator; Being a Complete Epitome of Navigation*, 17th ed. London: J. Johnson et al., 1807.

————. *The Seaman's Complete Daily Assistant and New Mariner's Compass*, 5th ed. London: B. Law et al., 1796.

Morrice, David. *The Young Midshipman's Instructor*. London: Knight & Compton, 1801.

Moutaine, William. *The Practical Sea-Gunner's Companion or, an Introduction to the Art of Gunnery*. London: W. & J. Mount & T. Page, 1747.

————. *The Seaman's Vade-Mecum and Defensive War by Sea*. London: J. Mount, T. Page and W. Mount, 1776.

Narborough, John, Jasmen Tasman, John Wood, and Frederick Marten. *An Account of Several Late Voyages & Discoveries to the South and North*. London: Sam Smith & Benj. Walford, 1694.

Naval Administration 1715–1750, ed. Daniel A. Baugh. London: Navy Records Society, 1977.

Newhouse, Daniel. *The Whole Art of Navigation*, 5th ed. London: T. Page & W. & F. Mount, 1727.

Norwood, Richard. *The Seaman's Practice*. London: Richard Mount, 1694.

O'Beire, Thomas. *Considerations on the Principles of Naval Discipline, and Naval Courts-Martial*, 2nd ed. London: J. Almon and J. Debrett, 1781.

Papers Relating to the Navy during the Spanish War, 1585–87, ed. Julian Corbett. London: Navy Records Society, 1898.

Park, Robert. *The Art of Sea-Fighting in 5 Parts*. London: Richard Mount and Thomas Page, 1706.

Patoun, Archibald. *A Complete Treatise of Practical Navigation Demonstrated for Its First Principles*. London: W. Mount & T. Page et al., 1751.

Pepys' Memoires of the Royal Navy 1679–1688, ed. J. R. Tanner. London: Clarendon Press, 1906.

Pringle, John. *A Discourse upon Some Late Improvements of the Means for Preserving the Health of Mariners*. London: Royal Society, 1776.

A Proposal for the Encouragement of Seamen &c. to Serve More Readily in His Majesty's Navy, for Preventing of Desertion, Supporting Their Wives and Families, and for the Easier and Quieter Government of His Majesty's Ships. London: A. Millar, 1758.

Raleigh, Walter. *Judicious and Select Essayes and Observations*. London: T. W. for Humphrey Mosele, 1650.

———.*The Last Fight of the Revenge*. London: Gibbings and Co., 1908.

———.*The Works of Sir Walter Raleigh*, 8 vols. Oxford: Oxford University Press, 1829.

Recorde, Robert. *The Castle of Knowledge*. London: R. Wolfe, 1556.

Regulations and Instructions Relating to His Majesty's Service at Sea, 2nd ed. London, 1734.

"Report of the Commissioners Appointed to Inquire into the Amount of Booty Taken at Cadiz in 1596." *Archaelogia* 22 (1829), 172–89.

Rowley, William. *Medical Advice, for the Use of the Army and Navy, in the Present American Expedition*. London: William Rowley, 1776.

St. Lo, George. *England's Safety; Or, a Bridle to the French King*. London: William Miller, 1693.

Select Pleas in the Court of Admiralty, vol. II, ed. R. G. Marsden. London: Selden Society, 1897.

Seller, John. *Practical Navigation (1680)*. Delmar, N.Y.: Scholars Facsimiles and Reprints, 1993.

Sinclair, John. *Thoughts on the Naval Strength of the British Empire*. London: T. Cadell, 1782.

Sir Francis Drake's West Indian Voyage 1585–6, ed. Mary Frear Keeler. London: Hakluyt Society, 1981.

Smith, John. *An Accidence or Pathway to Experience Necessary for All Young Seamen, or Those That Are Desirous to Goe to Sea*. London: Jonas Man and Benjamin Fisher, 1626.

———. *A Sea Grammar (with the Plaine Exposition of Smith Accidence for Young Sea-men Enlarged)*. London, 1627.

Some Considerations on the Reasonableness and Necessity of Encreasing and Encouraging the Seamen. London: J. Roberts, 1728.

Spavens, William. *The Seaman's Narrative*. Louth: Sheardown and Son, 1796.

The State of the Navy Consider'd in Relation to the Victualling, Particularly in the Straits, & the West Indies, 2nd ed. London: A. Baldwin, 1699.

State Papers Relating to the Defeat of the Spanish Armada, vols. I and II, 2nd ed., ed. John Knox Laughton. Aldershot, U.K.: Temple Smith for the Navy Records Society, 1987.

Statutes of the Realm, vols. II and IV. London: Dawsons of Pall Mall, 1963.

Steel, David. *The Ship-Master's Assistant and Owner's Manual*, 8th ed. London: Navigation Warehouse, 1799.

——. *Steel's Naval Remembrancer: or the Gentleman's Maritime Chronology of the Various Transactions of the Late War to 1783*. London: Printed for the author, 1784.

Synge, Edward. *An Essay towards Making the Knowledge of Religion Easy to the Meanest Capacity.*

——. *System of Naval Tactics; Combining the Established Theory with General Practice, and Particularly with the Present Practice of the British Navy*. London: David Steel, 1797.

Touch, P. *A Thanksgiving Sermon Preached at St. Lucia the Sunday after the Hurricaine in Oct. 1780 on Board His Majesty's Ship Vengeance*. London: Printed by the author, 1784.

Trinity House of Deptford Transactions, 1609–35, ed. G. G. Harris. London: London Record Society, 1983.

Tudor Economic Documents, 3 vols., ed. R. H. Tawney and E. Power. New York: Barnes and Noble, 1962.

Tudor Royal Proclamations, 3 vols., ed. Paul L. Hughes and James F. Larkin. New Haven, Conn.: Yale University Press, 1964–69.

A Voyage to the Antipodes. London, 1703.

The Voyage of Robert Dudley to the West Indies 1594–95, ed. George F. Warner. 1899; rpt. Nendeln, Leichtenstein: Kraus Reprint for the Hakluyt Society, 1991.

Voyages and Colonising Enterprises of Sir Humphrey Gilbert, 2 vols., ed. D. B. Quinn. London: Hakluyt Society, 1940.

The Voyages and Works of John Davis the Navigator, ed. Albert Hastings Markham. London: Hakluyt Society, 1880.

The Voyages of Captain Luke Foxe of Hull and Capt. Thomas James of Bristol in Search of a North-west Passage in 1631–32, vol. I, ed. Miller Christy. London: Hakluyt Society, 1894.

Wakerly, Andrew. *The Mariner's Compass Rectified*. London: Richard Mount, 1704.

Watson, George. *The Cures of the Diseased in Forraine Attempts of the English Nation*, ed. Charles Singer. 1598; Oxford, 1915.

Wood, John. *The True Honor of Navigation and Navigators or, Holy Meditations for Sea-Men*. London: Felix Kyngston, 1618.

Wright, Edward. *Certaine Errors in Navigation, Arising Either of the Ordinarie Erroneous Making or Vsing of the Sea Chart, Compasse, Crosse Staffe, and Tables of Declination of the Sunne, and Fixed Starres Detected and Corrected*. London: V. Sims, 1599.

Young, John. "Notes on Sea-Service." In William Monson, *The Naval Tracts of Sir William Monson*, Vol. IV, ed. M. Oppenheim. London: Navy Records Society, 1902.

SECONDARY SOURCES

Alsop, J. D. "The Career of William Towerson, Guinea Trader." *International Journal of Maritime History* 4 (1992), 45–82.

——. "From Muscovy to Guinea: English Seamen of the Mid-Sixteenth Century." *Terra Incognita* 19 (1987), 59–61.

———. "A Regime at Sea: The Navy and the 1553 Succession Crisis." *Albion* 24 (1992), 577–90.

———. "Religious Preambles in Early Modern English Wills as Formulae." *Journal of Ecclesiastical History* 40 (1989), 19–27.

———. "Sea Surgeons, Health and England's Maritime Expansion: The West African Trade 1553–1660." *Mariner's Mirror* 76 (1990), 215–20.

——— and K. R. Dick. "The Origin of Public Tendering for Royal Navy Provisions, 1699–1720." *Mariner's Mirror* 80 (1994), 395–402.

Amussen, Susan Dwyer. "Punishment, Discipline, and Power: The Social Meanings of Violence in Early Modern England." *Journal of British Studies* 34 (January 1995), 1–34.

Anderson, Michael. *Approaches to the History of the Western Family 1500–1914.* London: Economic History Society, 1980.

Andrews, Kenneth R. "Christopher Newport of Limehouse, Mariner." *William and Mary Quarterly* 11 (1954), 28–41.

———. *Drake's Voyages: A Re-Assessment of Their Place in Maritime Expansion.* London: Weidenfeld and Nicholson, 1967.

———. *Elizabethan Privateering: English Privateering during the Spanish War 1585–1603.* Cambridge: Cambridge University Press, 1964.

———. "The Elizabethan Seaman." *Mariner's Mirror* 68 (1982), 245–62.

———. *Ships, Money and Politics: Seafaring and Naval Enterprise in the Reign of Charles I.* Cambridge: Cambridge University Press, 1991.

———. "Sir Robert Cecil and Mediterranean Plunder." *Mariner's Mirror* 58 (1972), 513–32.

———. *Trade, Plunder and Settlement: Maritime Enterprise and the Genesis of the British Empire 1480–1630.* Cambridge: Cambridge University Press, 1984.

———. "The Voyage of the *Jaquet* of Falmouth to the West Indies and Newfoundland 1585–86." *Mariner's Mirror* 59 (1973), 101–3.

Appleby, A. B. "Diet in Sixteenth-Century England: Sources, Problems, Possibilities." In *Health, Medicine and Mortality in the Sixteenth Century*, ed. C. Webster. Cambridge: Cambridge University Press, 1979, 97–116.

———. *Famine in Tudor and Stuart England.* Stanford, Calif.: Stanford University Press, 1978.

———. "Nutrition and Disease: The Case of London, 1550–1750." *Journal of Interdisciplinary History* 6 (1975), 1–22.

Appleby, John C. "A Nursery of Pirates: The English Pirate Community in Ireland in the Early Seventeenth Century." *International Journal of Maritime History* 2 (1990), 1–27.

Aries, Philippe. *Centuries of Childhood*, trans. Robert Baldick. New York: Alfred A. Knopf, 1962.

Armstrong, E. "Venetian Despatches of the Armada and Its Results." *The English Historical Review* 12 (1897), 659–78.

Asher, G. M., ed. *Henry Hudson the Navigator.* New York: Burt Franklin, 1860.

Aydelotte, F. "Elizabethan Seamen in Mexico." *American Historical Review* 68 (1943), 1–19.

Baumber, M. L. "An East India Captain: The Early Career of Captain Richard Swanley." *Mariner's Mirror* 53 (1967), 265–79.

Baynham, Henry. *From the Lower Deck.* London: Hutchinson and Co., 1969.

Beier, Lucinda McCray. "The Good Death in Seventeenth-Century England." In *Death, Ritual, and Bereavement,* ed. Ralph Houlbrooke. London: Routledge, 1989, 43–61.

Bellamy, John. *Crime and Public Order in England in the Later Middle Ages.* London: Routledge and Kegan Paul, 1973.

Berckman, Evelyn. *Creators and Destroyers of the English Navy.* London: Hamish Hamilton, 1974.

———. *The Hidden Navy.* London: Hamish Hamilton, 1973.

Bindoff, S. T. *Tudor England.* 1950; rpt. Middlesex, U.K.: Penguin Books, 1983.

Bitterli, Urs. *Cultures in Conflict: Encounters between European and Non-European Cultures, 1492–1800,* trans. Ritchie Robertson. Stanford, Calif.: Stanford University Press, 1989.

Bohstedt, John. *Riots and Community Politics in England and Wales, 1790–1810.* Cambridge, Mass.: Harvard University Press, 1983.

Boulind, Richard. "Shipwreck and Mutiny in Spain's Galleys on the Santo Domingo Station, 1583." *Mariner's Mirror* 58 (1972), 297–330.

———. "Tudor Captains: The Beestons and the Tyrrells." *Mariner's Mirror* 59 (1973), 171–78.

Brenner, R. "The Social Basis of English Commercial Expansion, 1550–1630." *Journal of Economic History* 32 (1972), 361–84.

Bridenbaugh, Carl. *Vexed and Troubled Englishmen 1590–1642.* New York: Oxford University Press, 1968.

British Naval Documents 1204–1960, ed. John B. Hattendorf et al. London: Navy Records Society, 1993.

Brooks, Eric St. John. *Sir Christopher Hatton: Queen Elizabeth's Favorite.* London: Alden Press, 1946.

Brooks, F. W. "A Wage-Scale for Seamen, 1546." *English Historical Review* 60 (1945), 234–46.

Bryant, Arthur. *Freedom's Own Island: A History of Britain and the British People,* vol. 2. 1986; rpt. London: Grafton Books, 1987.

Burg, B. R. *Sodomy and the Pirate Tradition: English Sea Rovers in the Seventeenth-Century Caribbean.* New York: New York University Press, 1983.

Burke, Peter. *Popular Culture in Early Modern Europe.* New York: Harper and Row, 1978.

Burke's Peerage. London: Burke's Peerage, 1967.

Burton, Valerie. "The Myth of Bachelor Jack: Patriarchy and Seafaring Labour." In *Jack Tar in History: Essays in the History of Maritime Life and Labour,* ed. Colin Howell and Richard J. Twomey. Fredericton, N.B.: Acadiensis Press, 1991, 179–98.

Callender, Geoffrey. "Drake and His Detractors." *Mariner's Mirror* 7 (1921), 66–74, 98–105, 142–52.

———. "Fresh Light on Drake." *Mariner's Mirror* 9 (1923), 16–25.

———. "The Naval Campaign of 1587." *History* 3 (1919), 82–91.

———. "The Real Significance of the Armada's Overthrow." *History* 2 (1918), 174–77.

Capp, Bernard. *Cromwell's Navy: The Fleet and the English Revolution 1648–1660*. Oxford: Clarendon Press, 1989.

Carrington, C. E. *The British Overseas: Exploits of a Nation of Shopkeepers*, part I, 2nd ed. Cambridge: Cambridge University Press, 1968.

Cell, Gillian T. *English Enterprise in Newfoundland 1577–1660*. Toronto: University of Toronto Press, 1969.

Chaplin, W. R. "William Rainsborough (1587–1642) and His Associates of the Trinity House." *Mariner's Mirror* 31 (1945), 178–97.

Chaudhuri, K. N. "The East India Company and the Organization of Its Shipping in the Early Seventeenth Century." *Mariner's Mirror* 49 (1963), 27–41.

Christy, Miller. "Queen Elizabeth's Visit to Tilbury in 1588." *English Historical Review* 34 (1919), 43–61.

Cloudsley-Thompson, J. L. *Insects and History*. London: Weidenfeld and Nicholson, 1976.

Clowes, William Laird. "The Elizabethan Navy." In *Social England*, vol. III, ed. H. D. Traill. London: Cassell and Co., 1895, 458–77.

———. *The Royal Navy: A History from the Earliest Times to the Present*, vol. I. London: Sampson, Marston, and Co., 1897.

Coleman, D. C. *The Economy of England*. London: Oxford University Press, 1977.

Collins, Stephen. "British Stepfamily Relationships, 1500–1800." *Journal of Family History* 16 (1991), 331–44.

Collinson, T. B. "A Warning Voice from the Spanish Armada." *Journal of the Royal United Service Institution* 19 (1875), 285–333.

Copeman, W.S.C. *Doctors and Disease in Tudor Times*. London: Dawson's of Pall Mall, 1960.

Corbett, Julian S. *Drake and the Tudor Navy*, 2nd ed., 2 vols. New York: Burt Franklin, 1899.

Cordingly, David. *Under the Black Flag: The Romance and the Reality of Life among the Pirates*. New York: Random House, 1995.

Cox, Jane. *Wills, Inventories and Death Duties: The Records of the Prerogative Court of Canterbury and the Estate Duty Office*. London: Public Records Office, 1988.

Cox, Nancy and Jeff Cox. "Probate Inventories: The Legal Background." Parts 1 and 2 in *Local History* 16 (1984), 133–45, 217–27.

Creighton, Margaret S. "American Mariners and the Rites of Manhood, 1830–1870." In *Jack Tar in History: Essays in the History of Maritime Life and Labour*, ed. Colin Howell and Richard J. Twomey. Fredericton, N.B.: Acadiensis Press, 1991, 143–63.

Cressy, D. "Kinship and Kin Interaction in Early Modern England." *Past and Present* 113 (1986), 38–69.

———. *Literacy and the Social Order: Reading and Writing in Tudor and Stuart England*. Cambridge: Cambridge University Press, 1980.

Croft, Pauline. "English Mariners Trading to Spain and Portugal, 1558–1625." *Mariner's Mirror* 69 (1983), 253.

Cruickshank, C. G. *Elizabeth's Army*, 2nd ed. London: Oxford University Press, 1966.

Cuellar, Francisco. *A Story of the Spanish Armada*. Belfast: Athol Books, 1988.

Davies, C.S.L. "The Administration of the Royal Navy under Henry VIII: The Origins of the Navy Board." *The English Historical Review* 80 (1965), 268–88.

Davies, Margaret Gay. *The Enforcement of English Apprenticeship: A Study in Applied Mercantilism 1563–1642*. Cambridge, Mass.: Harvard University Press, 1956.

Davis, Natalie Zemon. "The Reasons of Misrule: Youth Groups and Charivaris in Sixteenth-Century France." *Past and Present* 50 (1971), 41–75.

Davis, Ralph. "England and the Mediterranean, 1570–1670." In *Essays in the Economic and Social History of Tudor and Stuart England*, ed. F. J. Fisher. Cambridge: Cambridge University Press, 1961, 117–37.

———. *The Rise of the English Shipping Industry in the Seventeenth and Eighteenth Centuries*. 1962; rpt. Newton Abbott, U.K.: David and Charles, 1972.

Dekker, Rudolf. "Labour Conflicts and Working-Class Culture in Early Modern Holland." *International Review of Social History* 35 (1990), 377–420.

Dietz, Brian. "The Royal Bounty and English Merchant Shipping in the Sixteenth and Seventeenth Centuries." *Mariner's Mirror* 77 (1991), 5–20.

Dixon, C. H. "Seamen and the Law: An Examination of the Impact of Legislation on the British Merchant Seamen's Lot, 1588–1918." Ph.D. diss., University College, London, 1981.

Dobson, C. R. *Masters and Journeymen: A Prehistory of Industrial Relations 1717–1800*. London: Croom Helm, 1980.

Duffy, Michael. "The Foundations of British Naval Power." In *The Military Revolution and the State, 1500–1800*, ed. Michael Duffy. Exeter: University of Exeter, 1980, 49–89.

Dyer, Florence E. "The Elizabethan Sailorman." *Mariner's Mirror* 10 (1924), 133–46.

Elliot, Vivien Brodsky. "Single Women in the London Marriage Market: Age, Status and Mobility, 1598–1619." In *Marriage and Society: Studies in the Social History of Marriage*, ed. R. B. Outhwaite. London: Europa Publications, 1981, 81–100.

Elton, G. R. *England under the Tudors*. 1955; rpt. London: Methuen, 1974.

Ewen, C. L'Estrange. "Organized Piracy round England in the Sixteenth Century." *Mariner's Mirror* 35 (1949), 29–42.

Farrant, John H. "The Rise and Decline of a South Coast Seafaring Town: Brighton, 1550–1750." *Mariner's Mirror* 71 (1985), 59–76.

Fernadez-Armesto, Felipe. "Armada Myths: The Formative Phase." In *God's Obvious Design: Papers for the Spanish Armada Symposium, Sligo, 1988*, ed. P. Gallagher and D. W. Cruickshank. London: Tamesis Books, 1990, 19–40.

———. *The Spanish Armada*. Oxford: Oxford University Press, 1988.

Fingard, Judith. *Jack in Port*. Toronto: University of Toronto Press, 1982.

Finlay, Roger A. P. "Population and Fertility in London 1586–1650." *Journal of Family History* 4 (1979), 26–35.

Flandrin, Jean-Louis. *Families in Former Times: Kinship, Household and Sexuality*, trans. Richard Southern. Cambridge: Cambridge University Press, 1979.

Flinn, M. W. "The Stabilisation of Mortality in Pre-Industrial Western Europe." *Journal of European Economic History* 3 (1974), 285–318.

Froude, James Anthony. *The Spanish Story of the Armada*. New York: Charles Scribner's Sons, 1892.

Fry, John, ed. *Seafaring in the Sixteenth Century*. San Francisco: Mellen Research University, 1991.

George, Timothy. "War and Peace in the Puritan Tradition." *Church History* 53 (1984), 492–503.

Gilbert, Arthur. "Buggery and the British Navy, 1700–1861." *Journal of Social History* 10 (1976), 72–98.

Glasgow, Tom (Jr.). "List of Ships in the Royal Navy from 1539 to 1588—The Navy from Its Infancy to the Defeat of the Spanish Armada." *Mariner's Mirror* 56 (1970), 299–307.

———. "Maturing of Naval Administration 1556–1564." *Mariner's Mirror* 56 (1970), 3–26.

———. "Vice Admiral Woodhouse and Shipkeeping in the Tudor Navy." *Mariner's Mirror* 63 (1977), 253–63.

Goldingham, C. S. "The Expedition to Portugal, 1589." *Journal of the Royal United Service Institution* 63 (1918), 469–78.

Gooddy, W. "Neurological Factors in Decision-Making." In *Starving Sailors*, ed. J. Watt, E. J. Freeman, and W. F. Bynum. Greenwich: National Maritime Museum, 1981, 187–98.

Goodman, W. L. "Bristol Apprentice Register 1532–1658: A Selection of Enrolments of Mariners." *Mariner's Mirror* 60 (1974), 27–31.

Graham, Winston. *The Spanish Armadas*. London: Collins, 1972.

Hainsworth, Roger and Christine Churches. *The Anglo-Dutch Naval Wars 1652–1674*. Stroud: Sutton Publishing, 1998.

Hair, P.E.H. "The Experience of the Sixteenth-Century English Voyages to Guinea." *Mariners Mirror* 83 (1997), 3–13.

———. "Protestants as Pirates, Slavers, and Proto-missionaries: Sierra Leone 1568 and 1582." *Journal of Ecclesiastical History* 21 (1970), 203–24.

——— and J. D. Alsop. *English Seamen and Traders in Guinea 1553–1565: The New Evidence of Their Wills*. Lewiston: Edwin Mellen Press, 1992.

Hale, J. R. *Renaissance Exploration*. New York: W. W. Norton and Co., 1968.

Hale, John. "Incitement to Violence? English Divines on the Theme of War, 1578 to 1631." *Renaissance War Studies* (1983), 487–517.

Hannay, David. "Raleigh's Orders." *Mariner's Mirror* 3 (1913), 212–15.

Harris, G. G. *The Trinity House of Deptford, 1514–1660*. London: Athlone Press, 1965.

Hassell Smith, A. "Labourers in Late Sixteenth-Century England: A Case Study from North Norfolk [Part II]." *Continuity and Change* 4 (1989), 367–94.

Hay, Douglas. "Property, Authority and the Criminal Law." In *Albion's Fatal Tree: Crime and Society in Eighteenth-Century England*, ed. Douglas Hay et al. New York: Pantheon Books, 1975, 17–63.

Herrup, Cynthia B. "Law and Morality in Seventeenth-Century England." *Past and Present* 106 (1985), 102–23.

Hill, L. M. *Bench and Bureaucracy: The Public Career of Sir Julius Caesar, 1580–1636*. Stanford, Calif.: Stanford University Press, 1988.

Hobsbawm, E. J. "Social Criminality." *Bulletin of the Society for the Study of Labour History* 25 (1972), 1–8.

Holmes, R. C. "Sea Fare." *Mariner's Mirror* 35 (1949), 139–45.

Houlbrooke, Ralph. "Death, Church, and Family in England between the Late Fifteenth and the Early Eighteenth Centuries." In *Death, Ritual, and Bereavement*, ed. Ralph Houlbrooke. London: Routledge, 1989, 25–42.

———. *The English Family 1450–1700*. London: Longman Group, 1984.

———. "The Making of Marriage in Mid-Tudor England: Evidence from the Records of Matrimonial Contract Litigation." *Journal of Family History* 10 (1985), 339–53.

Houston, Rab. "Coal, Class and Culture: Labour Relations in a Scottish Mining Community, 1650–1750." *Social History* 8 (1983), 1–18.

Hudson, Geoffrey L. "Ex-Servicemen, War Widows and the English County Pension Scheme, 1593–1679." Ph.D. diss., Oxford University, 1995.

———. "Negotiating for Blood Money: War Widows and the Courts in Seventeenth-Century England." In *Women, Crime and the Courts in Early Modern England*, ed. Jenny Kermode and Garthine Walker. London: UCL Press, 1994, 146–69.

———. "Negotiating for Relief: Strategies Used by Victims of War in Early Seventeenth Century England." Unpublished paper.

———. "The Origins of State Benefits for Ex-Servicemen in Elizabethan England." Unpublished paper.

Hume, Martin A. S. "Some Survivors of the Armada in Ireland." *Transactions of the Royal Historical Society* 11 (1897), 41–66.

Ingram, Martin. "Ridings, Rough Music and the 'Reform of Popular Culture' in Early Modern England." *Past and Present* 105 (1984), 79–113.

———. "Spousal Litigation in the English Ecclesiastical Courts c. 1350–c. 1640." In *Marriage and Society: Studies in the Social History of Marriage*, ed. R. B. Outhwaite. London: Europa Publications, 1981, 35–57.

Innes, Joanna and John Styles. "The Crime Wave: Recent Writing on Crime and Criminal Justice in Eighteenth-Century England." *Journal of British Studies* 25 (1986), 380–435.

Jeannin, Pierre. "The Sea-borne and Overland Trade Routes of Northern Europe in the XVIth and XVIIth Centuries." *Journal of European Economic History* 11 (1982), 5–59.

Jenner, G. "A Spanish Account of Drake's Voyages." *English Historical Review* 16 (1901), 46–68.

Jones, Gareth Stedman. *Outcast London: A Study in the Relationship between Classes in Victorian Society*. Oxford: Clarendon Press, 1971.

Jones, J. R. *The Anglo-Dutch Wars of the Seventeenth Century*. London: Longman, 1996.

Jorgensen, Paul A. "Elizabethan Religious Literature for Time of War." *Huntingdon Library Quarterly* 37 (1973–74), 1–17.

———. "Moral Guidance and Religious Encouragement for the Elizabethan Soldier." *Huntingdon Library Quarterly* 13 (1950), 241–59.

Joyce, Patrick. *Work, Society and Politics: The Culture of the Factory in Later Victorian England*. New Brunswick, N.J.: Rutgers University Press, 1980.

Jutte, Robert. "Poor Relief and Social Discipline in Sixteenth-Century Europe." *European Studies Review* 11 (1981), 25–52.

Kassmaul, Ann. *Servants in Husbandry in Early Modern England*. Cambridge: Cambridge University Press, 1981.

Keevil, J. J. *Medicine and the Navy 1200–1900*, vol. I. Edinburgh: E. and S. Livingstone, 1957.

Kelsey, Harry. *Sir Francis Drake: The Queen's Pirate*. New Haven, Conn.: Yale Nota Bene, 2000.

Kepler, J. S. "The Maximum Duration of Trading Voyages from Various Parts of Europe to London, c. 1577." *Mariner's Mirror* 65 (1979), 265–68.

Ker, W. P. "The Spanish Story of the Armada." *The Scottish Historical Review* 17 (1920), 165–76.

Laffin, John. *Jack Tar: The Story of the British Sailor*. London: Cassel and Co., 1969.

Laslett, Peter. *Family Life and Illicit Love in Earlier Generations: Essays in Historical Sociology*. Cambridge: Cambridge University Press, 1977.

———. *The World We Have Lost—Further Explored*, 3rd ed. London: Methuen, 1983.

Laslett, Peter and R. Wall, eds. *Household and Family in Past Times*. Cambridge: Cambridge University Press, 1972.

Laughton, L. G. Carr. "The Navy." In *Shakespeare's England*, vol. I. 1916; rpt. Oxford: Clarendon Press, 1950, 142–66.

———. "The Preamble to the Articles of War." *Mariner's Mirror* 7 (1921), 82–86.

———. "Shantying and Shanties." *Mariner's Mirror* 9 (1923), 52–55, 66–74.

Lavery, Brian. *The Colonial Merchantman Susan Constant 1605*. Annapolis: Naval Institute Press, 1988.

Le Goff, Jacques. *Medieval Civilization 400–1500*, trans. Julia Barrow. Oxford: Basil Blackwell, 1988.

———. *Time, Work and Culture in the Middle Ages*, trans. Arthur Goldhammer. Chicago: University of Chicago Press, 1980.

Levine, David. *Family Formation in an Age of Nascent Capitalism*. New York: Academic Press, 1977.

Levine, David and Keith Wrightson. *The Making of an Industrial Society Whickham 1560–1765*. Oxford: Clarendon Press, 1991.

Lewis, Michael. *The History of the British Navy*. Fair Lawn, N.J.: Essential Books, 1959.

———. *A Social History of the Navy 1793–1815*. London: George Allen and Unwin, 1960.

Lloyd, Christopher. *The British Seaman 1200–1860*. London: Collins, 1968.

———. *The Nation and the Navy*. 1954; rpt. London: Cresset Press, 1961.

———. "Victualling of the Fleet in the Eighteenth and Nineteenth Centuries." In *Starving Sailors*, ed. J. Watt, E. J. Freeman, and W. F. Bynum. Greenwich: National Maritime Museum, 1981, 9–16.

Loades, David M. *The Tudor Navy: An Administrative, Political and Military History*. Aldershot, U.K.: Scolar Press, 1992.

MacCarthy, Patrick Brian. "Her Majesty's Will and Pleasure: Volume XI of an Extensive Reconstruction, 1599–1601." *Mariner's Mirror* 43 (1957), 217–24.

———. "An Unsafe Treaty: How a Successful War Was Followed by an Injurious Peace, 1601–1618." *Mariner's Mirror* 44 (1958), 314–19.

Manwaring, G. E. "The Dress of the British Seamen." *Mariner's Mirror* 9 (1923), 162–73, 322–32.

Marcus, G. J. *A Naval History of England vol. I: The Formative Years.* London: Longmans, Green, and Co., 1961.

Marsden, R. G. "Early Prize Jurisdiction and Prize Law." *English Historical Review* 24 (1909), 675–97.

———. "Early Prize Jurisdiction and Prize Law." *English Historical Review* 25 (1910), 243–63.

———. "Early Prize Jurisdiction and Prize Law." *English Historical Review* 26 (1911), 34–56.

Mathew, David. "The Cornish and Welsh Pirates in the Reign of Elizabeth." *English Historical Review* 39 (1924), 337–48.

Mattingly, Garrett. *The Armada.* Boston: Houghton, Mifflin Co., 1959.

Maxwell, Susan. "Henry Seckford: Sixteenth-Century Merchant, Courtier and Privateer." *Mariner's Mirror* 82 (1996), 387–97.

McCracken, Grant. "The Exchange of Children in Tudor England: An Anthropological Phenomenon in Historical Context." *Journal of Family History* 8 (1983), 303–13.

McGrath, Patrick. "Merchant Shipping in the Seventeenth Century: The Evidence of the Bristol Deposition Books," Part II. *Mariner's Mirror* 41 (1955), 23–37.

McGurk, J.J.N. "A Levy of Seamen in the Cinque Ports, 1602." *Mariner's Mirror* 66 (1980), 137–44.

———. "Rochester and the Irish Levy of October 1601." *Mariner's Mirror* 74 (1988), 57–66.

McIntosh, Majorie K. "Servants and the Household Unit in an Elizabethan English Community." *Journal of Family History* 9 (1984), 3–23.

McLaughlin, Eve. *Wills before 1858.* 1979; rpt. Birmingham: Federation of Family History Societies, 1989.

Mead, Hilary P. *Trinity House.* London: Sampson, Low, Marston, and Co., 1947.

Meyerstein, E.H.W. "Troubles of Devonshire Mariners in Spanish Ports, 1550." *Mariner's Mirror* 35 (1949), 146–50.

Milford, Elizabeth. "The Navy at Peace—The Activities of the Early Jacobean Navy: 1603–1618." *Mariner's Mirror* 76 (1990), 23–36.

Milton-Thompson, G. J. "Two Hundred Years of the Sailor's Diet." In *Starving Sailors: The Influence of Nutrition upon Naval and Maritime History,* ed. J. Watt, E. J. Freeman, and W. F. Bynum. Greenwich: National Maritime Museum, 1981, 27–34.

Mollat, Michel. "The French Maritime Community—A Slow Progress up the Social Scale from the Middle Ages to the Sixteenth Century." *Mariner's Mirror* 69 (1983), 115–28.

Moore, Joseph Price. "The Greatest Enormity That Prevails: Direct Democracy and Workers' Self-Management in the British Naval Mutinies of 1797." In *Jack Tar in History: Essays in the History of Maritime Life and Labour,* ed. Colin Howell and Richard J. Twomey. Fredericton, N.B.: Acadiensis Press, 1991, 76–101.

Newman, Simon P. "Reading the Bodies of Early American Seafarers." *The William and Mary Quarterly* 55 (January 1998), 59–82.

Oppenheim, M. *A History of the Administration of the Royal Navy and of Merchant Shipping in Relation to the Navy, 1509–1660.* 1896; rpt. Hamden, Conn.: Shoe String Press, 1961.

———. "The Royal and Merchant Navy under Elizabeth." *English Historical Review* 6 (1891), 465–81.

Outhwaite, R. B. "Dearth, the English Crown and the 'Crisis of the 1590s.' " In *The European Crisis of the 1590s: Essays in Comparative History*, ed. Peter Clark. London: George Allen and Unwin, 1985, 23–43.

Padfield, Peter. *Armada.* London: Victor Gollancz, 1988.

Parker, Geoffrey. *The Army of Flanders and the Spanish Road 1567–1659.* Cambridge: Cambridge University Press, 1972.

Parry, J. H. *The Age of Reconnaissance*, 2nd ed. London: Weidenfeld and Nicholson, 1966.

———. "The Dreadnought Revolution of Tudor England." *Mariner's Mirror* 82 (1996), 269–300.

Pelling, Margaret. "Occupational Diversity: Barber-surgeons and the Trades of Norwich, 1550–1640." *Bulletin of the History of Medicine* 56 (1982), 484–511.

———. "Old People and Poverty in Early Modern Towns." *The Society for the Social History of Medicine Bulletin* 34 (1984), 42–47.

Perrin, W. G. "The Lord High Admiral and the Board of Admiralty." *Mariner's Mirror* 12 (1926), 178–97.

Pike, Ruth. "Penal Servitude in Early Modern Spain: The Galleys." *Journal of European Economic History* 11 (1982), 197–217.

Pollitt, Ronald. "Bureaucracy and the Armada: The Administrator's Battle." *Mariner's Mirror* 60 (1974), 119–32.

———. "John Hawkins's Troublesome Voyages: Merchants, Bureaucrats, and the Origin of the Slave Trade." *Journal of British Studies* 12 (1973), 26–40.

Porter, Roy. "Death and Doctors in Georgian England." In *Death, Ritual, and Bereavement*, ed. Ralph Houlbrooke. London: Routledge, 1989, 77–94.

———. *Disease, Medicine and Society in England 1550–1860.* Basingstoke: Macmillan Education, 1987.

———. "The Patient's View: Doing Medical History from Below." *Theory and Society* 14 (1985), 175–98.

Powell, Isobell G. "The Early Naval Lieutenant." *Mariner's Mirror* 9 (1923), 358–63.

———. "Early Ship Surgeons." *Mariner's Mirror* 10 (1923), 11–15.

———. "Seventeenth Century 'Profiteering' in the Royal Navy." *Mariner's Mirror* 7 (1921), 243–50.

———. " 'Shipkeepers' and Minor Officers Serving at Sea in the Early Stuart Navy." *Mariner's Mirror* 10 (1924), 156–72.

Prall, Stuart E. *Church and State in Tudor and Stuart England.* Arlington Heights, Ill.: Harlan Davidson, 1993.

Quinn, David B. "Christopher Newport in 1590." *The North Carolina Review* 29 (1952), 305–16.

Rappaport, Steve. "Social Structure and Mobility in Sixteenth-Century London: Part I." *London Journal* 9 (1983), 107–35.

Renard, G. and G. Weulersse. *Life and Work in Modern Europe.* 1926; rpt. London: Routledge and Kegan Paul, 1968.

Richmond, Herbert. *The Navy as an Instrument of Policy 1558–1727,* ed. E. A. Hughes. Cambridge: Cambridge University Press, 1953.

Ridley, Jaspar. *The Tudor Age.* London: Constable, 1988.

Roberts, Michael. "Waiting upon Chance: English Hiring Fairs and Their Meanings from the 14th to the 20th Century." *Journal of Historical Sociology* 1 (1988), 119–60.

Roberts, R. S. "The Personnel and Practice of Medicine in Tudor and Stuart England." *Medical History* 6 (1962), 363–82.

———. "The Personnel and Practice of Medicine in Tudor and Stuart England Part II." *Medical History* 8 (1964), 217–34.

Robinson, Gregory. "A Forgotten Life of Sir Francis Drake." *Mariner's Mirror* 7 (1921), 10–18.

———. "The Trial and Death of Thomas Doughty." *Mariner's Mirror* 7 (1921), 271–82.

Rodger, N.A.M. "The Development of Broadside Gunnery." *Mariner's Mirror* 82 (1996), 301–24.

———. *The Wooden World: An Anatomy of the Georgian Navy.* 1986; rpt. Glasgow: Fontana Press, 1990.

Rogers, Nicholas. "Liberty Road: Opposition to Impressment in Britain during the American War of Independence." In *Jack Tar in History: Essays in the History of Maritime Life and Labour,* ed. Colin Howell and Richard J. Twomey. Fredericton, N.B.: Acadiensis Press, 1991, 53–75.

Rose, J. Holland. "Was the Failure of the Spanish Armada Due to Storms?" *Proceedings of the British Academy* (1936), 207–44.

Rowse, A. L. *The England of Elizabeth.* 1950; rpt. London: Cardinal, 1973.

———. *The Expansion of Elizabethan England.* 1955; rpt. London: Reprint Society, 1957.

Ruddock, Alwyn A. "The Trinity House at Deptford in the Sixteenth Century." *English Historical Review* 65 (1950), 458–76.

Rule, John. *The Experience of Labour in Eighteenth-Century English Industry.* New York: St. Martin's Press, 1981.

Rule, Margaret. *The Mary Rose.* 1982; rpt. London: Conway Maritime Press, 1986.

———. *The Mary Rose: A Guide.* Portsmouth: Mary Rose Trust, 1986.

Rushton, Peter. "Property, Power and Family Networks: The Problem of Disputed Marriage in Early Modern England." *Journal of Family History* 11 (1986), 205–19.

Russell-Wood, A.J.R. "Seamen Ashore and Afloat: The Social Environment of the *Carreira Da India,* 1550–1750." *Mariner's Mirror* 69 (1983), 35–53.

Ruthven, J. F. "Wars by Land and Sea, 1588–1592: Tenison's *Elizabethan England,* vol. VIII." *Mariner's Mirror* 35 (1949), 240–45.

Scammell, G. V. "The English in the Atlantic Islands c. 1450–1650." *Mariner's Mirror* 72 (1986), 295–317.

———. "European Seamanship in the Great Age of Discovery." *Mariner's Mirror* 68 (1982), 357–76.

———. "Manning the English Merchant Service in the Sixteenth Century." *Mariner's Mirror* 56 (1970), 131–54.

————. "Shipowning in the Economy and Politics of Early Modern England."
    Historical Journal 15 (1972), 385–407.
————. *Ships, Oceans and Empire*. Aldershot, U.K.: Variorum, 1995.
————. "The Sinews of War: Manning and Provisioning English Fighting Ships c.
    1550–1650." *Mariner's Mirror* 73 (1987), 351–67.
Scarisbrick, J. J. *The Reformation and the English People*. Oxford: Basil Blackwell,
    1984.
Schofield, Roger. "English Marriage Patterns Revisited." *Journal of Family History*
    10 (1988), 2–20.
————. "The Impact of Scarcity and Plenty on Population Change in England,
    1541–1871." *Journal of Interdisciplinary History* 14 (1983), 265–91.
Senior, W. "Drake and the Suit of John Doughty." *Mariner's Mirror* 7 (1921),
    291–97.
————. "The Master-Mariner's Authority." *The Law Quarterly Review* 34 (1918),
    347–56.
Sharman, Ivan M. "Vitamin Requirements of the Human Body." In *Starving Sail-
    ors: The Influence of Nutrition upon Naval and Maritime History*, ed. J.
    Watt, E. J. Freeman, and W. F. Bynum. Greenwich: National Maritime Mu-
    seum, 1981, 17–26.
Sharp, B. "Popular Protest in Seventeenth-Century England." In *Popular Culture
    in Seventeenth-Century England*, ed. Barry Reay. London: Croom Helm,
    1985, 271–308.
Sharpe, J. A. "Such Disagreement betwyx Neighbours: Litigation and Human Re-
    lations in Early Modern England." In *Disputes and Settlements: Law and
    Human Relations in the West*, ed. John Bossy. Cambridge: Cambridge Uni-
    versity Press, 1983, 167–88.
Simon, Joan. *Education and Society in Tudor England*. Cambridge: Cambridge
    University Press, 1966.
Slack, Paul. "Books of Orders: The Making of English Social Policy, 1577–1631."
    Transactions of the Royal Historical Society 30 (1980), 1–22.
————, ed. *Rebellion, Popular Protest and the Social Order in Early Modern En-
    gland*. Cambridge: Cambridge University Press, 1984.
Smith, Lacey Baldwin. *Elizabeth Tudor*. Boston: Little, Brown, and Co., 1975.
Smith, R. M. "The Structural Dependency of the Elderly: A Twentieth-Century Cre-
    ation?" *The Society for the Social History of Medicine Bulletin* 34 (1984),
    35–41.
Smith, Steven R. "The Ideal and Reality: Apprentice–Master Relationships in
    Seventeenth-Century London." *History of Education Quarterly* 21 (1981),
    449–58.
————. "The London Apprentices as Seventeenth-Century Adolescents." *Past and
    Present* 61 (1973), 149–61.
Southey, Robert. *English Seamen: Howard, Clifford, Hawkins, Drake and Caven-
    dish*. London: Methuen and Co., 1895.
Spufford, Margaret. "First Steps in Literacy: The Reading and Writing Experiences
    of the Humblest Seventeenth Century Spiritual Autobiographers." *Social
    History* 4 (1979), 407–35.
Stephen, Leslie and Sidney Lee. *Dictionary of National Biography, Vol. II*. Oxford:
    Oxford University Press, 1917.

Stone, Lawrence. *The Family, Sex and Marriage in England 1500–1800*. New York: Harper & Row, 1977.

Taylor, Gordon. *The Sea Chaplains: A History of the Chaplains of the Royal Navy*. Oxford: Oxford Illustrated Press, 1978.

Thomas, David A. *The Illustrated Armada Handbook*. London: Harrap, 1988.

Thomas, E. G. "The Old Poor Law and Maritime Apprenticeship." *Mariner's Mirror* 63 (1977), 153–61.

———. "The Old Poor Law and Medicine." *Medical History* 24 (1980), 1–19.

Thomas, Keith. "Age and Authority in Early Modern England." *Proceedings of the British Academy* 62 (1976), 205–48.

Thompson, E. P. *Customs in Common*. London: Merlin Press, 1991.

———. "Eighteenth-Century English Society: Class Struggle without Class?" *Social History* 3 (1978), 133–65.

———. *The Making of the English Working Class*, 3rd ed. Harmondsworth, Middlesex: Penguin Books, 1984.

———. "Patrician Society, Plebeian Culture." *Journal of Social History* 7 (1975), 382–405.

———. "Time, Work-discipline and Industrial Capitalism." *Past and Present* 38 (1967), 56–97.

Tilly, Charles. "Food Supply and Public Order in Modern Europe." In *The Formation of National States in Western Europe*, ed. Charles Tilly. Princeton, N.J.: Princeton University Press, 1975, 380–455.

Traill, H. D., ed. *Social England*, vol. III. London: Cassell and Co., 1895.

Trevelyan, G. M. *History of England*, vol. II. New York: Doubleday and Co., 1953.

Unger, R. W. "The Tonnage of Europe's Merchant Fleets 1300–1800." *The American Neptune* 52 (1992), 247–61.

Unwin, Rayner. *The Defeat of John Hawkins*. Middlesex: Penguin Books, 1960.

Vann, R. T. "Wills and the Family in an English Town: Banbury, 1550–1800." *Journal of Family History* 4 (1979), 346–67.

Vines, Alice Gilmore. *Neither Fire nor Steel: Sir Christopher Hatton*. Chicago: Nelson-Hall, 1978.

Wall, Richard. "Beyond the Household: Marriage, Household Formation and the Role of Kin and Neighbours." *International Review of Social History* 44 (1999), 55–61.

Walter, John and Roger Schofield. "Famine, Disease and Crisis Mortality in Early Modern Society." In *Famine, Disease and the Social Order in Early Modern Society*, ed. John Walter and Roger Schofield. Cambridge: Cambridge University Press, 1989, 1–74.

———. "The Social Economy of Dearth." In *Famine, Disease and the Social Order in Early Modern Society*, ed. John Walter and Roger Schofield. Cambridge: Cambridge University Press, 1989, 75–128.

Walter, John and Keith Wrightson. "Dearth and the Social Order in Early Modern England." *Past and Present* 71 (1976), 22–42.

Waters, David W. *The Art of Navigation in England in Elizabethan and Early Stuart Times*. London: Hollis and Carter, 1958.

———. "The Elizabethan Navy and the Armada Campaign." *Mariner's Mirror* 35 (1949), 90–138.

———. "Limes, Lemons and Scurvy in Elizabethan and Early Stuart Times." *Mariner's Mirror* 41 (1955), 167–69.

Watt, James. "Some Consequences of Nutritional Disorders in Eighteenth Century British Circumnavigations." In *Starving Sailors: The Influence of Nutrition upon Naval and Maritime History*, ed. J. Watt, E. J. Freeman, and W. F. Bynum. Greenwich: National Maritime Museum, 1981, 51–72.

———. "Surgeons of the *Mary Rose*: The Practice of Surgery in Tudor England." *Mariner's Mirror* 69 (1983), 3–17.

Wear, Andrew. "Caring for the Sick Poor in St. Bartholomew's Exchange: 1580–1676." In *Living and Dying in London*, ed. W. F. Bynum and Roy Porter. London: Wellcome Institute for the History of Medicine, 1991, 41–60.

Webb, John. "Apprenticeship in the Maritime Occupations at Ipswich, 1596–1651." *Mariner's Mirror* 46 (1960), 29–34.

———. "William Sabyn of Ipswich: An Early Tudor Sea-Officer and Merchant." *Mariner's Mirror* 41 (1955), 209–21.

Webster, Charles. "Mortality Crises and Epidemic Disease in England 1485–1610." In *Health, Medicine and Mortality in the Sixteenth Century*, ed. Charles Webster. Cambridge: Cambridge University Press, 1979, 9–49.

Weir, David R. "Rather Never than Late: Celibacy and Age at Marriage in English Cohort Fertility, 1591–1871." *Journal of Family History* 9 (1984), 340–54.

White-Patarino, Vincent. "Living outside the Ordered Society: Discipline, Violence, and the Shipboard Culture of English Sailors, 1550–1688." Unpublished paper, 1997.

Whitlock, Peter. *At the Time of the Mary Rose: The King's Ships and the King's Men*. Portsmouth: Mary Rose Society, 1988.

Wiener, Carol. "The Beleaguered Isle: A Study of Elizabethan and Early Jacobean Anti-Catholicism." *Past and Present* 51 (1971), 27–62.

Williams, N. J. *The Maritime Trade of the East Anglian Ports, 1550–1590*. Oxford: Clarendon Press, 1988.

Williams, Neville. *The Sea Dogs: Privateers, Plunder and Piracy in the Elizabethan Age*. New York: Macmillan, 1975.

Williams, Penry. *The Tudor Regime*. 1979; rpt. Oxford: Clarendon Press, 1983.

Woodward, Donald. "Ships, Masters and Shipowners of the Wirral 1550–1650." *Mariner's Mirror* 63 (1977), 233–47.

Wrightson, Keith. "Alehouses, Order and Reformation in Rural England, 1590–1660." In *Popular Culture and Class Conflict 1590–1914: Explorations in the History of Labour and Leisure*, ed. Eileen Yeo and Stephen Yeo. Sussex: Harvester Press, 1981, 1–27.

———. *English Society 1580–1680*. London: Hutchinson, 1982.

———. "Household and Kinship in Sixteenth-Century England." *History Workshop* 12 (1981), 28–45.

Wrightson, Keith and David Levine. *Poverty and Piety in an English Village: Terling, 1525–1700*. London: Academic Press, 1979.

Wrigley, E. A. "Family Limitation in Pre-Industrial England." *Economic History Review* 19 (1966), 82–109.

Wroth, Lawrence C. "An Elizabethan Merchant and Man of Letters." *Huntington Library Quarterly* 17 (1954), 299–314.

Yarbrough, Anne. "Apprentices as Adolescents in Sixteenth Century Bristol." *Journal of Social History* 13 (1979), 67–81.

Youings, Joyce. "Raleigh's Country and the Sea." *Proceedings of the British Academy* 75 (1989), 267–90.

———, ed. *Raleigh in Exeter 1985: Privateering and Colonisation in the Reign of Elizabeth I.* Exeter: University of Exeter, 1985.

———. *Sixteenth-Century England.* 1984; rpt. London: Penguin Books, 1988.

Index

About the Author

CHERYL A. FURY teaches British and European History at the University of New Brunswick and St. Stephen's University. Born and raised in Fredericton, New Brunswick, she attended the University of New Brunswick, obtaining a B.A. (English and History Honours) and an M.A. (History) in 1990. She obtained her Ph.D. at McMaster University in Hamilton, Ontario, in 1998.